MMPI-A: ASSESSING ADOLESCENT PSYCHOPATHOLOGY

MMPI-A: ASSESSING ADOLESCENT PSYCHOPATHOLOGY

Robert P. Archer

Eastern Virginia Medical School

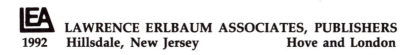
LAWRENCE ERLBAUM ASSOCIATES, PUBLISHERS
1992   Hillsdale, New Jersey   Hove and London

Lawrence Erlbaum Associates, Inc., Publishers
365 Broadway
Hillsdale, New Jersey 07642

Library of Congress Cataloging-in-Publication Data

Archer, Robert P.
    MMPI-A : assessing adolescent psychopathology /
Robert P. Archer.
        p.   cm.
    Includes bibliographical references and indexes.
    ISBN 0-8058-1113-3
    1. Minnesota Multiphasic Personality Inventory for Adolescents.
    2. Adolescent psychopathology--Diagnosis.   I. Title.
    [DNLM: 1. MMPI--in adolescence.   2. Personality Assessment--in
adolescence.   3. Psychopathology--in adolescence.   WM 145 A672m]
RJ503.7.M56A73   1992
616.89'022'0287--dc20
DNLM/DLC
for Library of Congress   91-47003
                                                                                      CIP

Printed in the United States of America
10 9 8 7 6 5 4 3 2 1

To my good friends and colleagues
Raymont A. Gordon and David L. Pancoast

The teacher is faced with an eternal dilemma,
whether to present the clear, simple, but
inaccurate fact, or the complex, confusing,
presumptive truth.
— KARL MENNINGER

CONTENTS

PREFACE

The purpose of this volume is to review the literature related to the use of the MMPI in adolescent populations and to provide an overview of a new form of the MMPI, the Minnesota Multiphasic Personality Inventory—Adolescent (MMPI-A). The MMPI-A represents an extensive revision of the MMPI involving the development of new adolescent norms (the first to be released for adolescents by the University of Minnesota Press), the modification of the traditional MMPI item pool and scales, and the inclusion of new items and scales. The University of Minnesota Press has recently released the MMPI-A after several years of intensive efforts to develop a form of the MMPI responsive to issues involving adolescent development and adolescent forms of psychopathology.

One of the primary objectives of this volume is to provide a clear and comprehensive guide to the clinician for using the MMPI or the MMPI-A in the clinical assessment of adolescents. Whenever possible, materials are presented to provide clear recommendations to the clinician concerning useful interpretive practices or procedures. The volume also provides a developmental perspective through which to understand adolescents' response patterns and the implications of various interpretation practices with adolescents. I have attempted to provide meaningful and useful information on such topics as selection of norms for T-score conversion, single-scale and codetype interpretation practices, and the use of a variety of supplementary and content scales. I have also tried to provide a useful overview of the development of the MMPI-A, and the manner in which this revision produced an instrument that differs from the original MMPI. Thus, it is hoped that this volume will provide the clinician with practical information based on sound empirical findings and a useful theoretical understanding of adolescent development.

This volume also seeks to stimulate future research efforts, particularly related to the MMPI-A. The MMPI has benefited greatly from the tremendous amount of research literature generated on this instrument. This research base has reflected the efforts of literally hundreds of researchers over five decades. Until fairly recently, most of this research attention had been focused on the use of the MMPI in adult populations with relatively little emphasis placed on the application of the MMPI in the assessment of adolescents. Over the past few years, however, I believe there is reassuring evidence that this trend is reversing. For example, the 1987 text, *Using the MMPI With Adolescents* reviewed the recent contributions of Robert Colligan and Kenneth Offord at the Mayo Clinic, and Irving Gottesman and his colleagues, in the development of adolescent norms for the original form of the MMPI. The development of the MMPI-A, in particular, has generated a substantial amount of research on many different aspects of the test instrument including the effects of modifications in original items, the congruence rate for codetypes generated from MMPI-A norms versus the traditional Marks and Briggs adolescent norms, and correlate investigations for both traditional and new scales that appear on the MMPI-A. It is important to emphasize, however, that the evaluation of the MMPI-A is in its infancy, and much important work remains to be done to understand comprehensively this test instrument. Many questions remain concerning, for example, the relatively low MMPI-A T-score elevations that will be found for many adolescents in clinical settings, and the effects of developing a "gray zone" or transitional area between T-score values of 60 through 65 to denote marginal elevations. Further, only preliminary data is available for many of the new scales developed for the MMPI-A, including content and supplementary scales. Additional research will also be needed in these areas including the usefulness of configural approaches to interpretation of the MMPI-A content scales. An effective understanding of the use of the MMPI-A will require several years of systematic research efforts. It is crucial that this research be conducted in an objective and impartial manner, and that researchers are as forceful in identifying possible problems in the use of the MMPI-A as in identifying potential advantages and assets. It is my hope that this text will provide the needed information for clinicians to effectively apply the MMPI and MMPI-A with adolescents, and will also help to provide the data base necessary to stimulate the future research that is crucial in this area.

ACKNOWLEDGMENT

I would like to mention several individuals who were centrally responsible for the creation of this text. Raymont A. Gordon, research associate at Eastern Virginia Medical School, has been very important in the development of this text, as well as my earlier MMPI text in 1987. I sincerely appreciate his intelligence, commitment, and friendship over the past 10 years. I would also like to express appreciation to Meda Moore who has worked with great dedication and patience in the preparation of this manuscript. I would be remiss if I did not note the extensive contributions of Eric A. Imhof and Radhika Krishnamurthy, graduate students in the Virginia Consortium for Professional Psychology (VCPP), who have read the manuscript in detail and made numerous helpful suggestions. I would also like to thank Donna Klinefelter of the VCPP program for her ample assistance in the preparation of materials for this text. I was very fortunate in having Mark Maruish, Senior Clinical Psychologist, National Computer Systems, and Grant W. Dahlstrom, Kenan Professor, University of North Carolina at Chapel Hill, who generously agreed to serve as reviewers for this text. Their comments and suggestions greatly improved the quality of the text. Any remaining errors or problems in this text are, of course, the result of my own deficits in scholarship. Finally, I would like to express much appreciation to the Charles G. Brown and Benjamin R. Brown Trust and the Norfolk Foundation for their crucial support of my efforts through a series of research grants.

FOREWORD

In his foreword to a previous volume by Dr. Archer on the use of the original MMPI with teenage subjects, Charles Spielberger noted approvingly that Archer "creatively links the assessment of adolescent personality to genetic and environmental theories of childhood and human development." Here too the reader will find this same innovative use of a developmental perspective, not only to place the overall task of appraising the adequacy of a given teenager's adjustment in a meaningful context but, more importantly, to make sense out of the patterns of answers to specific test items on which these young men and women differ from those of mature adults. Hathaway and Monachesi characterized these endorsement patterns as reflecting the fact that "youth is insurgent and held under control by the cultural mores and institutions with special difficulty." Archer goes well beyond this succinct summary of the struggles of individuals during this age period and matches specific item endorsement patterns to their life circumstances and concurrent experiences. In this way, he helps the reader comprehend the need for and the nature of the age-based norms employed by this instrument.

With the help of this volume, psychologists familiar with the use of the original MMPI with clients at this age level will have little difficulty in adapting their interpretive methods to the MMPI-A. The basic scales are essentially the same. However, in these new norms, only one age level is employed in place of the four levels used in the Marks–Briggs norms or the two levels provided in the norm-set devised by Gottesman and his coworkers. As expected, separate norms for each gender are still retained. The new content scales will require some effort to learn (and additional research to use appropriately). This volume does provide helpful linkages between these content scales and the more familiar Wiggins and Harris-Lingoes sets.

In the MMPI-A some of the original wordings of the MMPI items have been modified to reduce the need for the teenager to reinterpret some statements to their own special circumstances (e.g., having both parents still alive, having yet to complete their schooling, or being still in the midst of important decisions about career and educational goals). This seems a small refinement because thousands of adolescents had managed the task of answering the original MMPI with a minimum of difficulty and without experiencing any special encumbrance from the wording of the test items for adults in general. More important, perhaps, may be the limited ability of many subjects at this age now to read with comprehension the component items in either MMPI-A or MMPI-2. The addition of supplementary F scales to this version of the test (modeled after the F_B in MMPI-2) will undoubtedly prove to be particularly useful in assessing difficulties of this kind in the test records of some individuals in this age range.

The assessment of adolescent subjects has come a long way from the days when clinicians had to rely on the Mathews and Cady version of the Woodworth Personal Data Sheet (the device used with recruits in World War I) or on the Test of Personality Adjustment devised by Carl R. Rogers to appraise the extent to which a boy or girl was getting along in school, with friends, and among family members. The availability of this volume as an accompaniment to the MMPI-A will assure that the new version of Hathaway and McKinley's time-honored inventory will be used with effectiveness and insight by beginners and by experienced users alike.

W. Grant Dahlstrom

ADOLESCENT DEVELOPMENT AND PSYCHOPATHOLOGY

Much of the confusion and controversy that has traditionally surrounded the use of the MMPI with adolescent respondents has resulted from the application of this instrument without an adequate understanding of the unique characteristics of adolescent development. Unfortunately, many clinicians and researchers have attempted to interpret adolescents' MMPI profiles in a manner identical to procedures that have been established for the assessment of adults. There are a number of areas of interpretation strategy in which the approach developed for adults will work effectively in the understanding of adolescents' responses. There are also numerous areas, however, in which the use of practices or procedures derived for adults will result in substantial interpretive errors when applied to adolescents. Although development of the Minnesota Multiphasic Personality Inventory—Adolescent (MMPI-A) should substantially assist in deriving interpretive comments of direct relevance to adolescents, using this specialized form of the MMPI will not substitute for an awareness of salient developmental issues. Thus, the purpose of this chapter is to provide a brief overview of adolescent development and psychopathology, with particular attention focused on ways in which developmentally related issues may affect MMPI/MMPI-A interpretation practices.

DEVELOPMENTAL TASKS DURING ADOLESCENCE

Achenbach (1978) suggested that an understanding of psychopathology in children and adolescents must be firmly grounded in the study of normal development. Human development is a continuous process, but there may be critical periods in our development during which adaptational success or failure heavily influences the course of later development in the life cycle. Adolescence clearly is one of these critical developmental transitions. As noted by Petersen and Hamburg (1986), the number and extent of changes that occur simultaneously during adolescence present major challenges to the development of mature and effective coping strategies. Ineffective coping strategies may contribute to a variety of problem behaviors during adolescent development. Further, failures in adolescent development may result in psychopathology manifested during later life stages.

Three major areas of changes and challenges that face the individual during adolescence are reviewed, including physiological processes, cognitive processes, and psychological and emotional challenges.

Physiological/Sexual Maturation

Kimmel and Weiner (1985) defined puberty as "the process of becoming physically and sexually mature and developing the adult characteristics of one's sex" (p. 592). Petersen (1985) noted several characteristics of puberty that are important in understanding adolescent development. Puberty is a universal experience that may, however, be delayed, or in some cases even prevented, by the occurrence of physical disease or traumatic psychological events. Further, Petersen stressed that puberty is a process, rather than an isolated temporal event. This process involves changes that result in a sexually immature child achieving full reproductive potential. These physical changes are typically manifested in the growth of underarm and pubic hair, maturation of genitalia, and the first menstruation in girls. Often, the clearest signs of adolescent development are physical changes associated with the onset of puberty.

Fundamental physical changes occur during adolescence in terms of endocrinological, biochemical, and physiological processes. For example, Stone and Church (1957) noted that an individual is expected to increase 25% in height and 100% in weight during this developmental stage. Additionally, there is a marked increase in pituitary activity leading to increased production of hormones by the thyroid, adrenal, and other glands that are centrally involved in sexual maturation.

There are notable differences in the rate of physical maturation between boys and girls, and there are also very wide individual variations in sexual maturation within genders. Figures 1.1 and 1.2 show varying degrees of sexual maturation for 14 3/4-year-old boys and 12 3/4-year-old girls, and the velocity of growth in height by year of life (sources: J. M. Tanner, 1969 and J. M. Tanner, R. H. Whitehouse, & M. Takaishi, 1966, respectively). The data in Fig. 1.1 for pubertal

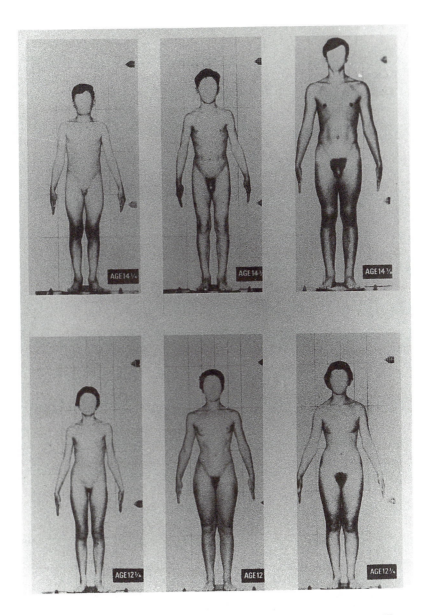

FIGURE 1.1 Variations in male and female pubertal development. (From Tanner, 1969. Copyright (c) by W. B. Saunders Company. Reprinted by permission)

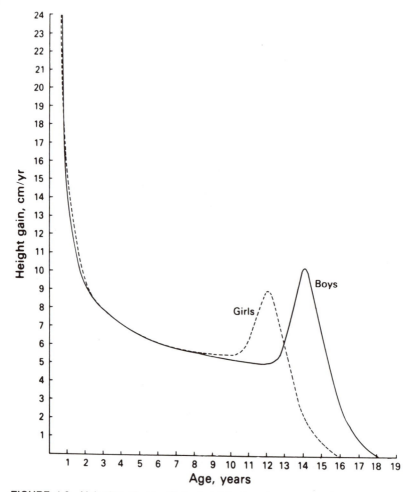

FIGURE 1.2   Velocity of growth in height at various ages. (From Tanner et al., 1966. Copyright (c) by the Archives of Disease in Childhood. Reprinted by permission)

development illustrates both the earlier maturation of females in relation to males, and the wide differences in pubertal development within genders at identical chronological ages. To the extent that pubertal development is precocious or significantly delayed, stress may occur that can be reflected in lower self-esteem or damaged self-concept for the adolescent during this period. Petersen (1985) observed that recent data indicate that the average age of menarche in the United States is now 12 1/2 years, or approximately 6 months earlier than that reported by Tanner (1962) in his British sample. For both boys and girls, rapid physical growth (i.e., the adolescent growth spurt) is typically completed by age 16. The most dramatic rate of physical growth, shown in Fig. 1.2, tends to occur between the ages of 12 and 15, with the peak of the growth curve occurring approximately 2 years earlier for females than for males.

An illustration of the influence of developmental forces on MMPI responses is provided by the item, "I am worried about sex." This item serves as a member of scales *3*, *5*, and *8*. The Minnesota Multiphasic Personality Inventory−2 (MMPI-2) Manual (Butcher, Dahlstrom, Graham, Tellegen, & Kaemmer, 1989) indicates that this item is endorsed in the *true* direction by 13% of adult female respondents in the MMPI-2 normative sample, and 15% of adult men. In contrast to adult samples, however, this item was endorsed as true by 37.2% of adolescent females and 30.2% of adolescent males in the MMPI-A normative sample (Butcher, Williams, Graham, Archer, Tellegen, Ben-Porath, & Kaemmer, 1992). The higher rate of endorsement of this item in the critical direction by the 14- to 18-year-old teenagers probably reflects the high level of stress for adolescents related to issues of sexual maturation as well as sexual identity.

Cognitive Maturation

Adolescence may also be defined in terms of changes that occur in cognitive processes. The work of Piaget and his colleagues offers an approach to understanding these cognitive changes, with the final stage of cognitive development in Piaget's (1975) paradigm unfolding during adolescence. Specifically, Piaget postulated that during early adolescence the individual typically makes the transition from Concrete Operations to the Formal Operation stage, the latter characterized by the capacity to manipulate ideas and concepts. According to Piaget, "The adolescent is an individual who is capable . . . of building and understanding ideas or abstract theories and concepts. The child does not build theories" (1975, p. 105). Thus, the adolescent is able to discern the real from the ideal, and to become passionately engaged by abstract concepts and notions. Adolescents begin to think of their world in new ways, including the ability to "think about thinking." Related to these changes in cognitive skills, Elkind (1978, 1980) argued that as adolescents become capable of thinking about their thoughts, they may also become excessively concerned with how they are perceived by others. This preoccupation includes an exaggerated view of the uniqueness of their own experiences, and the amount of time devoted by others to their appraisal. Elkind labeled the egocentric tendency of adolescents to believe that their behavior is intensely scrutinized by others as "the imaginary audience" (Elkind & Bowen, 1979).

Part of this self-absorption and belief in the uniqueness of one's own experiences may be reflected in the endorsement rate differences between adults and adolescents for the following item, which is a member of scales *Pt* and *Sc*:

"I have strange and peculiar thoughts."
(Endorsed true by 15% of MMPI-2 adult males and 10% of adult females, versus 45% of boys in the MMPI-A normative sample and 46% of MMPI-A teenage girls.)

and to the following item, a member of scales *Pd*, *Pa*, and *Sc*:
"No one seems to understand me."
(Endorsed true by 9% of adult men and 9% of adult women in the MMPI-2 normative sample, versus 25.6% of adolescent boys and 37.4% of adolescent girls in the MMPI-A normative sample.)

and to the following item, a member of the *Mf* and *Si* scales:
"It does not bother me that I am not better looking."
(Endorsed true by 77% and 59% of the MMPI-2 male and female normative samples, respectively, versus 49% of adolescent boys and 38% of adolescent girls in the MMPI-A normative sample.)

Psychological Development

Finally, a host of psychological and emotional tasks, including the processes of individuation, the formation of ego identity, and ego maturation, are accomplished during adolescence. Peter Blos (1967) discussed individuation as a process involved with the development of relative independence from family relationships, the weakening of infantile object ties, and an increased capacity to assume a functional role as a member of adult society. Blos defined and described this task as similar to the more primitive struggle for individuation in the attainment of object constancy that occurs toward the end of the third year of life. Thus, the early adolescent has marked ambivalence concerning issues of independence versus dependence, particularly in terms of their relationships to their parents. This ambivalence is likely to be seen in rapid and marked attitudinal and behavioral changes by the adolescent (e.g., one moment protesting any parental involvement or supervision and the next moment regressing to marked dependency on mother or father).

Erikson (1956) described ego identity formation during adolescence as the assembly of converging identity elements that occur at the end of childhood, achieved through a process of *normative crises*. Ego identity was viewed by Erikson as including the conscious sense of individual identity as well as an unconscious striving for a continuity of personal character. In this process of ego formation, the ego integrates previous childhood identifications into a new totality, which lays the foundation of the adult personality. Positive resolution to this issue leads to a sense of *ego identity*, or continuity in one's self-definition. Negative resolution of this challenge could result in *ego diffusion*, or uncertainty about who one is and what one will become in the future. This failure to achieve ego identity is related to the diagnostic category of identity disorder (313.82) as described in the American Psychiatric Association's (1980) *Diagnostic and Statistical Manual of Mental Disorders (DSM-III)*. Marcia (1966) further defined Erikson's concept of ego identity in terms of two variables: commitment (whether or not the individual has accepted a set of values) and crisis (whether or not the individual has experienced an inner struggle in arriving at personal acceptance of a set of values). These two variables combine to yield four identity statuses in Marcia's model: *diffusion* (no commitment, no crisis); *foreclosure* (commitment without crisis); *moratorium* (crisis without commitment); and *achievement* (commitment after crisis). Marcia argued that these categories, in the order given, represent developmental levels of increasingly advanced maturation.

The process of individuation is most clearly noted during early phases of adolescence, whereas the process of identity formation and consolidation is typically manifested during later stages of adolescence. As a result of these processes, adolescents will typically modify the way in which they interact and relate to others. Specifically, adolescents begin to increase their involvement with peers, while decreasing their immediate identification with family members. Further, the early stages of individuation may result in an increase in conflict with parents, as the adolescent attempts preliminary definitions of the self based on identifying the ways in which their feelings, thoughts, and attitudes may differ from those of their parents.

Loevinger (1976) articulated a concept of ego development in reference to the frameworks of meaning that individuals impose upon their life experiences. Within Loevinger's model, the concept of ego development is a dimension of individual differences, as well as a developmental sequence of increasingly complex functioning in terms of impulse control, character development, interpersonal relationships, and cognitive complexity. At the three lowest levels of ego development, collectively grouped into the *preconformist* stage, the individual may be described as impulsive, motivated by personal gain in the avoidance of punishment, and oriented to the present rather than the past or future. Cognitive styles are stereotyped and concrete, and interpersonal relationships are opportunistic, exploitive, and demanding. During the second broad stage of development, referred to as the *conformist* stage, the individual begins to identify his or her welfare with that of the social group. The individual places emphasis on conformity to socially approved norms and standards and on issues of social acceptability in terms of attitudes and behaviors. As the individual enters the *post-conformist* stages of development, self awareness, cognitive complexity, and interpersonal style become increasingly complex and a balance is achieved between autonomy and interdependence. The maturational stages described by Loevinger do not refer to specific age groups, but she notes that higher stages of ego development would rarely be achieved by adolescents. Loevinger's view of development is very comprehensive and served as a basis for the development of the MMPI-A Immaturity (*IMM*) scale described in Chapter 6.

The following five MMPI items illustrate substantial differences in endorsement frequency between adults in the MMPI-2 normative sample and adolescents in the MMPI-A normative sample:

"I have very few quarrels with members of my family."
   (True endorsement by 78% of adult women and 79% of adult men, versus 38% of adolescent girls and 46% of adolescent males.)
"Some of my family have habits that bother and annoy me very much."
   (Endorsed true by 66% of adult women and 48% of adult men, versus 79% of adolescent girls and 67% of adolescent boys.)
"My relatives are nearly all in sympathy with me."
   (Endorsed true by 53% of adult women and 56% of adult men, versus 31% of adolescent girls and 37% of adolescent boys.)
"Once in a while I feel hate towards members of my family whom I usually love."
   (Endorsed true by 44% of adult women and 32% of adult men, versus 72% of adolescent girls and 59% of adolescent boys.)
"My parents and other members of my family find more fault with me than they should."
   (Endorsed true by 14% of adult women and 11% of adult men, versus 43% of adolescent females and 40% of adolescent males.)

These differences in item endorsement patterns between adults and adolescents may be meaningfully viewed in reference to the adolescents' struggles with separation and individuation, and the tasks of identity formation and ego maturation. Tables 1.1 and 1.2 provide information on selected items that show at least a 30% endorsement rate difference between adolescents and adults, separated by gender, as noted in the normative data for the MMPI-2 and MMPI-A.

TABLE 1.1
Selected Items Showing Large Differences for Males in Percent Endorsement
as True Between the Adult (MMPI-2) Normative Sample and the Adolescent
(MMPI-A) Normative Sample

MMPI-A item no.	Item content	% endorsement as true	
		MMPI-2	MMPI-A
3	I wake up fresh and rested most mornings.	68.0	34.5
79	I have very few quarrels with members of my family.	79.0	46.2
82	I like to go to parties and other affairs where there is lots of loud fun.	45.0	75.3
128	At times I feel like picking a fist fight with someone.	16.0	47.7
137	I feel that I have often been punished without cause.	9.0	42.4
162	When I get bored I like to stir up some excitement.	43.0	73.0
208	I dream frequently about things that are best kept to myself.	28.0	62.9
296	I have strange and peculiar thoughts.	15.0	45.3
307	Bad words, often terrible words, come into my mind and I cannot get rid of them.	9.0	39.4
371	The future is too uncertain for a person to make serious plans.	12.0	42.1

Note. Items reproduced from the MMPI-2 and MMPI-A by permission. Copyright (c) by the Regents of the University of Minnesota.

The Effects of Maturation On MMPI Response Patterns

The preceding paragraphs discussed the implications of maturation for item-level response patterns. Maturational effects can also be demonstrated on the scale level, particularly in relation to scales F, Pd, Sc, and Ma. These latter scales have traditionally shown substantial differences in mean values obtained from adolescent and adult samples (Archer, 1984, 1987). For example, Fig. 1.3 presents the mean raw score values for adolescent and adult males and females on the MMPI-2 60-item F scale with findings presented separately by chronological age. As shown in this figure, mean raw score values on F continue to decrease as the chronological age of the groups increases. It is most reasonable to interpret these differences as a reflection of maturational processes rather than levels of psychopathology. Thus, MMPI scales are subject to maturational effects that may serve to obscure or confound the interpretation of psychopathology based on test scores. In this regard, Thomas Achenbach (1978) commented that:

TABLE 1.2

Selected Items Showing Large Differences for Females in Percent Endorsement as True Between the Adult (MMPI-2) Normative Sample and the Adolescent (MMPI-A) Normative Sample

MMPI-A item no.	Item content	% endorsement as true	
		MMPI-2	MMPI-A
3	I wake up fresh and rested most mornings.	66.0	29.3
21	At times I have fits of laughing and crying that I cannot control.	18.0	63.8
79	I have very few quarrels with members of my family.	78.0	37.5
81	At times I have a strong urge to do something harmful or shocking.	16.0	52.6
82	I like to go to parties and other affairs where there is lots of loud fun.	39.0	80.1
114	I like collecting flowers or growing house plants.	79.0	43.2
123	My conduct is mostly controlled by the behavior of those around me.	26.0	62.3
162	When I get bored I like to stir up some excitement.	43.0	80.1
205	I have periods of such great restlessness that I cannot sit long in a chair.	24.0	62.3
208	I dream frequently about things that are best kept to myself.	27.0	65.3
235	I have often felt that strangers were looking at me critically.	25.0	64.9
296	I have strange and peculiar thoughts.	10.0	46.1

Note. Items reproduced from the MMPI-2 and MMPI-A by permission. Copyright (c) by the Regents of the University of Minnesota.

An often overlooked complication of the search for individual differences in children is that developmental differences account for significant variance in almost every measurable behavior. One consequence is that measurements repeated on the same subjects more than a few weeks apart are likely to differ as a function of development, even if the subjects show stability with respect to their rank ordering within their cohort. A second consequence is that unless all subjects in a sample are at the same developmental level with respect to the behavior in question, individual differences in the behavior may in fact reflect differences in developmental level rather than traitlike characteristics. A third consequence is that covariation among several measures may merely reflect the variance that they all share with development rather than an independent trait. (p. 765)

This phenomenon is certainly not limited to adolescent populations, and Colligan, Osborne, Swenson, and Offord (1983) showed substantial

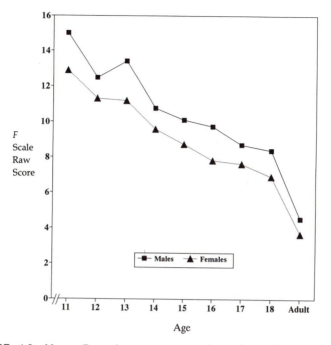

FIGURE 1.3 Mean *F* scale raw score values for male and female adolescents and adults.

age and maturational effects on standard MMPI scales studied in adult populations. Figures 1.4 and 1.5, for example, show cross-sectional changes in mean values on the *Hs* scale and on the *Ma* scale, respectively, for males and females across age categories ranging from 18/19 to 70+. Similarly, Pancoast and Archer (1992) reported substantial differences in mean MMPI profiles for large samples of adolescents, college students, and adults when the mean values of all three groups are plotted on the standard reference point of adult norms, as shown in Fig. 1.6.

Thus far, maturational influences have been discussed in relation to chronological age, but, as is seen later during the description of the development of the Immaturity scale for the MMPI-A, maturational effects can be clearly demonstrated on MMPI response patterns when chronological age is held constant and maturity is measured more directly.

Another method of examining maturational influences on MMPI scale-level data was provided in research by Pancoast and Archer (1988) that examined patterns of adolescent responses on the Harris–Lingoes subscales profiled on standard adult norms. Harris and Lingoes (1955) rationally divided six of the MMPI clinical scales (2, 3, 4, 6, 8, and 9) into subscales based on items that appeared logically similar in content. As is discussed later, the Harris–Lingoes subscales are frequently used in clin-

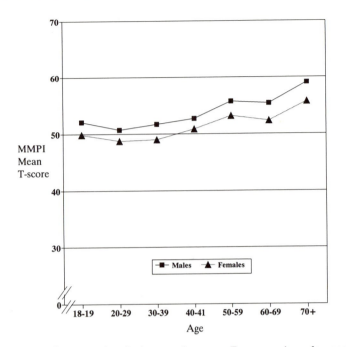

FIGURE 1.4   Cross-sectional changes in mean T-score values for scale *1* by age group and gender. (From Colligan et al., 1983. Copyright (c) by the Mayo Foundation. Reprinted by permission)

ical practice to determine which content areas of a standard clinical scale were critically endorsed in producing an overall T-score elevation on the parent or standard scale. Adult norms for these subscales have been developed, and adolescent norms are available for the Harris–Lingoes subscales of the MMPI and the MMPI-A. In the Pancoast and Archer study, adolescent values were examined on adult norms in order to evaluate the ways in which adolescent response patterns might differ from those typically found for normal adults. These mean data are based upon the adolescent normative data collected by Colligan and Offord (1989a) at the Mayo Foundation, and a smaller sample of adolescents collected in Virginia in 1987. Figure 1.7 presents findings for the Harris–Lingoes MMPI subscales on adult norms for MMPI scales D, Hy, and Pd. Results show a general trend for subscales related to the Pd scale to show more extreme elevations than subscales related to scales D or Hy. Although most of the subscales for Pd are elevated, the highest elevation occurs for Pd_1 (Familial Discord), which deals with a struggle against familial controls and the perception of marked family conflict. In contrast, there is no elevation for Pd_3 (Social Imperturbability), which deals with denial of social anxiety and the experience of discomfort in social situ-

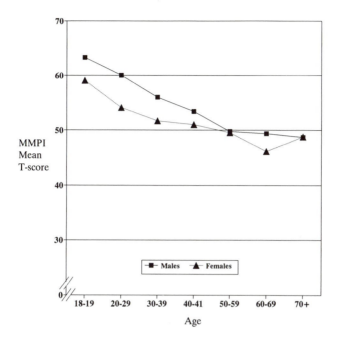

FIGURE 1.5   Cross-sectional changes in mean T-score values for scale *9* by age group and gender. (From Colligan et al., 1983. Copyright (c) by the Mayo Foundation. Reprinted by permission)

ations. Thus, although normal adolescents' experiences typically involve substantial degrees of family conflict, this struggle appears to be restricted primarily to familial issues and does not include a generalized social discomfort (Pd_3), nor does it necessarily include general conflicts with authority as measured by Pd_2 (Authority Conflicts).

Figure 1.8 presents Harris–Lingoes findings for the remaining three MMPI scales (*Pa, Sc,* and *Ma*). Findings from these scales also reveal an interpretable subscale pattern. For *Pa,* the highest subscale is Pa_1 (Persecutory Ideas), which primarily deals with the externalization of responsibility for one's problems and the perception of being treated unfairly and punished by others. On the *Sc* scale, the highest subscale is Sc_{2c} (Lack of Ego Mastery, Defective Inhibition), which deals with feelings of restlessness, hyperactivity, and not being in control of one's impulses. On the *Ma* scale, the elevated Ma_2 (Psychomotor Acceleration) subscale relates to restlessness, excitement, and pressure for action. Overall, the Harris–Lingoes subscale pattern suggests that the normal adolescent, as evaluated by adult norms or standards, is typically preoccupied with the familial struggle for independence, focused on the perception of family conflicts, and that there is a driven, restless, and

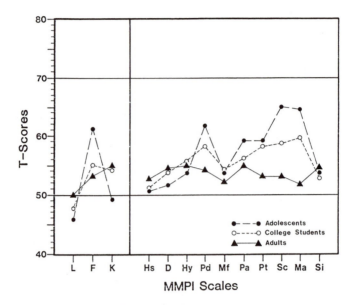

FIGURE 1.6   Mean MMPI T-score values for adolescents, college students, and adults as shown on adult non K-corrected norms. (From Pancoast & Archer, 1992. Copyright (c) by Clinical Psychology Publishing Company, Inc. Reprinted by permission)

excited quality to this developmental experience that often involves a sense of being confined or misunderstood.

In summary, the use of the MMPI or MMPI-A with adolescents requires a developmental perspective to understand and interpret test findings. This chapter briefly discussed the dramatic physiological/ sexual maturational changes, changes in cognitive processes, and some of the psychological challenges that occur during adolescence. These processes contribute to the observed differences between adults and adolescents in MMPI response patterns on the item, scale, and profile level. Recognition of the influence of these maturational and developmental factors was a major factor in the decision to create a specialized form of the MMPI for the assessment of adolescents, the MMPI-A. A focal point of this book is to accurately discriminate and describe those administration, scoring, and interpretive situations that require a unique approach when performed in relation to adolescent clients.

ADOLESCENCE AND PSYCHOPATHOLOGY

Methodological Issues

In addition to an awareness of adolescent developmental issues, it is important for the MMPI-A user to develop an understanding of the

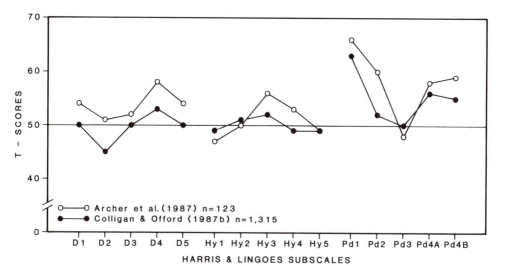

FIGURE 1.7   Harris-Lingoes subscale T-score values for adolescents based on adult norms: Subscales for *D*, *Hy*, and *Pd*. (From Pancoast & Archer, 1988. Copyright (c) by Lawrence Erlbaum Associates. Reprinted by permission)

nature and extent of psychopathology typically encountered during adolescence. Attempts to estimate the prevalence of psychiatric disturbance among adolescents, however, are directly affected by several methodological issues. These factors include the definition and measures employed to identify psychiatric disorders among adolescents, as well as the methods and informants employed (parents, teachers, direct psychiatric interviews) upon which such estimates are based. Weissman et al. (1987), for example, evaluated the results from independent interviews of 220 subjects between the ages of 6 and 23. The diagnostic data for this study were gathered by child interviews using the Schedule for Affective Disorders and Schizophrenia for School-Age Children and were also derived using *DSM-III*-related interviews with parents and other informants. The authors noted that considerable discrepancies were found between parents' and children's reports on the nature and degree of the child's psychopathology. They found that children's self-reports or self-descriptions produced evidence of considerably more psychopathology than did the descriptions of the child provided by their parents. Similar findings have also been reported by Reich and Earls (1987) when parental interview results are compared with the results of structured interview techniques used directly with children and adolescents, such as the Diagnostic Interview for Children and Adolescents (DICA). Further, an investigation by Rosenberg and Joshi (1986) found a significant relationship between the degree of marital discord and

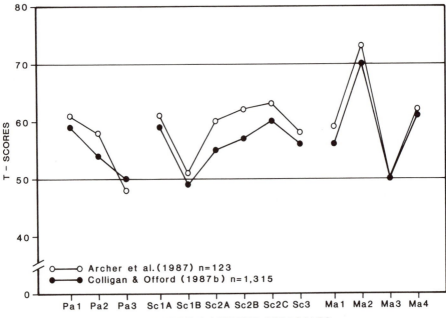

FIGURE 1.8   Harris-Lingoes subscale T-score values for adolescents based on adult norms: Subscales for *Pa*, *Sc*, and *Ma*. (From Pancoast & Archer, 1988. Copyright (c) by Lawrence Erlbaum Associates. Reprinted by permission)

discrepancies within parental reports of child behavior problems. These researchers reported that the greater the marital difficulty, the greater the difference in adults' ratings of child behavior difficulties on the Achenbach and Edelbrock (1983) Child Behavior Checklist (CBCL). Recently, Williams, Hearn, Hostetler, and Ben-Porath (1990) compared structured interview findings on the Diagnostic Interview Schedule for Children (DISC) with self-report measures of psychopathology that included the MMPI. In addition, subjects' parents completed the Achenbach and Edelbrock CBCL, and teachers completed the teacher form of the CBCL. Findings indicated substantial levels of disagreement between these measures in the identification of psychologically disturbed subjects. Thus, it is clear that our estimates of adolescent psychopathology relate not only to how diagnostic questions are asked, but to whom such questions are addressed. Despite these methodological problems and limitations, it appears possible to offer some general conclusions concerning the overall prevalence of psychiatric disorders during adolescence, as well as some meaningful observations concerning the form of these disorders.

Prevalence Findings

One of the most widely cited studies on the prevalence of child and adolescent psychiatric disorders is the "Isle of Wight" study reported by Rutter, Graham, Chadwick, and Yule (1976) and summarized by Graham and Rutter (1985). In the Isle of Wight study, a total population of over 2,000 British 14- and 15-year-olds were screened using questionnaires administered to parents and teachers to identify those adolescents with "deviant" adjustment patterns. Adolescents for whom deviant scores were produced on either questionnaire, along with a group of randomly selected control subjects, were then given individual psychiatric assessments involving direct interviews with parents, teachers, and the adolescent. All assessments were conducted in a blind fashion in terms of interviewer's knowledge of the adolescent's membership in the deviant or control groups. The authors estimated that the one-year period prevalence rate for psychiatric disorder in their sample was 21%. In general, psychiatric conditions appeared to occur with a slightly higher frequency during adolescence, in contrast to data available for middle childhood. Certain psychiatric conditions, however, did show substantial increases during adolescence, including the occurrence of affective disorders and depressive conditions. Along with the increase in depression, there was also a dramatic increase in the frequency of attempted and completed suicide.

In the United States, Gould, Wunsch-Hitzig, and Dohrenwend (1981) reported that the median prevalence rate for clinical maladjustment among children and adolescents was 11.8%, based on a review of 25 prevalence studies conducted between 1928 and 1975. The majority of these studies employed teachers' reports as a means of identifying psychiatrically disturbed children. Brandenburg, Friedman, and Silver (1989) noted that more recent epidemiologic field studies of child and adolescent psychopathology have employed diverse methods of case definition and have more frequently used a multi-method, multi-stage approach to case identification. Based upon a review of eight recent studies, these authors placed the prevalence estimate of psychiatric disorder in children and adolescents at 14% to 20%.

Beyond these prevalence studies of general psychopathology, several studies have attempted to identify the relative prevalence of specific types of psychiatric symptomatology or disorder within adolescent samples. Kashani et al. (1987) utilized both child and parent structured interviews to determine the prevalence of psychiatric disorder among 150 adolescents selected in a community sample. Roughly 41% were found to have at least one *DSM-III* diagnosis, and 19% were judged to have a diagnosis *and* to be functionally impaired to a degree indicating the need for psychiatric treatment. The three most common diagnoses found in this total sample were anxiety disorder (8.7%), conduct disorder (8.7%), and depression (combined categories of major depression and dysthymic disorder) with a frequency of 8%.

Kashani and Orvaschel (1988) randomly selected 150 adolescents between the ages of 14 and 16 from a roster of 1,703 students in a Midwestern public school system. In this study of anxiety disorders during adolescence, both children and their parents were interviewed in their homes using the standard and parental interview forms of the DICA. Interview results were videotaped and scored by three trained raters with established interrater reliability. Additionally, subjects received several objective personality assessment instruments related to self-concept, affect, and coping. Seventeen percent of this sample were found to meet the criteria for one or more forms of psychiatric disorder, and 8.7% were identified as positive cases of anxiety disorder. The most frequently occurring anxiety disorder in this sample was overanxious disorder. Results of this study tend to support the view that anxiety disorders are a major form of psychopathology in adolescent populations. In other research, Hillard, Slomowitz, and Levi (1987) studied 100 adult and 100 adolescent admissions to a university hospital psychiatric emergency service. The authors reported that adolescents were less likely to receive diagnoses of personality disorders or psychoses, but were more likely to receive diagnoses involving conduct disorder and adjustment disorder. Further, self-destructive ideation or behavior was present in 40% of the adolescents seen in the emergency room visits.

The issue of suicidal ideation and behavior has received special focus in recent studies of adolescence. Friedman, Asnis, Boeck, and DiFiore (1987), for example, investigated 300 high school students who were anonymously surveyed regarding their experiences with suicidal ideation and behaviors. Roughly 53% of this sample stated that they had thought about killing themselves but did not actually try, and 9% of the total sample stated that they had attempted suicide at least once. These findings indicated that suicidal ideation is relatively common among adolescents, but also suggested that actual suicide attempts were disturbingly frequent. In this regard, Kimmel and Weiner (1985) noted that suicide is the third most common cause of death for adolescents aged 15 to 19, with the suicide rate particularly marked for White male adolescents. Further, the rate of adolescent suicide has nearly doubled from 1960 to 1975, and about 10% of adolescents seen in mental health clinics, and more than 25% of those admitted to psychiatric units in general hospitals, have threatened or attempted suicide (Kimmel & Weiner, 1985). Boys appear four times more likely than girls to actually kill themselves, whereas girls appear three times more likely to make a suicide attempt. Within the MMPI-A normative sample, 21% of boys and 38% of girls responded true to item 177, "I sometimes think about killing myself."

Several general conclusions seem possible from these and other investigations of psychopathology during adolescence. First, the majority of adolescents do not show evidence of psychopathology that would result in psychiatric diagnosis. The rate of psychopathology during adolescence appears "only slightly higher than that found earlier in childhood or later in life" (Petersen & Hamburg, 1986, p. 491). There is evidence that the frequency and severity of depression does increase during adolescence, and there is a marked increase in both suicide attempts and suicide fatalities during this period of development. Several disorders tend to make their first appearance during adolescence, including anorexia nervosa, bipolar illness, bulimia, obsessive-compulsive disorder, schizophrenia, and substance abuse, although other disorders, such as enuresis and encopresis, become less frequent (Burke, Burke, Regier, & Rae, 1990; Graham & Rutter, 1985). Although the rate of anxiety disorders and conduct disorders may show little change during adolescence, the expression of symptoms related to these disorders do change. The rate of specific phobic disorders appears to decrease during adolescence, whereas conduct disorders more frequently involve violence (Graham & Rutter, 1985; Petersen & Hamburg, 1986).

The "Storm and Stress" Model and Psychopathology

G. Stanley Hall (1904), considered by many to be the father of child psychology in the United States, was the formulator of the "Sturm und Drang" or Storm and Stress model of adolescent development. This view, consistent with that of Anna Freud (1958), postulates that adolescence is typically accompanied by emotional upheavals and behavioral turbulence. Anna Freud postulated that adolescents who did not demonstrate turbulent features of adjustment were at risk for the development of serious psychopathological symptoms in adulthood. Freud's formulation of this view is represented in her statement that, "the upholding of a steady equilibrium during the process [of adolescence] is, in itself, abnormal" (p. 275). Freud's view of adolescent development may be best illustrated by the following quotation:

> I take it that it is normal for an adolescent to behave for a considerable length of time in an inconsistent and unpredictable manner; to fight his impulses and to accept them; to ward them off successfully and to be overrun by them; to love his parents and to hate them; to revolt against

them and to be dependent on them; to be deeply ashamed to acknowledge his mother before others and, unexpectedly, to desire heart-to-heart talks with her; to thrive on imitation and identification with others while searching unceasingly for his own identity; to be more idealistic, artistic, generous, unselfish than he will ever be again, but also the opposite — self-centered, egoistic, calculating. Such fluctuations between extreme opposites would be deemed highly abnormal at any other time of life. At this time they may signify no more than that an adult structure of personality takes a long time to emerge, that the ego of the individual in question does not cease to experiment and is in no hurry to close down on possibilities. (1958, p. 276)

Peter Blos (1962) also felt that the psychiatric symptoms typically presented during adolescence were often ill-defined, unstable, and transitory in nature and did not signify stable markers of psychiatric illness. Similarly, Erikson (1956) proposed that the adolescent's struggles for self-definition frequently resulted in deviations from expected or normal behavior, which he termed "identity diffusion" or "identity confusion," and differentiated from stable psychopathology.

Many have objected to the Storm and Stress view of adolescent development, particularly the implication that normal adolescent development is characterized by substantial turbulence and lability. Bandura (1964), for example, argued that many adolescents establish more trusting and relaxed relations with their parents during adolescence while also increasing contact with peer groups. Thus, the shifting away from the nuclear family to the peer group is not necessarily and inevitably a source of family tension. Offer and Offer (1975) investigated suburban male adolescents and found that, although transient episodes of nondisabling depression and anxiety were common, only 20% of adolescents demonstrated moderate to severe symptomatology. This estimate, as we have seen, is generally consistent with reports of the prevalence of significant psychopathology in adolescent populations. Further, these investigators also found that 20% of their sample did not appear to experience any significant turmoil during their adolescent development and were able to successfully cope with the wide variety of challenges it presented.

Rutter et al. (1976) examined the concept of adolescent turmoil within the context of their findings in the Isle of Wight study of 14- and 15-year-olds. These authors concluded that parent-child alienation was not a feature common to adolescents in general, but rather appeared restricted to adolescents who already showed signs of psychiatric problems. On the other hand, "inner turmoil," which was defined by the researchers as feelings of misery and self-depreciation, appeared to be frequently associated with adolescence. The authors concluded that "adolescent turmoil is a fact, not a fiction, but its psychiatric importance has probably been overestimated in the past. Certainly it would be most unwise to assume that adolescents will grow out of their problems to a greater extent than do younger children" (p. 55).

In their review of the literature on adolescent psychopathology, Weiner and Del Gaudio (1976) offered the following three conclusions: First, psychiatric symptoms are not a normal feature of adolescence; second, boundaries between normal and abnormal adolescence may be drawn despite inherent difficulties; and third, rather than a passing phase, psychological disturbance during adolescence typically requires treatment for remission. This concept has also been expressed by Kimmel and Weiner (1985) in their statement that, "by and large, people remain basically the same in how they think, handle interpersonal relationships, and are perceived by others. For better or worse, adults tend to display many of the same personality characteristics and same relative level of adjustment they did as adolescents" (p. 449). The view that many of the characteristics displayed during adolescence are recapitulated across the remainder of the life cycle is expressed in Fig. 1.9, a cartoon commentary by Jules Feiffer.

Viewed within the context of our data on the prevalence of psychiatric disorders during adolescence, the debate surrounding the stability of adolescent symptomatology appears to center on the distinction be-

FEIFFER®

FIGURE 1.9   Copyright (c) 1986, Jules Feiffer. Reprinted with permission of Universal Press Syndicate. All rights reserved.

tween psychopathology as defined by *DSM-III* categories, and terms such as *turbulence* and *Storm and Stress*. Prevalence estimates of psychopathology during adolescence appear to fall within a reasonably stable range of 12% to 22% (National Institute of Mental Health, 1990). The adolescents identified in these studies do, in fact, appear to suffer from stable *DSM-III* related disorders that would not be expected to remit without active and effective treatment. For example, it is estimated that almost half of children or adolescents receiving conduct disorder diagnoses will become antisocial adults, and that untreated depression and anxiety disorders during adolescence often persist into adulthood (National Institute of Mental Health, 1990). On the other hand, many more adolescents go through a period of turbulence and lability during adolescent development that would *not* qualify as a *DSM-III* disorder, but is commonly associated with accomplishing the mastery of the various adaptational challenges presented during this developmental period. Although it is clear that the dividing line between these two groups is frequently blurred and difficult to discern, it serves little purpose to view these groups as homogeneous in terms of the severity of their symptoms or implications for long-term adjustment. It might be expected that MMPI-A test results, based on contemporary adolescent norms for this instrument, should prove of substantial value to the clinician in rendering this important diagnostic distinction.

Stability of Adolescents' MMPI/MMPI-A Features

Whether adolescent symptomatology is stable or transitory, it appears relatively clear that those features and characteristics measured by the MMPI or MMPI-A in the assessment of adolescents serve to accurately describe the teenager at the moment of testing. Adolescents' test scores often do not, however, provide the types of data necessary to make accurate long-term predictions concerning psychopathology or personality functioning. The MMPI/MMPI-A is best used as a means of deriving an overall estimate and current description of adolescent psychopathology, rather than as a method of making long-range predictions regarding future adjustment.

An illustration of the variability inherent in adolescent personality structure may be found in data reported by Hathaway and Monachesi (1963) in their classic study of adolescents' MMPI response patterns. These authors evaluated 15,300 Grade 9 children within Minnesota school systems between 1948 and 1954, and retested 3,856 students when they reached Grade 12 during the 1956-57 school year. Examining adolescents who were tested in both the 9th and 12th grade, Hathaway and Monachesi found test-retest correlation coefficients ranging from the low to mid .30s on scales such as *Pd* and *Pa*, to values in the high .50s and low .60s for scale *Si*. Hathaway and Monachesi concluded that these correlations underscored the degree of change that may occur within an adolescent's MMPI profile, reflecting the fluid nature of adolescents' overall personality organizations. Hathaway and Monachesi noted, however, that the stability of an adolescent's profile tends to increase when T-score values are substantially elevated in the initial testing. Thus, clinically elevated profile characteristics may be subject to less change than marginally elevated profile features. Even in clinical or preclinical adolescent populations, however, substantial change often occurs in MMPI profile features. Similar to the Hathaway and Monachesi results, Lowman, Galinsky, and Gray-Little (1980) reported that relatively pathological MMPI profiles of eighth graders in a rural county in North Carolina were generally not predictive of level of psychological disturbance or achievement for this sample at young adulthood.

Gottesman and Hanson (1990) recently reported pilot findings from a study that has continued to follow the Hathaway and Monachesi data set of adolescents administered the MMPI in the late 1940s and early 1950s. These authors located individuals admitted to Minnesota psychiatric hospitals or correctional facilities more than 20 years following their initial ninth-grade MMPI assessment. The researchers identified 183 men and women admitted to these public institutions, of which 26 cases were identified as schizophrenics. Figure 1.10 shows the MMPI profiles of 16 boys, evaluated in the ninth grade, who later received a diagnosis of schizophrenia, and a group of normal matched control subjects from the ninth-grade testing. Figure 1.11 shows similar findings for 10 girls, evaluated in the ninth-grade sample, who later manifested schizophrenia, and their matched cohorts. These remarkable data illustrate the difficulties involved in attempting to make long-term predictions from MMPI profiles of adolescents. Differences did occur in these ninth-grade samples between groups of adolescents who did, and did not, develop schizophrenia. These differences, however, clearly would not permit for specific diagnostic predictions. As noted by Hanson, Gottesman, and Heston (1990) in reference to these data, an effort to predict schizophrenia from ninth-grade test results would have been an "exercise in futility."

Hathaway and Monachesi (1963) indicated that MMPI profiles produced by an adolescent often change across time because of the "transient organization of the personality" during adolescence. They noted that such psychometric changes, rather than indicating difficulties in test construction, indicate the sensitivity of instruments such as the MMPI to the ongoing change in maturational process. These phenomena do, however, limit the utility of tests such as the MMPI when

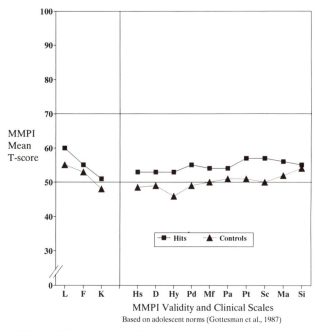

MMPI Validity and Clinical Scales
Based on adolescent norms (Gottesman et al., 1987)

FIGURE 1.10 MMPI mean profiles for boys who grew up to be schizophrenic (*N*=16) and their normal matched controls. (From Gottesman & Hanson, 1990, August. Copyright (c) by I. I. Gottesman. Reprinted by permission)

such instruments are applied in a long-range predictive, rather than descriptive, manner.

SUMMARY

This chapter has provided a brief review of adolescent development and issues related to developmental psychopathology during this maturational stage. As is discussed in the following chapters in this text, the MMPI-A presents a variety of features that could potentially improve the identification and description of psychopathology among adolescents in contrast to the original test instrument. For example, the development of the MMPI-A included extensive revisions of the original MMPI item pool to improve item clarity and relevance for adolescents. New items were also included in the MMPI-A that are related to forms of psychopathology of importance during adolescent development, including suicidal ideation, alcohol and drug abuse, and eating disorders. On the scale level, the MMPI-A has incorporated new measures of

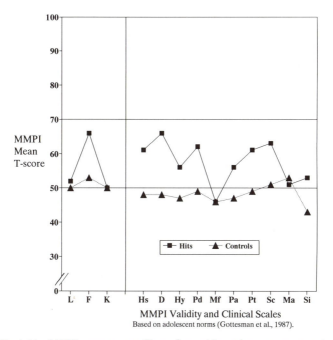

MMPI Validity and Clinical Scales
Based on adolescent norms (Gottesman et al., 1987).

FIGURE 1.11 MMPI mean profiles for girls who grew up to be schizophrenic (N = 10) and their normal matched controls. (From Gottesman & Hanson, 1990, August. Copyright (c) by I. I. Gottesman. Reprinted by permission)

psychopathology of particular relevance to adolescents, including conduct disorder, school problems, depression, anxiety, and immaturity. Additionally, the MMPI-A development included the collection of an adolescent normative sample of 1,620 adolescents representing varying geographic, socioeconomic, and ethnic groups. The release of an official set of adolescent norms for the MMPI-A by the University of Minnesota Press is likely to substantially assist in eliminating the inappropriate, but widespread, practice of the application of adult norms in the interpretation of adolescent response patterns.

Finally, the MMPI-A profile sheet contains a "gray zone" area denoting a range of marginal or transitional elevation in place of the traditional use of a specific T-score designation as a cutoff between normal range scores and clinically elevated values. This use of a range of T scores to mark the transition between normal range values and clinical values is particularly important in the assessment of adolescents, where the conceptual and psychometric dividing line between normalcy and pathology may be less clear than during adult development. Thus, the MMPI-A contains a number of features that may improve the assessment of adolescent psychopathology when employed by a clinician who is sensitive to developmental issues in this population.

REFERENCES

Achenbach, T. M. (1978). Psychopathology of childhood: Research problems and issues. *Journal of Consulting and Clinical Psychology, 46,* 759–776.

Achenbach, T. M., & Edelbrock, C. S. (1983). *Manual for the Child Behavior Checklist and revised child behavior profile.* Burlington, VT: University of Vermont.

American Psychiatric Association. (1980). *Diagnostic and statistical manual of mental disorders* (3rd ed.). Washington, DC: Author.

Archer, R. P. (1984). Use of the MMPI with adolescents: A review of salient issues. *Clinical Psychology Review, 4,* 241–251.

Archer, R. P. (1987). *Using the MMPI with adolescents.* Hillsdale, NJ: Lawrence Erlbaum Associates.

Archer, R. P., Gordon, R. A., & Pancoast, D. L. (1987). [MMPI responses from normal adolescents in southeastern Virginia]. Unpublished raw data.

Bandura, A. (1964). The stormy decade: Fact or fiction? *Psychology in the School, 1,* 224–231.

Blos, P. (1962). *On adolescence: A psychoanalytic interpretation.* New York: The Free Press.

Blos, P. (1967). The second individuation process of adolescence. *Psychoanalytic Study of the Child, 22,* 162–186.

Brandenburg, N. A., Friedman, R. M., & Silver, S. E. (1989). The epidemiology of childhood psychiatric disorders: Prevalence findings from recent studies. *Journal of the American Academy of Child and Adolescent Psychiatry, 29,* 76–83.

Burke, K. C., Burke, J. D., Regier, D. A., & Rae, D. S. (1990). Age at onset of selected mental disorders in five community populations. *Archives of General Psychiatry, 47,* 511–518.

Butcher, J. N., Dahlstrom, W. G., Graham, J. R., Tellegen, A., & Kaemmer, B. (1989). *Minnesota Multiphasic Personality Inventory–2 (MMPI-2). Manual for administration and scoring.* Minneapolis: University of Minnesota Press.

Butcher, J. N., Williams, C. L., Graham, J. R., Archer, R. P., Tellegen, A., Ben-Porath, Y. S., & Kaemmer, B. (1992). *MMPI-A (Minnesota Multiphasic Personality Inventory– Adolescent): Manual for administration, scoring, and interpretation.* Minneapolis: University of Minnesota Press.

Colligan, R. C., & Offord, K. P. (1987a). Today's adolescent and the MMPI: Patterns of MMPI responses from normal teenagers of the 1980s. In R. P. Archer, *Using the MMPI with adolescents* (pp. 215–239). Hillsdale, NJ: Lawrence Erlbaum Associates.

Colligan, R. C., & Offord, K. P. (1987b). [Adolescent mean values for the Harris & Lingoes subscales]. Unpublished raw data.

Colligan, R. C., & Offord, K. P. (1989). The aging MMPI: Contemporary norms for contemporary teenagers. *Mayo Clinic Proceedings, 64,* 3–27.

Colligan, R. C., Osborne, D., Swenson, W. M., & Offord, K. P. (1983). *The MMPI: A contemporary normative study.* New York: Praeger.

Elkind, D. (1978). Understanding the young adolescent. *Adolescence, 13,* 127–134.

Elkind, D. (1980). Egocentrism in adolescence. In R. E. Muuss (Ed.), *Adolescent behavior and society: A book of readings* (3rd ed., pp. 79–88). New York: Random House.

Elkind, D., & Bowen, R. (1979). Imaginary audience behavior in children and adolescents. *Developmental Psychology, 15,* 38–44.

Erikson, E. H. (1956). The concept of ego identity. *The Journal of the American Psychoanalytic Association, 4,* 56–121.

Freud, A. (1958). Adolescence. *Psychoanalytic Study of the Child, 13*, 255–278.

Friedman, J. M. H., Asnis, G. M., Boeck, M., & DiFiore, J. (1987). Prevalence of specific suicidal behaviors in a high school sample. *American Journal of Psychiatry, 144*, 1203–1206.

Gottesman, I. I., Hanson, D. R., Kroeker, T. A., & Briggs, P. F. (1987). New MMPI normative data and power-transformed T-score tables for the Hathaway-Monachesi Minnesota cohort of 14,019 fifteen-year-old and 3,674 eighteen-year-olds. In R. P. Archer, *Using the MMPI with adolescents* (pp. 241–297). Hillsdale, NJ: Lawrence Erlbaum Associates.

Gottesman, I. I., & Hanson, D. R. (1990, August). Can the MMPI at age 15 predict schizophrenics-to-be? In R. C. Colligan (Chair), *The MMPI and adolescents: Historical perspective, current research, future developments.* Symposium presentation to the annual meeting of the American Psychological Association, Boston, MA.

Gould, M. S., Wunsch-Hitzig, R., & Dohrenwend, B. (1981). Estimating the prevalence of child psychopathology: A critical review. *Journal of the American Academy of Child Psychiatry, 20*, 462–476.

Graham, P., & Rutter, M. (1985). Adolescent disorders. In M. Rutter & L. Hovsov (Eds.), *Child and adolescent psychiatry: Modern approaches* (pp. 351–367). Oxford, England: Blackwell.

Hall, G. S. (1904). *Adolescence: Its psychology and its relationship to physiology, anthropology, sociology, sex, crime, religion, and education.* New York: Appleton.

Hanson, D. R., Gottesman, I. I., & Heston, L. L. (1990). Long-range schizophrenia forecasting: Many a slip twixt cup and lip. In J. E. Rolf, A. Masten, D. Cicchetti, K. Neuchterlein, & S. Weintraub (Eds.), *Risk and protective factors in the development of psychopathology* (pp. 424–444). New York: Cambridge University Press.

Harris, R. E., & Lingoes, J. C. (1955). *Subscales for the MMPI: An aid to profile interpretation.* Mimeographed materials, Department of Psychology, University of California–San Francisco.

Hathaway, S. R., & Monachesi, E. D. (1963). *Adolescent personality and behavior.* Minneapolis: University of Minnesota Press.

Hillard, J. R., Slomowitz, M., & Levi, L. S. (1987). A retrospective study of adolescents' visits to a general hospital psychiatric emergency service. *American Journal of Psychiatry, 144*, 432–436.

Kashani, J. H., Beck, N., Hoeper, E. W., Fallahi, C., Corcoran, C. M., McAllister, J. A., Rosenberg, T. K., & Reid, J. C. (1987). Psychiatric disorders in a community sample of adolescents. *American Journal of Psychiatry, 144*, 584–589.

Kashani, J. H., & Orvaschel, H. (1988). Anxiety disorders in mid-adolescence: A community sample. *American Journal of Psychiatry, 145*, 960–964.

Kimmel, D. C., & Weiner, I. B. (1985). *Adolescence: A developmental transition.* Hillsdale, NJ: Lawrence Erlbaum Associates.

Loevinger, J. (1976). *Ego development: Conceptions and theories.* San Francisco: Jossey-Bass.

Lowman, J., Galinsky, M. D., & Gray-Little, B. (1980). *Predicting achievement: A ten-year follow-up of black and white adolescents.* The University of North Carolina at Chapel Hill: Institute for Research in Social Science (IRSS Research Reports).

Marcia, J. E. (1966). Development and validation of ego identity status. *Journal of Personality and Social Psychology, 3*, 551–558.

National Institute of Mental Health. (1990). *National plan for research on child and adolescent mental disorders* (DHHS Publication No. ADM 90-1683). Washington, DC: U.S. Government Printing Office.

Offer, D., & Offer, J. B. (1975). *From teenager to young manhood.* New York: Basic Books.

Pancoast, D. L., & Archer, R. P. (1988). MMPI adolescent norms: Patterns and trends across 4 decades. *Journal of Personality Assessment, 52*, 691–706.

Pancoast, D. L., & Archer, R. P. (1992). MMPI response patterns of college students: Comparisons to adolescents and adults. *Journal of Clinical Psychology, 48,* 47–53.

Petersen, A. C. (1985). Pubertal development as a cause of disturbance: Myths, realities, and unanswered questions. *Genetic, Social, and General Psychology Monographs, 111,* 205–232.

Petersen, A. C., & Hamburg, B. A. (1986). Adolescence: A developmental approach to problems and psychopathology. *Behavior Therapy, 17,* 480–499.

Piaget, J. (1975). The intellectual development of the adolescent. In A. H. Esman (Ed.), *The psychology of adolescence: Essential reading* (pp. 104–108). New York: International Universities Press.

Reich, W., & Earls, F. (1987). Rules for making psychiatric diagnoses in children on the basis of multiple sources of information: Preliminary strategies. *Journal of Abnormal Child Psychology, 15,* 601–616.

Rosenberg, L. A., & Joshi, P. (1986). Effect of marital discord on parental reports on the Child Behavior Checklist. *Psychological Reports, 59,* 1255–1259.

Rutter, M., Graham, P., Chadwick, O. F. D., & Yule, W. (1976). Adolescent turmoil: fact or fiction? *Journal of Child Psychology and Psychiatry, 17,* 35–56.

Stone, L. J., & Church, J. (1957). Pubescence, puberty, and physical development. In A. H. Esman (Ed.). *The psychology of adolescence: Essential readings* (pp. 75–85). New York: International Universities Press.

Tanner, J. M. (1969). Growth and endocrinology of the adolescent. In L. Gardner (Ed.), *Endocrine and genetic diseases of childhood* (pp. 19–60). Philadelphia: Saunders.

Tanner, J. M., Whitehouse, R. H., & Takaishi, M. (1966). Standards from birth to maturity for height, weight, height velocity, and weight velocity: British children, 1965, Part I. *Archives of Disease in Childhood, 41,* 454–471.

Weiner, I. B., & Del Gaudio, A. C. (1976). Psychopathology in adolescence: An epidemiological study. *Archives of General Psychiatry, 33,* 187–193.

Weissman, M. M., Wickramaratne, P., Warner, V., John, K., Prusoff, B. A., Merikangas, K. R., & Gammon, G. D. (1987). Assessing psychiatric disorders in children: Discrepancies between mothers' and children's reports. *Archives of General Psychiatry, 44,* 747–753.

Williams, C. L., Hearn, M. D., Hostetler, K., & Ben-Porath, Y. S. (1990). *A comparison of several epidemiological measures for adolescents: MMPI, DISC, and YSR.* Unpublished manuscript, University of Minnesota, Minneapolis.

DEVELOPMENT OF THE MMPI AND THE MMPI-A

DEVELOPMENT OF THE MMPI

Work on the instrument that was to become the Minnesota Multiphasic Personality Inventory (MMPI) was begun in 1937 by Stark R. Hathaway, a psychologist, and J. C. McKinley, a neuropsychiatrist. The test authors were stimulated to develop a "personality inventory" based on their pursuit of several objectives. First, they had noticed that a large proportion of patients presenting for medical treatment manifested "one or more complaints that turn out to be psychoneurotic in nature" (McKinley & Hathaway, 1943, p. 161). The two test authors sought to develop an instrument that would be useful in identifying and describing these patients in a manner that was more efficient and effective than the psychiatric interview techniques traditionally used for psychological evaluations of medical patients. Apparently, Hathaway also believed that such an instrument might assist researchers in attempting to evaluate the efficacy of new treatment interventions by allowing for the systematic matching and evaluation of treatment groups. For example, Hathaway (1964), in reference to the use of insulin therapy, which was prevalent in the 1930s, noted:

> There was no way that our hospital staff could select a group of patients for the new treatment who would be surely comparable in diagnosis and severity of illness to those from some other setting. It became an obvious possibility that one might devise a personality test which, like intelligence tests, would somehow stabilize the identification of the illness and provide an estimate of its severity. Toward this problem the MMPI research was initiated. (p. 205)

Finally, Hathaway was also interested in the development of a personality assessment instrument that could assess changes in symptomatology across time. Further, when such a measure was administered at various stages of the treatment process, it would provide the clinician with an index of therapeutic change. In this regard, Hathaway (1965) stated that the MMPI was designed to serve as an "objective aid in the routine psychiatric case workup of adult patients and as a method of determining the severity of the condition. As a corollary to this, the inventory was expected to provide an objective estimate of psychotherapeutic effect and other changes in the severity of their conditions over time" (p. 463).

As noted by Colligan, Osborne, Swenson, and Offord (1983), the first published reference to the MMPI project was listed as a footnote to a 1939 paper (Hathaway, 1939). The MMPI was initially referred to as the "Medical and Psychiatric Inventory," later titled the "Multiphasic Personality Schedule" in a 1940 paper by Hathaway and McKinley, and finally designated the Minnesota Multiphasic Personality Inventory in the 1943 publication of the instrument through the University of Minnesota Press. Hathaway and McKinley had initial difficulty in finding a publisher for the MMPI, and Hathaway noted that "Dr. McKinley and I had faith sufficient to carry us through several rejections before the University of Minnesota Press finally undertook publication" (cited in Dahlstrom & Welsh, 1960, p. vii). Despite this humble beginning, the MMPI has become the most widely used objective personality assessment instrument across a wide variety of clinical settings (Lubin, Larsen, & Matarazzo, 1984; Lubin, Larsen, Matarazzo, & Seever, 1985; Lubin, Wallis, & Paine, 1971; Piotrowski & Keller, 1989). Butcher (1987) estimated that over 10,000 books and articles have been produced on the MMPI, and Butcher and Owen (1978) reported that 84% of all research on personality inventory instruments has been focused on the MMPI.

Historical Context

In their development of the MMPI, Hathaway and McKinley were sensitive to many of the problems that existed in the personality inventories of that era. For example, the Woodworth Personal Data Sheet (Woodworth, 1920) was a 169-item, self-rating scale designed to detect neurotic maladjustment and was used in screening draftees during World War I. Respondents answered *yes* or *no* to the series of questions, and the total number of positive answers was used to determine whether the individual was referred for additional psychiatric interview. Following the development of the Woodworth Personal Data Sheet, several other rationally developed questionnaires were created, including the Bell Adjustment Inventory (Bell, 1934), and the Bernreuter Personality Inventory (Bernreuter, 1933). Rational scale construction involves the selection of items that logically or rationally appear to measure important areas. The selection of these items is based on the developer's theory, clinical experience, and intuition. A fundamental assumption inherent in this test construction method was that the items actually measured what the authors assumed they measured. Over time, however, it became clear that items selected exclusively on a rational basis were not always indicative of deviant behavior, and that test subjects did not always respond accurately and honestly to test instruments. As noted by Greene (1980), critical studies and reviews appeared by several authors, including Landis and Katz (1934) and Super (1942), that strongly criticized the effectiveness of these rationally derived personality inventories. For example, test scores produced by normal subjects and subjects in clinical settings were often found to show little difference on these measures.

Hathaway and McKinley were also aware of the rudimentary efforts to develop validity scales as employed in the Humm-Wadsworth Temperament Scale (Humm & Wadsworth, 1935). This symptom check-list measure contained a "no count" score consisting of the number of items or symptoms denied (i.e., not endorsed by the subject) in responding to the instrument. Thus, a high no count score was seen as reflective of a subject who was excessively guarded or defensive, whereas a very low no count score might indicate a tendency to exaggerate or overreport symptoms. Additionally, Hathaway and McKinley began work on the MMPI following Strong's use of criterion groups in the development (1927, 1943) of a vocational or occupational-interest inventory (i.e., the Strong Vocational Interest Blank). Thus, Hathaway and McKinley had available a model of scale construction that stood in contrast to the rational development procedures that had typically been used for personality measures. They were also motivated by the need for the creation of an inventory that would be of practical use in clinical settings. By the late 1930s, much of personality assessment was seen as irrelevant by applied psychologists, as acknowledged by Hathaway (1965) in his comment that "it was so widely accepted that personality inventories were valueless that some program directors did not feel that any course work in their nature and interpretation was worth the effort" (p. 461).

Development Methods for the Original MMPI

Greene (1991) dramatically noted that "Out of the psychiatric wilderness of the early 1930s appeared two men, Stark Hathaway and J. C.

McKinley, who, under the banner of empiricism, waged a new battle for the scientific advancement of personality assessment" (p. 4). Numerous descriptions of the developmental procedures used in the creation of the MMPI have been extensively documented by authors including Colligan et al. (1983); Dahlstrom, Welsh, and Dahlstrom (1972, 1975); Friedman, Webb, and Lewak (1989); Graham (1990); and Greene (1991). The procedures employed by Hathaway and McKinley are therefore only briefly summarized in this text.

A salient feature of Hathaway and McKinley's approach to the creation of the MMPI was their use of the *criterion keying* method, or the empirical method of inventory construction. Indeed, the MMPI is usually cited as the outstanding example of this test construction method (e.g., Anastasi, 1982). In the criterion keying approach, items are presented to two or more groups of subjects. One subject group serves as a criterion group that manifests a defining diagnosis or characteristic that the test is meant to measure, and there are one or more comparison groups that do not manifest the trait or characteristic under study. Responses of the criterion and comparison groups are compared, and items are then selected for inventory membership that empirically demonstrate significant differences in response frequency. As noted by Friedman et al. (1989), scales constructed utilizing this methodology are usually named after the criterion group. For example, if the criterion group consisted of clinically depressed patients, the scale would probably be labeled a *Depression scale*. Further, scoring is usually accomplished by assigning one point to each item answered in the direction that is more frequently endorsed by criterion subjects. Additionally, the higher an individual scores on this type of measure, the more items he or she has answered in a direction consistent with that of the criterion group members.

Much as earlier researchers did, Hathaway and McKinley began their construction of the MMPI by generating an extensive pool of items from which various scales might be constructed. Specifically, they created nearly 1,000 self-referenced statements inspired from a wide variety of sources, including psychiatric examination forms, psychiatric textbooks, previously published scales of personality and social attitudes, and their own clinical experience (Hathaway & McKinley, 1940). They then reduced this list to 504 items by deleting items that duplicated content, or that the authors subjectively felt had relatively little significance or value. Thus, the authors used a subjective and rational method to create the initial item pool. To simplify the task of identifying item duplication, Hathaway and McKinley constructed 25 content categories for the original MMPI item pool, which are shown in Table 2.1. In addition to the items shown in Table 2.1, 55 items were subsequently added

TABLE 2.1
Content Categories of the Original 504 MMPI Items as Determined by
Hathaway and McKinley

No.	Category	Number of Items
1.	General health	9
2.	General neurologic	19
3.	Cranial nerves	11
4.	Motility and coordination	6
5.	Sensibility	5
6.	Vasomotor, trophic, speech, secretory	10
7.	Cardiorespiratory	5
8.	Gastrointestinal	11
9.	Genitourinary	6
10.	Habits	20
11.	Family and marital	29
12.	Occupational	18
13.	Educational	12
14.	Sexual attitudes	19
15.	Religious attitudes	20
16.	Political attitudes — law and order	46
17.	Social attitudes	72
18.	Affect, depressive	32
19.	Affect, manic	24
20.	Obsessive, compulsive	15
21.	Delusions, hallucinations, illusions, ideas of reference	31
22.	Phobias	29
23.	Sadistic, masochistic	7
24.	Morale	33
25.	Items to "indicate whether the individual is trying to place himself in an improbably acceptable or unacceptable light"	15

Note. From Colligan, Osborne, Swenson, and Offord (1983). Copyright (c) 1983
by the Mayo Foundation. Adapted by permission of the Mayo Foundation.

"primarily related to masculinity-femininity" (McKinley & Hathaway, 1943, p.162) and nine items were apparently deleted (Colligan et al., 1983), resulting in the creation of a final pool of 550 items. These items were then employed to construct scales by comparing the item responses of normal individuals against those of psychiatric patients who held membership in relatively homogeneous clinical criterion groups.

Normative Groups

The normal criterion group primarily used in developing the MMPI consisted of individuals ($N = 724$) who were visiting friends or relatives receiving treatment at the University of Minnesota Hospital. These subjects, ages 16 years and older, were approached in the halls or waiting rooms of the hospital and invited to participate in the research project if preliminary screening indicated that they were not receiving treatment for any psychiatric or medical illness. The overall age, gender, and marital status of this University of Minnesota group was reported to be comparable to the 1930 United States Census findings (Hathaway & McKinley, 1940). Dahlstrom et al. (1972) described the Minnesota normative sample as follows: "In 1940, such a Minnesota normal adult was about thirty-five years old, was married, lived in a small town or rural area, had had eight years of general schooling, and worked at a skilled or semiskilled trade (or was married to a man with such an occupational level) (p. 8).

In addition, Hathaway and McKinley collected data from two other samples of "normals." One of these samples consisted of 265 high school graduates who were coming to the University of Minnesota Testing Bureau for college counseling and guidance, and 265 individuals who were contacted through the local Works Progress Administration (WPA), a federally funded employment project. This latter group consisted of skilled workers who were "all white-collar workers and were used as controls for urban background and socioeconomic level" (Dahlstrom & Welsh, 1960, p. 46).

Colligan et al. (1983) noted that the original normative data collected by Hathaway and McKinley are no longer available. However, a subsample of these data, referred to as the Minnesota normal "purified" sample, was developed by Hathaway and Briggs (1957). The Hathaway and Briggs sample consists of 225 males and 315 females drawn from the general Minnesota normal sample. These data have been preserved and were the basis for the development of Appendix K in the MMPI-2 Manual (Butcher, Dahlstrom, Graham, Tellegen, & Kaemmer, 1989). Appendix K provides T-score values, based on the purified sample of the original Hathaway/ McKinley norms, for MMPI-2 basic scales.

Clinical Scales

The clinical criterion groups utilized by Hathaway and McKinley defined the eight basic MMPI scales and consisted of carefully selected psychiatric patients in the following diagnostic categories: Hypochondriasis (scale 1), Depression (scale 2), Hysteria (scale 3), Psychopathic Deviate (scale 4), Paranoia (scale 6), Psychasthenia (scale 7), Schizophrenia (scale 8), and Hypomania (scale 9). Detailed descriptions of these clinical criterion groups were provided by Colligan et al. (1983), Dahlstrom and Dahlstrom (1980), Dahlstrom et al. (1972), and Greene (1980, 1991). In addition, a group consisting of "homosexual invert males" was employed by Hathaway and McKinley in the development of the Masculinity-Femininity scale (scale 5). Finally, the Social Intro-version-Extroversion scale, developed by Drake (1946), was eventually added as the 10th basic scale of the MMPI (scale 0). The *Si* scale remains the only standard scale that was developed outside of the original Hathaway group, and the only scale for which a psychiatric criterion group was not obtained (Colligan et al., 1983).

Validity Scales

In addition to the 10 standard clinical scales, Hathaway and McKinley also developed 4 validity scales for the MMPI, the purpose of which was to detect deviant test-taking attitudes or response sets. These measures included the Cannot Say or (?) scale, which was simply the total number of MMPI items that were either omitted or endorsed as both true and false, and the *L* or Lie scale, which consisted of 15 rationally derived items that present common human faults or foibles. The *L* scale was designed to detect crude attempts to present oneself in an unrealistically favorable manner. The *F* scale was composed of 64 items that were selected because they were endorsed in a particular direction by 10% or fewer of the Minnesota normal group. Hathaway and McKinley (1943) suggested that high scores on the *F* scale would imply that the clinical scale profile was invalid because the subject was careless, unable to comprehend the items, or that extensive scoring errors had occurred. The T-score conversion values for *F*, like those for the Cannot Say scale and scale *L*, were arbitrarily assigned by McKinley and Hathaway rather than based on a linear transformation of raw score data from the Minnesota normal sample.

The final validity scale developed for the MMPI was the *K* scale. The *K* scale was developed by selecting 25 male and 25 female psychiatric patients who produced normal-range clinical scale values (i.e., T-score values ≤69 on all clinical scales). These subjects, therefore, could be considered to be false negatives (Meehl & Hathaway, 1946). The profiles of these false-negative patients were compared with the responses of the Minnesota normal cases, that is, true negatives. Item analysis revealed 22 items that discriminated the "true- and false-negative profiles in their item endorsements by at least 30%" (Dahlstrom et al., 1972, p. 124). Eight additional items were eventually added to the *K* scale to aid in the accurate discrimination of depressed and schizophrenic patients from subjects in the normative group. The main function of the *K* scale was to improve the discriminative power of the clinical scales in detecting psychopathology, and varying proportions of the *K* scale raw score total have traditionally been added to scales 1, 4, 7, 8, and 9 when using the

K-correction procedure with adult respondents. The standard validity and clinical scales are discussed in more detail in later chapters of this book dealing with validity assessment and clinical interpretation strategies.

Important Features

Before leaving the topic of the development of the original form of the MMPI, two general points should be made regarding characteristics of the instrument that have largely contributed to its popularity among clinical practitioners. First, as discussed by Graham (1990), it rapidly became apparent following the publication of the MMPI that its interpretation was considerably more complex than was initially anticipated. Rather than producing an elevated score on a single clinical scale, many psychiatric patients produced multiple elevations involving several scales. Thus, for example, depressed patients often produced elevations on the Depression scale, but also obtained high scores on other standard clinical scales of this instrument. According to Graham, this phenomenon resulted from several factors, including a high degree of intercorrelation among the MMPI standard scales. Indeed, a variety of approaches have been used with MMPI data over the past 40 years in attempts to yield useful diagnostic information. No approach has produced more than modest correspondence between MMPI-derived diagnoses and psychiatric diagnoses based upon clinical judgment or standard diagnostic interviews (e.g., Pancoast, Archer, & Gordon, 1988).

For these reasons, the MMPI has come to be used in a manner different from that originally envisioned by Hathaway and McKinley, particularly in terms of profile interpretation. Specifically, the usefulness of the particular scale labels or names has been deemphasized, a practice reflected in the tendency of MMPI interpreters to refer to MMPI scales by their numbers rather than criterion group labels (e.g., references to scale 7 rather than to the Psychasthenia scale). Accompanying this change, numerous researchers have set about to establish the meaning of clinical scales through extensive clinical correlate research. In this research approach, the actual extra-test correlates of the MMPI scales are identified through empirical research efforts based on careful studies of individuals who produce certain patterns of MMPI scale elevations. The net impact of this shift in interpretive focus has been that the MMPI is standardly used as a *descriptive* instrument, and that this descriptive capacity of the MMPI is based upon the accumulation of numerous research studies concerning the test characteristics of specific MMPI configuration groups. As noted by Graham (1990):

Thus, even though the MMPI was not particularly successful in terms of its original purpose (differential diagnosis of clinical groups believed in the 1930s to be discrete psychiatric types), it has proven possible subsequently to use the test to generate descriptions of and inferences about individuals (both normal and patients) on the basis of their own profiles. It is this behavioral description approach to the utilization of the test in everyday practice that has led to its great popularity among practicing clinicians. (p. 8)

It should also be noted that this approach to the interpretation of the MMPI has linked the usefulness of the test, not to aspects of its original psychometric construction, but rather to the massive accumulation of research literature that has been developed for this test instrument. Thus, the major clinical value of the MMPI lies in what we have come to know about what test results "mean."

A second important feature of the MMPI concerns the development of a broad variety of validity scales and indices through which to evaluate the consistency and accuracy of the clients' self-reports. The MMPI was among the first personality assessment instruments to strongly emphasize the use of validity scales to assist in determining the interpretability of clinical test findings. Thus, the MMPI interpreter can estimate the degree to which test findings are influenced by a number of factors related to the respondents' willingness and capacity to respond in a valid manner. This feature, in turn, has allowed the extension of the MMPI to assessment issues not originally envisioned by Hathaway and McKinley. These latter tasks have included the psychological screening of individuals in personnel and forensic settings, situations that differ substantially from those of the typical psychological treatment setting. Beyond the original four validity scales, numerous other MMPI measures have been subsequently developed to assess issues related to technical profile validity (e.g., the Carelessness scale and the Test-Retest Index). Many of these have been recently reviewed by Greene (1989, 1991).

MMPI-2

The MMPI was updated and restandardized, resulting in the release of the MMPI-2 in 1989 (Butcher et al., 1989), 46 years after the original publication of this instrument. The revision involved a modernization of the content and language of test items, the elimination of objectionable items, and the creation of new scales, including a series of 15 content scales. The development of the MMPI-2 also involved the collection of a nationally representative normative data sample of 2,600 adult men and women throughout the United States. The MMPI-2 contains 567 items that heavily overlap with items from both the original form of the MMPI and the adolescent form of the MMPI (MMPI-A). Several comprehensive guides to the MMPI-2 are now available (Butcher, 1990; Graham, 1990; Greene, 1991), and a text has been specifically devoted to a description of the MMPI-2 content scales (Butcher, Graham, Williams, & Ben-Porath, 1990). In addition, an extensive research base is rapidly developing for refinement of interpretation strategies for the MMPI-2 (Archer, in press). It should be specifically noted, however, that the MMPI-2 was designed and normed for individuals who are 18 years of age or older. Adolescent norms were *not* developed for the MMPI-2, nor was it intended for use in the assessment of adolescents.

THE USE OF THE MMPI WITH ADOLESCENTS

The application of the MMPI to adolescent populations for both clinical and research purposes occurred early in the development of this instrument. Although the MMPI was originally intended for administration to individuals who were 16 years of age or older, Dahlstrom et al. (1972) noted that the test could be used effectively with "bright children as young as 12" (p. 21). The delineation of age 12 as the lower limit for administration of the MMPI was probably related to the estimate that a sixth-grade reading level was a prerequisite for understanding the MMPI item pool (Archer, 1987).

Early Applications

The first research application of the MMPI with adolescents appears to have been made by Dora Capwell in 1941, two years prior to the formal publication of the MMPI in 1943. Capwell (1945a) demonstrated the ability of the MMPI to accurately discriminate between groups of delinquent and non-delinquent adolescent girls based upon *Pd* scale elevation. Further, the MMPI *Pd* scale differences between these groups were maintained in a follow-up study that reevaluated MMPI profiles 4 to 15 months following the initial MMPI administration (Capwell, 1945b). Early studies by Monachesi (1948, 1950) also served to provide validity data concerning the *Pd* scale by demonstrating that delinquent boys scored significantly higher on this measure than normal male adolescents. In addition, the 1950 study by Monachesi included a sample of incarcerated female delinquents who produced findings that replicated the earlier reports of Capwell. Following these initial studies, the MMPI was used with adolescents in various attempts to predict, diagnose, and plan treatment programs for delinquent adolescents (e.g., Ball, 1962; Hathaway & Monachesi, 1951, 1952). Pursuing this research topic, Hathaway and Monachesi eventually collected the largest MMPI data set ever obtained on adolescents, in a longitudinal study of the relationship between MMPI findings and delinquent behaviors.

Hathaway and Monachesi administered the MMPI to 3,971 Minnesota ninth-graders during the 1947–1948 school year in a study that served as a prelude to the collection of a larger sample, termed the *statewide sample*. The statewide sample was collected during the spring of 1954, when Hathaway and Monachesi tested 11,329 ninth graders in 86 communities in Minnesota. Their combined samples involved approximately 15,000 adolescents, including a wide sample of Minnesota children from both urban and rural settings. In addition to the MMPI, subjects' school records were obtained and teachers were asked to indicate which students they felt were most likely either to have psychiatric or legal difficulty. Hathaway and Monachesi also gathered information concerning test scores on such instruments as intelligence tests and the Strong Vocational Interest Blank. The MMPI was then repeated on a sample of 3,976 of these children when they reached 12th grade during the 1956–1957 school year.

Follow-up data were obtained by field workers in the children's community area, who searched files of public agencies, including police and court records. The authors continued to acquire biographical information on members of this sample until the mid-1960s (e.g., Hathaway, Reynolds, & Monachesi, 1969) and other researchers are currently performing follow-up studies on various subsections of the sample (e.g., Hanson, Gottesman, & Heston, 1990). A summary of the early findings from this investigation was published in a 1963 book by Hathaway and Monachesi entitled, *Adolescent Personality and Behavior: MMPI Patterns of Normal, Delinquent, Dropout, and Other Outcomes*.

Hathaway and Monachesi (1953, 1961, 1963) undertook the collection of this massive data set in order to implement a longitudinal/prospective study that would identify personality variables related to the onset of delinquency. Rather than retroactively identifying a group of delinquent adolescents based on psychosocial histories, they chose to follow adolescents longitudinally to *predict* involvement in antisocial or delinquent behaviors. Thus, Hathaway and Monachesi hoped to identify MMPI predictors that could serve as indicators of risk factors associated with the later development of delinquent behaviors. Monachesi and Hathaway summarized their results as follows:

> Scales 4, 8, and 9, the excitatory scales, were found to be associated with high delinquency rates. When profiles were deviant on these scales, singly

or in combination, delinquency rates were considerably larger than the overall rate. Thus, it was found that boys with the excitatory MMPI scale codes (where scales 4, 8, and 9 in combination were the most deviant scales in the profile) had a delinquency rate of 41.9% in contrast to the overall rate of 34.6%. Again, scales 0, 2, and 5 are the suppressor scales and were the dominant scales in the profiles of boys with low delinquency rates (27.1% as against 34.6%). The variable scales 1, 3, 6, and 7 were again found to have little relationship with delinquency. Of great interest is the fact that some of these relationships are even more marked for girls. In this case, the MMPI data are so closely related to delinquency that it was found that girls with the excitatory code profile had a delinquency rate twice as large as the overall rate. Again, the more deviant scores on scales 4, 8, and 9, the higher the delinquency rate. Girls with inhibitor or suppressor scale scores have lower delinquency rates than the overall rate. (1969, p. 217)

Systematic follow-up and extensions of this work, usually based on further analyses of the Minnesota statewide sample, have provided consistent support for the concept that elevations on scales *Pd*, *Sc*, and *Ma* serve an *excitatory* function. Higher scores on these scales are predictive of higher rates of "acting out" or delinquent behavior in adolescent samples (e.g., Briggs, Wirt, & Johnson, 1961; Rempel, 1958; Wirt & Briggs, 1959). Findings by Briggs et al. indicated that the accuracy of prediction to delinquent behaviors increased when MMPI data were combined with data regarding the family history of severe disease or death. Specifically, Briggs et al. found that when elevations on excitatory scales were combined with positive histories for family trauma, the frequency of delinquent behavior was twice that of the general population. Similarly, Rempel reported that he could accurately identify 69.5% of a delinquent sample based on analysis of MMPI scales. When MMPI data were combined with school record data in a linear regression procedure, the accurate identification rate for delinquent boys rose to 74.2%. More recently, Huesmann, Lefkowitz, and Eron (1978) found that a simple linear summation of the sums of scales *Pd*, *Ma* and *F* served as the best predictor of delinquent and aggressive behavior in a sample of 426 nineteen-year-old adolescents. This procedure was effective in predicting concurrent incidents of aggression and delinquency as well as retroactively accounting for significant proportions of variance in the ratings of aggressiveness for subjects at age 9.

The research by Hathaway and Monachesi has proved to be very valuable in several ways. First, this research established that the MMPI could usefully predict at least one broad area of important behavior displayed by adolescents: delinquency. Second, the results of their investigation also provided a body of crucial information concerning differences in item endorsement for male versus female adolescents, for adolescents versus adults, and also identified important longitudinal test-retest differences in item endorsement patterns occurring between middle to late adolescence. Third, the data collected by Hathaway and Monachesi provided a major component of the traditionally used adolescent norms later developed by Marks and Briggs (1972), and have also served as the exclusive data source for another set of adolescent norms developed by Gottesman, Hanson, Kroeker, and Briggs (published in Archer, 1987). Further, Hathaway and Monachesi empirically established the clinical correlates of high and low scores for each of the 10 standard clinical scales, separately for each gender. Finally, this project has provided an extraordinarily rich source of data in follow-up investigations of the original Hathaway and Monachesi subjects, spanning topics from the prediction of juvenile delinquency to the personality precursors of schizophrenia (e.g., Hanson, Gottesman, & Heston, 1990).

Development of Adolescent Norms and Codetype Correlates

The most frequently used adolescent norms for the original MMPI form were derived by Marks and Briggs in 1967 and first published in Dahlstrom et al. (1972, pp. 388–399). These norms have also been published in several other texts, including Marks, Seeman, and Haller (1974, pp. 155–162) and Archer (1987, pp. 197–213), and are included in Appendix A of this text. The Marks and Briggs adolescent norms were based on the responses of approximately 1,800 normal adolescents, and reported separately for males and females at age groupings of 17, 16, 15, and a category of 14 and below. The sample sizes used to create these norms ranged from 166 males and 139 females at age 17, to 271 males and 280 females at ages 14 and below.

The Marks and Briggs adolescent norms were based on responses of 720 adolescents selected from the data collected by Hathaway and Monachesi (1963) in the Minnesota statewide sample, combined with additional data from 1,046 adolescents collected during 1964 and 1965 in six states: Alabama, California, Kansas, Missouri, North Carolina, and Ohio. Marks et al. (1974) reported that this sample consisted of White adolescents who were not receiving treatment for emotional disturbance at the time of their MMPI evaluation. Much of the research that has been performed on the use of the MMPI with adolescent populations has been based on the Marks and Briggs normative set.

Like the original Minnesota adult norms, the norms developed by Marks and Briggs converted raw scores to T scores using the standard linear transformation procedure. T scores were therefore determined by taking the nearest integer value of T through the use of the following formula:

$$T = 50 + \frac{10\ (X_i - M)}{SD}$$

In this formula, M and SD represent the mean and standard deviation of the raw scores for a particular scale based upon the normative distribution of subjects in the appropriate age category and gender, and X_i is equal to the raw score value earned by a particular subject. Also similar to the Minnesota normal adult sample, the adolescent norms were based on White respondents.

There were several distinguishing features to the adolescent norms developed by Marks and Briggs (1972). First, Marks and Briggs did not develop a K-correction procedure for use with their adolescent norms. Marks et al. (1974) listed several reasons for this decision. They noted that the original K weights were developed on a small sample of adults and their applicability and generalizability to adolescents was questionable. Further, they cited research findings indicating that K-correction procedures with adolescents reduced, rather than increased, relationships to external criteria. Second, the normative data reported by Marks and Briggs included the scores from all respondents, without screening out subjects based on validity criteria related to scores on L, F, or K. Thus, all profiles were utilized in this data set, regardless of validity scale values. The most extensive description of the adolescent norms developed by Marks and Briggs is provided in the Marks et al. (1974) text entitled, *The Actuarial Use of the MMPI With Adolescents and Adults.*

In addition to adolescent norms, the Marks et al. (1974) text also contained actuarial-based personality descriptors for a series of 29 MMPI high-point codetypes. The main subject pool utilized by Marks and his colleagues to derive these codetype descriptors involved 834 adolescents between the ages of 12 and 18. These adolescents were evaluated after receiving at least 10 hours of psychotherapy between 1965 and 1970. They were described as White teenagers who were not "mentally deficient or retarded" (p. 138). Marks et al. also reported that they later added an additional sample of 419 adolescents who received psychiatric services in the years 1970 to 1973. Adolescents in their samples completed the MMPI and a personal data form that included a self-description adjective checklist and questions covering such topics as attitudes toward self, attitudes toward others, motivational needs, and areas of conflict. The study also employed 172 therapists from 30 states, who provided descriptive ratings on the adolescents. According to Marks et al.:

Of the 172 psychotherapists who provided patient ratings, 116 were either Board certified psychiatrists, Ph.D. level clinical psychologists, or M.S.W. level social workers with two additional years of therapy experience. These "experienced" therapists rated 746 patients or 90% of the cases; an additional 24 therapists who were either third- or fourth-year clinical psychology interns, third-year psychiatric residents, or recent M.S.W. graduates rated 83 patients or 10% of the cases. (1974, p. 139)

Clinician ratings involved multiple instruments, including a case data schedule, an adjective checklist, and a Q-sort of personality descriptors. Therapists' ratings were based on available evidence, including case records, chart notes, and psychological test findings excluding MMPI results.

Taken together, the preliminary codetype pool available to Marks et al. consisted of 2,302 descriptors that were potentially relevant to adolescents' experiences. The authors then selected from these potential correlates or descriptors 1,265 descriptors that were deemed to be relevant for both male and female respondents, that occurred with sufficient frequency to allow for statistical analyses, and that offered information that was clinically relevant in terms of patient description. Data from adolescents were then grouped into descriptive categories related to 29 high-point codetypes with an average sample size of 13.4 respondents per codetype. Descriptors were developed that differentiated between *high* and *low* profiles (profiles above and below the median two-point codetype elevation for that grouping, respectively), as well as between two-point code reversals (e.g., 2-4 in contrast to 4-2 codes). A detailed discussion of the codetype procedures used in this correlate study is presented in Marks et al. (1974) and in Archer (1987).

The Marks et al. (1974) clinical correlate study was crucial in providing clinicians with the first correlate information necessary to interpret adolescents' codetype patterns. Further, the information provided by Marks et al. was sufficiently comprehensive, and flexible in terms of application, so that their system was capable of classifying a large proportion of adolescent profiles typically obtained in clinical settings. The Marks et al. actuarial data descriptions for adolescents represented a substantial improvement over the Hathaway and Monachesi (1961) text, *An Atlas of Juvenile MMPI Profiles*, which was composed of 1,088 MMPI codes representing individual profile configurations from their sample of Minnesota ninth graders. Each profile was accompanied by a short case history and a brief description of that subject's most salient personality features. Clinicians using this atlas identified the cases with profiles most similar to the one produced by their patient, and read the accompanying case description. The clinicians had to derive their own summary of personality features commonly found for the codetype, without the assistance of statistical evaluations to identify the most relevant descriptors for the codetype in general.

Recent Contributions

Since the publication of Marks et al. (1974), substantial work has been done in applying the MMPI to adolescents. This work was summarized in Archer (1984, 1987) and in Colligan and Offord (1989). Specifically, Archer reviewed the numerous studies indicating that adolescent response patterns should be evaluated exclusively with reference to adolescent norms, in contrast to the application of adult norms. Colligan and Offord (1989) noted research done with adolescent samples in the areas of medical evaluation, school adjustment, and juvenile delinquency. Of particular interest is the work that has been done subsequent to Marks et al. in the areas of adolescent norm development and clinical correlates.

In addition to the adolescent norms developed by Marks and Briggs (1972), adolescent MMPI norms for the traditional MMPI instrument were developed by Gottesman et al. (published in Archer, 1987), and by Colligan and Offord (1989) at the Mayo Clinic. The norms developed by Gottesman and his colleagues represent a comprehensive analysis of the approximately 15,000 ninth-grade adolescents tested between 1948 and 1954, and the approximately 3,500 12th graders tested during 1956–1957 by Hathaway and Monachesi in their statewide sample. The sample sizes, validity criteria, raw score, and T-score data for this project are reported in Archer (1987) in Appendix C. In addition to standard scale data, Gottesman et al. provided T-score conversions for a variety of MMPI special scales, including Barron's (1953) Ego Strength scale, MacAndrew's (1965) Alcoholism scale, Welsh's (1956) Anxiety and Repression scales, the Wiggins (1969) Content scales, and the special scales developed by Rosen (1962) for differential diagnosis of psychiatric patients.

Colligan and Offord (1989) also collected normative data for the original form of the MMPI based on the responses of 691 girls and 624 boys between the ages of 13 and 17, inclusive. In collecting these data during the mid-1980s, the authors randomly sampled from 11,930 households in Minnesota, Iowa, and Wisconsin that were within a 50-mile radius of the Mayo Clinic, which is located in Rochester, Minnesota. Telephone interviews established that slightly more than 10% of these households contained adolescents within the appropriate age groups, and after excluding adolescents with potentially handicapping disabilities, 1,412 adolescents were targeted for evaluation. MMPI materials were then mailed to these households, resulting in return rates of 83% for female adolescents and 72% for male adolescents. Colligan and Offord found little evidence of significant differences in mean raw score values across age groups, and therefore the final norms are based on normalized T-score conversions for 13- through 17-year-olds, with conversions presented separately by gender. Colligan and Offord (1991) also recently provided K-corrected T-score values for these norms.

Both the Gottesman et al. (1987) and the Colligan and Offord (1989) adolescent norm projects have substantial strengths. Although the Gottesman et al. data are based upon MMPI responses of adolescents tested nearly 40 years ago, their current analyses are the first to comprehensively evaluate this very large and important data set. Additionally, the Marks and Briggs (1972) norms and the Gottesman et al. (1987) norms share common subjects and produce T-score conversion values for the standard MMPI scales that are similar. The Gottesman et al. MMPI special scale T-score values are, therefore, probably relatively close to those that would have been provided by Marks and Briggs had they attempted to derive normative data for MMPI special scales. The work of Colligan and Offord is based upon a solid methodology employed with a contemporary sample of adolescents, and therefore provides very useful data concerning how modern teenagers respond to the original form of the MMPI. A complete evaluation of both of these adolescent norm sets, however, will require several years of investigation.

Preliminary studies by Archer, Pancoast, and Klinefelter (1989), and by Klinefelter, Pancoast, Archer, and Pruitt (1990) examined the degree to which the Gottesman et al. (1987) and Colligan and Offord (1989) norm sets produce profile elevations and configurations that differ from the traditional Marks and Briggs (1972) norms. These studies employed samples of normal, outpatient, and inpatient adolescents scored on all three normative sets. Results indicated significant differences in profile elevation by norm set, with the lowest T-score values typically produced by the Colligan and Offord norms. Using standardized criteria to judge profile congruence, the congruence rates ranged from 53% for profiles generated by Marks and Briggs versus Colligan and Offord, to approximately 60% for profiles scored on the Marks and Briggs and Gottesman et al. norms. These data suggest that the more recent norms generate codetypes that may often differ from the traditional Marks and Briggs norms. Therefore, the existing codetype literature related to the traditional form of the MMPI may not apply for all profiles generated by these recently published adolescent norms. Given this observation, it seems most reasonable to apply Gottesman et al. or Colligan and Offord norms in conjunction with the traditional Marks and Briggs norms on the original MMPI form, rather than employing either of these normative values as a substitute for the Marks and Briggs norms.

In addition to the work that has been done on adolescent normative values, several investigations have also been conducted recently that examined the clinical correlates of single-scale and two-point codetypes based on the traditional Marks and Briggs adolescent norms. Archer, Gordon, Giannetti, and Singles (1988), for example, examined descriptive correlates of single-scale high-point elevations for scales 2, 3, 4, 8, and 9 in a sample of 112 adolescent inpatients. Clinical descriptors were collected for subjects based on their psychometric self-reports and patient ratings by parents, nursing staff, and individual psychotherapists. In general, findings from this study produced correlate patterns that were highly similar to those reported for basic MMPI scales in the adult literature. Using a similar methodology, Archer, Gordon, Anderson, and Giannetti (1989) also investigated the clinical correlates of the MacAndrew Alcoholism scale, Welsh's Anxiety and Repression scales, and Barron's Ego Strength scale in a sample of 68 adolescent inpatients. Results from this study also indicated patterns of clinically relevant descriptors that were largely consistent with findings derived from studies of adult respondents. Ball, Archer, Struve, Hunter, and Gordon (1987) found evidence of subtle, but detectable, neurological differences between adolescent psychiatric inpatients with and without elevated scale 1 values. Further, Archer and Gordon (1988) found that scale 8 elevations were an effective and sensitive indicator of the presence of schizophrenic diagnoses in a sample of adolescent inpatients.

Williams and Butcher (1989a) also examined single-scale correlates in a sample of 492 boys and 352 girls primarily evaluated in either substance abuse or psychiatric inpatient units. Standard scale values were investigated in relationship to data derived from psychiatric records and parental and treatment staff ratings and reports. Similar to Archer et al. (1988), the authors concluded that single-scale descriptors found for these adolescents were consistent with those reported in adult studies. Additionally, Williams and Butcher (1989b) investigated codetype correlates for this sample of 844 adolescents and found that although some of the codetype descriptors reported by Marks et al. (1974) were replicated in this study, other descriptor patterns were not supported. Recent studies by Lachar and Wrobel (1990) and by Wrobel and Lachar (1990) examined the issue of gender differences in correlate patterns and found evidence of substantially different correlate patterns for male and female adolescents. This latter work underscores the need for more emphasis to be placed on the issue of potential gender differences in MMPI clinical correlate studies of adolescents.

Several researchers have also examined the effects of using both adolescent and adult norms in terms of profile elevation and configuration. Specifically, studies by Archer (1984); Ehrenworth and Archer (1985); Klinge, Lachar, Grissell, and Berman (1978); Klinge and Strauss (1976); and Lachar, Klinge, and Grissell (1976) examined the effects of using adolescent and adult norms in profiling responses of male and female adolescents admitted to inpatient psychiatric services. These studies have consistently shown that the degree of psychopathology displayed by adolescent respondents tends to be more pronounced when adult norms are employed, particularly on scales *F*, *4*, and *8*. Finally, factor analytic studies have been reported based on scale level data by Archer (1984), and by Archer and Klinefelter (1991) on both the item and scale level. In general, the results of these studies produced factor patterns that are reasonably consistent with those that have been typically derived from factor analytic findings in adult samples.

Frequency of Use of the MMPI in Adolescent Assessments

As we have seen, research attention has been increasingly focused on the use of the MMPI in adolescent populations. Until very recently, however, no surveys of test usage were specifically targeted with practitioners who worked mainly with adolescents. Therefore, the relative popularity of instruments such as the MMPI among such practitioners remained unclear. In addressing this issue, Archer, Maruish, Imhof, and Piotrowski (1991) asked psychologists how frequently they used each of 67 instruments in their assessment of adolescent clients. Table 2.2 shows the results for the top 20 assessment instruments, with findings presented by total mention as well as weighted scores that were adjusted for frequency of test usage. As shown in this table, the MMPI is the third most frequently mentioned assessment instrument with adolescents, and the sixth most frequently employed instrument when scores are adjusted for frequency of use. The MMPI is the most frequently employed objective personality assessment instrument with teenagers when either total mentions or weighted scores are evaluated.

Respondents were also asked to indicate those instruments used in their standard test batteries with adolescents, with the results of this question shown in Fig. 2.1. As shown in this figure, the Wechsler IQ measures and the Rorschach are the most frequently reported tests included within standard batteries. The MMPI ranked fifth and was included by roughly half of the survey respondents. In contrast, the only other objective personality assessment included in Fig. 2.1 is the

TABLE 2.2
Frequency of Use of Psychological Assessment Instruments With Adolescents

Instrument	Usage Rating Totals							
	a	b	c	d	e	f	TM	WS
WISC-R/WAIS-R	17	6	20	16	26	77	145	583
Rorschach	25	15	23	15	16	68	137	510
Bender-Gestalt	41	17	24	11	20	49	121	423
TAT	40	18	20	20	22	42	122	416
Sentence Completion	41	21	23	14	20	43	121	404
MMPI	36	23	23	27	21	32	126	394
Human Figure Drawing	61	22	13	15	13	38	101	335
House-Tree-Person	57	25	22	15	15	28	105	314
WRAT	59	17	35	10	16	25	103	306
Kinetic Family Drawing	64	24	22	13	12	27	98	290
Beck Depression Inventory	59	36	46	7	7	7	103	212
MAPI	88	34	10	5	9	16	74	185
MacAndrew Alcoholism Scale	87	33	14	8	8	12	75	177
CBCL	90	30	18	5	4	15	72	172
Woodcock Johnson	94	24	16	11	8	9	68	166
PPVT	78	33	41	6	1	3	84	152
Conners Behavior Rating	94	26	24	9	5	4	68	141
Beery VMI	92	33	18	11	4	4	70	138
Reynolds Adolescent Depression Scale	103	31	13	3	4	8	59	122
Children's Depression Inventory	101	27	18	7	9	0	61	120

Note. From Archer, Maruish, Imhof, and Piotrowski (1991). Copyright (c) 1991 by the American Psychological Association. Reprinted by permission. a = Never; b = Infrequently; c = Occasionally; d = About 50% of the Time; e = Frequently; f = Almost Always. TM = Total Mentions; WS = Weighted Score (sum of n x numerical weight of ratings: a = 0, b = 1, c = 2, d = 3, e = 4, f = 5).

Millon Adolescent Personality Inventory (Millon, Green, & Meagher, 1977), which is included in only 17% of the standard test batteries reported by the respondents. Overall, the results of the survey by Archer et al. (1991) indicate that the MMPI, consistent with surveys of test use in adult populations (e.g., Lubin, Larsen, Matarazzo, & Seever, 1985) is the most frequently used objective personality assessment instrument in evaluations of adolescents.

DEVELOPMENT OF THE MMPI-A

Despite the popularity of the MMPI, researchers and clinicians have expressed concerns regarding several aspects of the use of the MMPI to assess teenagers. For example, Archer et al. (1991) asked survey

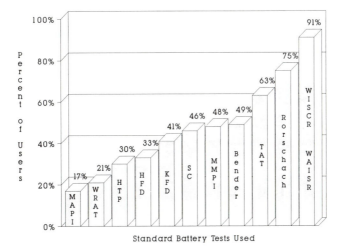

Figure 2.1   Most frequently used psychological instruments in "standard batteries" with adolescents. (From Archer et al., 1991. Copyright (c) by the American Psychological Association. Reprinted by permission)

respondents to indicate their perceptions concerning the major advantages and disadvantages of using the MMPI with adolescents. Major advantages reported included the comprehensive and accurate nature of clinically relevant descriptors, the relative ease of administration and scoring, and the extensive adolescent research data base available for this instrument. Forty-nine percent of respondents, however, indicated that they felt the test was too long, 20% of respondents had concerns regarding inadequate or outdated adolescent norms, 18% felt that the reading level of the original MMPI was too high, and 17% of respondents objected to the use of inappropriate or outdated language in the item pool. Consistent with most of the survey respondents' views, Table 2.3 summarizes a variety of factors pointing to the need for revision of the original test instrument.

Serious concerns have been expressed regarding the nature of the adolescent norms available for the original MMPI. Specifically, the Marks and Briggs (1972) adolescent norms were based on data samples collected in the late 1940s through mid-1960s on White adolescents. This adolescent data set is therefore substantially dated, and dramatically limited in terms of ethnic representation. Pancoast and Archer (1988) examined the adequacy of the traditional adolescent norms in a meta-analysis of normal adolescent samples collected between 1947 and 1965, and contemporary normal adolescent samples collected since 1975. Findings supported the adequacy of the traditional adolescent norms for evaluations of samples of normal adolescents collected between 1947

TABLE 2.3
Factors Contributing to the Development of the MMPI-A

I.   Need for contemporary norms.
   A.   Current norms.
   B.   National sample.
   C.   Ethnic representation.
II. Need for revision of item pool.
   A.   Elimination of offensive items.
   B.   Elimination of items inappropriate for adolescents.
   C.   Rewritten items to simplify wording or sentence structure.
   D.   Inclusion of new items of specific relevance for adolescents.
III. Need for creation of scales to assess adolescent problem areas.
   A.   New supplementary scales including the Immaturity scale.
   B.   Several new content scales including School Problems and Conduct Problems.
IV. Need to standardize MMPI assessment practices for adolescents.
   A.   Confusion regarding appropriate norms.
   B.   Confusion regarding interpretation practices.
   C.   Fostering interest in special scale use.

and 1965. This interval of time coincides with the data collection period for the adolescent samples used in the Marks and Briggs (1972) norms. MMPI patterns produced by contemporary samples of adolescents, however, are elevated above the Marks and Briggs mean values on most clinical scales. These findings suggest that the traditional adolescent norms may not provide an accurate normative baseline, in terms of mean fit, for evaluations of contemporary adolescents.

There have also been criticisms of some of the item content of the original MMPI as inappropriate or offensive in the assessment of teenagers. Most clinicians who have used the traditional form with teenagers are probably aware that an item concerning "drop the handkerchief" has little meaning for today's adolescents, and that questions concerning "deportment" are not readily understood by many adolescents. Similarly, questions such as "my sex life is satisfactory" may have a substantially different meaning when asked of a 13-year-old in contrast to a 30-year-old. Further, awkwardly worded items, a source of concern in terms of administration of the MMPI to adults, has been a major problem in the assessment of adolescents. Finally, the MMPI item pool, although quite extensive, has historically lacked items of specific relevance to adolescent experiences, including problem areas that typically emerge during the teenage years such as drug use, eating disorders, and school-related problems. In addition to modifications at the item level, the creation of MMPI items related to adolescence would provide an opportunity to develop scale measures of specific relevance to adolescent development and psychopathology. Although several special MMPI scales, developed for adults, have been applied to adolescents (e.g., Welsh Anxiety and Repression scales, the MacAndrew Alcoholism scale), these scales were not specifically developed for this population.

On July 1, 1989, the MMPI Adolescent Project Committee, consisting of James N. Butcher, Beverly Kaemmer, Auke Tellegen, and Robert P. Archer, was appointed by the University of Minnesota Press to consider the advisability of creating an adolescent form of the MMPI, and the features such a form should incorporate if development was undertaken.

Goals of the MMPI-A Project

A number of goals were envisioned in the creation of the MMPI-A. Some of these goals were in conflict, and required varying degrees of compromise for work to move forward on the adolescent form. It was clear that adult norms would not be applicable to an adolescent form (Archer, 1984, 1987, 1990; Williams, Graham, & Butcher, 1986) and that a national normative sample representative of the general population of American teenagers would be required for the MMPI-A. An emphasis was also placed on shortening the length of the MMPI, to the extent that this could be achieved without loss of substantive clinical information. Maintaining the continuity between the original MMPI and the MMPI-A was also stressed, including preservation of the standard or basic MMPI validity and clinical scales. Within this context, however, opportunities were taken to modify and improve MMPI scales F, Mf, and Si, based on observations concerning adolescent response characteristics on these measures in the MMPI-A normative sample. If a form was to be developed for adolescent assessment, it was also deemed desirable to include items and scales directly relevant to adolescent development and expression of psychopathology. Finally, it was anticipated that the release of an adolescent form of the MMPI would help to standardize assessment practices with adolescents. As noted by Archer (1984, 1987), there has been considerable controversy and confusion regarding the optimal approach to interpreting adolescents' MMPI profiles. Questions concerning the most appropriate administration criteria, norm sets, special scales, and clinical correlates have been the subject of substantial debate, without clear and consistent resolution. The development and release of the MMPI-A, and the extensive manual for this instrument (Butcher et al. 1992), should serve to standardize and improve assessment practices for both clinician and researcher.

The Experimental Booklet (Form TX)

The development of the MMPI-A was initiated with the creation of an experimental test booklet for adolescents, identified as MMPI Form TX. This experimental test booklet contained 704 items to be used in normative data collection efforts, and in preliminary analyses to determine the feasibility of creating an adolescent form. The first section of this booklet contained 550 items from the traditional MMPI form, followed by the presentation of a new experimental item pool for which scale membership and clinical correlates had not yet been established. The 154 items included in the latter part of the test booklet involved content areas including negative peer group influence, alcohol and drug abuse, family relationship difficulties, school and achievement problems, eating disorders, and identity problems (Archer, 1987). Of the original 550 items, approximately 13% had been reworded to increase content clarity or quality. The 16 repeated items found on the traditional MMPI form were eliminated from MMPI Form TX. In addition to MMPI Form TX, adolescents in the normative samples were administered a 16-item Biographical Information Form and a 74-item Life Events Form. The biographical questionnaire obtained data on a number of variables including age, ethnic background, family structure, parental education and occupation, and academic performance. The life events questionnaire requested information on the occurrence and effect of life events including major illnesses, loss of family members, and parental separation or divorce.

The MMPI-A Normative Sample

The collection of adolescent normative data was undertaken in eight states, seven of which also served as primary sites for adult normative data collection for the MMPI-2. Adolescent normative subjects were generally solicited by mail from the rosters of junior and senior high schools in predetermined areas, and subjects were tested in group sessions generally conducted within school settings. Adolescents who participated in the MMPI-A normative data collection (except at the New York site) were paid for their voluntary participation. A total of approximately 2,500 adolescents were evaluated with the MMPI Form TX in data collection procedures in Minnesota, Ohio, California, Virginia, Pennsylvania, New York, North Carolina, and Washington. Various exclusion criteria were applied to these data including the following: (a) subjects with incomplete data; (b) Carelessness scale values > 35; (c) original F scale value > 25; (d) subject age < 14 or > 18. Employing these exclusion criteria resulted in the creation of a

TABLE 2.4
Geographic Distribution of Adolescents in the MMPI-A Normative Sample

| Location | Males (N = 805) | | Females (N = 815) | |
	Frequency	%	Frequency	%
California	99	12.3	127	15.6
Minnesota	201	25.0	300	36.8
New York	168	20.9	0	00.0
North Carolina	119	14.8	84	10.3
Ohio	101	12.5	109	13.4
Pennsylvania	34	4.2	55	6.7
Virginia	82	10.2	127	15.6
Washington State	1	0.1	13	1.6

Note. From Butcher, Williams, Graham, Archer, Tellegen, Ben-Porath, and Kaemmer (1992). Copyright (c) 1992 by the Regents of the University of Minnesota. Reproduced by permission.

final adolescent normative sample that included 805 males and 815 females. Table 2.4 shows the geographic distribution of this adolescent sample, and Table 2.5 provides age distribution data. The mean age of male adolescents in the MMPI-A normative sample was 15.5 years (SD = 1.17 years), and the mean age for females was 15.6 years (SD = 1.18 years).

Table 2.6 provides information concerning the ethnic origins of adolescents in the MMPI-A normative sample. The ethnic distribution of the MMPI-A normative sample represents a reasonable match against U.S. Census figures, with approximately 76% of data derived from Whites, 12% from Black adolescents, and the remaining 12% of data coming from other ethnic groups.

Tables 2.7 and 2.8 provide data on fathers' and mothers' educational levels, respectively, for adolescents in the MMPI-A normative sample. In general, these data show that the parents of adolescents used in the MMPI-A normative sample are well educated, and overrepresent higher

TABLE 2.5
Age Distribution of Adolescents in the MMPI-A Normative Sample

| Age | Males (N = 805) | | Females (N = 815) | |
	Frequency	%	Frequency	%
14	193	24.0	174	21.3
15	207	25.7	231	28.3
16	228	28.3	202	24.8
17	135	16.8	163	20.0
18	42	5.2	45	5.5

Note. From Butcher, Williams, Graham, Archer, Tellegen, Ben-Porath, and Kaemmer (1992). Copyright (c) 1992 by the Regents of the University of Minnesota. Reproduced by permission.

TABLE 2.6
Ethnic Origin of Adolescents in the MMPI-A Normative Sample

Ethnicity	Males (N = 805)		Females (N = 815)	
	Frequency	%	Frequency	%
White	616	76.5	619	76.0
Black	100	12.4	100	12.3
Asian	23	2.9	23	2.8
Native American	21	2.6	26	3.2
Hispanic	18	2.2	16	2.0
Other	20	2.5	21	2.6
None reported	7	0.9	10	1.2

Note. From Butcher, Williams, Graham, Archer, Tellegen, Ben-Porath, and Kaemmer (1992). Copyright (c) 1992 by the Regents of the University of Minnesota. Reproduced by permission.

TABLE 2.7
Fathers' Educational Level for Adolescents in the MMPI-A Normative Sample

Educational Level	Males (N = 805)		Females (N = 815)	
	Frequency	%	Frequency	%
Less than high school	17	2.1	15	1.8
Some high school	59	7.3	88	10.8
High school graduate	173	21.5	191	23.4
Some college	114	14.2	108	13.3
College graduate	272	33.8	262	32.1
Graduate school	152	18.9	122	15.0
None reported	18	2.2	29	3.6

Note. From Butcher, Williams, Graham, Archer, Tellegen, Ben-Porath, and Kaemmer (1992). Copyright (c) 1992 by the Regents of the University of Minnesota. Reproduced by permission.

educational levels in comparison to the 1980 U.S. Census data. Specifically, roughly 50% of the fathers and 40% of the mothers of children in the MMPI-A normative sample reported an educational level of a bachelors degree or higher. This may be compared with 20% of males and 13% of females in the 1980 U.S. Census data who reported comparable educational levels. This degree of overrepresentation of better-educated individuals is very similar to that found in the MMPI-2 adult normative sample (Archer, in press). This phenomenon is probably related to the use of volunteer subjects in normative data collection procedures, in which better-educated and higher socioeconomic status subjects are differentially more likely to participate.

Finally, Table 2.9 provides data concerning the living situation of the adolescents in the MMPI-A normative sample in terms of the family members with whom they resided. As shown in this table, approxi-

TABLE 2.8
Mothers' Educational Level for Adolescents in the MMPI-A Normative Sample

Educational Level	Males (N = 805)		Females (N = 815)	
	Frequency	%	Frequency	%
Less than high school	9	1.1	11	1.3
Some high school	38	4.7	54	6.6
High school graduate	250	31.1	230	28.2
Some college	145	18.0	183	22.5
College graduate	260	32.3	244	30.0
Graduate school	91	11.3	68	8.3
None reported	12	1.5	25	3.0

Note. From Butcher, Williams, Graham, Archer, Tellegen, Ben-Porath, and Kaemmer (1992). Copyright (c) 1992 by the Regents of the University of Minnesota. Reproduced by permission.

TABLE 2.9
Family Characteristics of Adolescents in the MMPI-A Normative Sample

In home with	Males (N = 805)		Females (N = 815)	
	Frequency	%	Frequency	%
Mother and father	557	69.2	518	63.6
Father only	28	3.5	34	4.2
Mother only	191	23.7	229	28.0
Other	29	3.6	34	4.2
Total	805		815	

Note. From Butcher, Williams, Graham, Archer, Tellegen, Ben-Porath, and Kaemmer (1992). Copyright (c) 1992 by the Regents of the University of Minnesota. Reproduced by permission.

mately two thirds of the adolescents in the MMPI-A normative sample reported that they lived with both parents, approximately 24% reported that they lived with their biological mother only, approximately 3.4% reported living with their biological father, approximately 2% reported living in other home settings, and 4.2% of the sample did not provide information on this variable.

Structure of the MMPI-A

After examining the preliminary data, a decision was reached by the MMPI Adolescent Project Committee during January, 1990 to recommend the creation of the MMPI-A instrument. The final version of the MMPI-A contains 478 items. Administration of the first 350 items of the MMPI-A booklet are sufficient to score validity scales L, F, and K, and the standard clinical scales. The remaining 128 items are scored predominantly on supplementary or content scales. The standard MMPI clinical scales were retained in the MMPI-A form. Fifty-eight standard scale items were deleted from the original scales, however, with about 88% of these item deletions occurring on scales *F, Mf,* or *Si.* Items deleted from the MMPI-A standard scales included the 13 items that were also deleted from the traditional MMPI in the creation of the MMPI-2. In general, items deleted from the MMPI-A dealt with religious attitudes and practices, sexual preferences, bowel and bladder functioning, or items deemed inappropriate in terms of adolescents' life experiences. A variety of empirical criteria were used to delete items from scales *F, Mf,* and *Si.* Specifically, items deleted from the *F* scale were endorsed with a frequency of 21% or greater for either boys or girls in the MMPI-A normative sample. Items were deleted from *Mf* or *Si* if the item loaded only on that particular scale (i.e., did not overlap on other standard measures) and did not demonstrate significant gender differences for the *Mf* scale or did not contribute to factor patterns established for the *Si* scale. Table 2.10 indicates the number of items deleted and retained for each of the standard MMPI-A validity and clinical scales, and Table 2.11 provides a listing of items deleted from the basic validity and clinical scales.

The final form of the MMPI-A includes the original 13 standard scales combined with 4 new validity scales, 15 content scales and 6 supple-

TABLE 2.10
Item Changes in Original MMPI Basic Scales and Resulting Effects on the MMPI-A Basic Scales

MMPI-A Scale	Items Retained	Number of Items Deleted
L	14	1
F	66[a]	27
K	30	0
1 (Hs)	32	1
2 (D)	57	3
3 (Hy)	60	0
4 (Pd)	49	1
5 (Mf)	44	16
6 (Pa)	40	0
7 (Pt)	48	0
8 (Sc)	77	1
9 (Ma)	46	0
0 (Si)	62	8

a = 12 items were deleted from the MMPI-A *F* scale, but retained in the MMPI-A item pool, 12 items from original test which were not scored on the *F* scale were transferred to the MMPI-A scale *F*, and 17 new items were also added to the MMPI-A *F* scale.

TABLE 2.11

Item Deletions from the Original MMPI Basic Validity and Clinical Scales

MMPI Scale	Item No.	Item
L	255	Sometimes at elections I vote for men about whom I know very little.
F	14	I have diarrhea once a month or more.
	20	My sex life is satisfactory.
	*31	I have nightmares every few nights.
	*40	Most any time I would rather sit and daydream than to do anything else.
	53	A minister can cure disease by praying and putting his hand on your head.
	85	Sometimes I am strongly attracted by the personal articles of others such as shoes, gloves, etc., so that I want to handle or steal them though I have no use for them.
	*112	I frequently find it necessary to stand up for what I think is right.
	*115	I believe in a life hereafter.
	139	Sometimes I feel as if I must injure either myself or someone else.
	146	I have the wanderlust and am never happy unless I am roaming or traveling about.
	*156	I have had periods in which I carried on activities without knowing later what I had been doing.
	*164	I like to study and read about things that I am working at.
	169	I am not afraid to handle money.
	197	Someone has been trying to rob me.
	199	Children should be taught all the main facts of sex.
	206	I am very religious (more than most people).
	211	I can sleep during the day but not at night.
	*215	I have used alcohol excessively.
	218	It does not bother me particularly to see animals suffer.
	227	I have been told that I walk during sleep.
	*245	My parents and family find more fault with me than they should.
	246	My neck spots with red often.
	*247	I have reason for feeling jealous of one or more members of my family.
	*256	The only interesting part of newspapers is the "funnies."
	258	I believe there is a God.
	*269	I can easily make other people afraid of me.
	*276	I enjoy children.
1	63	I have had no difficulty in starting or holding my bowel movement.
2	58	Everything is turning out just like the prophets of the Bible said it would.
	95	I go to church almost every week.
	98	I believe in the second coming of Christ.

(Continued)

TABLE 2.11 (Continued)

MMPI Scale	Item No.	Item
4	20	My sex life is satisfactory.
5	4	I think I would like the work of a librarian.
	19	When I take a new job, I like to be tipped off on who should be gotten next to.
	25	I would like to be a singer.
	69	I am very strongly attracted by members of my own sex.
	70	I used to like drop-the-handkerchief.
	87	I would like to be a florist.
	126	I like dramatics.
	133	I have never indulged in any unusual sex practices.
	198	I daydream very little.
	203	If I were a reporter I would very much like to report news of the theater.
	204	I would like to be a journalist.
	214	I have never had any breaking out on my skin that has worried me.
	229	I should like to belong to several clubs or lodges.
	249	I believe there is a Devil and a Hell in afterlife.
	261	If I were an artist I would like to draw flowers.
	295	I liked "Alice in Wonderland" by Lewis Carroll.
8	20	My sex life is satisfactory.
0	25	I would like to be a singer.
	126	I like dramatics.
	229	I should like to belong to several clubs or lodges.
	371	I am not unusually self-conscious.
	427	I am embarrassed by dirty stories.
	440	I try to remember good stories to pass them on to other people.
	455	I am quite often not in on the gossip and talk of the group I belong to.
	462	I have had no difficulty starting or holding my urine.

Note. From Butcher, Williams, Graham, Archer, Tellegen, Ben-Porath, and Kaemmer (1992). Copyright (c) 1992 by the Regents of the University of Minnesota. Reproduced by permission. * Original MMPI *F* scale item not appearing on the MMPI-A *F* scale but appearing on other MMPI-A scales.

mentary scales, and the 28 Harris-Lingoes and 3 *Si* subscales. Table 2.12 provides an overview of the scale structure of the MMPI-A. The new validity measures for the MMPI-A include the F_1 and F_2 subscales of the standard *F* scale, and the True Response Inconsistency scale (*TRIN*) and the Variable Response Inconsistency scale (*VRIN*) developed by Auke Tellegen. The supplementary scales for the MMPI-A involve measures that were developed for the original MMPI, including the Anxiety (*A*) scale, the Repression (*R*) scale, and the MacAndrew Alcoholism scale (*MAC*). In addition, the supplementary scales include a variety of new

TABLE 2.12
Overview of the MMPI-A Scales and Subscales

Basic Profile Scales (17 scales)

Standard Scales (13)
  L through *Si*
Additional Validity Scales (4)
  F_1/F_2 (Subscales of *F* Scale)
  VRIN   (Variable Response Inconsistency)
  TRIN   (True Response Inconsistency)
    Content and Supplementary Scales (21 scales)

Content Scales (15)
  A-anx   (Anxiety)
  A-obs   (Obsessiveness)
  A-dep   (Depression)
  A-hea   (Health Concerns)
  A-aln   (Alienation)
  A-biz   (Bizarre Mentation)
  A-ang   (Anger)
  A-cyn   (Cynicism)
  A-con   (Conduct Problems)
  A-lse   (Low Self-esteem)
  A-las   (Low Aspirations)
  A-sod   (Social Discomfort)
  A-fam   (Family Problems)
  A-sch   (School Problems)
  A-trt   (Negative Treatment Indicators)
Supplementary Scales (6)
  MAC-R (MacAndrew Alcoholism-Revised)
  ACK   (Alcohol/Drug Problem Acknowledgment)
  PRO   (Alcohol/Drug Problem Potential)
  IMM   (Immaturity)
  A   (Anxiety)
  R   (Repression)
    Harris-Lingoes and Si Subscales (31 subscales)

Harris-Lingoes Subscales (28)
  D_1 (Subjective depression)
  D_2 (Psychomotor retardation)
  D_3 (Physical malfunctioning)
  D_4 (Mental dullness)
  D_5 (Brooding)
  Hy_1 (Denial of social anxiety)
  Hy_2 (Need for affection)
  Hy_3 (Lassitude-malaise)
  Hy_4 (Somatic complaints)
  Hy_5 (Inhibition of aggression)
  Pd_1 (Familial discord)
  Pd_2 (Authority problems)
  Pd_3 (Social imperturbability)
  Pd_4 (Social alienation)
  Pd_5 (Self-alienation)

(Continued)

TABLE 2.12 *(Continued)*

Pa_1	(Persecutory ideas)
Pa_2	(Poignancy)
Pa_3	(Naivete)
Sc_1	(Social alienation)
Sc_2	(Emotional alienation)
Sc_3	(Lack of ego mastery, cognitive)
Sc_4	(Lack of ego mastery, conative)
Sc_5	(Lack of ego mastery, defective inhibition)
Sc_6	(Bizarre sensory experiences)
Ma_1	(Amorality)
Ma_2	(Psychomotor acceleration)
Ma_3	(Imperturbability)
Ma_4	(Ego inflation)
Si Subscales (3)	
Si_1	(Shyness/Self-Consciousness)
Si_2	(Social Avoidance)
Si_3	(Alienation-Self and others)

measures developed for the MMPI-A, including the Immaturity (*IMM*) scale, the Alcohol/Drug Problem Acknowledgment (*ACK*) scale, and the Alcohol/Drug Problem Potential (*PRO*) scale. Most of the 15 content scales developed for the MMPI-A overlap with similar measures developed for the MMPI-2, but several of these scales were created specifically and uniquely for the adolescent form. The Harris-Lingoes content subscales developed for the original MMPI were carried over to the MMPI-A, with a few item deletions resulting from the deletion of items on the basic scales. The *Si* subscales were directly carried over from their counterparts in the MMPI-2. The MMPI-A manual by Butcher et al. (1992) contains a listing of each MMPI-A item accompanied by data concerning endorsement frequencies and reading requirements. Appendix B of this text provides the composition of each of the MMPI-A basic scales, content and supplementary scales, and Harris-Lingoes and *Si* subscales. Finally, Butcher et al. (1992) shows item number conversion information for the group form of the original MMPI and MMPI-A, and for conversions between items in the MMPI-2 and MMPI-A.

The MMPI-A is an instrument that is heavily interrelated to both the original form of the MMPI, and to the MMPI-2. The MMPI-A, however, also contains distinctive features that are found only in this form. It is anticipated that much of the research done on the original form of the MMPI with adolescents will be generalizable to the MMPI-A. It is also anticipated that much of the research currently being generated on the MMPI-2 (e.g., validation of many of the MMPI-2 content scales and studies focused on codetype congruence) will also have relevance for the use of the MMPI-A. The development of the MMPI-A, however, represents the first time in the roughly 50-year history of this instrument that a specialized set of adolescent norms, and a specific adolescent form, has been released by the test publisher. The MMPI-A, therefore, has the potential to produce significant improvements in the assessment of psychopathology in adolescents by underscoring the unique aspects of MMPI interpretation necessary with this age group.

REFERENCES

Anastasi, A. (1982). *Psychological testing* (5th ed.). New York: MacMillan.

Archer, R. P. (1984). Use of the MMPI with adolescents: A review of salient issues. *Clinical Psychology Review, 4,* 241–251.

Archer, R. P. (1987). *Using the MMPI with adolescents.* Hillsdale, NJ: Lawrence Erlbaum Associates.

Archer, R. P. (1990). Responses of adolescents on the MMPI-2: Comparisons with MMPI findings. In R. C. Colligan (Chair) *The MMPI and adolescents: Historical perspective, current research, and future developments.* A symposium presented to the annual convention of the American Psychological Association, Boston, MA.

Archer, R. P. (in press). Review of the Minnesota Multiphasic Personality Inventory-2 (MMPI-2). *The Tenth Mental Measurements Yearbook.* Lincoln, NE: Buros Institute of Mental Measurements.

Archer, R. P., & Gordon, R. A. (1988). MMPI and Rorschach indices of schizophrenic and depressive diagnoses among adolescent inpatients. *Journal of Personality Assessment, 52,* 276–287.

Archer, R. P., Gordon, R. A., Anderson, G. L., & Giannetti, R. (1989). MMPI special scale clinical correlates for adolescent inpatients. *Journal of Personality Assessment, 53,* 654–664.

Archer, R. P., Gordon, R. A., Giannetti, R., & Singles, J. (1988). MMPI scale clinical correlates for adolescent inpatients. *Journal of Personality Assessment, 52,* 707–721.

Archer, R. P., & Klinefelter, D. (1991). MMPI factor analytic findings for adolescents: Item- and scale-level factor structures. *Journal of Personality Assessment, 57,* 356–367.

Archer, R. P., Maruish, M., Imhof, E. A., & Piotrowski, C. (1991). Psychological test usage with adolescent clients: 1990 survey findings. *Professional Psychology: Research and Practice, 22,* 247–252.

Archer, R. P., Pancoast, D. L., & Klinefelter, D. (1989). A comparison of MMPI code types produced by traditional and recent adolescent norms. *Psychological Assessment: A Journal of Consulting and Clinical Psychology, 1,* 23–29.

Ball, J. C. (1962). *Social deviancy and adolescent personality: An analytical study with the MMPI.* Lexington, KY: University of Kentucky Press.

Ball, J. D., Archer, R. P., Struve, F. A., Hunter, J. A., & Gordon, R. A. (1987). MMPI correlates of a controversial EEG pattern among adolescent psychiatric patients. *Journal of Clinical Psychology, 43,* 708–714.

Barron, F. (1953). An ego-strength scale which predicts response to psychotherapy. *Journal of Consulting Psychology, 17,* 327–333.

Bell, H. M. (1934). *Adjustment Inventory.* Stanford, CA: Stanford University Press.

Bernreuter, R. G. (1933). The theory and construction of the Personality Inventory. *Journal of Social Psychology, 4,* 387–405.

Briggs, P. F., Wirt, R. D., & Johnson, R. (1961). An application of prediction tables to the study of delinquency. *Journal of Consulting Psychology, 25,* 46–50.

Butcher, J. N. (Ed.). (1987). *Computerized psychological assessment: A practitioner's guide*. New York: Basic Books.

Butcher, J. N. (1990). *MMPI-2 in psychological treatment*. New York: Oxford University Press.

Butcher, J. N., Dahlstrom, W. G., Graham, J. R., Tellegen, A., & Kaemmer, B. (1989). *Minnesota Multiphasic Personality Inventory-2 (MMPI-2): Manual for administration and scoring*. Minneapolis: University of Minnesota Press.

Butcher, J. N., Graham, J. R., Williams, C. L., & Ben-Porath, Y. S. (1990). *Development and use of the MMPI-2 content scales*. Minneapolis: University of Minnesota Press.

Butcher, J. N., & Owen, P. L. (1978). Objective personality inventories: Recent research and some contemporary issues. In B. B. Wolman (Ed.), *Clinical diagnosis of mental disorders: A handbook* (pp. 475–545). New York: Plenum.

Butcher, J. N., Williams, C. L., Graham, J. R., Archer, R. P., Tellegen, A., Ben-Porath, Y. S., & Kaemmer, B. (1992). *MMPI-A (Minnesota Multiphasic Personality Inventory—Adolescent): Manual for administration, scoring, and interpretation*. Minneapolis: University of Minnesota Press.

Capwell, D. F. (1945a). Personality patterns of adolescent girls. I. Girls who show improvement in IQ. *Journal of Applied Psychology, 29*, 212–228.

Capwell, D. F. (1945b). Personality patterns of adolescent girls. II. Delinquents and non-delinquents. *Journal of Applied Psychology, 29*, 284–297.

Colligan, R. C., & Offord, K. P. (1989). The aging MMPI: Contemporary norms for contemporary teenagers. *Mayo Clinic Proceedings, 64*, 3–27.

Colligan, R. C., & Offord, K. P. (1991). Adolescents, the MMPI, and the issue of K correction: A contemporary normative study. *Journal of Clinical Psychology, 47*, 607–631.

Colligan, R. C., Osborne, D., Swenson, W. M., & Offord, K. P. (1983). *The MMPI: A contemporary normative study*. New York: Praeger.

Dahlstrom, W. G., & Dahlstrom, L. E. (Eds.). (1980). *Basic readings on the MMPI: A new selection on personality measurement*. Minneapolis: University of Minnesota Press.

Dahlstrom, W. G., & Welsh, G. S. (1960). *An MMPI handbook: A guide to use in clinical practice and research*. Minneapolis: University of Minnesota Press.

Dahlstrom, W. G., Welsh, G. S., & Dahlstrom, L. E. (1972). *An MMPI handbook: Vol. 1. Clinical interpretation* (rev. ed.). Minneapolis: University of Minnesota Press.

Dahlstrom, W. G., Welsh, G. S., & Dahlstrom, L. E. (1975). *An MMPI handbook: Vol. II. Research applications* (rev. ed.). Minneapolis: University of Minnesota Press.

Drake, L. E. (1946). A social I-E Scale for the MMPI. *Journal of Applied Psychology, 30*, 51–54.

Ehrenworth, N. V., & Archer, R. P. (1985). A comparison of clinical accuracy ratings of interpretive approaches for adolescent MMPI responses. *Journal of Personality Assessment, 49*, 413–421.

Friedman, A. F., Webb, J. T., & Lewak, R. (1989). *Psychological assessment with the MMPI*. Hillsdale, NJ: Lawrence Erlbaum Associates.

Gottesman, I. I., Hanson, D. R., Kroeker, T. A., & Briggs, P. F. (1987). New MMPI normative data and power-transformed T-score tables for the Hathaway-Monachesi Minnesota Cohort of 14,019 15-year-olds and 3,674 18-year-olds. In R. P. Archer, *Using the MMPI with adolescents* (pp. 241–297). Hillsdale, NJ: Lawrence Erlbaum Associates.

Graham, J. R. (1990). *MMPI-2: Assessing personality and psychopathology*. New York: Oxford University Press.

Greene, R. L. (1980). The MMPI: An interpretive manual. Boston: Allyn & Bacon.

Greene, R. L. (1989). Assessing the validity of MMPI profiles in clinical settings. *Clinical notes on the MMPI, No. 11*. Minneapolis: National Computer Systems.

Greene, R. L. (1991). *The MMPI-2/MMPI: An interpretive manual*. Boston: Allyn & Bacon.

Hanson, D. R., Gottesman, I. I., & Heston, L. L. (1990). Long-range schizophrenic forecasting: Many a slip twixt cup and lip. In J. E. Rolf, A. S. Masten, D. Cicchetti, K.

N. Nuechterlein, & S. Weintraub (Eds.), *Risk and protective factors in the development of psychopathology* (pp. 424–444). New York: Cambridge University Press.

Hathaway, S. R. (1939). The personality inventory as an aid in the diagnosis of psychopathic inferiors. *Journal of Consulting Psychology, 3,* 112–117.

Hathaway, S. R. (1964). MMPI: Professional use by professional people. *American Psychologist, 19,* 204–210.

Hathaway, S. R. (1965). Personality inventories. In B. B. Wolman (Ed.), *Handbook of clinical psychology* (pp. 451–476). New York: McGraw-Hill.

Hathaway, S. R., & Briggs, P. F. (1957). Some normative data on new MMPI scales. *Journal of Clinical Psychology, 13,* 364–368.

Hathaway, S. R., & McKinley, J. C. (1940). A multiphasic personality schedule (Minnesota): I. Construction of the schedule. *Journal of Psychology, 10,* 249–254.

Hathaway, S. R., & McKinley, J. C. (1943). *The Minnesota Multiphasic Personality Inventory* (rev. ed.). Minneapolis: University of Minnesota Press.

Hathaway, S. R., & Monachesi, E. D. (1951). The prediction of juvenile delinquency using the Minnesota Multiphasic Personality Inventory. *American Journal of Psychiatry, 108,* 469–473.

Hathaway, S. R., & Monachesi, E. D. (1952). The Minnesota Multiphasic Personality Inventory in the study of juvenile delinquents. *American Sociological Review, 17,* 704–710.

Hathaway, S. R., & Monachesi, E. D. (Eds.). (1953). *Analyzing and predicting juvenile delinquency with the MMPI.* Minneapolis: University of Minnesota Press.

Hathaway, S. R., & Monachesi, E. D. (1961). *An atlas of juvenile MMPI profiles.* Minneapolis: University of Minnesota Press.

Hathaway, S. R., & Monachesi, E. D. (1963). *Adolescent personality and behavior: MMPI patterns of normal, delinquent, dropout, and other outcomes.* Minneapolis: University of Minnesota Press.

Hathaway, S. R., Reynolds, P. C., & Monachesi, E. D. (1969). Follow-up of the later careers and lives of 1,000 boys who dropped out of high school. *Journal of Consulting and Clinical Psychology, 33,* 370–380.

Huesmann, L. R., Lefkowitz, M. M., & Eron, L. D. (1978). Sum of MMPI Scales F, 4, and 9 as a measure of aggression. *Journal of Consulting and Clinical Psychology, 46,* 1071–1078.

Humm, D. G., & Wadsworth, G. W. (1935). The Humm-Wadsworth Temperament Scale. *American Journal of Psychiatry, 92,* 163–200.

Klinefelter, D., Pancoast, D. L., Archer, R. P., & Pruitt, D. L. (1990). Recent adolescent MMPI norms: T-score elevation comparisons to Marks and Briggs. *Journal of Personality Assessment, 54,* 379–389.

Klinge, V., Lachar, D., Grissell, J., & Berman, W. (1978). Effects of scoring norms on adolescent psychiatric drug users' and nonusers' MMPI profiles. *Adolescence, 13,* 1–11.

Klinge, V., & Strauss, M. E. (1976). Effects of scoring norms on adolescent psychiatric patients' MMPI profiles. *Journal of Personality Assessment, 40,* 13–17.

Lachar, D., Klinge, V., & Grissell, J. L. (1976). Relative accuracy of automated MMPI narratives generated from adult norm and adolescent norm profiles. *Journal of Consulting and Clinical Psychology, 44,* 20–24.

Lachar, D., & Wrobel, N. H. (1990, August). Predicting adolescent MMPI correlates: Comparative efficacy of self-report and other-informant assessment. In R. C. Colligan (Chair), *The MMPI and adolescents: Historical perspective, current research, and future developments.* A symposium presented to the annual convention of the American Psychological Association, Boston, MA.

Landis, C., & Katz, S. E. (1934). The validity of certain questions which purport to measure neurotic tendencies. *Journal of Applied Psychology, 18,* 343–356.

Lubin, B., Larsen, R. M., & Matarazzo, J. D. (1984). Patterns of psychological test usage in the United States: 1935–1982. *American Psychologist, 39,* 451–454.

Lubin, B., Larsen, R. M., Matarazzo, J. D., & Seever, M. F. (1985). Psychological test usage patterns in five professional settings. *American Psychologist, 40,* 857–861.

Lubin, B., Wallis, R. R., & Paine, C. (1971). Patterns of psychological test usage in the United States: 1935–1969. *Professional Psychology, 2,* 70–74.

MacAndrew, C. (1965). The differentiation of male alcoholic out-patients from nonalcoholic psychiatric patients by means of the MMPI. *Quarterly Journal of Studies on Alcohol, 26,* 238–246.

Marks, P. A., & Briggs, P. F. (1972). Adolescent norm tables for the MMPI. In W. G. Dahlstrom, G. S. Welsh, & L. E. Dahlstrom, *An MMPI handbook: Vol. 1. Clinical interpretation* (rev. ed., pp. 388–399). Minneapolis: University of Minnesota Press.

Marks, P. A., Seeman, W., & Haller, D. L. (1974). *The actuarial use of the MMPI with adolescents and adults.* Baltimore: Williams & Wilkins.

McKinley, J. C., & Hathaway, S. R. (1943). The identification and measurement of the psychoneuroses in medical practice. *Journal of the American Medical Association, 122,* 161–167.

Meehl, P. E., & Hathaway, S. R. (1946). The K factor as a suppressor variable in the MMPI. *Journal of Applied Psychology, 30,* 525–564.

Millon, T., Green, C. J., & Meagher, R. B. (1977). *Millon Adolescent Personality Inventory.* Minneapolis: National Computer Systems.

Monachesi, E. D. (1948). Some personality characteristics of delinquents and non-delinquents. *Journal of Criminal Law and Criminology, 38,* 487–500.

Monachesi, E. D. (1950). Personality characteristics of institutionalized and non-institutionalized male delinquents. *Journal of Criminal Law and Criminology, 41,* 167–179.

Monachesi, E. D., & Hathaway, S. R. (1969). The personality of delinquents. In J. N. Butcher (Ed.), *MMPI: Research developments and clinical applications* (pp. 207–219). Minneapolis: University of Minnesota Press.

Pancoast, D. L., & Archer, R. P. (1988). MMPI adolescent norms: Patterns and trends across 4 decades. *Journal of Personality Assessment, 52,* 691–706.

Pancoast, D. L., Archer, R. P., & Gordon, R. A. (1988). The MMPI and clinical diagnosis: A comparison of classification system outcomes with discharge diagnoses. *Journal of Personality Assessment, 52,* 81–90.

Piotrowski, C., & Keller, J. W. (1989). Psychological testing in outpatient mental health facilities: A national study. *Professional Psychology: Research and Practice, 20,* 423–425.

Rempel, P. P. (1958). The use of multivariate statistical analysis of Minnesota Multiphasic Personality Inventory scores in the classification of delinquent and nondelinquent high school boys. *Journal of Consulting Psychology, 22,* 17–23.

Rosen, A. (1962). Development of MMPI scales based on a reference group of psychiatric patients. *Psychological Monographs, 76,* (8, Whole No. 527).

Strong, E. K., Jr. (1927). Differentiation of certified public accountants from other occupational groups. *Journal of Educational Psychology, 18,* 227–238.

Strong, E. K., Jr. (1943). *Vocational interests of men and women.* Stanford, CA: Stanford University Press.

Super, D. E. (1942). The Bernreuter Personality Inventory: A review of research. *Psychological Bulletin, 39,* 94–125.

Welsh, G. S. (1956). Factor dimensions A and R. In G. S. Welsh & W. G. Dahlstrom (Eds.), *Basic reading on the MMPI in psychology and medicine* (pp. 264–281). Minneapolis: University of Minnesota Press.

Wiggins, J. S. (1969). Content dimensions in the MMPI. In J. N. Butcher (Ed.), *MMPI: Research developments and clinical applications* (pp. 127–180). New York: McGraw-Hill.

Williams, C. L., & Butcher, J. N. (1989a). An MMPI study of adolescents: I. Empirical validity of standard scales. *Psychological Assessment: A Journal of Consulting and Clinical Psychology, 1,* 251–259.

Williams, C. L., & Butcher, J. N. (1989b). An MMPI study of adolescents: II. Verification and limitations of code type classifications. *Psychological Assessment: A Journal of Consulting and Clinical Psychology, 1,* 260–265.

Williams, C. L., Graham, J. R., & Butcher, J. N. (1986, March). *Appropriate MMPI norms for adolescents: An old problem revisited.* Paper presented at the 21st Annual Symposium on Recent Developments in the Use of the MMPI, Clearwater, FL.

Wirt, R. D., & Briggs, P. F. (1959). Personality and environmental factors in the development of delinquency. *Psychological Monographs: General and Applied,* Whole No. 485, 1–47.

Woodworth, R. S. (1920). Personal data sheet. Chicago: Stoelting.

Wrobel, N. H., & Lachar, D. (1990, August). Refining adolescent MMPI interpretation: Is sex a moderator variable? In R. C. Colligan (Chair), *The MMPI and adolescents: Historical perspective, current research, and future developments.* A symposium presented to the annual convention of the American Psychological Association, Boston, MA.

ADMINISTRATION AND SCORING ISSUES

QUALIFICATION AND BACKGROUND OF TEST USERS

The use of the MMPI-A with adolescents requires specific training and experience in several areas. First, the clinician should be adequately trained in the essential features of test theory and test construction, as well as more specifically in the development and uses of the MMPI and MMPI-A. Therefore, the test user should have completed graduate-level courses in psychological testing and reviewed texts, such as the MMPI handbooks (Dahlstrom, Welsh, & Dahlstrom, 1972, 1975), that have served as definitive references on the MMPI. Those seeking greater familiarity with the development of the MMPI or MMPI-2, including the composition of the basic validity and clinical scales, or basic interpretive strategies, should also refer to the general guides provided by Friedman, Webb, and Lewak (1989); Graham (1987, 1990); or Greene (1980, 1991). Archer (1987), Hathaway and Monachesi (1963), and Marks, Seeman, and Haller (1974) provide reference works concerning the use of the original MMPI form in the assessment of adolescents. Before administering the MMPI-A, the clinician should also thoroughly review the MMPI-A manual (Butcher et al., 1992) which provides a summary of the development, administration, scoring, and interpretation of this instrument.

In addition to background and training in psychological assessment issues, individuals who apply the MMPI/MMPI-A with adolescents should also have additional preparation in the areas of adolescent development, personality, psychopathology, and psychodiagnosis.

Administration Personnel

Because the actual administration of the MMPI or MMPI-A appears deceptively simple, this task is frequently entrusted to individuals operating under the supervision of a psychologist. If these individuals are carefully trained, closely supervised, and well informed concerning appropriate test procedures, such a test administration procedure should not negatively affect test validity. Unfortunately, there are many instances of invalid MMPI findings that are related to incorrect administration procedures used by untrained or unsupervised clerks or secretaries. Greene (1991) noted that although a clinician may delegate the task of MMPI administration to an assistant, a clinician cannot delegate responsibility for proper administration. Responsibility for appropriate administration remains with the clinician utilizing and interpreting test findings. Because testing conditions, test instructions, and response to clients' questions concerning test materials or purposes can all profoundly affect test results, the clinician must ensure that these areas meet the accepted standards for administration procedures.

Purpose of MMPI-A Administration

The MMPI-A is designed to assess psychopathology for adolescents ages 14 through 18, inclusive, and may be selectively used with 12- and 13-year-old adolescents under certain circumstances which are discussed later. As noted in the MMPI-A manual (Butcher et al., 1992), 18-year-olds may be evaluated with this instrument if they are living with their parents in a dependent environment, but should be assessed with the adult form of the revised MMPI, that is, the MMPI-2, if living independently. The MMPI-A is appropriate for evaluating adolescents who are experiencing, or may be suspected of experiencing, some form or type of psychopathology. The MMPI-A has two major functions in the assessment of adolescent psychopathology. First, the MMPI-A provides the ability to objectively evaluate and describe an adolescent's level of functioning in relation to selected standardized dimensions of psychopathology. We may examine MMPI-A test findings, for example, in order to assess the degree to which an adolescent's psychological functioning deviates from that typically reported by normal adolescents. For these purposes, we compare an adolescent's test scores against those obtained by the MMPI-A normative sample. If an adolescent produces clinical levels of psychopathology on the MMPI-A, we may also consult the clinical literature on the MMPI and the MMPI-A to find the most appropriate descriptors for that adolescent. These descriptors are established based on research with adolescents who have produced similar MMPI-A patterns. Second, the repeated administration of the MMPI-A can provide the clinician with a means of assessing changes in psychopathology across time. The ability to assess temporal changes is particularly important in dealing with adolescents, because this developmental stage is defined by rapid changes in personality and psychopathology. When the MMPI-A is administered at various stages in the treatment process, test results may also provide the clinician with a sensitive index of therapeutic change. Because the MMPI-A was developed as a means of describing psychopathology, it was not intended to serve as a primary measure for describing normal-range personality traits or functioning.

ADMINISTRATION ISSUES

A number of administration guidelines or criteria may be offered for using the MMPI-A with adolescents. Table 3.1 provides an overview of these criteria, with suggested responses that may be utilized by the clinician in dealing with specific administration issues and problems.

Age Criteria

General administration guidelines for the use of the MMPI with adolescents were provided by Dahlstrom et al. (1972), and more recently by Williams (1986) and Archer (1987, 1989). Dahlstrom et al. stated that the MMPI can be administered to "bright subjects" as young as age 12, and

TABLE 3.1
Administration Guidelines for Adolescents Using the MMPI-A

Criteria	Possible Responses
1. Adolescent should be 14 to 18 years old.	A. 12–13-year-old adolescents may be evaluated with MMPI-A if they meet all other criteria.
	B. Above 18 administer MMPI-2.
	C. Under age 12 do not administer MMPI (any form).
2. Adolescent must be able to read and understand item pool.	A. Evaluate reading ability on standardized measure of reading comprehension.
	B. If below seventh-grade reading level, administer MMPI-A orally by tape administration.
	C. If IQ is below 70 or reading level below third grade, do not administer MMPI (any form).
3. Adolescent must have appropriate supervised environment to take MMPI-A.	A. Provide continuous supervision by trained personnel in appropriate setting.
	B. Do not attempt MMPI-A testing in nonsupervised environment.
4. Adolescent must be willing to tolerate testing with lengthy instument.	A. Establish rapport with subject prior to testing.
	B. Discuss the importance of MMPI-A testing.
	C. Clearly explain to adolescents that they will with lengthy receive test feedback.
	D. Consider administering only standard scale items, but do not administer "short forms."
	E. Consider dividing testing session into two or more segments.

both Archer (1987) and Williams recommended that younger subjects, that is, those aged 12 and 13, be carefully evaluated before MMPI administration is undertaken. The majority of the MMPI Adolescent Project Committee was of the opinion that the validity of the data for 13-year-olds was too questionable to warrant inclusion in the normative sample. The decision was therefore made to limit the MMPI-A norms to the age categories of 14 through 18, inclusive. However, it is the present author's opinion that elimination of the 13-year-olds' data from all further consideration is not warranted. If a 12- or 13-year-old adolescent meets all administration criteria including adequate reading ability and cognitive and social maturity, it is often possible to administer the MMPI-A to these adolescents. A set of MMPI-A adolescent norms for 13-year-old boys and girls, based on linear T-score conversions and using the same exclusion criteria employed for the 14- through 18-year-old MMPI norms (e.g., original F scale raw score >25), is included in Appendix C of this text. Tables 3.2 and 3.3 show comparisons between T-score elevations produced by these norms for 13-year-olds versus the standard MMPI-A norms. In general, it may be seen that the MMPI-A norms based on 13-year-old respondents produce lower T-score values on most clinical scales. These normative values for 13-year-olds have been developed to promote further research in this area and to allow the clinician to plot the 13-year-old norms in *conjunction* with the standard MMPI-A norms for 13-year-old respondents to identify the degree to which standard interpretive comments might be modified based on a consideration of the adolescent's age. The profile interpretation, however, should be primarily based on the standard MMPI-A norms, and modified or refined by consideration of the specific 13-year-old normative values. It is cautioned, however, that 13-year-old adolescents typically represent a difficult age group to evaluate with either the MMPI or the MMPI-A. All criteria for administration must be carefully assessed to determine if these adolescents are capable of producing valid responses. Younger adolescents may not have a wide enough range of life experiences, including exposure to cultural and educational opportunities commonly encountered in the American society, to render the item content psychologically and semantically meaningful. Limitations in developmental opportunities as well as reading abilities, clearly contraindicate the administration of the MMPI or MMPI-A to younger adolescents.

Reading Requirements

Reading level is obviously a crucial factor in determining whether an adolescent can complete the MMPI-A. Inadequate reading ability may serve as one of the major causes of invalid test protocols for adolescents. Ball and Carroll (1960) found that adolescents with lower IQs and below-average academic records tended to produce higher Cannot Say

TABLE 3.2
Comparison of T Scores Generated for Non-Elevated Profiles by MMPI-A
Norms for 13-Year-Olds, Standard MMPI-A Norms (14–18 Years Old) and Marks
and Briggs Adolescent Norms for the Original MMPI (Age 14 and Below)

			T-scores					
MMPI-A	Raw Score		MMPI-A (13)		MMPI-A		MMPI	
Scale	Male	Female	Male	Female	Male	Female	Male	Female
VRIN	6	5	50	49	54	54	—	—
TRIN	10	9	52F	52F	54T	54T	—	—
F1	6	4	50	49	55	53	—	—
F2	6	7	50	50	52	55	—	—
F	14	11	50	50	56	55	64	65
L	4	3	52	50	55	54	56	50
K	12	11	51	51	49	49	48	44
1 (Hs)	7	7	50	50	49	46	55	54
2 (D)	23	23	51	50	56	53	66	64
3 (Hy)	21	21	50	50	50	46	58	53
4 (Pd)	20	20	49	50	50	48	56	57
5 (Mf)	21	26	51	50	49	56	62	55
6 (Pa)	15	13	51	50	54	49	63	56
7 (Pt)	21	22	50	50	53	50	59	60
8 (Sc)	29	26	50	50	55	51	63	64
9 (Ma)	23	22	50	49	52	48	60	62
0 (Si)	29	29	50	49	54	53	56	54
Additional Scales								
A-anx	9	9	49	50	52	48	—	—
A-obs	8	8	51	49	51	48	—	—
A-dep	9	9	50	51	52	51	—	—
A-hea	11	11	50	50	54	53	—	—
A-aln	7	7	50	51	52	53	—	—
A-biz	6	5	50	49	55	53	—	—
A-ang	8	9	48	49	48	49	—	—
A-cyn	13	14	49	49	48	50	—	—
A-con	10	9	49	51	49	51	—	—
A-lse	6	6	50	49	52	50	—	—
A-las	7	6	51	49	52	48	—	—
A-sod	10	9	51	50	53	53	—	—
A-fam	14	13	51	49	53	49	—	—
A-sch	8	7	49	51	53	53	—	—
A-trt	11	7	50	51	52	45	—	—
MAC-R	22	21	51	51	52	53	—	—
ACK	4	4	49	49	50	51	—	—
PRO	17	16	51	49	56	48	—	—
IMM	18	16	51	50	57	57	—	—
A	17	17	50	50	53	50	—	—
R	14	15	49	51	51	55	—	—

TABLE 3.3

Comparison of T scores generated for elevated profiles by MMPI-A norms for 13-year-olds, standard MMPI-A norms (14–18 Years Old) and Marks and Briggs adolescent norms for the original MMPI (Age 14 and Below)

MMPI-A	Raw Score		MMPI-A (13)		MMPI-A		MMPI	
Scale	Male	Female	Male	Female	Male	Female	Male	Female
VRIN	11	10	67	65	69	75	–	–
TRIN	13	13	66F	66T	71T	73T	–	–
F1	11	9	64	65	68	69	–	–
F2	15	14	64	65	70	70	–	–
F	25	22	65	65	69	70	79	91
L	7	6	64	64	67	70	71	64
K	18	17	66	66	61	62	60	60
1 (Hs)	12	12	65	64	58	54	70	66
2 (D)	32	34	65	65	75	75	86	87
3 (Hy)	30	30	65	65	66	65	78	73
4 (Pd)	29	28	65	65	70	64	76	74
5 (Mf)	26	21	65	65	62	69	76	69
6 (Pa)	21	19	65	64	73	65	79	69
7 (Pt)	32	33	65	65	71	67	74	76
8 (Sc)	43	42	65	65	74	71	78	84
9 (Ma)	30	28	65	64	72	64	74	75
0 (Si)	38	39	65	64	65	65	68	68
Additional Scales								
A-anx	15	14	66	65	69	61	–	–
A-obs	13	13	66	66	72	70	–	–
A-dep	16	15	65	65	69	61	–	–
A-hea	19	19	65	65	72	68	–	–
A-aln	12	11	65	64	70	66	–	–
A-biz	10	10	64	65	70	69	–	–
A-ang	13	13	65	65	69	67	–	–
A-cyn	19	20	64	65	69	72	–	–
A-con	16	14	64	64	68	66	–	–
A-lse	13	11	65	66	79	65	–	–
A-las	12	10	66	65	81	66	–	–
A-sod	15	14	66	64	66	66	–	–
A-fam	21	21	66	65	70	67	–	–
A-sch	12	12	65	66	69	71	–	–
A-trt	18	16	65	64	77	67	–	–
MAC-R	28	27	66	66	66	68	–	–
ACK	8	8	67	66	67	68	–	–
PRO	24	23	65	66	67	65	–	–
IMM	27	25	66	66	72	71	–	–
A	27	26	65	65	67	62	–	–
R	20	21	65	66	65	72	–	–

scores, suggesting that the failure to respond to MMPI items often reflects problems in item comprehension. An inverse relationship ($r =$ -.10, $p < .05$) between reading grade level and raw score values on the Cannot Say scale was also found by Archer and Gordon (1991). This study was based on a sample of 495 normal adolescents who received the MMPI-A and the Ohio Literacy Test, a measure of reading comprehension. Thus, adolescents who have difficulty reading MMPI or MMPI-A items tend to omit items at a higher frequency than other adolescents. Unfortunately, many adolescents also attempt to respond to items that they cannot adequately read or comprehend, often resulting in invalid test protocols.

For many years a sixth-grade reading level was generally accepted as a requirement for MMPI evaluation. Johnson and Bond (1950), for example, assessed the readability of MMPI items using the Flesch Reading Ease Formula (Flesch, 1948), and derived an overall estimate of sixth-grade reading difficulty for a sample of MMPI items. The sixth-grade reading level estimate was used in most standard texts on the MMPI. Ward and Ward (1980), however, reevaluated the MMPI items using the Flesch readability measure and reported that MMPI items on the basic scales have an average reading difficulty level at the 6.7 grade level. Individual scale readability levels range from a 6.4 grade level on the *Mf* scale to a 7.2 grade level for the *K* scale. Their findings resulted in the recommendation of a seventh-grade reading level for individuals taking the MMPI. Further increasing reading ability requirements, Butcher, Dahlstrom, Graham, Tellegen, and Kaemmer (1989) recommended that clients have at least an eighth-grade reading level in order to ensure adequate comprehension of the MMPI-2 item pool. This recommendation was based on the analysis of MMPI-2 items using item difficulty ratings referred to as *Lexile* ratings in the MMPI-2 manual. When the MMPI-2 item pool is evaluated using other standardized measures of reading difficulty such as the Flesch Reading Ease Formula (Flesch, 1948), however, there are some indications that the Lexile ratings may have produced an overestimate of reading requirements. In the highest estimate of reading difficulty, Blanchard (1981) reported that nine years of education was necessary to meet the criterion of accurate comprehension of 90% of the MMPI items. As noted by Greene (1991), this reading level appears particularly restrictive in that most freshman-level college textbooks are written at a ninth-grade reading level.

Part of the complexity in attempting to evaluate the reading requirements of the MMPI involves the differences in standardized methods of estimating the reading difficulty of individual items. Additionally, lack of agreement on the number or percentage of items that must be successfully read and comprehended before an individual is deemed suitable to take the inventory has added to variations in estimates. Unfortunately, reading ability is frequently discussed in a dichotomous manner, that is, the subject either does or does not have the reading ability to take the MMPI. Many subjects, however, can successfully comprehend some, but not all, of the MMPI or MMPI-A item pool. The central question concerns the number of items that must be successfully read in order to ensure the overall validity of the test findings.

The MMPI-A manual (Butcher et al., 1992) provides an analysis of the reading difficulty for each of the MMPI-A items using several standardized measures of reading difficulty. The measures include the Flesch-Kincaid method, which has been used in previous studies of the MMPI and other assessment instruments. Based on the Flesch-Kincaid, the MMPI-A item pool varies in reading difficulty from the 1st to the 16th-grade level. Employing a criterion that at least 80% of the MMPI-A item pool should be accurately read and comprehended in order to ensure valid test findings, a seventh-grade reading level would be required for the MMPI-A, based on the Flesch-Kincaid reading comprehension standard. This seventh-grade reading level serves as the current recommendation for adolescents evaluated with the MMPI-A.

Adolescents' reading abilities may be evaluated by the use of any of a number of reading comprehension instruments, including the Gray Oral Reading Tests, (GORT: Gray & Robinson, 1963; GORT-R: Wiederholt & Bryant, 1986), the Peabody Individual Achievement Test—Revised (PIAT-R: Markwardt, 1989), or the reading component of the Wide Range Achievement Test—Revised (WRAT-R: Jastak & Wilkinson, 1984). A reasonably accurate reading screen can also be accomplished, however, by requesting the adolescent to read aloud and explain several MMPI-A items. The items that appear to be the most useful markers in this regard are items that have an eighth-grade reading level difficulty rating. Among the initial MMPI-A test statements, eighth-grade level items include the following:

5. I am easily awakened by noise.
17. I am troubled by attacks of nausea and vomiting.
18. I am very seldom troubled by constipation.
25. I am bothered by an upset stomach several times a week.
29. I have had very peculiar and strange experiences.

An adolescent may have difficulty in responding to the MMPI-A because of specific reading ability deficits, in contrast to limitations in overall intellectual cognitive functioning. Under these circumstances, an administration may still be undertaken using the standardized audiotape versions of this instrument available through National Computer Systems. Generally, procedures in which an examiner reads test items to the adolescent are not recommended because of the degree of intrusion on the response process associated with this method. Research by Newmark (1971), for example, indicated that MMPI profiles produced by adolescents for whom items were read aloud by an examiner resulted in higher K scale scores than results obtained with traditional administration methods. If an adolescent scores below 70 on the standardized IQ assessment measure, or has less than a fourth-grade reading level, administration of the MMPI-A should not be attempted through any format.

When questions are asked by adolescents concerning the specific meaning of an MMPI-A statement or word, the examiner should attempt to provide useful but neutral information. For example, dictionary definitions can be given to commonly misunderstood words (e.g., *constipation, nausea,* or *diarrhea*). However, the frequency with which adolescents encounter unfamiliar or awkwardly worded items should be reduced on the MMPI-A, in comparison with the original test instrument, because 69 of the original items have been reworded or modified in order to improve the readability or relevance of the MMPI-A to contemporary adolescents' life experiences. Table 3.4 provides examples of item revisions designed to accomplish these tasks. Research by Archer and Gordon (1992) indicated that these revised items may be considered to be psychometrically equivalent to the original items in terms of response characteristics. When questions are raised by the adolescent concerning items that he or she clearly understands and comprehends, however, the examiner must always be careful to remind the subject to respond to the item as it applies to him or her, based on the adolescent's own judgments and opinions.

Despite reasonable efforts to evaluate reading ability, the clinician is likely to encounter adolescents who have responded to the MMPI-A item pool without reading and/or understanding many items. These problems may occur because of reading deficits, motivational issues, or a combination of these factors. A simple method of checking for most types of random response patterns involves recording the total MMPI-A administration time. Total administration time provides one useful index for aiding in the identification of random response sets among adolescents, particularly for adolescents who provide unusually brief administration times of less than 40 minutes for the full-length MMPI-A. Unless test administration time is recorded, however, this valuable information source is lost. Other methods of detecting potential problems in reading ability, based on MMPI-A scales including *TRIN* and *VRIN*, are discussed in the following chapter.

TABLE 3.4
Examples of MMPI-A Item Revisions

MMPI Item No.	MMPI Content	MMPI-A Item No.	MMPI-A Content
38	During one period when I was a youngster I engaged in petty thievery.	32	I have sometimes stolen things.
56	As a youngster I was suspended from school one or more times for cutting up.	80	I have been suspended from school one or more times for bad behavior.
124	Most people will use somewhat unfair means to gain profit or an advantage rather than to lose it.	107	Most people will use somewhat unfair means to get what they want.
313	The man who provides temptation by leaving valuable property unprotected is about as much to blame for its theft as the one who steals it.	263	A person who leaves valuable property unprotected is about as much to blame when it is stolen as the one who steals it.
471	In school my marks in deportment were quite regularly bad.	389	In school my grades in classroom behavior (conduct) are quite regularly bad.

Note. Items reproduced from the MMPI and MMPI-A by permission. Copyright (c) by the Regents of the University of Minnesota.

Supervision Requirements

It is important that the adolescent be provided with an appropriate testing environment in which to complete the MMPI or MMPI-A. This environment should include adequate privacy and supervision. The testing environment should be as comfortable as possible, minimizing the presence of extraneous noise or other distracting influences. It is inappropriate to allow an adolescent to complete the MMPI in any unsupervised setting, or in settings in which privacy cannot be assured, such as at home or in a clinic waiting room. Unsupervised test administration does not provide adequate data for valid test interpretation, and is subject to legal challenge if such findings are presented in a courtroom setting. Adequate test supervision means that a proctor or examiner is available to continuously monitor the test-taking process, and to provide appropriate assistance when necessary. Adequate proctoring does not require, however, that the proctor monitor each individual response by the subject, or otherwise become overly intrusive in the testing process.

Increasing Adolescents' Cooperation with Testing Procedures

A final criterion in the evaluation of adolescents involves their willingness to answer the lengthy item pool of the MMPI or MMPI-A. For the angry and oppositional adolescent, the MMPI-A may present a welcomed opportunity to exhibit hostility and resistance by refusing to respond to items, or responding in an inappropriate or random manner (Newmark & Thibodeau, 1979). Once the adolescent has entered into an "anal-retentive" struggle with the examiner over test completion, there is often little the examiner can do that will effectively decrease the conflict. Prior to the administration of the MMPI-A, however, several steps may be taken to increase the motivation of most adolescents. These procedures include the following: (a) establishing adequate rapport with the adolescent prior to testing; (b) providing clear and concise instructions concerning the purposes of testing; and (c) providing the adolescent with an opportunity to receive testing feedback.

Clear and concise instructions should be given to the adolescent that provide him or her with a general understanding of the purposes of the MMPI-A administration. When clear instructions are not provided, many adolescents will project their own meaning onto the testing in a manner that may serve to render test results invalid. For example, an adolescent may erroneously believe that test results are being utilized to determine whether a psychiatric hospitalization is indicated, or are being used by the therapist in order to attribute blame or punishment for family conflict or family dysfunction. Poorly worded instructions may also negatively influence a subject's test-taking attitude and cooperation with testing procedures. The instructions, therefore, should be carefully worded and standardized. The adolescent should read the instructions provided in the MMPI-A test booklet and also receive a verbal summary, which might, for example, include the following: "Read each statement and decide whether it is true as applied to you or false as applied to you. Remember to give your own opinion of yourself. There are no right or wrong answers. Your test results will help us to understand you."

In addition to these introductory instructions, adolescents frequently ask questions concerning various aspects of testing, which often reflect their anxiety concerning the evaluation process. The following are frequently encountered questions, with suggested responses, as adapted from the Caldwell Report (Caldwell, 1977a) and from Friedman et al. (1989).

1. Q. How long will this take?
   A. About an hour to an hour and a half, usually. Some teenagers take longer, whereas other teenagers finish in less time.
2. Q. Will it make any difference if I skip some questions and come back to them?
   A. If you do it carefully, skipping some questions and returning to them probably will not make any difference. But it is easy to get mixed up in marking your answers, and that will make a difference, so it is better to do them in order, if possible.
3. Q. Suppose I cannot answer all the questions?
   A. Try to answer all of them. If you omit a few items, it will not matter, but try to do them all. When you are finished, take a few minutes to check your answer sheet for any missing answers, incomplete erasures, or double-answered questions.
4. Q. What is the MMPI-A?
   A. The MMPI-A is short for the Minnesota Multiphasic Personality Inventory—Adolescent. It is a widely used test to help understand the kinds of problems that happen to teenagers.
5. Q. How do I try to answer these questions?
   A. Answer the questions as you currently feel. Work quickly, and do not spend time worrying over your answers.
6. Q. What if I don't agree with the results from the test or the test results are wrong?
   A. That is something that you and I will get a chance to discuss during the feedback process. Teenagers often learn some things about themselves that they did not know, and the therapist often learns which parts of the testing were more accurate than others. It is hoped we will *both* learn something from the feedback process.

It is important to present the MMPI-A to adolescents in a careful and serious manner that underscores the importance of the testing process. Attempts to assist the adolescent in feeling more comfortable by minimizing the importance of the MMPI-A evaluation are usually counterproductive. A "casual" presentation of the MMPI-A may actually result in a reduction in the adolescent's cooperation and motivation to complete testing because his or her doubts concerning the importance of test findings will have been validated.

Providing Test Results Feedback

In addition to establishing rapport with the adolescent prior to testing, and providing clear and concise test instructions, it is very helpful to inform the adolescent that he or she will receive feedback on the test results. If an adolescent does not have the opportunity to learn from the testing experience, there is often little inherent motivation to cooperate with the demanding testing procedures. The MMPI test feedback process has served as a central focus in two recent texts entitled *MMPI-2 in Psychological Treatment* (Butcher, 1990), and in *Therapist Guide to the MMPI and MMPI-2: Providing Feedback and Treatment* (Lewak, Marks, & Nelson, 1990). In addition, a computer software package has been developed by Marks and Lewak (1991) to assist the clinician in providing meaningful MMPI test feedback to adolescent clients. The interpretive information provided within this report includes statements designed to be provided directly to the client. A sample output from this report is provided, with the permission of Western Psychological Services, in the appendix to this chapter.

Butcher (1990) provided general guidelines for MMPI-2 feedback that are also applicable to the MMPI-A. Among Butcher's recommendations are suggestions that the test be explained to the patient, including a brief description of the meaning of scales and T scores, and that the therapist then review the patient's scores in relation to test norms. Furthermore, responses are encouraged from the client during the feedback session in order to make feedback an interactive experience. Butcher also underscores the therapist's need to appraise the degree of acceptance of test feedback by asking the client to summarize his or her understanding of, and reaction to, major findings. Butcher cautions that therapists should present feedback as "provisional" information, and that the therapist should gauge how much feedback the client can realistically absorb or incorporate without becoming overwhelmed or excessively defensive.

The origin and rationale of the feedback approach taken by Lewak et al. (1990), and by Marks and Lewak (1991) is described as an empirical-phenomenological approach based upon the theoretical formulations of Alex Caldwell. Caldwell (1976, 1977b) postulated that MMPI scales measure dimensions of psychopathology that are related to fear-conditioned defensive responses. These defensive responses are acquired as a result of the interaction between individuals' predispositions and the occurrence of certain environmental stresses during their development. Table 3.5 lists each of the 8 clinical scales for which Caldwell has described an associated fear-conditioned defensive response.

The use of the Caldwell model provides a basis upon which to offer nonthreatening feedback to adolescent and adult clients. Much of the traditional descriptive literature regarding MMPI interpretation, however, has contained psychological terms that may be viewed by the client as negative, pejorative, evaluative, or irrelevant. The Lewak et al. (1990) approach to providing patient feedback attempts to move beyond

TABLE 3.5
MMPI Clinical Scales and the Associated Fear-Conditioned Defensive
Responses Postulated by Alex Caldwell.

Scale	Fear	Response
1	Physical pain, illness or death.	Overprotecting the body.
2	Significant and irretrievable loss.	Stopping of wanting or needing.
3	Emotional pain, anger or sadness.	Denying or positivizing feelings.
4	Being unwanted, rejected or abandoned.	"Numbing out" emotional involvements.
6	Being criticized, devalued or humiliated.	Maintaining hypersensitivity and vigilance.
7	Unexpected and unpleasant events.	Thinking ahead and worrying.
8	Hostility, being disliked or despised by those upon whom one depends.	"Shutting down" cognitive processing.
9	Failing significant others.	Increasing activity and expectations.

Note. Adapted from Friedman, Webb, and Lewak (1989). Copyright (c) 1989 by Lawrence Erlbaum Associates, Inc. Reprinted by permission.

this problem. Their feedback strategy focuses on the patient's phenomenological experience of the stressors that initially induced maladaptive response patterns, rather than providing an objective clinical description of the defenses themselves. For example, Lewak et al. note that high T-score values for MMPI scale *1* are typically related to descriptions that emphasize personality characteristics including immaturity, dependency, psychological naivete, and excessive preoccupation with somatic concerns. From the patient's perspective, however, high scale *1* elevations may represent a reasonable response to the perception that one's physical health is fragile, and that physical integrity may be threatened by pain, illness, or even death. Therefore, their feedback statements for marked elevations on scale *1* include the following:

> Your body is a constant source of anxiety and fear for you, so right now your worries about health take up most of your time and energy. This constant fear and worry about your physical health may be taking its toll and leaving you feeling extremely defeated, pessimistic, and bitter. You may even find yourself resigned to living the rest of your life chronically ill and in pain . . . . You probably have to rely on others to help you in your daily living; this is usually very frustrating for you. (Lewak et al., 1990, pp. 55–56)

Test Administration Procedures to Increase Cooperation

Several additional steps may be taken in order to increase adolescents' willingness to cooperate with testing procedures. For example, it is often feasible to divide the administration of the MMPI across several sessions, when the total test administration can be accomplished over a few days. If administration is attempted in one session, it is advisable to provide rest periods if an adolescent is becoming fatigued during the testing process. Placement of the MMPI at the earlier stages of an extensive test battery decreases the probability that an adolescent may employ a random response set in order to finish the testing session as quickly as possible. Finally, a clinician may elect to administer only the first 349 items in the MMPI-A form, or the first 399 items in the original MMPI Form R, as an abbreviated administration of the test. This administration format utilizes only those items necessary to score the standard validity and clinical scales. If the motivation or cooperation of an adolescent would be increased significantly by an abbreviated administration format, or if time restrictions impose such limitations, this option allows the clinician to fully score and interpret the standard clinical scales and the Harris-Lingoes and *Si* subscales. Abbreviated administrations do not, however, provide information concerning the content scales, several of the supplementary scales, or the validity scales *VRIN*, *TRIN*, *F*, and *F$_2$*.

Short Form Issues

In response to the problems created by the lengthy MMPI item pool, Newmark and Thibodeau (1979) recommended the development and use of short forms of the MMPI in the assessment of adolescents. As defined by Butcher and Hostetler (1990), the term *short form* is "used to describe sets of scales that have been decreased in length from the standard MMPI form. An MMPI short form is a group of items that is thought to be a valid substitute for the full scale score even though it might contain only 4 or 5 items from the original full scale" (p. 12).

The MMPI-168 was developed by utilizing the first 168 items to appear in the group booklet form of the MMPI (Overall & Gomez-Mont, 1974). The 71-item Mini-Mult was devised by Kincannon (1968) based upon factor analyses used to identify item cluster groups. Investigations of MMPI-168 characteristics in adolescent samples were provided by MacBeth and Cadow (1984) and Rathus (1978). In addition, Mlott (1973) reported Mini-Mult findings for adolescent inpatients.

Butcher (1985) and Butcher and Hostetler (1990) noted a series of potential problems with the use of MMPI short forms: The reduced number of items within MMPI scales entailed in short form versions reduces the overall reliability of the measurement of scale constructs. The shortened versions of the MMPI have also not been sufficiently validated against external criteria. Additionally, the short form profiles and codetypes are frequently different from results that would have been achieved for an individual based on the administration of the full MMPI item pool. Research by Hoffmann and Butcher (1975), for example, showed that the Mini-Mult and administration of the standard MMPI tend to produce the same MMPI codetypes in only 33% of cases, and that the full MMPI and the MMPI-168 produce similar codetypes in only 40% of adult cases. Consistent with these findings, Lueger (1983) reported that two-point codetypes derived from standard and MMPI-168 forms were different in over 50% of their sample of male adolescents. Greene (1982) suggested that short forms of the MMPI may constitute new test measures that require additional validation to identify external correlates. In addition to issues related to scale reliability and codetype congruence, Butcher and Hostetler (1990) questioned the ability of the MMPI short forms to accurately determine profile validity.

The problems with MMPI short forms, as identified in studies with adult populations, appear to have important implications for clinical and/or research uses of the MMPI-A. In particular, there is a significant loss of valuable clinical information when short forms are used in place of the full MMPI. The use of a short form procedure, although it saves administration time with adolescent respondents, appears likely to introduce more than an acceptable range of confusion and "noise" into the interpretation process for adolescent profiles. In recognition of these problems, no efforts were made by the MMPI-2 or MMPI-A advisory committees to preserve any of the currently existing MMPI short forms. Consequently, as noted by Butcher and Hostetler (1990), "Some of the items constituting previously developed MMPI short forms may have been deleted from the MMPI in the revision process" (p. 18).

The use of MMPI short forms, in contrast to an abbreviated administration, is not recommended in the assessment of adolescents. As previously noted, however, the abbreviated form of the MMPI may serve as a reasonable resource in coping with poorly motivated or resistant adolescents. Additionally, several approaches to abbreviating the administration of the MMPI item pool by adapting the presentation of MMPI items to computer administration are currently being developed and evaluated (e.g., Ben-Porath, Slutske, & Butcher, 1989; Roper, Ben-Porath, & Butcher, 1991). Computer-adapted administration approaches are strategies of presenting only those items that add to clinically relevant information about the patient, given the patient's prior MMPI responses. Several approaches have been developed for this purpose, including strategies based on Item Response Theory (IRT). Butcher and Hostetler (1990) noted that although none of these approaches are currently practical, it is likely that effective, adaptive programs will be developed in the future for automated administration of the MMPI-2 and MMPI-A.

TEST MATERIALS

Original MMPI Forms

Several forms of the original MMPI have been developed, including the MMPI Group Form which is a reusable group booklet form, and MMPI Form R which is a hard cover, spiral-bound test booklet. Of these two forms, the Group Form is more widely used. Furthermore, as Greene (1980) noted, most of the MMPI research literature has been based on data derived from the Group Form. The Form R booklet has been particularly useful, however, when a subject does not have a hard surface on which to enter responses to the test items. The Form R answer sheet is inserted over two pegs in the back of the test booklet. Form R pages follow a step-down format in which the turning of each consecutive page reveals another column of answer spaces matched with the booklet column of the corresponding questions. The step-down procedure reveals only one column of questions and answers at a time, thereby reducing the possibility of misplacing a response to a specific question. An audio cassette version of the group form is also available through the Professional Assessment Services of National Computer Systems, the authorized distributor of MMPI, MMPI-2, and MMPI-A materials. Materials are made available only to individuals who meet user qualification standards established by NCS.

The numbering system for items in the group booklet form and Form R of the original MMPI are identical for the first 366 items, but diverge for the latter parts of the item pool. This discrepancy has created substantial confusion for both researchers and clinicians. Dahlstrom et al (1972), however, have provided item conversion tables between the Group Form and Form R formats. Administration of the first 399 items on Form R allows for an abbreviated testing permitting the scoring of all basic standard and validity scales. Unfortunately, there is not a straight-forward method of providing an abbreviated administration for the Group Form booklet.

MMPI-A Test Materials

In addition to test materials related to the original MMPI, new materials are also available for the MMPI-A. Fortunately, the order of the 478 items in the soft cover, hard cover, and audiotape versions of the MMPI-A are identical and arranged such that the standard validity (except scale *F*) and clinical scales may be scored based on the admin-istration of the first 350 items. It should again be noted, however, that the content scales and several of the supplementary scales of the MMPI-A cannot be scored when abbreviated administrations are utilized and therefore valuable information may be lost. The audio cassette version of the MMPI-A is useful for the visually impaired, as well as for adolescents with significant reading-related disabilities that make the standard form administration impractical. A Hispanic item booklet and audiotape are planned for development for the MMPI-A.

Different answer sheets are available for the MMPI-A, depending on whether the examiner intends to score the test by the use of hand-scoring keys, or by computer scoring. Therefore, the examiner should consider the scoring mechanism that will be utilized before selecting the answer sheet to be used for the MMPI-A. Additionally, it should be noted that answer sheets designed for the original MMPI or the MMPI-2 are not applicable to the MMPI-A.

SCORING THE MMPI-A

The examiner should take substantial care to eliminate the common sources of error that occur in scoring and profiling MMPI-A responses. This process should start with a careful examination of the adolescent's answer sheet to ensure that items were not left unanswered, or endorsed in both the true and false directions. Additionally, answer sheets should be examined for evidence of response patterns indicative of random markings, or all true or all false response sets.

Obtaining the raw scores for all of the MMPI-A standard and supplementary scales may be accomplished by computer or hand scoring keys. If hand scoring is used, conversion of raw scores to T-score values should be done using MMPI-A profile sheets based on the gender-specific adolescent norms for this instrument. Adolescent profile sheets for the MMPI-A are available through National Computer Systems, which utilize the normative values for the MMPI-A described and presented in the MMPI-A manual (Butcher et al., 1992) and in Appendix D of this text. When using the original form of the MMPI, adolescent age-appropriate norm tables may be found in texts including Archer (1987), Dahlstrom et al. (1972), Marks et al. (1974), and in Appendix A of this text. Additionally, adolescent profile sheets, based on the Marks and Briggs (1972) norms for the original test instrument, are available through Psychological Assessment Resources, Inc. It is important to clarify that the raw-score K-correction procedure is *not* used in deriving or profiling T scores for adolescents with either the original test instrument or the MMPI-A. As previously noted, Marks et al. (1974) reported several reasons why the K-correction procedure was not developed for adolescent norms, including their preliminary evidence that adolescent MMPI profiles achieve greater discrimination between adolescent subgroups without the addition of a *K*-correction factor.

As reviewed by Archer (1989), the procedures for scoring and profiling adolescent responses may be summarized as follows: First, carefully examine the answer sheet for evidence of deviant response sets, unanswered items, or double-marked items. Second, obtain the raw score value for each scale, utilizing the computer scoring methods available from National Computer Systems or the hand-scoring keys. Third, convert the non-*K*-corrected raw scores to T scores for each scale using the appropriate adolescent norm tables, with particular attention to the gender of the respondent. Fourth, plot T-score values on the MMPI-A profile sheet for the revised instrument, or the adolescent MMPI profile sheet available through Psychological Assessment Resources, Inc. for the original test instrument. The MMPI-A Profile for Basic Scales (Male Form) is shown in Fig. 3.1.

Scoring of the MMPI-A may be accomplished through several different methods. A computer software program is available through National Computer Systems that permits test users to administer and score the standard validity and clinical scales, as well as all content and supplementary scales, using personal microcomputers. The test may also be administered via the standard paper-pencil format, with the responses key-entered later by trained support staff. High-volume test users might wish to consider the scanner option for their personal computer, in which answer sheets are scanned and responses tabulated by the scoring program. In addition, answer sheets may be mailed to National Computer Systems (NCS) in Minneapolis, where test responses will be scored and returned to the test user. A teleprocessing service is also available through NCS, which provides the option of entering the item responses via the personal computer unit keyboard to NCS using a telephone modem. Responses are immediately scored at NCS and results are printed on the user's personal computer printer. NCS consultants are available to discuss the details and prices connected with each of these systems, and may be reached at 1–800–627–7271.

In addition to computerized scoring services, hand-scoring templates, for use with specialized answer sheets, are available for all MMPI-A standard, content, and supplementary scales, and for all subscales. Templates for each scale are placed over the answer sheet, and the number of darkened spaces is counted, representing the raw score for the scale being scored. Special care should be taken when scoring scale 5 (Masculinity-Femininity) to use the scoring key designed for the adolescent's gender, and caution should also be used in scoring *TRIN* (True Response Inconsistency) and *VRIN* (Variable Response Inconsistency), given the complexity of the scoring for these scales.

MMPI-A

Minnesota Multiphasic Personality Inventory-A™

Profile for Basic Scales

James N. Butcher, Carolyn L. Williams, John R. Graham, Robert P. Archer, Auke Tellegen, Yossef S. Ben-Porath, and Beverly Kaemmer

S. R. Hathaway and J. C. McKinley

Minnesota Multiphasic Personality Inventory-A™
Copyright © by THE REGENTS OF THE UNIVERSITY OF MINNESOTA 1942, 1943 (renewed 1970), 1992. This Profile Form 1992.
All rights reserved. Distributed exclusively by NATIONAL COMPUTER SYSTEMS, INC. under license from The University of Minnesota.

"MMPI-A" and "Minnesota Multiphasic Personality Inventory-A" are trademarks owned by The University of Minnesota. Printed in the United States of America.

MALE

Name _____

Address _____

Grade Level _____ Date Tested / /

Setting _____ Age _____

Referred By _____

Scorer's Initials _____

Raw Score

? Raw Score

LEGEND

Ts	T score
VRIN	Variable Response Inconsistency
TRIN	True Response Inconsistency
F₁	Infrequency 1
F₂	Infrequency 2
F	Infrequency
L	Lie
K	Correction
Hs	Hypochondriasis
D	Depression
Hy	Conversion Hysteria
Pd	Psychopathic Deviate
Mf	Masculinity-femininity
Pa	Paranoia
Pt	Psychasthenia
Sc	Schizophrenia
Ma	Hypomania
Si	Social Introversion
?	Cannot Say

NATIONAL COMPUTER SYSTEMS
PROFESSIONAL ASSESSMENT SERVICES
25000

FIGURE 3.1 MMPI-A Profile for Basic Scales (Male).

Computer Administration and Scoring Issues

There are several special considerations that should be evaluated when using computer software for administering or scoring the MMPI/MMPI-A. With on-line administration of the inventory, clear instructions for entering and changing responses should be provided to the respondent. The examiner should ensure that the respondent is instructed in how to accurately enter or change his or her responses. The respondents' entry of responses should be monitored to ensure that they have understood the instructions. Computer administration programs often have summary or editing screens that permit the monitoring of item omissions.

As previously noted, a mail-in scoring service is available for the MMPI-A. When this option is utilized, the respondent enters his or her responses on the computer-scored MMPI-A answer sheet, which is sent to NCS for scoring and reporting. As with the hand-scored version of the MMPI-A, the computer-scored answer sheet should be checked by the examiner for item omissions, double-marking, and deviant response sets before the answer sheet is sent to NCS for processing. The clinician should also eliminate any stray marks or incomplete erasures because these may be interpreted as valid responses in the computer scoring process. These same cautions apply to those examiners who use in-office scanning equipment for response entry.

Along with the cautions just mentioned, those who elect to enter MMPI responses into teleprocessing systems (via modem) by keyboard entry or who use an in-office scoring system should remember to check the accuracy of their entries. These systems often have summary or editing features to facilitate this task.

Selection of Appropriate Norms

The profiling of adolescent scale values should be based on adolescent norms appropriate to the form (MMPI or MMPI-A) that was used in the evaluation. The adolescent norms that should be employed for the original form of the MMPI are those derived by Marks and Briggs (1972) and provided in Appendix A. The adolescent norm set to be utilized with the MMPI-A is based on the MMPI-A normative sample described in Chapter 2 and provided in Appendix D of this text. Because the MMPI-2 was specifically created for adult respondents, and adolescent norms have not been developed for this form, the MMPI-2 should *not* be utilized with respondents under the age of 18 (Butcher et al., 1989).

Archer (1984, 1987) discussed in detail the statistical and interpretive problems that are related to the use of adult norms when applied to adolescent response patterns. In particular, the use of adult norms with adolescent clients tends to overestimate the occurrence and degree of symptomatology related to conduct disorder and antisocial personality features, as well as psychotic and schizophrenic disorders.

Adolescent Norm Transformation Procedures

The adolescent norms developed by Marks and Briggs (1972) for the original form of the MMPI were based on linear transformation procedures that convert raw scores to T-score values. This is identical to the transformation procedures used in developing the adult norms for the original MMPI by Hathaway and McKinley (Dahlstrom et al., 1972). The MMPI-A retains the use of linear T scores for the validity scales (i.e., VRIN, TRIN, F_1, F_2, F, L, and K), for scales 5 (Masculinity-Femininity), and 0 (Social Introversion), and for the supplementary scales, including MacAndrew Alcoholism Scale—Revised (MAC-R), Alcohol/Drug Problem Acknowledgment (ACK), Alcohol/Drug Problem Proneness (PRO), Immaturity (IMM), Repression (R), and Anxiety (A). Eight of the clinical scales on the MMPI-A (1, 2, 3, 4, 6, 7, 8, and 9) and all of the 15 content scales have T-score values derived from uniform T-score transformation procedures.

Uniform transformation procedures were developed to address a problem that has been associated with the use of linear T-score values for the MMPI. This problem is that identical T-score values do not represent the same percentile equivalents across the standard MMPI scales when derived using linear procedures. This phenomenon occurs because MMPI scale raw score distributions are not normally distributed, and the degree to which they vary from the normal distribution fluctuates from scale to scale. Thus, using linear T-score conversion procedures, a T-score value of 70 on one scale does not represent an equivalent percentile value that may be represented by a T = 70 score on another MMPI clinical scale. This discrepancy results in difficulty when directly comparing T-score values across the MMPI scales. The problems related to use of linear T-score conversion procedures for the MMPI were first discussed in detail by Colligan, Osborne, Swenson, and Offord (1983).

In the development of the MMPI-2, uniform T-score transformation procedures were used in order to provide equivalent T-score values across the clinical and content scales. This same approach was taken in the development of the MMPI-A. Uniform T-score values were developed for the clinical scales by examining the distributions for scales 1, 2, 3, 4, 6, 7, 8, and 9 for males and females separately. MMPI-A scales 5 and 0 were not included in the uniform T-score procedures because these scales were derived in a manner different than the other clinical scales, and the distribution of scores on scales 5 and 0 are less skewed, that is, more normally distributed. A composite or averaged distribution of raw scores was then created across the eight basic scales for each gender, adjusting the distribution of each individual scale so that it would match the composite distribution. The purpose of developing a composite distribution was to allow for the assignment of T-score conversion values for each scale such that a given T-score value would convert to equivalent percentile values across each of these scales. Uniform T-score conversions were separately derived for the 15 content scales based on the distribution of scores for this group of measures.

Since uniform T scores represent composite linear T scores, this procedure serves to produce equivalent percentile values across scales for a given T score. This procedure, however, also maintains the underlying positive skew in the distribution of scores from these measures. Thus, uniform T scores are generally similar to values that would be obtained from linear T scores. Nevertheless, differences in T-score transformation procedures, combined with marked differences in mean raw score values produced by the Marks and Briggs (1972) and the MMPI-A (Butcher et al., 1992) normative sample, result in adolescent norms that will often produce differences in overall elevation and profile configuration for a particular response pattern. This topic is discussed in more detail in Chapter 5 in the section on codetype congruence issues. At this point, it is important to stress that the clinician should not assume that the traditional MMPI and the MMPI-A will necessarily produce equivalent profiles, either in elevation or in codetype.

Honaker examined the issue of equivalency between the MMPI and MMPI-2 in the assessment of adults at a 1990 symposium. According to Honaker, the issue of psychometric equivalence between the MMPI and MMPI-2 is critically important because this factor determines, to a large extent, the degree to which the vast research literature on the original instrument may be generalized to the revised and restandardized form. Honaker noted that psychometric theory and standards require four conditions to be met in order to consider two forms equivalent or parallel. These conditions are as follows:

1. Both forms should yield identical scores (e.g., equal mean scores, high-point codes, etc.).
2. Both forms should yield the same distribution of scores.
3. Individual rank ordering produced by both forms should be identical (e.g., individuals should be ranked on a given dimension in the same order based on test scores from each form).
4. Scores generated from each form should correlate equally well with independent external criteria.

In evaluating this issue, Honaker examined a sample of 101 adult psychiatric patients who had received both the MMPI and the MMPI-2 in a counterbalanced, repeated-measures design. Findings indicated that the MMPI and the MMPI-2 did produce parallel score dispersion and rank ordering of respondents, but did not yield equivalent mean scores. MMPI-2 scores were consistently lower for scales *F, 2, 4, 8, 9,* and *0.* Further, the congruence of high-point codes between the MMPI and MMPI-2 was lower than that found for repeated administrations of the MMPI or the MMPI-2. These findings indicate that the MMPI and MMPI-2 are highly interrelated, but not equivalent, test forms. A similar conclusion was supported in research findings by Archer and Gordon (1991) who administered the MMPI-A and the MMPI to a sample of normal high school students. Findings from this study indicate significant and pervasive elevation differences between T scores produced by these two instruments, with MMPI-A scores significantly lower on most clinical scales.

A major focus of future research with the MMPI-A should be directed to examining the congruence between adolescents' profiles produced on the original MMPI versus the MMPI-A. As previously noted, this issue is a central determinant of the degree to which the research literature developed for adolescents using the original test instrument may be validly generalized to the use of the MMPI-A.

Deriving the Welsh Code

Two major coding systems have been developed for MMPI profiles, the first by Stark Hathaway (1947), which in turn was modified and made more comprehensive in a revision by George Welsh (1948). Because the Welsh system is more widely used than the Hathaway code, and allows for a more precise classification of profile features, this system is recommended for classification of adolescents' MMPI responses. A comprehensive description of both the Hathaway and Welsh systems, however, is contained in such texts as Dahlstrom et al. (1972) and Friedman, Webb, and Lewak (1989).

The general function of profile coding is to provide a quick notation that summarizes the most salient features of the profile. These features include the range of elevation of scales and the pattern of relationships between the scales when ordered from highest to lowest elevation. The code provides a quick and convenient way of summarizing the major features of the profile, without the loss of substantial information.

The Welsh Code requires that all standard clinical scales (designated by number) be arranged (left to right) in descending order of magnitude of T-score elevation. The traditional validity scales (*L, F,* and *K*) are then coded immediately to the right of the clinical scales, again arranged from most to least elevated. The relative degree of elevation for any scale within the code is denoted by the following system of symbols (as modified for the MMPI-A and described in the test manual for this instrument):

T-score Values	Symbol
100 and above	**
90–99	*
80–89	"
70–79	'
65–69	+
60–64	−
50–59	/
40–49	:
30–39	#
29 and below	No symbol (scale is presented to the right of the # symbol)

In the Welsh Coding System, the relevant symbol is placed to the immediate right of the scale or scales related to that range of elevation. For example, if scale 2 has a T-score value of 98 and scale 4 has a T-score value of 92, the expression 24* would symbolically represent this occurrence. Further, if two or more scales are within 1 T-score point of each other, this occurrence is denoted by underlining all affected scales. For example, if scale 2 were elevated at 53 and scale 3 were elevated at 52, they would be denoted as follows: 23/. The following example, adapted from Friedman et al. (1989), illustrates the Welsh Coding System for the MMPI-A.

Example:
   Scales: L F K 1 2 3 4 5 6 7 8 9 0
   T scores: 44 60 49 49 99 62 50 67 62 79 63 38 70
   Welsh Code: 2* "70'5 + 836-4/1:9#   F-/KL:

Several features of this illustration may be noted. For example, scales 3 and 6 both produced an identical T-score value of 62, and therefore by convention the scale identified by the lowest numerical value (i.e., scale 3) is presented first in the descending order. Additionally, scales 3, 6, and 8, vary by only one T-score value and therefore all three scales are underlined in the code. Finally, the " is immediately adjacent to the * that follows scale 2. This indicates that no MMPI scale produced values in the T-score range of 80 to 89, illustrating the convention that although no value in this specific T-score range may occur, the appropriate symbol should nevertheless be recorded in the code. Typically, most clinicians apply the Welsh Code first to the standard clinical scales, and then repeat the coding exercise for the validity scales. An example of the use of Welsh coding for the MMPI-A is also provided in the manual for this test instrument (Butcher et al., 1992).

APPENDIX 3.1

MINNESOTA MULTIPHASIC PERSONALITY INVENTORY (MMPI)
The Marks Adolescent Feedback and Treatment Report
by Philip A. Marks, Ph.D. and Richard W. Lewak, Ph.D.

A WPS TEST REPORT by Western Psychological Services
12031 Wilshire Boulevard
Los Angeles, California   90025-1251
Version: 1.000
Copyright (c) 1991 by Western Psychological Services

```
NAME: WPS SAMPLE                        ID NUMBER: 000000001
SEX: MALE                               EDUCATION(IN YEARS): 8
AGE: 15                                 INPATIENT/OUTPATIENT: INPATIENT
BIRTHDATE: 07-18-1976                   MMPI ADMIN DATE: 09-19-1991
ETHNICITY: NATIVE AMERICAN              REPORT DATE: 09-19-1991
```

CONTENT OF THE MMPI REPORT

This report is designed to be used by professionals in providing
teens with an individualized, empathic, and nontechnical understanding
of their MMPI test results, and to assist in the treatment process. It
was developed from research and clinical work with adolescents, ages 12
through 17, who had six or more years of education and came from families
earning at least lower-middle-level incomes, and who were seen in clinic,
office, or outpatient settings for personal, family, and school- or work-
related reasons.

The report was developed for use with results of initial or
pretreatment testing, and it is based on MMPI T-scores derived from the
adolescent norms of Marks, Seeman, and Haller (1974). The material
contained in this report would not be appropriate for use with adults or
with any T-scores that are K-corrected. Users employing this report for
treatment purposes would benefit from an understanding of the treatment
procedures described in the "Therapist Guide to the MMPI and MMPI-2:
Providing Feedback and Treatment" (WPS Catalog No. AE-4).

The report consists of three sections. Section 1, "Notes to the
Provider," determines the validity of the test results, highlights salient
features of the test scores, and provides suggestions for treatment. This
section is written specifically for the professional. It is considered a
professional-to-professional consultation and should not be shown to the
client. The second section describes the teen's approach to the test and
lists his or her uppermost thoughts, feelings, and concerns under the
heading "Issues." This section is to be given directly to the client, who
is then asked to read and validate each of the issues. The final section,
Self-Help," offers suggestions for "homework" that, at the discretion of
the provider, may be given to the client for practice at home.

```
+--------------------------------------------------------------------+
|   Users of this WPS Report should be familiar with the interpretive |
|   guidelines, psychometric properties, and limitations of the MMPI. |
+--------------------------------------------------------------------+
```

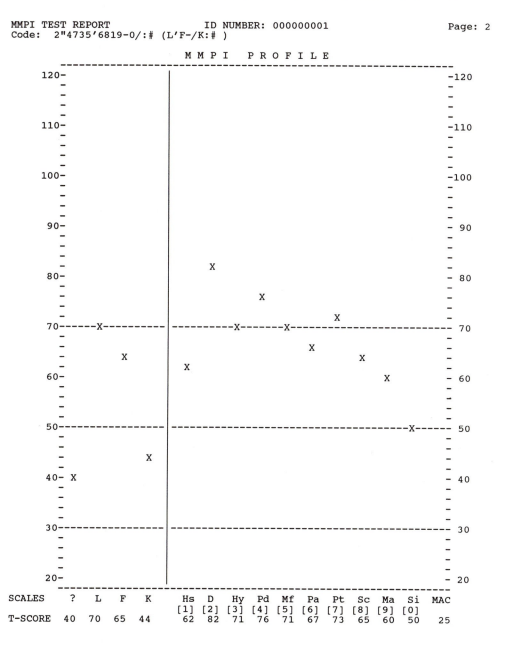

Code: 2"4735'6819-0/:# (L'F-/K:#)

M M P I   P R O F I L E

SCALES	?	L	F	K		Hs	D	Hy	Pd	Mf	Pa	Pt	Sc	Ma	Si	MAC
						[1]	[2]	[3]	[4]	[5]	[6]	[7]	[8]	[9]	[0]	
T-SCORE	40	70	65	44		62	82	71	76	71	67	73	65	60	50	25

NOTE TO THE PROVIDER

This is a clinically elevated profile of a youngster who was cooperative, understood the instructions, and answered the questions in a consistent manner. The results are valid.

This can be characterized as the "escape" or "nothing to lose" codetype. The adolescent with this codetype shares with his or her adult counterparts a sense of being trapped, angry, and hopeless. Angry with authority figures, he or she feels that rules and regulations are made for the sake of adults and used to control teens against their interests. Consequently, these youngsters feel justified in bending the rules and even in breaking them. They are difficult in therapy because they have little trust in adults, and do not believe that what they say will be kept confidential. They are often sullen, and their treatment tends to feel laborious and difficult for the therapist. In some instances, the behavior of these young people can engage the therapist's anger, which then confirms their negative view of authority. For teens from lower socioeconomic backgrounds, this codetype is associated with legal problems including arrests and court actions.

Many of these teens abuse alcohol and drugs. If scale 0 is less than 50T, then sexual promiscuity and self-defeating behaviors are common. In most cases, this codetype reflects the teen's sense of somehow being in a hopeless situation from which there is little to lose by escaping. They have difficulties in concentration at school, where they lack interest and have low motivation. Those with average or lower IQs typically lack the necessary perseverance to finish high school, and they often drop out. They tend to drift into heavy metal music, drugs, and other avenues of escape that reflect their alienation, anger, and sense of hopelessness. They are dissatisfied with their home situations and feel that there is no one they can trust in their families. They also have a poor self-image and, therefore, little confidence in their own ability to take care of themselves. Under these circumstances, they feel that they have nothing to lose by "going for it" in terms of whatever feels good to them now. If the teen is of average or below average intelligence, it is important to determine how far "behind" in school he or she may be, compared to his or her peers. Then, a program to catch up should be instituted with specific rewards provided for success. These youngsters tend to work well if given consistent, small rewards within short-term intervals, whereas they do very poorly when working toward long-term rewards. Treatment should ideally involve a combination of family therapy and individual support. Limit-setting for both the parents and the teen would be important to help the teen learn to trust rules and ultimately benefit from them. In cases where there is a chaotic background or an absence of consistent parenting, then hospitalization or treatment in a residential setting would probably be the best alternatives.

Teenagers with elevated scale 0 scores are shy, socially introverted, insecure, and very uncomfortable in social situations. Timid and submissive, they lack self-confidence and are subassertive. Even when scales 4 and 9 are also elevated, elevations on scale 0 act as a suppressor and decrease the potential for impulsive acting out. Teens from rural settings tend to score higher on this scale, and those from professional families tend to score lower.

MMPI TEST REPORT

Dear HIGH CODE,

The responses you gave to the statements on the MMPI are valuable because they are one way of measuring your thoughts and feelings. The MMPI interprets your thoughts and feelings in comparison to average responses; this interpretation is sometimes called a "profile". Only you can decide if the interpretations feel right for you, and your therapist can help you.

YOUR APPROACH TO THE TEST

Your MMPI results indicated that you have completed the test in the following manners:

Your answers to the questions suggest that you are very concerned about doing "the right thing," and that you do not like to break any rules that might get you into trouble. Being criticized for doing something wrong or bad is very hurtful to you, and you usually try hard to avoid it.

Your answers suggest that you're feeling pretty uptight, unhappy, and confused right now. You might be scared about what is happening to you, and perhaps you feel that you're in need of help from someone. You may be worried about some of your thoughts and even about something being wrong with your health.

The way that you answered the questions suggests that you are an open teenager, and that you are willing to talk about the things that trouble you. You might not be feeling too good about yourself right now, but you seem to be willing to accept help.

ISSUES (Current thoughts, feelings and concerns)

Your test profile suggests that the following issues may be important to you. Please read each issue, then circle the number corresponding to how well it applies to you right now.

4	3	2	1	0
Very True	Mostly True	Partially True	Mostly False	False

1. Right now, you seem to be feeling trapped and angry.   4 3 2 1 0
2. There are times when you feel that you have nothing to lose anymore, and you don't care about anything.   4 3 2 1 0
3. There have been times when you felt things were so bad that you thought of taking your life or just giving up...   4 3 2 1 0
4. There are times when you feel so angry and hopeless that you impulsively do things that can get you into trouble...   4 3 2 1 0
5. For example, you may "blow up" at some adult who you feel is "bugging" you, or you may decide to not do your homework, or you may do something else that winds

	up causing problems for you.........................	4	3	2	1	0
6.	Once you feel like doing something, even if it will get you into trouble, it's hard to say no to yourself and to not do it....................................	4	3	2	1	0
7.	Your impulsiveness sometimes gets you into trouble with people in authority and even the law...........	4	3	2	1	0
8.	You tend to be independent-minded and hate to be controlled...	4	3	2	1	0
9.	You argue a lot with adults because you feel they often don't know what they are talking about.........	4	3	2	1	0
10.	It's hard for you to believe that adults care about you or that anybody really cares about anybody else...	4	3	2	1	0
11.	You typically feel that you have to take care of yourself because nobody else will...................	4	3	2	1	0
12.	The reason why you feel this way is because you have been let down by the adults in your life, and now you don't feel that you can trust anybody...............	4	3	2	1	0
13.	You feel that your parents are overly critical, uncaring, or too "into" themselves...................	4	3	2	1	0
14.	You have always felt that you had nobody to turn to for help when you had a problem, and therefore you've learned to take care of yourself.............	4	3	2	1	0
15.	You tend to do what feels good at the moment, without thinking too much of what might happen later on......	4	3	2	1	0
16.	It is difficult for you to face problems, and so you frequently run away from them......................	4	3	2	1	0
17.	You often use alcohol or drugs as a means to escape from what is bothering you........................	4	3	2	1	0
18.	In school, you have a great deal of difficulty concentrating, much more so than others..............	4	3	2	1	0
19.	Physically, you feel well and you rarely have illnesses or injuries..............................	4	3	2	1	0
20.	You are a very responsible teenager and you worry about accomplishing all of the things that you're supposed to do......................................	4	3	2	1	0
21.	It's hard for you to relax, because you feel that something bad will take you by surprise if you do....	4	3	2	1	0
22.	You tend to be a tense and worried person...........	4	3	2	1	0
23.	In fact, you are a "worrywart" who is always frightened that something bad or unpredictable will happen......	4	3	2	1	0
24.	You are neither shy nor extraverted; you can enjoy attending parties as well as being alone...........	4	3	2	1	0
25.	You are able to assert yourself if you have to.......	4	3	2	1	0
26.	You can be both playful and responsible..............	4	3	2	1	0
27.	You can enjoy loud parties, but you also need to have some time to be alone..................................	4	3	2	1	0
28.	You are a sensitive teenager........................	4	3	2	1	0
29.	You have a number of cultural interests, such as theater and art......................................	4	3	2	1	0
30.	You value literature, philosophy, music, and ideas.	4	3	2	1	0
31.	You believe that girls are interesting as friends as well as girlfriends..................................	4	3	2	1	0

SELF-HELP (SUGGESTIONS OF THINGS YOU CAN DO)

    -Whenever you find yourself arguing with someone, take a moment
to consider whether you really believe in what you are saying or if you
are just arguing automatically.
    -Any time that people in authority "come on strong," try not to
respond as if they are your parents, with whom you feel angry.
    -Even though you may not feel up to it, it is important to develop
a regular exercise program, and also to eat properly.
    -Although you probably feel too angry and hopeless to do anything
right now, it is important that you make a commitment to change one small
thing about yourself and then follow it through.
    -Whenever you feel like giving up on something that you've started,
take a moment to think about the consequences of quitting.
    -Notice how often you look at what is wrong at any given time, rather
than looking at what may be right. When things do go right, allow yourself
to enjoy them.
    -If you are drinking or using drugs, reduce your intake. Try to find
ways of relieving your stress other than the use of alcohol or drugs.

    It is hypothesized that scale 5 reflects gender identity and not sexual
preference. High scores for boys indicate intellectual, aesthetic, and verbal
interests, and a rejection of stereotypic masculine values. Boys scoring above
64T usually avoid aggressive and competitive sports, and they tend to be fussy,
sensitive teens who have difficulty being assertive with girls, unless scales
4 and 9 are also elevated. These boys tend to make friends with girls before
being able to ask them for dates, perhaps as a way of minimizing the
possibility of rejection. They are rather passive teens who need a great deal
of feminine reassurance and approval. Often comfortable exploring their own
feelings and intimate reactions, they make good therapy patients and tend to
be responsive to shaping. Psychotherapy should concentrate on helping them to
become more assertive and able to meet their own needs in heterosexual
relationships.

REFERENCES

Archer, R. P. (1984). Use of the MMPI with adolescents: A review of salient issues. *Clinical Psychology Review, 4,* 241–251.

Archer, R. P. (1987). *Using the MMPI with adolescents.* Hillsdale, NJ: Lawrence Erlbaum Associates.

Archer, R. P. (1989). MMPI assessment of adolescent clients. *Clinical Notes on the MMPI, No. 12.* Minneapolis: National Computer Systems.

Archer, R. P., & Gordon, R. A. (1991). [Correlational analysis of the MMPI-A normative data set]. Unpublished raw data.

Archer, R. P., & Gordon, R. A. (1992). *Psychometric stability of MMPI-A item modifications.* Manuscript submitted for review.

Ball, J. C., & Carroll, D. (1960). Analysis of MMPI Cannot Say scores in an adolescent population. *Journal of Clinical Psychology, 16,* 30–31.

Ben-Porath, Y. S., Slutske, W. S., & Butcher, J. N. (1989). A real-data simulation of computerized adaptive administration of the MMPI. *Psychological Assessment: A Journal of Consulting and Clinical Psychology, 1,* 18–22.

Blanchard, J. S. (1981). Readability of the MMPI. *Perceptual and Motor Skills, 52,* 985–986.

Butcher, J. N. (1985). Why MMPI short forms should not be used for clinical predictions. In J. N. Butcher & J. R. Graham (Eds.), *Clinical applications of the MMPI* (pp. 10–11). Minneapolis: University of Minnesota Department of Conferences.

Butcher, J. N. (1990). *MMPI-2 in psychological treatment.* New York: Oxford University Press.

Butcher, J. N., Dahlstrom, W. G., Graham, J. R., Tellegen, A., & Kaemmer, B. (1989). *Minnesota Multiphasic Personality Inventory–2 (MMPI-2): Manual for administration and scoring.* Minneapolis: University of Minnesota Press.

Butcher, J. N., & Hostetler, K. (1990). Abbreviating MMPI item administration: What can be learned from the MMPI for the MMPI-2? *Psychological Assessment: A Journal of Consulting and Clinical Psychology, 2,* 12–21.

Butcher, J. N., Williams, C. L., Graham, J. R., Archer, R. P., Tellegen, A., Ben-Porath, Y. S., & Kaemmer, B. (1992). *MMPI-A (Minnesota Multiphasic Personality Inventory–Adolescent): Manual for administration, scoring, and interpretation.* Minneapolis: University of Minnesota Press.

Caldwell, A. B. (1976, January). *MMPI profile types.* Paper presented at the Eleventh Annual MMPI Workshop and Symposium, sponsored by the University of Minnesota Press, Minneapolis, MN.

Caldwell, A. B. (1977a). *Questions people ask when taking the MMPI.* (Special Bulletin No. 3, available from Caldwell Report, 1545 Sawtelle Blvd., Ste. 14, Los Angeles, CA 90025).

Caldwell, A. B. (1977b, February). *Treatment recommendations for patients with different MMPI types.* Paper presented at the Twelfth Annual MMPI Workshop and Symposium sponsored by the University of Minnesota, St. Petersburg Beach, FL.

Colligan, R. C., Osborne, D., Swenson, W. M., & Offord, K. P. (1983). *The MMPI: A contemporary normative study.* New York: Praeger.

Dahlstrom, W. G., Welsh, G. S., & Dahlstrom, L. E. (1972). *An MMPI handbook: Vol. I. Clinical interpretation* (rev. ed.). Minneapolis: University of Minnesota Press.

Dahlstrom, W. G., Welsh, G. S., & Dahlstrom, L. E. (1975). *An MMPI handbook: Vol. II. Research applications* (rev. ed.). Minneapolis: University of Minnesota Press.

Flesch, R. (1948). A new readability yardstick. *Journal of Applied Psychology, 32,* 221–233.

Friedman, A. F., Webb, J. T., & Lewak, R. (1989). *Psychological assessment with the MMPI.* Hillsdale, NJ: Lawrence Erlbaum Associates.

Graham, J. R. (1987). *The MMPI: A practical guide* (2nd ed.). New York: Oxford University Press.

Graham, J. R. (1990). *MMPI-2: Assessing personality and psychopathology.* New York: Oxford University Press.

Gray, W. S., & Robinson, H. M. (1963). *Gray Oral Reading Test.* Indianapolis: Bobbs-Merrill.

Greene, R. L. (1980). *The MMPI: An interpretive manual.* Boston: Allyn & Bacon.

Greene, R. L. (1982). Some reflections on "MMPI short forms: A literature review." *Journal of Personality Assessment, 46,* 486–487.

Greene, R. L. (1991). *The MMPI-2/MMPI: An interpretive manual.* Boston: Allyn & Bacon.

Hathaway, S. R. (1947). A coding system for MMPI profiles. *Journal of Consulting Psychology, 11,* 334–337.

Hathaway, S. R., & Monachesi, E. D. (1963). *Adolescent personality and behavior: MMPI patterns of normal, delinquent, dropout, and other outcomes.* Minneapolis: University of Minnesota Press.

Hoffmann, N. G., & Butcher, J. N. (1975). Clinical limitations of three MMPI short forms. *Journal of Consulting and Clinical Psychology, 43,* 32–39.

Honaker, L. M. (1990). MMPI and MMPI-2: Alternate forms or different tests? In M. E. Maruish (Chair), *The MMPI and MMPI-2: Comparability examined from different perspectives.* A symposium conducted at the Annual Convention of the American Psychological Association, Boston, MA.

Jastak, S., & Wilkinson, G. S. (1984). *Wide Range Achievement Test — Revised.* Wilmington, DE: Jastak Associates.

Johnson, R. H., & Bond, G. L. (1950). Reading ease of commonly used tests. *Journal of Applied Psychology, 34,* 319–324.

Kincannon, J. C. (1968). Prediction of the standard MMPI scale scores from 71 items: The Mini-Mult. *Journal of Consulting and Clinical Psychology, 32,* 319–325.

Lewak, R. W., Marks, P. A., & Nelson, G. E. (1990). *Therapist guide to the MMPI & MMPI-2: Providing feedback and treatment.* Muncie, IN: Accelerated Development, Inc.

Lueger, R. J. (1983). The use of the MMPI-168 with delinquent adolescents. *Journal of Clinical Psychology, 39,* 139–141.

MacBeth, L., & Cadow, B. (1984). Utility of the MMPI-168 with adolescents. *Journal of Clinical Psychology, 40,* 142–148.

Marks, P. A., & Briggs, P. F. (1972). Adolescent norm tables for the MMPI. In W. G. Dahlstrom, G. S. Welsh, & L. E. Dahlstrom, *An MMPI handbook: Vol. I. Clinical interpretation* (rev. ed., pp. 388–399). Minneapolis: University of Minnesota Press.

Marks, P. A., & Lewak, R. W. (1991). *The Marks MMPI adolescent feedback and treatment report* [Computer program]. Los Angeles: Western Psychological Services.

Marks, P. A., Seeman, W., & Haller, D. L. (1974). *The actuarial use of the MMPI with adolescents and adults.* New York: Oxford University Press.

Markwardt, F. C. (1989). *Peabody Individual Achievement Test — Revised.* Circle Pines, MN: American Guidance Service.

Mlott, S. R. (1973). The Mini-Mult and its use with adolescents. *Journal of Clinical Psychology, 29,* 376–377.

Newmark, C. S. (1971). MMPI: Comparison of the oral form presented by a live examiner in the booklet form. *Psychological Reports, 29,* 797–798.

Newmark, C. S., & Thibodeau, J. R. (1979). Interpretive accuracy and empirical validity of abbreviated forms of the MMPI with hospitalized adolescents. In C. S. Newmark (Ed.), *MMPI: Clinical and research trends* (pp. 248–275). New York: Praeger.

Overall, J. E., & Gomez-Mont, F. (1974). The MMPI-168 for psychiatric screening. *Educational and Psychological Measurement, 34,* 315–319.

Rathus, S. A. (1978). Factor structure of the MMPI-168 with and without regression weights. *Psychological Reports, 42,* 643–646.

Roper, B. L., Ben-Porath, Y. S., & Butcher, J. N. (1991). Comparability of computerized adaptive and conventional testing with the MMPI-2. *Journal of Personality Assessment, 57,* 278–290.

Ward, L. C., & Ward, J. W. (1980). MMPI readability reconsidered. *Journal of Personality Assessment, 44,* 387–389.

Welsh, G. S. (1948). An extension of Hathaway's MMPI profile coding system. *Journal of Consulting Psychology, 12,* 343–344.

Wiederholt, J. L., & Bryant, B. R. (1986). *Gray Oral Reading Tests, Revised.* Austin, TX: PRO-ED.

Williams, C. L. (1986). MMPI profiles from adolescents: Interpretive strategies and treatment considerations. *Journal of Child and Adolescent Psychotherapy, 3,* 179–193.

VALIDITY SCALES AND VALIDITY ASSESSMENT INTERPRETATION

There are several methods of assessing the technical validity of adolescents' MMPI-A profiles. These methods have traditionally involved the individual and configural interpretation of standard validity scale findings, and have often extended to include an analysis of the overall MMPI basic scale profile configuration for evidence of atypical response set features. Additional methods of evaluating profile validity have also been developed. These methods include the Test-Retest (TR) Index and the Carelessness (CLS) scale for the original form of the MMPI. On the MMPI-A, new validity measures were developed which are the Variable Response Inconsistency (VRIN) and True Response Inconsistency (TRIN) scales, and the F_1 and F_2 subscales. The inclusion of these four new validity scales at the beginning of the MMPI-A basic scale profile (in conjunction with reordering L, F, and K to F, L, and K) is among the most readily apparent changes associated with the revised instrument. In addition to these validity assessment tools, this chapter also reviews a conceptual model developed by Roger Greene (1989, 1991) for interpreting technical validity patterns. This model emphasizes the distinction between response consistency and response accuracy as components of technical validity.

MMPI-A VALIDITY SCALES

Traditional Validity Scales and Derivative Subscales

The traditional validity (F, L, and K) scales originally developed by Hathaway and McKinley were created to detect deviant test-taking attitudes and responses. Determining the technical validity of the adolescents' MMPI-A profiles is particularly important because invalid profiles probably occur with a higher frequency in adolescent samples, resulting from problems related to response consistency as well as response accuracy. As research has accumulated on the standard validity measures, however, Graham (1987) noted that we have come to view the traditional validity scales as additional sources of inferences about the respondents' extra-test behaviors. Thus, these validity scales provide data regarding not only the technical validity of the MMPI response pattern, but also valuable information concerning behavioral correlates or descriptors that are likely to apply to the respondent.

The Cannot Say (?) Scale

The Cannot Say (?) scale consists of the total number of items that a respondent fails to answer, or answers in both the true and false directions. Thus, the Cannot Say scale is not a formal MMPI scale because it does not have a consistent or fixed item pool. Profile sheets for the traditional MMPI have shown the ? scale as the first in the series of standard validity scales on the profile grid. The MMPI-2 and MMPI-A profile sheets, although still providing a space to record the raw score for the ? scale, have deemphasized its role as a "scale" by its new placement in the lower left-hand portion of the profile sheet.

Although several studies have examined the characteristics of Cannot Say values in adult populations (as reviewed in Greene, 1980, 1989, 1991), very little research has been focused on this issue among adolescent respondents. Ball and Carroll (1960) examined correlates of the Cannot Say scores among 262 ninth-grade public school students in Kentucky. They reported that male respondents had a higher mean number of Cannot Say responses than females. The items omitted by these adolescents tended to fall into broad categories, including statements not applicable to adolescents, religious items, items related to sexuality and bodily functions, and items that require adolescents to make a decision concerning personal characteristics about which they are ambivalent. Similarly, Hathaway and Monachesi (1963) found 23 items that were left unanswered by at least 2% of the male or female respondents in their statewide Minnesota sample of normal adolescents. They reported that content related to religion and sex appeared to be the most frequently omitted items for both boys and girls. Additionally, girls tended to leave a significantly larger number of sex-related items unanswered.

In general, findings on the original MMPI by Ball and Carroll (1960) and on the MMPI-A by Archer and Gordon (1991) indicated a relationship between intellectual functioning/reading ability and Cannot Say scale scores. Ball and Carroll found no evidence of a relationship between Cannot Say scores and delinquent behaviors in their sample, but did find higher ? scale scores to be inversely associated with adolescents' scores on intelligence measures and their academic grades. Archer and Gordon (1991) found a significant relationship ($r = -.10$, p < .05) between the number of unanswered MMPI-A items and adolescents' reading abilities in a sample of 495 junior high and high school students. These findings suggest that the adolescents' failure to complete items may often be related to intellectual and reading limitations, rather than oppositional and defiant characteristics.

Table 4.1 provides information from Greene (1991) concerning the frequency of omitted items for the original MMPI in psychiatric samples of adults and adolescents. This table shows approximately equivalent rates of item omissions between these two age groups.

Gottesman, Hanson, Kroeker, and Briggs (1987) reported that the mean Cannot Say scale value for normal adolescents in the Hathaway and Monachesi (1963) data set was roughly three. Further, a raw score value of five to six converts to a T-score range of 70 to 80 in the Gottesman et al. adolescent norms. It should be noted, however, that the Marks and Briggs (1972) adolescent norms for the traditional MMPI indicate that a Cannot Say raw score value of 30 converts to a T-score value of 50 for both male and female adolescents. This T-score conver-

TABLE 4.1

Frequency of Omitted Items on the MMPI in Adult and Adolescent Psychiatric Samples by Gender

| Number of omitted items | Psychiatric patients (Hedlund & Won Cho, 1979) | | | |
| | Adults | | Adolescents | |
	Male (N = 8646)	Female (N = 3743)	Male (N = 693)	Female (N = 290)
0	29.8%	28.4%	28.0%	27.9%
1–5	32.3%	30.4%	31.0%	30.8%
Cumulative (0–5)	62.1%	58.8%	59.0%	58.7%
6–10	16.8%	17.2%	21.1%	21.7%
Cumulative (0–10)	78.9%	76.0%	80.1%	80.4%
11–30	14.7%	17.4%	14.6%	13.1%
Cumulative (0–30)	93.6%	93.4%	94.7%	93.5%
31+	6.4%	6.6%	5.3%	6.5%
M	8.7	9.3	7.7	8.4
SD	18.1	19.2	13.1	15.1

Note. Adapted by permission from Greene (1991). Copyright (c) 1991 by Allyn & Bacon.

sion appears to be a continuation of the arbitrary assignment of T-score values to Cannot Say raw score values of 30 used by Hathaway and McKinley (1967) in the original adult MMPI norms. In both adolescent and adult samples, however, a raw score value of 30 on the ? scale occurs *much* less frequently than is implied by the T = 50 value. The data from the MMPI-A normative sample indicate that the mean raw score value for the ? scale is 1.01 for males (*SD* = 3.70) and .80 for females (*SD* = 2.50).

Table 4.2, adapted from Greene (1991), shows the traditional MMPI items most frequently omitted in a sample of 983 adolescent psychiatric patients. Of these 17 items, 10 were deleted in the formation of the

TABLE 4.2

Content of Original MMPI Items Most Frequently Omitted by Male and Female Adolescent Psychiatric Patients

MMPI		% Omitted	
item no.	Item content	Male	Female
[a]58	Everything is turning out just like the prophets of the Bible said it would.	14.3	12.1
[a]513	I think Lincoln was greater than Washington.	10.2	14.8
[a]255	Sometimes at elections I vote for men about whom I know very little.	11.7	11.0
[a]483	Christ performed miracles such as changing water into wine.	9.2	6.9
[b]42	My family does not like the work I have chosen (or the work I intend to choose for my life work).	5.8	8.6
[a]441	I like tall women.	<5.0	9.3
558	A large number of people are guilty of bad sexual conduct.	6.9	6.6
[a]98	I believe in the second coming of Christ.	6.1	6.9
[a]70	I used to like drop-the-handkerchief.	8.2	<5.0
[a]53	A minister can cure disease by praying and putting his hand on your head.	6.8	<5.0
[b]57	I am a good mixer.	6.3	5.5
[b]17	My father was a good man.	5.2	6.6
232	I have been inspired to a program of life based on duty which I have since carefully followed.	5.6	5.5
[a]476	I am a special agent of God.	5.8	5.9
168	There is something wrong with my mind.	5.2	5.2
400	If given the chance I could do some things that would be of great benefit to the world.	5.2	<5.0
[a]295	I liked "Alice in Wonderland" by Lewis Carroll.	<5.0	5.2

Note. Data in this table are based on research by Hedlund and Cho (1979) as reported in Greene (1991). Copyright (c) 1991 by Allyn & Bacon. Adapted by permission. [a] item deleted in MMPI-A. [b] item revised in MMPI-A.

MMPI-A, and 3 additional items underwent revision. The very low *?* scale mean raw score values found for the MMPI-A normative sample suggests that the MMPI-A item revision process may have been successful in creating a test booklet of increased relevance to adolescents when contrasted with the original test form. It should be noted, however, that MMPI-A *?* scale mean values were affected by the elimination of adolescents from the normative sample with *?* scale raw score values ≥ 35. Tables 4.3 and 4.4 show the items most frequently omitted by 805 boys and 815 girls, respectively, in the MMPI-A normative sample.

Table 4.5 provides interpretive guidelines for the MMPI-A based on raw score values. As noted in this table, adolescents who omit more than 30 items should be requested to complete the unanswered items or retake the entire test. Research findings relating omissions to intelligence and reading ability, however, strongly indicate that the examiner assess an adolescent's capacity to comprehend items before instructing the teenager to respond to unanswered MMPI-A statements. Clopton and Neuringer (1977) demonstrated that random omissions of 30 items or fewer from the traditional MMPI do not seriously distort MMPI profile features when scored on adult norms. As previously noted, a substantial majority of adolescents would be expected to omit fewer than 10 items on either the traditional MMPI or the MMPI-A. Raw score

TABLE 4.3

Most Frequently Omitted Items for 805 Male Adolescents in the MMPI-A Normative Sample

MMPI item number	*Item content*	*Freq. of omission*	*% of sample*
203	I brood a great deal.	25	3.1
441	People do not find me attractive.	13	1.6
16	I am sure I get a raw deal from life.	10	1.2
199	I have been inspired to a program of life based on duty which I have since carefully followed.	8	1.0
395	I have often worked for people who take credit for good work but who pass off mistakes on those who work for them.	8	1.0
404	I sometimes feel that I am about to go to pieces.	8	1.0
177	I sometimes think about killing myself.	7	.9
406	A large number of people are guilty of bad sexual conduct.	7	.9
448	Most people think they can depend on me.	7	.9
467	I enjoy using marijuana.	7	.9

Note. Items reproduced from the MMPI-A by permission. Copyright (c) 1992 by the Regents of the University of Minnesota.

TABLE 4.4
Most Frequently Omitted Items for 815 Female Adolescents in the MMPI-A
Normative Sample

Item number	Item content	Freq. of omission	% of sample
203	I brood a great deal.	24	2.9
199	I have been inspired to a program of life based on duty which I have since carefully followed.	12	1.5
93	There seems to be a fullness in my head or nose most of the time.	10	1.2
16	I am sure I get a raw deal from life.	8	1.0
31	I have never been in trouble because of my sex behavior.	7	.9
213	I don't blame people for trying to grab everything they can get in this world.	7	.9
431	Talking over problems and worries with someone is often more helpful than taking drugs or medicines.	7	.9
196	I hardly ever notice my heart pounding and I am seldom short of breath.	6	.7
244	I have very few fears compared to my friends.	6	.7
251	I wish I were not bothered by thoughts about sex.	6	.7
429	I have some habits that are really harmful.	6	.7
432	I recognize several faults in myself that I will not be able to change.	6	.7
442	People should always follow their beliefs even if it means bending the rules to do it.	6	.7

Note. Items reproduced from the MMPI-A by permission. Copyright (c) 1992 by the Regents of the University of Minnesota.

values of 11 to 30 on the Cannot Say scale represent substantially more omissions than might typically be expected. This degree of item omission may be produced by adolescents who have impaired reading ability, or have limitations in their life experiences that render some items meaningless or unanswerable. It is unlikely, however, that this range of Cannot Say scale values will result in profile elevation or configuration distortions unless omitted items are concentrated within a few scales.

The F (Frequency) Scale and the F_1 and F_2 Subscales

The original MMPI F scale consisted of 64 items selected using the criterion that no more than 10% of the Minnesota normative adult sample answered these items in the deviant direction. As a result of this development procedure, the F scale was often referred to as the Frequency or Infrequency scale. The F scale includes a variety of items related to strange or unusual experiences, thoughts, sensations, para-

TABLE 4.5
Interpretation Guidelines for the Cannot Say (?) Scale

Raw score	Interpretation
0–3	*Low.* These adolescents are willing and capable of responding to the item pool and were not evasive of item content.
4–10	*Moderate.* These adolescents have omitted a few items in a selective manner. Their omissions may be the result of limitations in life experiences that rendered some items unanswerable. There is little probability of profile distortions unless all omissions occurred from a single scale.
11 – 30	*Marked.* These adolescents are omitting more items than expected and may be very indecisive. Their omissions may have distorted their profile elevations. Check the scale membership of missing items to evaluate profile validity.
31 and above	*Invalid.* Adolescents in this range have left many items unanswered, possibly as a result of a defiant or uncooperative stance or serious reading difficulties. The profile is invalid. If possible, the adolescent should complete unanswered items or retake the entire test.

Note. Adapted from Archer (1987). Copyright (c) 1987 by Lawrence Erlbaum Associates, Inc. Reprinted by permission.

noid ideation, and antisocial attitudes and behaviors. The *F* scale on the original MMPI was also one of the most problematic scales when applied in adolescent populations, because adolescents typically produced much higher *F* scale raw scores than adults. Significant *F* scale mean raw score differences between adolescent and adult respondents have been consistently reported in both normal and clinical samples (e.g., Archer, 1984, 1987). Because of the typically high *F* scale values found for adolescents, the use of *F* scale validity criteria to assess the technical validity of teenagers' MMPI profiles is very complex and often ineffective.

In the development of the MMPI-A, it was apparent that adolescents produced marked elevations on the *F* scale because many of the *F* scale items did not function effectively for this age group. Specifically, 11 of the 60 *F* items that appear on the MMPI-2 form for adults produced item endorsement frequencies exceeding 20% in the MMPI-A normative sample. For example, roughly 26% of both male and female adolescents in the MMPI-A normative sample responded *true* to the traditional *F* scale item, "Sometimes I feel as if I must injure either myself or someone else," and roughly 36% of males and 45% of females answered *true* to the item, "Most any time I would rather sit and daydream than to do anything else." Table 4.6 provides the item content and endorsement frequencies for the 11 *F* scale items most frequently endorsed by adolescents in the MMPI-A normative sample using the MMPI-TX experimental test form.

TABLE 4.6

MMPI-2 F Scale Items Producing Endorsement Frequencies Exceeding 20% in the MMPI-A Normative Data Collection Sample

MMPI-2 item number	Item content	Endorsement frequency[a]
48	Most anytime I would rather sit and daydream than do anything else.	40.9%
288	My parents and family find more fault with me than they should.	41.4%
174	I like to study and read about things that I am working at.	32.2%
132	I believe in a life hereafter.	29.0%
168	I have had periods in which I carried on activities without knowing later what I had been doing.	29.2%
324	I can easily make other people afraid of me, and sometimes do for the fun of it.	28.1%
312	The only interesting part of newspapers is the comic strips.	24.8%
264	I have used alcohol excessively.	22.4%

Note. Items reproduced from the MMPI-A by permission. Copyright (c) 1992 by the Regents of the University of Minnesota.

[a] Analyses based on 1,620 adolescents sampled in the MMPI-A normative data collection for those items retained in the MMPI-A. MMPI-2 items number 12, 150, and 300 also exceeded a 20% endorsement frequency in the MMPI-A normative sample but were deleted from the MMPI-A form.

The traditional F scale also contains several items that might be deemed offensive because statement content was related to religious beliefs (e.g., "I believe there is a God"), or sexual attitudes and functioning (e.g., "Children should be taught all the main facts of sex"). Based on these observations, the F scale underwent a major revision in the development of the MMPI-A, leading to the creation of a new 66-item F scale, which is subdivided into the F_1 and F_2 subscales.

The MMPI-A F scale was created by the selection of items endorsed in a deviant direction by no more than 20% of the 805 boys and 815 girls in the MMPI-A normative sample. In creating the MMPI-A F scale, 27 items were deleted from the original F scale because adolescents' endorsement of these items exceeded the 20% criterion for selection, or because the items contained content deemed inappropriate for inclusion in the MMPI-A. In addition, 12 items that appeared on the original form of the MMPI but were not traditionally scored on F were included on the MMPI-A F scale because these items met the 20% criterion rule. Finally, the MMPI-A F scale includes 17 new items that appear only on the MMPI-A.

Table 4.7 provides five levels of interpretive suggestions for the MMPI-A F scale. Adolescents who produce marked or extreme elevations on the MMPI-A F scale may be suffering from severe psychiatric illnesses, may be attempting to "fake-bad" or overreport symptomatology, or may be engaging in a random response pattern either through conscious intent or as a result of inadequate reading ability. For example, Krakauer (1991) investigated the relationship between MMPI-A F scale elevation and reading ability in a sample of 495 adolescents. She found that 11% of adolescents scored below a sixth-grade reading level in the total sample. In a subsample of 231 adolescents who produced F scale T-score values $\geq$ 65, however, the percentage of adolescents reading below the sixth-grade level increased to 18%. Similarly, the examination of 120 adolescents who produced an F scale T-score value of 80 or greater, yielded a base rate of 24% for poor readers. This further increased to 29% when considering 68 adolescents who produced F scale T-score values of 90 or greater.

The F_1 scale is a direct descendant of the original F scale and consists of 33 items, of which 24 appeared on the original. The remaining 9 F_1 items are new items which do not appear on the original instrument. All of the F_1 items occur in the first 350 items of the MMPI-A booklet, and

TABLE 4.7
Interpretation Guidelines for the MMPI-A F Scale

T score	Interpretation
45 and below	*Low.* Scores in this range may reflect very conventional life experiences among normal adolescents, and possible "fake good" attempts among disturbed adolescents.
46–59	*Normal.* Adolescents in this range have endorsed unusual experiences to a degree that is common during adolescence.
60–65	*Moderate.* These adolescents are endorsing a range of F scores typically found among teenagers exhibiting some evidence of psychopathology.
66–89	*Marked.* Validity indicators should be checked carefully for adolescents in this range. Valid profiles most likely reflect significant psychopathology including symptoms typically exhibited by adolescents in inpatient settings.
90 and above	*Extreme.* Protocols with F scores in this range are likely to be invalid. If "fake-bad" and other response set issues are ruled out, may reflect severely disorganized or psychotic adolescents.

Note. Adapted from Archer (1987). Copyright (c) 1987 by Lawrence Erlbaum Associates, Inc. Reprinted by permission.

therefore may be used even when the MMPI-A is given in the abbreviated format. The F_2 scale also consists of 33 items, all of which occur after item 242, and 16 of which occur after item 350. The F_2 scale consists predominantly of items that appeared on the original MMPI (28 of the 33 F_2 items), but only 12 of these items were scored on the F scale in the original instrument. Eight of the F_2 items are new items that did not appear on the original MMPI. Table 4.8 provides examples of MMPI-A F scale items with the F_1 and F_2 membership indicated within the parentheses. All F_1 and F_2 items, as part of the MMPI-A F scale, were selected based on the criterion that fewer than 20% of normal adolescent subjects in the MMPI-A normative data collection endorsed the item in the scored or critical direction.

The F_1 and F_2 scales for the MMPI-A may be used in an interpretive strategy similar to that employed for the F and F_B scales found in the MMPI-2 (Butcher, Dahlstrom, Graham, Tellegen, & Kaemmer, 1989). Specifically, the F_1 scale provides information concerning the validity of the adolescent's responses to the basic MMPI-A scales, whereas F_2 provides information concerning the adolescent's responses to the latter part of the MMPI-A test booklet, and data necessary to score the MMPI-A content scales and supplementary scales. If an adolescent's F_1 score is within acceptable ranges, but F_2 is extremely elevated (T $\geq$ 90), this pattern is indicative of the possible use of a random response

TABLE 4.8

Sample Items From the MMPI-A F Scale With F_1 or F_2 Subscale Membership

---

Items scored if true

22.   Evil spirits possess me at times. (F_1)

51.   My family doesn't like the kind of work I plan to do. (F_1)

80.   I have been suspended from school one or more times for bad behavior. (F_1)

250. My soul sometimes leaves my body. (F_2)

463. I have no close friends. ($F2$)

470. I have a cough most of the time. (F_2)

Items scored if false

74.   I am liked by most people who know me. (F_1)

98.   I get angry sometimes. (F^1)

258. I love my mother, or (if your mother is dead) I loved my mother. (F_2)

289. At times I am all full of energy. (F_2)

447. I usually expect to succeed in things I do. (F_2)

Items deleted from F Scale

Most anytime I would rather sit and daydream than do anything else.

I have had periods in which I carried on activities without knowing later what I had been doing.

Note. Items reproduced from the MMPI-A by permission. Copyright (c) 1992 by the Regents of the University of Minnesota.

pattern during the latter half of the MMPI-A test booklet. Under these conditions, it may be possible to interpret data from the standard scales, while treating content scale and supplementary scale findings as invalid. If F_1 scores exceed acceptable ranges, however, the entire protocol should be treated as invalid and further interpretation should not be undertaken.

Because the F_1 and F_2 Scales are newly developed for the MMPI-A, research data is currently unavailable concerning the optimal cutoff score for identifying invalid records with these scales. Further, there is not sufficient data to pinpoint the optimal method by which these scales may be used in conjunction to identify invalid protocols. Regarding this latter issue, Greene (1991) suggested that the raw score formula $F - F_B$ produces values useful in the detection of invalid response sets on the MMPI-2. A similar formula, based on raw score values from F_1 and F_2, is likely to be found useful in detecting invalid response sets on the MMPI-A, but systematic research is necessary on this topic before clinicians apply this approach. Because the item selection criteria and number of items are identical in F_1 and F_2, the same interpretive statements would appear to be applicable to both scales for given levels of T-score elevation, and would be expected to parallel the F scale guidelines provided in Table 4.7.

Lie (L) Scale

The Lie scale in the traditional MMPI consists of 15 items that were originally selected to identify individuals deliberately attempting to lie, or to avoid answering the item pool in an open and honest manner. The Lie scale is keyed in the false direction for all items, and was created based on a rational/intuitive identification of items. The MMPI-A Lie scale retains all but one item from the original measure, resulting in a 14-item scale. The traditional Lie scale item deleted in the creation of the MMPI-A L scale was, "Sometimes in elections I vote for men about whom I know very little," based on the limited relevance of this item for many adolescents. Table 4.9 presents examples of the items contained in the MMPI-A L scale.

The MMPI-A Lie scale covers a variety of content areas, including the denial of aggressive or hostile impulses that constitute areas of common human failings for the majority of individuals. Higher range L scale values have been related to longer treatment duration for hospitalized adolescents (Archer, White, & Orvin, 1979). In general, the clinical correlates of Lie scale elevations for adolescents appear to be similar to the meaning of these elevations in adult populations. Thus, moderate elevations, in the range of T-score values of 60 to 65, are related to an

TABLE 4.9
Sample Items From the L Scale (14 items)

Items scored if true
  None
Items scored if false
  26.   At times I feel like swearing.
  38.   I do not always tell the truth.
  89.   Sometimes when I am not feeling well I am irritable.
  98.   I get angry sometimes.
  117. If I could get into a movie without paying and be sure I was not
        seen, I would probably do it.
  133. I would rather win than lose in a game.
  192. I gossip a little at times.
  243. Once in a while I laugh at a dirty joke.
Item deleted from L Scale
Sometimes at elections I vote for men about whom I know very little.

Note. Items reproduced from the MMPI-A by permission. Copyright (c) 1992 by the Regents of the University of Minnesota.

emphasis on conformity and the use of denial among adolescent respondents. Marked elevations in excess of T-score values of 65 raise questions concerning the possible use of a "nay-saying" response set or an unsophisticated attempt by a respondent to present personal characteristics in a favorable light and in a "saintly" manner. Because all *L* scale items are keyed in the false direction, scores on this measure (in conjunction with the *TRIN* scale discussed later in this chapter) serve as a valuable index in detecting all-true and all-false response patterns. Table 4.10 presents a variety of interpretive suggestions for four levels of *L* scale elevations on the MMPI-A.

The *K* (Defensiveness) Scale

In contrast to the extensive changes to the *F* scale, the *K* scale did not undergo any item deletions in the development of the MMPI-A, and only two items were modified in terms of wording. Thus, the MMPI-A *K* scale consists of 30 items that were empirically selected to identify individuals who display significant degrees of psychopathology but produced profiles that were within normal limits (Meehl & Hathaway, 1946). Only one of these items is scored in the true direction. Table 4.11 provides examples of items from the MMPI-A *K* scale.

Item content on the *K* scale is quite diverse and covers issues ranging from self-control to family and interpersonal relationships (Greene, 1980). Although the *K*-correction procedure for basic scales 1, 4, 7, 8, and 9 has become standard practice with adult respondents, *K*-correction is

TABLE 4.10
Interpretation Guidelines for the MMPI-A L Scale

T score	Interpretation
45 and below	*Low.* May reflect an open, confident stance among normal adolescents. "All-true" or "fake-bad" response sets are possible in this range.
46–55	*Normal.* Scores in this range reflect an appropriate balance between the admission and denial of common social faults. These adolescents tend to be flexible and non-rigid.
56–65	*Moderate.* May reflect an emphasis on conformity and conventional behaviors among adolescents. Scores in this range for adolescents in psychiatric settings may reflect the use of denial as a central defense mechanism.
66 and above	*Marked.* Scores in this range reflect extreme use of denial, poor insight, and lack of sophistication. Treatment efforts are likely to be longer and associated with guarded prognosis. An "all-false" or "fake-good" response set may have occurred.

Note. Adapted from Archer (1987). Copyright (c) 1987 by Lawrence Erlbaum Associates, Inc. Reprinted by permission.

TABLE 4.11
Sample Items from the MMPI-A K Scale

Item scored if true (one only)
79.   I have very few quarrels with members of my family.
Items scored if false
34.   At times I feel like smashing things.
72.   It takes a lot of argument to convince most people of the truth.
111.   Often I can't understand why I have been so irritable and grouchy.
121.   Criticism or scolding hurts me terribly.
124.   I certainly feel useless at times.
289.   At times I am all full of energy.
317.   People often disappoint me.
325.   I have often met people who were supposed to be experts who were no better than I.
327.   I often think, "I wish I were a child again."
333.   I find it hard to set aside a task that I have undertaken, even for a short time.
341.   I like to let people know where I stand on things.

Note. Items reproduced from the MMPI-A by permission. Copyright (c) 1992 by the Regents of the University of Minnesota.

not used with adolescent profiles, either with the original MMPI or the MMPI-A. Marks, Seeman, and Haller (1974) presented three reasons why K-correction procedures should not be employed with adolescents. First, they noted that K-correction was originally developed on a small sample of adult patients and "hence its applicability to adolescents is at best questionable" (1974, p. 134). Second, they noted that Dahlstrom,

Welsh, and Dahlstrom (1972), as well as other authorities, have repeatedly cautioned against the use of K weights with samples that differ significantly from those employed by Meehl in the development of the original K-correction weights. Finally, Marks et al. cited previous research using adolescent samples that indicated that adolescents' MMPI scores produced a stronger relationship to external criteria without use of the K-correction procedure. This latter pattern was also recently reported by Weed, Ben-Porath, and Butcher (1990) in MMPI data collected in adult samples, raising questions concerning the usefulness of K-correction even in interpretation of adult profiles.

In general, the K scale is unique (relative to the basic clinical scales) in that K scale mean raw score values for adolescents tend to be *lower* than that found for adult samples. For example, the K scale mean raw score value for males and females in the MMPI-2 adult normative sample was 15.30 and 15.03, respectively (Butcher et al., 1989), whereas the normative values for males and females in the MMPI-A normative sample was 12.7 for males and 11.5 for females (Butcher et al., 1992). Although little research has been devoted to this issue, the available data indicates that K scale elevations in adolescents may be related to the same clinical correlate patterns that have been established for adult respondents. Thus, markedly low elevations on the K scale tend to be produced by adolescents who may be consciously or unconsciously exaggerating their degree of symptomatology in an attempt to fake-bad, or as a "cry for help" in response to acute distress. Conversely, elevations on the K scale are often produced by adolescents who are defensive and who underreport psychological problems and symptoms. Further, this latter group of adolescents often fail to perceive a need for psychological treatment and attempt to deny psychological problems. They often hide behind a facade of adequate coping and adjustment. In both the adolescent and adult MMPI literatures, high K scale profiles have been linked to a poor prognosis for positive response to psychological intervention because of the respondent's inability or refusal to cooperate with treatment efforts (Archer et al., 1979). Table 4.12 offers interpretive guides for four elevation levels on the MMPI-A K scale.

Traditional Validity Scale Configurations

A configural approach to validity scale interpretation may be applied to adolescents' MMPI-A profiles in a manner analagous to Friedman, Webb, and Lewak (1989), Graham (1987, 1990), and Greene's (1980, 1991) interpretive suggestions for adults. The reordering of the traditional validity scales, however, in the MMPI-A (i.e., F, L, and K) requires a shift in our expectations of validity scale configural patterns acquired

TABLE 4.12
Interpretation Guidelines for the MMPI-A K Scale

T score	Interpretation
40 and below	*Low.* These adolescents may have poor self-concepts and limited resources for coping with stress. Scores in this range may be related to "fake bad" attempts among normals, or acute distress for adolescents in psychiatric settings.
41–55	*Normal.* Scores in this range reflect an appropriate balance between self-disclosure and guardedness. Prognosis for psychotherapy is often good.
56–65	*Moderate.* Scores in this range among normal adolescents may reflect a self-reliant stance and reluctance to seek help from others. For adolescents in psychiatric settings, this level of *K* is related to an unwillingness to admit psychological problems and a denial of the need for treatment or psychiatric help.
66 and above	*Marked.* Scores in this range reflect extreme defensiveness often related to poor treatment prognosis and longer treatment duration. The possibility of a "fake-good" response set should be considered.

Note. Adapted from Archer (1987). Copyright (c) 1987 by Lawrence Erlbaum Associates, Inc. Reprinted by permission.

based on use of the original MMPI. Figure 4.1 provides a dimension along which to evaluate possible MMPI-A validity scale configurations. The "most closed" validity configuration occurs when scales *L* and *K* are markedly elevated, and scale *F* (including F_1 and F_2) is below a T score of 50. The greater the degree of elevation manifested in scales *L* and *K* relative to the *F* scale and its subscales, the more the adolescent is attempting to present a self-report in an extremely favorable light that minimizes or denies the occurrence of any psychological problems. This type of validity configuration would most likely be encountered among adolescents who were involuntarily placed in treatment by parents or court officials. At the opposite extreme is the "most open" profile configuration characterized by elevated *F* scale and subscale values that occur with *L* and *K* scale T-score values below 50. As the elevation difference between *F* and the *L* and *K* scales becomes more pronounced or extreme, it is increasingly likely that the adolescent is exaggerating symptomatology or psychological problems as a cry for help. This pattern may reflect a conscious or unconscious effort to overreport symptomatology.

On the original form of the MMPI, configural approaches to validity scale interpretation were rendered complex because adolescents' *F* scale values were typically higher than those found for adults, and thus interpretive inferences needed to be adjusted accordingly. The "most

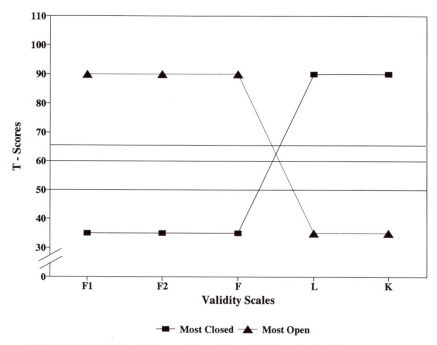

FIGURE 4.1   Validity Scale configurations: Most open to most closed.

open" profile type was very frequently encountered for adolescents on the original instrument, whereas the "most closed" profile type occurred infrequently. Additionally, related to the issue of high F scale elevations, the $F-K$ index was not useful when used with adolescents (Archer, 1987). Because of the major revision that has occurred in creating the MMPI-A F scale, it is expected that validity scale configuration patterns will become correspondingly more useful for this instrument. However, until research has been conducted using an $F-K$ index on the MMPI-A in adolescent samples, the use of this index is not advised.

ADDITIONAL VALIDITY SCALES FOR THE MMPI-A

Variable Response Inconsistency (*VRIN*) and True Response Inconsistency (*TRIN*) Scales

A Variable Response Inconsistency (*VRIN*) scale and a True Response Inconsistency (*TRIN*) scale were originally developed for the MMPI-2, and served as models for their counterparts in the MMPI-A instrument. Both *VRIN* and *TRIN* provide data concerning an individual's tendency to respond to MMPI-A items in a consistent manner. The *VRIN* scale consists of 50 pairs of items with either similar or opposite content. Each time an adolescent answers an item pair inconsistently, one raw score point is added to the *VRIN* scale score. Table 4.13 provides illustrations of *VRIN* scale items. As shown in this table, the content of the item pairs determines the response combination that would result in a point added to the *VRIN* total. For some item pairs, two true responses are scored, for other combinations two false responses are scored, and for others a combination of true and false responses produces an inconsistent response pattern resulting in a point added to the raw score value. The *VRIN* findings can serve as a warning that an adolescent has responded to the MMPI-A in an indiscriminate and random manner. Elevated *VRIN* scale values, for example, can be used to support the inference that an elevation on the *F* scale is likely to reflect carelessness or a random response pattern. It should be noted, however, that *VRIN* T-score values within acceptable ranges do not necessarily imply that an MMPI-A profile is subject to valid interpretation. While *VRIN* scale values are related to inferences concerning the consistency of an adolescent's response pattern, findings from this scale do not permit judgments concerning the accuracy of the subjects' responses. The distinction between accuracy and consistency as subcomponents of validity assessment are discussed later in this chapter.

The True Response Inconsistency (*TRIN*) scale for the MMPI-A, like its counterpart on the MMPI-2, was developed to detect an individual's

TABLE 4.13
Examples of Variable Response Inconsistency (VRIN) Scale Items

---

Sample VRIN pairs that add one point when both marked true
 70. I am certainly lacking in self-confidence.
  223. I am entirely self-confident.
146. I do not tire quickly.
  167. I feel weak all over much of the time.

Sample VRIN pairs that add one point when both marked false
 46. I am a very sociable person.
  475. I am usually very quiet around other people.
304. Whenever possible I avoid being in a crowd.
  335. I enjoy the excitement of a crowd.

Sample VRIN pairs scored when marked differently (T–F or F–T)
  6. My father is a good man, or (if your father is dead) My father was a good man.
  86. I love my father, or (if your father is dead) I loved my father.
 77. I think most people would lie to get ahead.
  107. Most people will use somewhat unfair means to get what they want.

Note. Items reproduced from the MMPI-A by permission. Copyright (c) 1992 by the Regents of the University of Minnesota.

tendency to indiscriminately respond to items as either *true* (acquiescence response set), or *false* (nay-saying), regardless of item content. This MMPI-A scale consists of 24 pairs of items that are negatively correlated and semantically opposite in content. The *TRIN* scale was developed in such a manner that raw score values must convert to T scores that are ≥ 50 (that is, raw scores cannot convert to T-score values below 50). *TRIN* T scores > 50 may represent deviations from the mean in either the acquiescent or nay-saying direction. In the computer scoring of the MMPI-A provided by National Computer Systems, the direction of deviation is indicated by a "T" or "F" which occupies the T score plot assigned to the *TRIN* scale. For example, a T on the profile sheet would indicate inconsistency in the true-response direction, whereas an F would represent an equal magnitude of inconsistency in the direction of false responding. Table 4.14 provides examples of *TRIN* items. As shown in Table 4.14, *true* responses to some item pairs, and *false* responses to other item pairs, result in scores on the *TRIN* scale. *TRIN* scores may be used to provide data concerning the degree to which an adolescent has tended to employ an acquiescent or nay-saying response style. As noted by Greene (1991), however, scores on the *TRIN* scale should not be used to determine whether an adolescent has endorsed MMPI-A items in a random manner. As will be shown later in this chapter in the example of a random profile, the *TRIN* scale may often produce acceptable T-score values under a random response set condition. The specific formula for *TRIN* scoring, as provided in the MMPI-A manual (Butcher et al., 1992), is as follows:

TABLE 4.14
Examples of True Response Inconsistency (TRIN) Scale Items

Sample TRIN pairs that add one point when both marked true

   14.   I work under a great deal of tension.
       424.   I am not feeling much stress these days.
   37.   Much of the time my head seems to hurt all over.
       168.   I have very few headaches.
   60.   My feelings are not easily hurt.
       121.   Criticism or scolding hurts me terribly.

Sample TRIN pairs that subtract one point when both marked false

   46.   I am a very sociable person.
       475.   I am usually very quiet around other people.
   71.   I usually feel that life is worthwhile.
       283.   Most of the time I wish I were dead.
  304.   Whenever possible I avoid being in a crowd.
       335.   I enjoy the excitement of a crowd.

Note. Items reproduced from the MMPI-A by permission. Copyright (c) 1992 by the Regents of the University of Minnesota.

1. For each of the following response pairs *add* one point:

14 T–424 T	119 T–184 T
37 T–168 T	146 T–167 T
60 T–121 T	242 T–260 T
62 T–360 T	264 T–331 T
63 T–120 T	304 T–335 T
70 T–223 T	355 T–367 T
71 T–283 T	463 T–476 T
95 T–294 T	

2. For each of the following response patterns *subtract* one point:

46 F–475 F	128 F–465 F
53 F–91 F	158 F–288 F
63 F–120 F	245 F–257 F
71 F–283 F	304 F–335 F
82 F–316 F	

3. Then add 9 points to the total raw score.

Both *TRIN* and *VRIN* are new MMPI-A scales and limited information is currently available concerning the characteristics of these measures in adolescent samples. Because both scales include items beyond item 350, the full MMPI-A must be administered to score *TRIN* or *VRIN*. The following rough guidelines in interpreting these scales are tentatively recommended:

> *VRIN* T scores of 70–79 indicate marginal levels of response inconsistency.
> *VRIN* T scores $\geq$ 80 indicate unacceptable levels of response inconsistency.
> *TRIN* T scores of 70–79 indicate marginal levels of response inconsistency.
> *TRIN* T scores $\geq$ 80 indicate unacceptable levels of response inconsistency.

Inconsistent item endorsement patterns for adolescents may be related to inadequate reading ability, limited intellectual ability, active noncompliance or test resistance, or thought disorganization related to substance abuse-induced toxicity, or active psychosis.

EFFECTS OF RESPONSE SETS ON STANDARD SCALES

Graham (1990) described the characteristics of MMPI-2 profiles that are generated by adults based on systematic response sets such as "all-true," "all-false," and random patterns, and Graham, Watts, and Timbrook (1991) described MMPI-2 fake-good and fake-bad profiles. Similar response set data for adolescents on the original test instrument was presented by Archer, Gordon, and Kirchner (1987) and summarized in Archer (1987, 1989). Archer (1989) noted that adolescents employing all-true and all-false response sets on the original test instrument are easily detected, and profile features are similar to those produced by their adult counterparts. Additionally, the fake-bad response set found for adolescents is relatively easy to identify based on the occurrence of an extremely elevated F scale combined with clinical-range elevations on all clinical scales (excluding Mf and Si). In contrast, adolescents' production of random response sets and fake-good response sets were more difficult to detect on the original test instrument. The following section provides a summary of the effects of a variety of response sets on the MMPI-A.

All-true

The all-true response pattern is indicated by extremely low scores on scales L and K, and markedly elevated scores (T > 90) on scales F, F_1 and F_2. The male and female all-true profile on MMPI-A norms is presented in Fig. 4.2. The raw score value for TRIN (raw score = 24) clearly indicates inconsistent responses, with TRIN indicative of an extreme "yea-saying" response style, whereas VRIN (raw score = 5) is within acceptable limits. In addition to the extreme "most open" validity scale pattern formed by scales F_1, F_2, F, L, and K, there is a very noticeable positive or psychotic slope to the profile, with elevations on Scales 6, 7, 8, and 9. These characteristics are similar to those found for all-true response patterns among adolescents on the original form of the MMPI (Archer, 1989).

Figure 4.3 provides the content scale and supplementary scale profile for the all-true response pattern. Because the majority of items in the content scales are keyed in the true direction, this profile exhibits very elevated T-score values for most content scales.

All-false

The profile shown in Fig. 4.4 will be produced if an adolescent responds *false* to all MMPI-A items. The TRIN raw score value is zero (T > 100) and the VRIN raw score value is 4. The TRIN value indicates response inconsistency, exhibiting an extreme nay-saying response style. In addition, F_1 values produce marginally elevated T scores whereas F_2 and F T scores fall within normal limits. The all-false profile is characterized

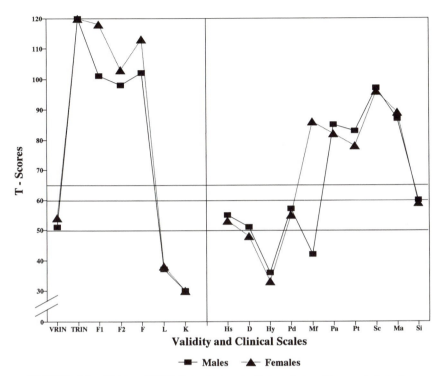

FIGURE 4.2   All-true MMPI-A response patterns for males and females. (*TRIN* T score = 120T for males and females)

by extreme elevations on validity scales *L* and *K*, and on the first three clinical scales of the MMPI, which are frequently referred to as the *neurotic triad*. The clinical scale profile has a distinctive negative slope, that is, scale values decrease as the scale's numerical designation increases. These findings are similar to the adolescent all-false profile for the original MMPI reported by Archer et al. (1987) and for adults on the MMPI-2 reported by Graham (1990). The characteristic profile features of both the all-true and the all-false patterns are easily discernible as invalid profiles. It should be clearly noted, however, that these deviant response sets should typically be detected by the inspection of the completed answer form prior to the profiling of response features.

Figure 4.5 shows the content and supplementary scale profile associated with an all-false pattern. Because all content scales except Health Concerns (*A-hea*) and Low Aspirations (*A-las*) are composed of items predominantly keyed in the *true* direction, an all-false response set produces low T scores for these scales. In contrast, the Repression (*R*) scale is composed of items exclusively keyed in the *false* direction and therefore produces a very elevated T-score value under this response set.

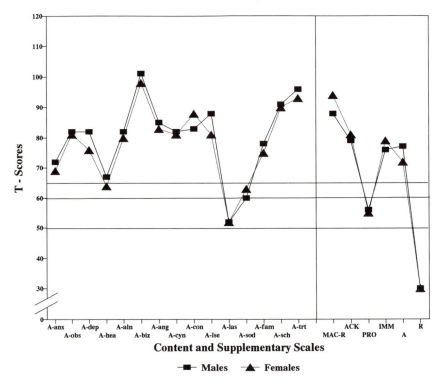

FIGURE 4.3   All-true MMPI-A content and supplementary scale patterns for males and females.

Random Response Sets

An adolescent may also respond to MMPI-A items in a random response pattern. The profile resulting from equal numbers of true and false item endorsements on each MMPI-A basic scale (i.e., the effect of an infinite number of random sorts) is presented in Fig. 4.6.

Consistent with the findings for adolescents on the original test instrument (Archer, Gordon, & Kirchner, 1987), random MMPI-A profiles are more difficult to detect than other response sets. The new MMPI-A validity scale *VRIN* is a useful indicator of random response sets in adolescents. The *TRIN* scale, however, may often produce acceptable T-score values under a random response set condition. The random profile is also characterized by an unusual validity scale configuration in which clinical-range elevations on scales F, F_1, and F_2 are accompanied by a clinical-range L scale elevation. The actual profile characteristics for a random response set will vary substantially, depending on the particular approach used to randomize the response

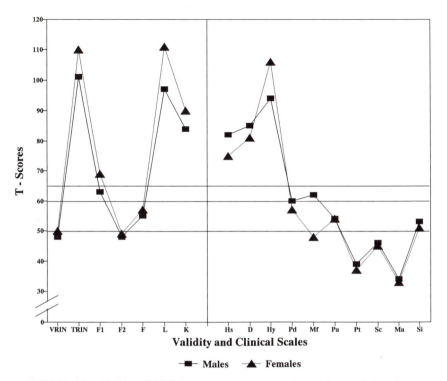

FIGURE 4.4   All-false MMPI-A response patterns for males and females. (*TRIN* T score = 101F for males and 110F for females)

pattern. Random response patterns should always be considered when an adolescent completes the MMPI-A too quickly, that is, in less than 40 minutes.

Figure 4.7 shows the effects of random response patterns on the MMPI-A content and supplementary scales. Similar to the corresponding basic scale profile, this profile is relatively difficult to detect based on shape and elevation features.

Fake-good (underreporting)

Another response set issue concerns the characteristics of MMPI-A profiles produced by adolescents who distort the accuracy of their responses. Adolescents may fake-good, or underreport problems on the MMPI-A, or they may fake-bad, completing the MMPI-A in a manner that overreports symptomatology. Because these types of profiles may be produced by individuals who consciously or unconsciously distort their responses, Greene (1989, 1991) emphasized the use of the terms

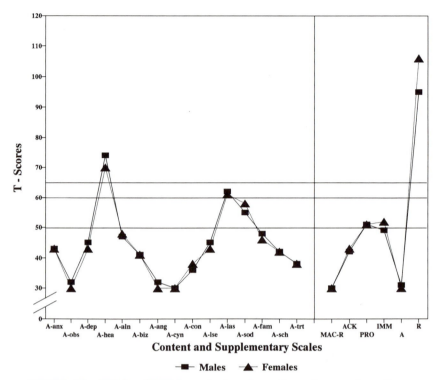

FIGURE 4.5   All-false MMPI-A content and supplementary scale patterns for males and females.

underreporting and *overreporting,* respectively, to describe these response sets. Graham (1990) used the terms *positive self-presentation* and *negative self-presentation* to describe these distortions in the accuracy of a subject's test responses.

Studies with adult psychiatric patients have found that the ability to simulate a normal profile is significantly related to a favorable treatment outcome among schizophrenics (Newmark, Gentry, Whitt, McKee, & Wicker, 1983) and across psychiatric diagnoses (Grayson & Olinger, 1957). Additionally, Bonfilio and Lyman (1981) investigated the ability of college students to simulate the profile of "well-adjusted" peers. Results from this study indicated that simulations produced by college students classified as *neurotic, normal,* and *psychopathic,* based on their actual MMPIs administered under normal instructions, were essentially within normal limits. Simulated profiles produced by psychotic or hypomanic college students, however, contained clearly pathological or clinical-range features. Graham (1990) provided MMPI-2 fake-good response features generated by college students who were administered the

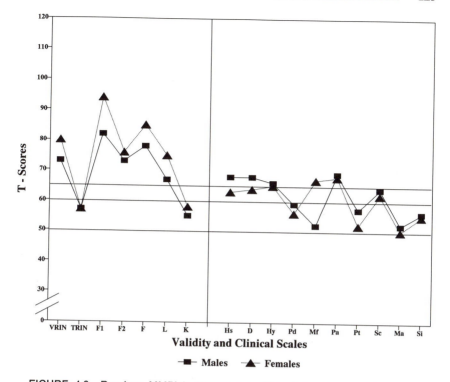

FIGURE 4.6   Random MMPI-A response profiles for males and females. (*TRIN* T score = 60T for males and females)

MMPI with instructions to respond as they would if they were applying for a highly valued job. The clearest indication of a fake-good profile in these data was the occurrence of the "most closed" validity scale configuration in which marked elevations occurred for scales *L* and *K*.

To investigate fake-good profiles in an adolescent sample, Archer et al. (1987) administered the original form of the MMPI to a group of 22 adolescents (mean age = 14.76 years) in an inpatient psychiatric setting. Ten of these adolescents were female and 12 were male. These adolescents were individually administered the MMPI with the following instructions:

> We would like you to respond to the MMPI as you believe a well-adjusted teenager would who is not experiencing emotional or psychological problems. By well-adjusted, we mean an adolescent who is doing well and is comfortable in school, at home, and with their peers. As you read the items in the MMPI, please respond to them as you believe a well-adjusted adolescent would who is not in need of psychiatric counseling, and who is relatively happy and comfortable. (pp. 508–509)

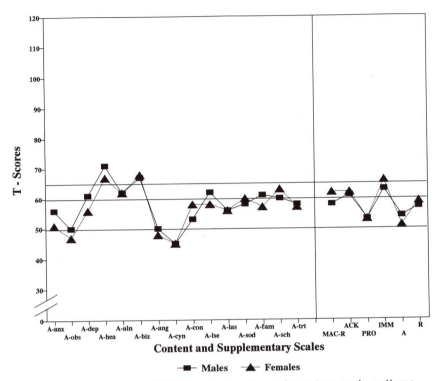

FIGURE 4.7   Random MMPI-A content and supplementary scale patterns for males and females.

As noted by Archer et al. (1987), two distinct profile groups emerged in response to this fake-good instructional set. One profile, produced by eight adolescents and termed *ineffective*, consisted of a very poor simulation of a normal profile, as defined by one or more clinical scales being elevated in excess of a T-score value of 70. In contrast, a group of 14 adolescents were able to simulate a normal profile (termed *effective*) to the extent that none of their clinical scale values were elevated within clinical ranges. In general, adolescents in the effective group tended to be older and have less severe diagnoses, and they produced less elevated profiles under the standard administration conditions.

These data were reanalyzed by the use of information provided in the MMPI-A manual (Butcher et al., 1992), and are reproduced in Appendix E of this text, which allows for T-score conversions between the MMPI and the MMPI-A. Figure 4.8 presents the corresponding MMPI-A T-score profiles produced for the effective and ineffective groups under fake-good instructions.

These data indicate a validity scale configuration for the effective

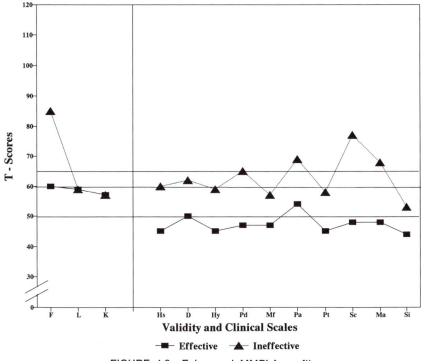

FIGURE 4.8   Fake-good MMPI-A profile.

group characterized by elevations on scales *L*, *F*, and *K*, which are generally within acceptable ranges. Clinical scale values present a "hypernormal" configuration, with T scores at or below 50 on most clinical scales. Therefore, the mean fake-good profile for the effective group would be difficult to distinguish from the responses of a somewhat guarded and defensive normal adolescent without significant psychiatric problems. The following guidelines, however, should serve to improve screening for adolescents who attempt to fake-good on the MMPI-A:

1. Elevations on validity scales *L* and *K*.
2. All clinical scale T-score values are ≤ 60, but produced by an adolescent with known or established psychopathology.

Fake-bad (overreporting)

The ability of normal adults to simulate psychopathology, or to fake-bad, has been investigated by numerous researchers, including

Anthony (1976); Exner, McDowell, Pabst, Stackman, and Kirk (1963); Gough (1947, 1954); Lanyon (1967); and Meehl and Hathaway (1946). Results have consistently shown that adults fail to accurately simulate the types of symptomatology typically reported by psychiatric patients. In general, normals tend to overreport psychopathology on the MMPI in an exaggerated and non-specific manner that is easily detected as a fake-bad attempt (Dahlstrom, Welsh, & Dahlstrom, 1975; Greene, 1980). Graham (1990) requested male and female college students to take the MMPI-2 with instructions to present themselves "as if they had serious psychological or emotional problems" (p. 42). The fake-bad profiles were characterized by highly elevated F scale values and clinical-range elevations on all standard clinical scales except Mf and Si.

Research by Archer et al. (1987) investigated the characteristics of fake-bad profiles among normal adolescents. The original form of the MMPI was administered to a group of 94 public high school students in four psychology classes, with the subjects ranging in age from 14 to 18 years and roughly equally divided in terms of gender and ethnic background (Black-White). Subjects were administered the MMPI with the following instructions:

> We would like you to respond to the MMPI as you believe you would if you were experiencing serious emotional or psychological problems. By serious problems, we mean problems that were severe enough that hospitalization for treatment would be necessary. As you read the items in the MMPI, please respond to them as if you were seriously disturbed and in need of hospital treatment for psychiatric care. (p. 508)

The mean profile produced by this group showed a grossly exaggerated picture of symptomatology that included a very elevated mean F scale value of $T = 130$, and clinical-range elevations on all MMPI clinical scales except Mf and Si. Data from the fake-bad administration was reprofiled, using the values provided in Appendix E of this text to derive MMPI-A norm-based T-score values. Figure 4.9, plotted on these MMPI-A norms, presents this fake-bad profile (the $TRIN$ and $VRIN$ scales cannot be derived from these data). Consistent with the findings by Archer et al. (1987) for the original MMPI, and the MMPI-2 results reported by Graham (1990) for college students, the fake-bad profile on the MMPI-A is characterized by extremely elevated F scale T-score values, and multiple clinical-range elevations on the standard clinical scales. These data indicate that adolescents will probably encounter substantial difficulty in successfully simulating psychiatric illness on the MMPI-A. The $TRIN$ and $VRIN$ raw score values for fake-bad and fake-good profiles, although not shown in Figs. 4.8 and 4.9, would probably be within

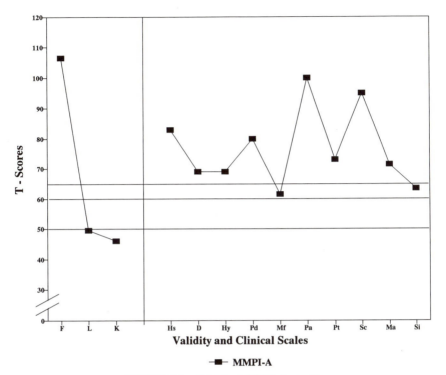

FIGURE 4.9   Fake-bad MMPI-A profile.

acceptable limits for response consistency, underscoring the difference between response inconsistency and response accuracy issues. Greene (1989) noted that individuals who attempt to underreport or overreport on the MMPI often produce highly consistent (although inaccurate and invalid) response patterns.

The F scale and clinical scale criteria summarized below should serve to effectively screen for most adolescents who attempt to fake-bad on the MMPI-A:

1. F scale T score value $\geq$ 90.
2. Presence of a floating profile characterized by clinical scale elevations within the clinical ranges (shaded zone or higher), with the exception of Mf and Si scale values.

A CONCEPTUAL MODEL FOR VALIDITY ASSESSMENT

Greene (1989) recently presented a conceptual approach or model for understanding validity assessment issues, as well as a number of empirical criteria through which to assess the validity of MMPI profiles. Figure 4.10 provides an overview of Greene's model.

Greene emphasizes the use of sequential steps or stages in the validity assessment process. The first stage involves the determination of the number of omitted items (i.e., the Cannot Say scale raw score value), with the omission of more than 30 items requiring test readministration. Greene notes that excessive item omissions may reflect not only characteristics of the respondent, but can also serve as a signal of problems in the MMPI administration process.

Consistency of Item Endorsement

The next step in evaluating the validity of patients' responses involves an assessment of the consistency of item endorsement. As noted by Greene (1989):

Consistency of item endorsement verifies that the patient has endorsed the items in a reliable manner. This procedure is necessary to ensure that

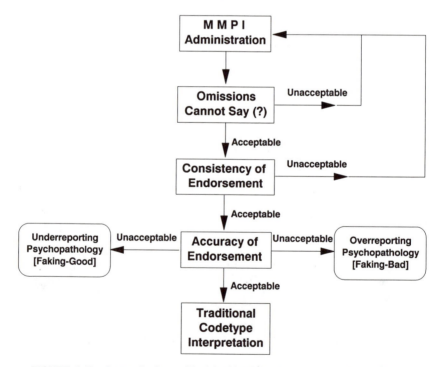

FIGURE 4.10   Greene's Stage Model of Validity Assessment. (From Greene, 1991. Copyright (c) 1991 by Allyn & Bacon. Adapted by permission)

the patient has endorsed the items consistently before any assessment of their accuracy is made. To highlight these differences, consistency of item endorsement may be conceptualized as being independent of or irrelevant to item content, while accuracy of item endorsement is dependent upon or relevant to item characteristics. (p. 7)

On the original form of the MMPI, item endorsement consistency has been measured by the use of the Test-Retest (*TR*) Index (Buechley & Ball, 1952) and by the Carelessness (*CLS*) scale developed by Greene (1978).

The *TR* Index consists of the 16 items that are repeated in the original form of the MMPI, and utilizes this duplication to yield a measure of inconsistency. The *TR* score is the total number of the 16 repeated items that the patient has endorsed in an inconsistent manner. Greene (1989) suggested that a score of three to five on the *TR* Index indicates questionable response reliability, and values in excess of five clearly indicate unacceptable reliability problems. Table 4.15 provides a list of *TR* Index items as they appear in the group booklet form of the original MMPI. Greene (1979) reported the number of inconsistent responses

TABLE 4.15
Original MMPI Group Form Items Used in the TR Index

Pair number	Item numbers	Items
1	8–318	My daily life is full of things that keep me interested.
2	13–290	I work under a great deal of tension.
3	15–314	Once in a while I think of things too bad to talk about.
4	16–315	I am sure I get a raw deal from life.
5	20–310	My sex life is satisfactory.
6	21–308	At times I have very much wanted to leave home.
7	22–326	At times I have fits of laughing and crying that I cannot control.
8	23–288	I am troubled by attacks of nausea and vomiting.
9	24–333	No one seems to understand me.
10	32–328	I find it hard to keep my mind on a task or job.
11	33–323	I have had very peculiar and strange experiences.
12	35–331	If people had not had it in for me I would have been much more successful.
13	37–302	I have never been in trouble because of my sex behavior.
14	38–311	During one period when I was a youngster I engaged in petty thievery.
15	305–366	Even when I am with people I feel lonely much of the time.
16	317–362	I am more sensitive than most other people.

Note. Adapted from Friedman, Webb, and Lewak (1989). Copyright (c) 1989 by Lawrence Erlbaum Associates, Inc. Reprinted by permission.

produced by subjects in four samples, including a sample of predominantly male adolescents in a juvenile probation setting. Table 4.16 shows the percentage of inconsistent responses provided for each sample. These findings provide evidence that the frequency of inconsistent responses is higher for adolescents in contrast to college students and adults. The mean *TR* Index score for the adolescent sample in this study was slightly more than four, whereas the mean *TR* values for the remaining three samples were all less than two.

The Carelessness scale (Greene, 1978) consists of 12 pairs of empirically selected items that were judged to be either psychologically opposite or similar in content. One raw score point is added to the Carelessness scale each time the test-taker responds inconsistently to a pair of synonymous items, or responds in the same manner (T-T or F-F) to items that are semantically opposite. Table 4.17 provides a list of Carelessness scale items from the original form of the MMPI. Greene (1989) indicated that *CLS* scale values of four to five indicate potential reliability problems, and values greater than five represent unacceptable levels of respondent inconsistency. Several authors (e.g., Bond, 1986), however, have noted that response inconsistency may be the result of

TABLE 4.16

Percentage of Inconsistent Responses on the Original MMPI for the Test-Retest (TR) Index Items by Sample

MMPI Group Booklet item numbers	Percentage of inconsistent responses by sample			
	VA Hospital (N = 50)	Psychology clinic (N = 50)	College students (N = 50)	Juvenile probation (N = 50)
8–318	20%	8%	12%	42%
13–290	6%	6%	16%	18%
15–314	28%	20%	28%	34%
16–315	2%	12%	16%	26%
20–310	12%	6%	6%	20%
21–308	6%	2%	20%	14%
22–326	10%	14%	18%	18%
23–288	4%	14%	0%	14%
24–333	20%	14%	14%	34%
32–328	12%	14%	16%	30%
33–323	16%	10%	14%	28%
35–331	8%	14%	0%	28%
37–302	10%	16%	6%	28%
38–311	4%	4%	2%	32%
305–366	8%	8%	4%	28%
317–362	12%	12%	12%	22%

Note. From Greene (1979). Copyright (c) 1979 by the Society for Personality Assessment, Inc. Adapted by permission. VA = Veterans Administration

TABLE 4.17
Original MMPI Group Form Items Used in the Carelessness (CLS) Scale

Pair number	Item number	Item	Careless answer
1	10	There seems to be a lump in my throat much of the time.	
	405	I have no trouble swallowing.	Same
2	17	My father was a good man.	
	65	I loved my father.	Different
3	18	I am very seldom troubled by constipation.	
	63	I have had no difficulty in starting or holding my bowel movement.	Different
4	49	It would be better if almost all laws were thrown away.	
	113	I believe in law enforcement.	Same
5	76	Most of the time I feel blue.	
	107	I am happy most of the time.	Same
6	88	I usually feel that life is worth while.	
	526	The future seems hopeless to me.	Same
7	137	I believe that my home life is as pleasant as that of most people I know.	
	216	There is very little love and companionship in my family as compared to other homes.	Same
8	177	My mother was a good woman.	
	220	I loved my mother.	Different
9	178	My memory seems to be all right.	
	342	I forget right away what people say to me.	Same
10	286	I am never happier than when alone.	
	312	I dislike having people about me.	Different
11	329	I almost never dream.	
	425	I dream frequently.	Same
12	388	I am afraid to be alone in the dark.	
	480	I am often afraid of the dark.	Different

Note. Adapted from Greene (1978). Copyright (c) 1978 by *The Journal of Clinical Psychology*. Adapted by permission. The term *same* refers to T-T or F-F response patterns, whereas *different* is defined as a T-F or F-T response.

processes other than carelessness, including marked indecisiveness or high levels of maladjustment. Table 4.18 provides data from Greene (1991) on the frequency of *CLS* scale inconsistent responses in adult and adolescent psychiatric patients.

The *TR* Index and the *CLS* scale are not applicable to the MMPI-A because of the changes in item content in the creation of this instrument. In particular, the repeated presentation of 16 items that occurred in the original MMPI has been eliminated in the MMPI-A. Nevertheless, as previously noted, there are new measures available on the MMPI-A to evaluate response consistency. The True Response Inconsistency scale (*TRIN*) and the Variable Response Inconsistency scale (*VRIN*) are

TABLE 4.18
Frequency of Inconsistent Responses on the Original MMPI for the Carelessness (CLS) Scale in Psychiatric Samples by Age and Gender

Number of inconsistent responses	Psychiatric patients (Hedlund & Won Cho, 1979)			
	Adults		Adolescents	
	Male (N = 8,646)	Female (N = 3,743)	Male (N = 693)	Female (N = 290)
0	12.6%	8.8%	9.7%	10.0%
1	22.1%	19.7%	16.9%	19.0%
2	23.5%	22.8%	21.9%	24.1%
3	17.8%	19.0%	20.6%	16.9%
4	11.8%	14.9%	12.7%	14.1%
Cumulative (0–4)	87.8%	85.2%	81.8%	84.1%
5	6.4%	8.0%	9.1%	9.0%
6	3.4%	3.9%	5.2%	3.8%
7	1.7%	1.8%	2.9%	2.8%
8+	0.7%	1.1%	1.0%	0.3%
Raw Score				
M	2.40	2.67	2.79	2.64
SD	1.74	1.77	1.85	1.78

Note. Adapted from Greene (1991). Copyright (c) 1991 by Allyn & Bacon.
Adapted by permission.

descendants of Greene's CLS measure and provide substantial information concerning the adolescent's response consistency. Further, the
comparison of values from F_1 and F_2 may allow for the detection of
inconsistent response patterns that occur during the latter stages of the
MMPI-A test booklet.

Regardless of the cause, substantial inconsistency renders the MMPI-
A profile invalid and further profile interpretation should not be
undertaken. Greene's model of validity assessment indicates that unac-
ceptably high levels of response inconsistency require readministration
of the MMPI in order to obtain interpretable clinical data.

Accuracy of Item Endorsement

The next step in the process of assessing MMPI or MMPI-A validity is to
derive an estimate of item endorsement accuracy. Greene (1989) noted
several assumptions relevant to this stage of validity assessment. First,
overreporting and underreporting represent a continuum, and any
particular respondent may be placed at some point along this dimension. Second, attempts to overreport and underreport symptomatology
tend to be generalized rather than specific. For example, adults who

underreport tend to deny the presence of any type or dimension of psychopathology, and individuals engaging in overreporting tend to endorse psychopathology related to a wide variety of mental disorders. Third, Greene points out that the occurrence of overreporting or underreporting is relatively independent from the patient's actual psychopathology. It would be inaccurate to assume that evidence of underreporting or overreporting can be used to conclude that a patient does or does not have actual psychopathology. A patient may overreport *and* manifest actual and severe symptomatology, or substantially underreport and also be relatively free from actual symptomatology.

Greene recommends the use of several indices in determining response accuracy with the original form of the MMPI, including the Wiener-Harmon Subtle-Obvious subscales (Wiener, 1948) and the Lachar-Wrobel (1979) Critical Item List. Because of the empirical method of scale construction used by Hathaway and McKinley in the development of the original form of the MMPI, the clinical scales contain numerous *subtle* items that seem, or appear to be, unrelated to the construct that is the focus of measurement. Wiener and Harmon rationally developed Subtle and Obvious subscales for five of the MMPI clinical scales: *D*, *Hy*, *Pd*, *Pa*, and *Ma*. Greene (1989) noted that when individuals overreport symptomatology, scores on Obvious subscales would be expected to increase relative to Subtle scale values. Conversely, when individuals attempt to underreport symptomatology, Subtle scale values will become elevated in relation to Obvious subscale values.

The Lachar and Wrobel (1979) critical items consist of 111 empirically selected MMPI items related to symptoms that may motivate individuals to seek psychological treatment, or symptomatology crucial in the clinician's diagnostic decision making. Greene recommends that the total number of Lachar and Wrobel critical items endorsed be used as an index of accuracy of item endorsement. A patient who is attempting to overreport symptomatology, for example, might be expected to endorse a large number of these items, whereas a patient underreporting psychopathology would be expected to endorse relatively few critical items.

Very little is known concerning the usefulness of the Wiener-Harmon Subtle-Obvious subscales, or the Lachar and Wrobel critical items, in the assessment of adolescents. Herkov, Archer, and Gordon (1991) provided the only study of the Wiener-Harmon subscales in an adolescent sample. These investigators compared the use of the standard validity scales in relation to the Wiener-Harmon subscales in terms of ability to accurately identify adolescents from four assessment groups. These groups included normal adolescents, psychiatric inpatients, normal adolescents instructed to fake-bad, and psychiatric inpatients instructed to fake-good. Table 4.19 presents the classification accuracy achieved by the use of the sum of the difference in T-score values between the Wiener-Harmon subscales (Obvious minus Subtle) in contrast to predictions based solely on the traditional validity scales. Several points may be made in relation to these findings. First, the optimal Obvious minus Subtle subscale difference value used in identifying overreporting ($\geq$ 140) and underreporting ($\leq$ 0) differ substantially from recommendations provided by Greene (1989) for adult respondents. Additionally, it might be noted that the Subtle-Obvious subscales were of use in identifying various response sets, but were not as useful as simple prediction rules applied to the standard validity scales to identify response sets. Specifically, predicting that adolescents who produced F scale T-score values $\geq$ 100 were overreporters, and that adolescents producing L scale T-score values $\geq$ 55 were underreporters, proved more accurate than predictions based on the Subtle-Obvious subscales.

The only available data on adolescent response patterns for the Lachar and Wrobel (1979) critical items is provided by Greene (1991). This author reported the frequencies of the critical item endorsement produced by adolescents and by adults receiving services in the Missouri public mental health system. These data, shown in Table 4.20, indicate roughly comparable levels of critical item endorsement for these two groups. The degree to which these findings would be generalizable to adolescents in other psychiatric settings, and the degree to which

TABLE 4.19

Response Set Prediction Accuracy Based on the Wiener-Harmon Subtle-Obvious Subscales and Traditional Validity Indices of the Original MMPI

Accuracy measure	Fake-bad versus inpatient			Fake-good versus normal	
	Predictors			Predictors	
	Obv.-Sub. $\geq +140$	$F + K +$ $Pa - Obv.$	$F \geq T =$ 100	Obv.-Sub. ≤ 0	L $\geq T = 55$
Hit Rate	84.7%	94.1%	93.5%	77.7%	89.3%
Sensitivity	71.9%	92.2%	92.2%	50.0%	71.4%
Specificity	92.5%	95.3%	94.3%	79.5%	90.4%
PPP	85.2%	92.2%	90.1%	13.5%	32.3%
NPP	84.5%	95.3%	95.2%	96.1%	98.0%

Note. Adapted from Herkov, Archer, and Gordon (1991). Copyright (c) 1991 by the American Psychological Association. Reproduced by permission.
Obv.-Sub. = Obvious minus Subtle difference score;
Pa − Obv. = Obvious subscale for the Paranoia basic scale.
PPP = Positive Predictive Power;
NPP = Negative Predictive Power.

TABLE 4.20
Distribution of the Total Number of Lachar and Wrobel (1979) Critical Items
Endorsed on the Original MMPI in Psychiatric Samples Grouped by Age and
Gender

| Total critical items | Psychiatric patients (Hedlund & Cho, 1979) | | | |
| | Adults | | Adolescents | |
	Male (N = 8646)	Female (N = 3743)	Male (N = 693)	Female (N = 290)
91+	0.3%	0.3%	0.7%	0.0%
81–90	1.8	1.4	2.6	1.7
71–80	3.9	3.2	4.8	4.2
61–70	6.9	7.3	6.6	11.7
51–60	10.7	12.7	13.0	13.8
41–50	14.3	18.0	16.2	19.3
31–40	18.6	18.7	16.7	15.2
21–30	20.3	19.3	21.7	14.4
11–20	17.3	14.1	13.9	16.9
0–10	5.9	5.0	3.8	2.8
Raw Score				
M	36.5	38.0	39.2	40.5
SD	19.3	18.3	19.5	19.3

Note. Adapted from Greene (1991). Copyright (c) 1991 by Allyn & Bacon. Adapted by permission.

comparable patterns would be found in comparisons of normal adolescents and adults, is unknown. Appendix F of this text provides a listing of the 99 Lachar-Wrobel critical items that were retained in the MMPI-A. Although these critical items may or may not prove to be useful in future research studies of the assessment of MMPI-A response accuracy, these items have utility to the clinician in leading to further areas of important discussion during the test feedback process with the adolescent.

Overall, there are currently insufficient data to support the use of either the Wiener-Harmon Subtle-Obvious subscales or the Lachar-Wrobel critical items in the standard assessment of the accuracy of adolescents' MMPI-A responses. In contrast to the MMPI-2, for example, the MMPI-A Advisory Committee did not recommend the creation of MMPI-A Subtle-Obvious subscale profile sheets because of the lack of empirical evidence supporting the use of these measures in adolescent populations. The use of the traditional validity scales, individually and configurally, is recommended for the evaluation of response accuracy on the MMPI-A. As previously noted, elevations of L and K, singly or in combination, in relation to the F scale and subscales, have been related to conscious and unconscious efforts to underreport symptomatology.

Further, the most open validity configuration is related to conscious or unconscious efforts to overreport symptomatology on the original MMPI and on the MMPI-A.

Adolescents are most likely to overreport psychopathology as a conscious or unconscious plea for help in order to communicate their desire for attention and support. Conversely, adolescents are most likely to underreport symptomatology when they have been involuntarily placed in treatment by their parents or court officials, and wish to underscore their perception that they do not have any significant problems. Additionally, adolescents will often underreport or overreport on the MMPI-A as a result of inappropriate test instructions or testing procedures that influence the adolescent, either consciously or unconsciously, to distort the accuracy of their responses.

SUMMARY

This chapter provided an overview of the traditional MMPI validity scales in the assessment of MMPI-A technical validity, and reviewed a number of MMPI-A profile features produced by various response sets. In addition, this chapter reviewed several sets of new validity-related measures developed for the MMPI-A including *TRIN* and *VRIN*, and the F_1 and F_2 Subscales. Finally, emphasis was placed on the validity assessment model developed by Greene (1989, 1991). In particular, a sequential approach to MMPI and MMPI-A validity assessment was presented, with particular attention to the distinction between the consistency of item endorsement and the accuracy of item endorsement. Within the Greene model, consistency of item endorsement may be viewed as a necessary, but not sufficient, component of valid response patterns.

REFERENCES

Anthony, N. (1976). Malingering as role taking. *Journal of Clinical Psychology, 32*, 32–41.

Archer, R. P. (1984). Use of the MMPI with adolescents: A review of salient issues. *Clinical Psychology Review, 4*, 241–251.

Archer, R. P. (1987). *Using the MMPI with adolescents.* Hillsdale, NJ: Lawrence Erlbaum Associates.

Archer, R. P. (1989). MMPI assessment of adolescent clients. *Clinical Notes on the MMPI, No. 12.* Minneapolis: National Computer Systems.

Archer, R. P., & Gordon, R. A. (1991). [Correlational analysis of MMPI-A normative data set]. Unpublished raw data.

Archer, R. P., Gordon, R. A., & Kirchner, F. H. (1987). MMPI response-set characteristics among adolescents. *Journal of Personality Assessment, 51*, 506–516.

Archer, R. P., White, J. L., & Orvin, G. H. (1979). MMPI characteristics and correlates among adolescent psychiatric inpatients. *Journal of Clinical Psychology, 35*, 498–504.

Ball, J. C., & Carroll, D. (1960). Analysis of MMPI Cannot Say scores in an adolescent population. *Journal of Clinical Psychology, 16*, 30–31.

Bond, J. A. (1986). Inconsistent responding to repeated MMPI items: Is its major cause really carelessness? *Journal of Personality Assessment, 50*, 50–64.

Bonfilio, S. A., & Lyman, R. D. (1981). Ability to simulate normalcy as a function of differential psychopathology. *Psychological Reports, 49*, 15–21.

Buechley, R., & Ball, H. (1952). A new test of "validity" for the group MMPI. *Journal of Consulting Psychology, 16*, 299–301.

Butcher, J. N., Dahlstrom, W. G., Graham, J. R., Tellegen, A., & Kaemmer, B. (1989). *Minnesota Multiphasic Personality Inventory–2 (MMPI-2): Manual for administration and scoring*. Minneapolis: University of Minnesota Press.

Butcher, J. N., Williams, C. L., Graham, J. R., Archer, R. P., Tellegen, A., Ben-Porath, Y. S., & Kaemmer, B. (1992). *MMPI-A (Minnesota Multiphasic Personality Inventory–Adolescent): Manual for administration, scoring, and interpretation*. Minneapolis: University of Minnesota Press.

Clopton, J. R., & Neuringer, C. (1977). MMPI Cannot Say scores: Normative data and degree of profile distortion. *Journal of Personality Assessment, 41*, 511–513.

Dahlstrom, W. G., Welsh, G. S., & Dahlstrom, L. E. (1972). *An MMPI handbook: Vol. 1. Clinical interpretation* (rev. ed.). Minneapolis: University of Minnesota Press.

Dahlstrom, W. G., Welsh, G. S., & Dahlstrom, L. E. (1975). *An MMPI handbook: Vol. II. Research applications* (rev. ed.). Minneapolis: University of Minnesota Press.

Exner, J. E., Jr., McDowell, E., Pabst, J., Stackman, W., & Kirk, L. (1963). On the detection of willful falsifications in the MMPI. *Journal of Consulting Psychology, 27*, 91–94.

Friedman, A. F., Webb, J. T., & Lewak, R. (1989). *Psychological assessment with the MMPI*. Hillsdale, NJ: Lawrence Erlbaum Associates.

Gottesman, I. I., Hanson, D. R., Kroeker, T. A., & Briggs, P. F. (1987). New MMPI normative data and power-transformed T-score tables for the Hathaway-Monachesi Minnesota cohort of 14,019 15-year-olds and 3,674 18-year-olds. In R. P. Archer, *Using the MMPI with adolescents* (pp. 241–297). Hillsdale, NJ: Lawrence Erlbaum Associates.

Gough, H. G. (1947). Simulated patterns on the MMPI. *Journal of Abnormal and Social Psychology, 42*, 215–225.

Gough, H. G. (1954). Some common misconceptions about neuroticism. *Journal of Consulting Psychology, 18*, 287–292.

Graham, J. R. (1987). *The MMPI: A practical guide* (2nd ed.). New York: Oxford University Press.

Graham, J. R. (1990). *MMPI-2: Assessing personality and psychopathology*. New York: Oxford University Press.

Graham, J. R., Watts, D., & Timbrook, R. E. (1991). Detecting fake-good and fake-bad MMPI-2 profiles. *Journal of Personality Assessment, 57*, 264–277.

Grayson, H. M., & Olinger, L. B. (1957). Simulation of "normalcy" by psychiatric patients on the MMPI. *Journal of Consulting Psychology, 21*, 73–77.

Greene, R. L. (1978). An empirically derived MMPI carelessness scale. *Journal of Clinical Psychology, 34*, 407–410.

Greene, R. L. (1979). Response consistency on the MMPI: The TR Index. *Journal of Personality Assessment, 43*, 69–71.

Greene, R. L. (1980). *The MMPI: An interpretive manual*. Boston: Allyn & Bacon.

Greene, R. L. (1989). Assessing the validity of MMPI profiles in clinical settings. *Clinical notes on the MMPI, No. 11*. Minneapolis: National Computer Systems.

Greene, R. L. (1991). *The MMPI-2/MMPI: An interpretive manual*. Boston: Allyn & Bacon.

Hathaway, S. R., & McKinley, J. C. (1967). *Minnesota Multiphasic Personality Inventory manual* (rev. ed.). New York: Psychological Corporation.

Hathaway, S. R., & Monachesi, E. D. (1963). *Adolescent personality and behavior: MMPI patterns of normal, delinquent, dropout, and other outcomes.* Minneapolis: University of Minnesota Press.

Hedlund, J. L., & Cho, D. W. (1979). [MMPI data research tape for Missouri Department of Mental Health patients]. Unpublished raw data.

Herkov, M. J., Archer, R. P., & Gordon, R. A. (1991). MMPI response sets among adolescents: An evaluation of the limitations of the Subtle-Obvious subscales. *Psychological Assessment: A Journal of Consulting and Clinical Psychology, 3,* 424–426.

Krakauer, S. (1991). *Assessing reading-deficit patterns among adolescents' MMPI profiles.* Unpublished doctoral dissertation, Virginia Consortium for Professional Psychology, Norfolk, Virginia.

Lachar, D., & Wrobel, T. A. (1979). Validating clinicians' hunches: Construction of a new MMPI critical item set. *Journal of Consulting and Clinical Psychology, 47,* 277–284.

Lanyon, R. I. (1967). Simulation of normal and psychopathic MMPI personality patterns. *Journal of Consulting Psychology, 31,* 94–97.

Marks, P. A., & Briggs, P. F. (1972). Adolescent norm tables for the MMPI. In W. G. Dahlstrom, G. S. Welsh, & L. E. Dahlstrom, *An MMPI handbook: Vol. 1. Clinical interpretation* (rev. ed., pp. 388–399). Minneapolis: University of Minnesota Press.

Marks, P. A., Seeman, W., & Haller, D. L. (1974). *The actuarial use of the MMPI with adolescents and adults.* New York: Oxford University Press.

Meehl, P. E., & Hathaway, S. R. (1946). The K factor as a suppressor variable in the MMPI. *Journal of Applied Psychology, 30,* 525–564.

Newmark, C. S., Gentry, L., Whitt, J. K., McKee, D. C., & Wicker, C. (1983). Simulating normal MMPI profiles as a favorable prognostic sign in schizophrenia. *Australian Journal of Psychology, 35,* 433–444.

Weed, N. C., Ben-Porath, Y. S., & Butcher, J. N. (1990). Failure of the Wiener and Harmon Minnesota Multiphasic Personality Inventory (MMPI) subtle scales as personality descriptors and as validity indicators. *Psychological Assessment: A Journal of Consulting and Clinical Psychology, 2,* 281–285.

Wiener, D. N. (1948). Subtle and Obvious keys for the MMPI. *Journal of Consulting Psychology, 12,* 164–170.

CLINICAL SCALE AND CODETYPE CORRELATES FOR ADOLESCENTS

PROFILE ELEVATION ISSUES AND THE MMPI-A PROFILE "SHADED" ZONE

As noted in previous chapters, adolescent MMPI responses should be interpreted exclusively through the use of age-appropriate adolescent norms. The conclusion that adolescent norm conversion is the most appropriate means of interpreting adolescent responses does not imply that such a procedure renders the evaluation of adolescent MMPI or MMPI-A profiles to be either simple or straightforward. The most important difficulties that occur when interpreting adolescent responses scored on adolescent norms is that resulting profiles typically produce subclinical elevations, even for adolescents in inpatient psychiatric settings, if a T-score value ≥ 70 is employed as the criterion for determining clinical-range elevation. The inherent contradiction in interpreting a normal-range profile for an adolescent who exhibits evidence of serious psychopathology has probably contributed to the inappropriate practice of using adult norms for adolescents. Thus, just as the application of adult norms to adolescent patterns tends to produce profiles that grossly overemphasize or exaggerate psychiatric symptomatology, so the application of adolescent norms, either on the original form of the MMPI or the MMPI-A, produces profiles that may often appear to underestimate an adolescent's psychopathology.

Normal-range mean profiles (e.g., mean T-score values <70) for inpatient adolescent populations on the original form of the MMPI have been reported by Archer (1987); Archer, Ball, and Hunter (1985); Archer, Stolberg, Gordon, and Goldman (1986); Ehrenworth and Archer (1985); and Klinge and Strauss (1976). The result of this phenomenon for adolescent MMPI profile interpretation on the original MMPI instrument was that the application of a T-score criterion of ≥ 70, traditionally found useful in defining clinical symptomatology for adult respondents, had substantially less utility with adolescents. Based on these observations, Ehrenworth and Archer (1985) recommended the use of a T-score value of 65 for defining clinical-range elevations for adolescents on the original instrument. Employment of this criterion in inpatient and outpatient adolescent samples served to substantially reduce the frequency of normal-range profiles obtained for adolescents (Archer, 1987). For example, Archer, Pancoast, and Klinefelter (1989) found that the use of clinical scale T-score values of 65 or greater (rather than ≥ 70) to detect the presence of psychopathology resulted in increased sensitivity in accurately identifying profiles produced by normal adolescents versus adolescents from outpatient and inpatient samples. Archer (1987) speculated that the "within normal limits" T-score elevations typically found for adolescents on the original instrument was partially related to the absence of K-correction procedures as well as the high base rate of endorsement of clinical symptoms typically found in samples of normal adolescents.

Figure 5.1 presents the profile of normal adolescents, scored on the Marks and Briggs (1972) traditional adolescent norms, from eight studies conducted between 1947 to 1965, in contrast to the mean profile

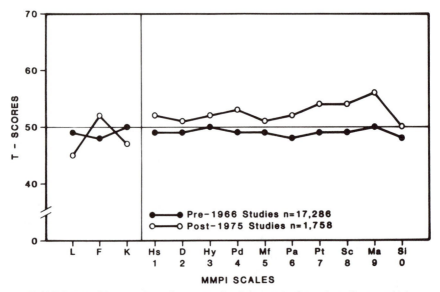

FIGURE 5.1 Mean values for normal adolescents from two time periods plotted on adolescent norms by Marks and Briggs (1972). (From Pancoast & Archer, 1988. Copyright (c) 1988 by Lawrence Erlbaum Associates. Reprinted by permission)

produced by normal adolescents in four studies conducted between 1975 and 1987 (Pancoast & Archer, 1988). These profiles (which present the validity scales in the traditional order) suggest that detectable changes have occurred in adolescent MMPI response patterns over the past 40 years, with these results lending support to the effort to create a contemporary adolescent MMPI norm set.

Figures 5.2 and 5.3 compare the post-1975 mean profile from the Pancoast and Archer (1988) review with the MMPI-A normative response patterns, separately by gender, as profiled on the Marks and Briggs (1972) adolescent norms using the conversion table in Appendix E. These data show that mean values from the MMPI-A normative sample are relatively consistent with other samples of normal adolescents that have been collected across the past decade. Because the MMPI-A normative set is based on adolescent response patterns that have higher mean scale raw score values than do the original Marks and Briggs adolescent norms, a major effect of the MMPI-A norms will be to reduce profile elevation for a given set of raw score values in comparison with the original Marks and Briggs norms. This may be illustrated in Figs. 5.4 and 5.5, which provide a comparison of the MMPI profile

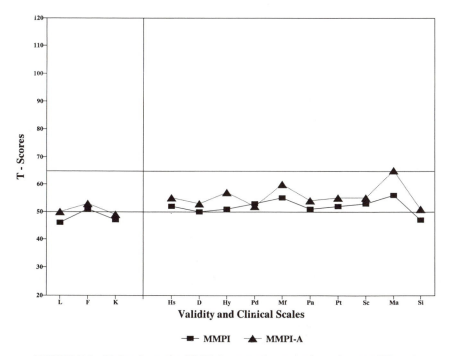

FIGURE 5.2   Males from the MMPI-A normative sample and post-1975 male adolescents on the original MMPI: Profiles on Marks and Briggs (1972) adolescent norms.

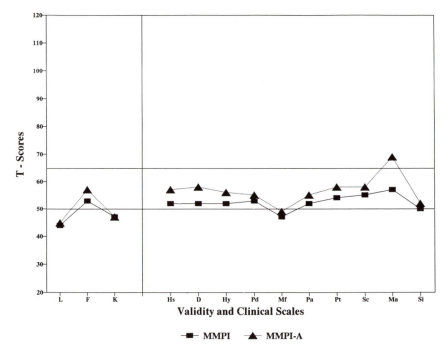

FIGURE 5.3 Females from the MMPI-A normative sample and post-1975 female adolescents on the original MMPI: Profiles on the Marks and Briggs (1972) adolescent norms.

elevations produced for a group of female ($N = 1,032$) and male ($N = 730$) adolescent psychiatric patients as profiled on the traditional Marks and Briggs (1972) norms, and on the MMPI-A adolescent norms based on the use of Appendix E. A comparison of profile elevations in these figures clearly demonstrates a reduction in MMPI scale T-score elevations related to the use of the more recent adolescent norm set.

In response to the profile elevation issues related to the use of the MMPI with adolescents, and the further reduction in profile elevations produced by the MMPI-A adolescent norms, an innovative strategy for determining clinical-range elevations was developed for the MMPI-A. Specifically, the use of a "black line" value, that is, a single T-score value that denotes the beginning of clinical-range elevations, was abandoned in favor of the creation of a range of values that serve as a transitional area or zone between normal-range and clinical-range elevations. The use of this zone concept explicitly recognizes that T-score values between ≥ 60 and ≤ 65 constitute a marginal range of elevation in which the adolescent may be expected to show some, but not necessarily all, of the clinical correlate patterns or traits associated with higher-range elevations for a specific MMPI-A scale. Conceptually, the use of a

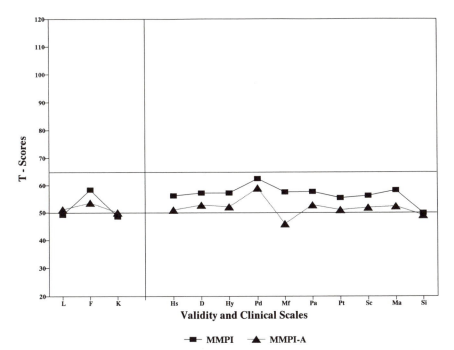

FIGURE 5.4   Male adolescent patients profiled on Marks and Briggs (1972) norms and MMPI-A adolescent norms.

"shaded" zone recognizes that the demarcation point or dividing line between normalcy and psychopathology during adolescence may be less clear than during adult development. Adolescents who are not deviant in a statistical sense (i.e., who do not produce clinical-range elevations in excess of a particular T-score value) may still display behaviors or report experiences disturbing enough to be labeled as clinically significant, and to require psychological intervention. As noted by Archer (1987), the "typical" adolescent may experience sufficient psychological turbulence and distress during adolescent development such that relatively minor deviations in the course of normal develop-ment may warrant psychiatric intervention and response. Thus, in addition to the traditional categories of *within normal limits* and *clinical range* elevations that have been typically associated with MMPI re-sponses, the MMPI-A has included a new category of *marginally or moderately elevated* T-score values.

UNIFORM T-SCORE TRANSFORMATION PROCEDURES FOR THE MMPI-A

As previously noted, the traditional adolescent norms developed by Marks and Briggs (1972), as well as the original MMPI norms for adults,

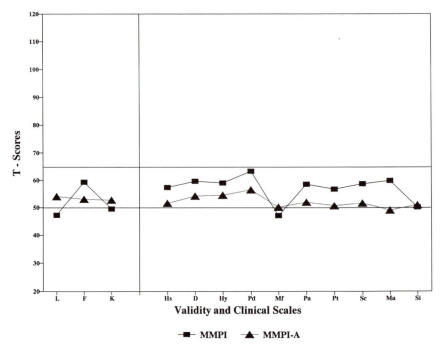

FIGURE 5.5 Female adolescent patients profiled on Marks and Briggs (1972) norms and MMPI-A adolescent norms.

utilized linear T-score transformations to convert raw score values to T scores. As noted by Colligan, Osborne, and Offord (1980, 1984), and by Butcher, Dahlstrom, Graham, Tellegen, and Kaemmer (1989) in the manual for the MMPI-2, linear T-score values have presented problems in the interpretation of MMPI profiles because a given linear T-score value typically converts to differing percentile equivalents across the various MMPI scales. Thus, a given T-score value on the original Marks and Briggs (1972) norms may convert to a percentile equivalent value that ranges as much as 10 to 15 percentile points across the ten MMPI basic scales. This occurs because the raw-score distribution for different MMPI scales varies in shape (e.g., in skewness), whereas a linear T-score transformation procedure will produce equivalent percentile values for a given T score only if the raw score distributions for the basic scales were each normally distributed. Because the basic scales display varying degrees of skewness, the same linear T-score value will have a different percentile equivalency score across the different scales. Uniform T scores represent composite or averaged linear T scores, which serve to promote percentile equivalence across MMPI-A clinical scales (excluding 5 and 0), and the content scales. Uniform T scores do not, however, have major effects on the underlying distribution of raw scores, and do not serve to "normalize" the underlying raw score distributions. This is important in that the "true" distribution of scores on the MMPI scales may in fact *not* be normal and, therefore, a normalizing procedure may actually serve to distort T-score values by artificially lowering those in the higher range. Table 5.1 shows the percentile values of uniform T scores as derived for the basic scales on the MMPI-A, and for the MMPI-2 as reported by Ben-Porath (1990). As shown in this table, uniform T scores do not correct or normalize the underlying raw score distributions such that a T-score value of 50 equals a percentile value of 50. Rather, the uniform T-score procedure makes relatively small adjustments in individual scale raw score distributions, achieved by creating a composite or overall distribution across the affected scales. These adjustments permit comparable percentile equivalents to be assigned to T-score values such that a given T score will yield equivalent percentile ranks across the eight clinical scales and the content scales. Appendix D contains uniform T-score transformations for the basic scales (with linear T scores for validity scales and *Mf* and *Si*) and content scales. Appendix D also contains linear T-score transformations for the supplementary scales and for the Harris-Lingoes and *Si* subscales.

CODETYPE CONGRUENCE ISSUES

A major area of controversy concerning the development of the MMPI-2 has centered on the degree to which adult profiles produced by the

TABLE 5.1
Percentile Values of Uniform T-scores for MMPI-A and MMPI-2

T-score	MMPI-A Percentile	MMPI-2[a] Percentile
30	0.6	0.2
35	4.2	3.7
40	15.1	15.1
45	36.5	34.2
50	59.1	54.9
55	76.0	72.3
60	85.7	84.7
65	92.2	92.1
70	95.8	96.0
75	98.3	98.1
80	99.4	99.3
85	99.9	99.8

[a] = MMPI-2 values reported by Ben-Porath (1990).

revised instrument were comparable to, or congruent with, adult profiles derived from the original MMPI (Archer, in press). This issue has received substantial focus because it relates to the degree to which the research literature available on the interpretation of the traditional MMPI may be generalized to the MMPI-2. Empirical research has slowly been accumulating on this crucial issue of congruence between the MMPI and MMPI-2. The MMPI-2 manual (Butcher et al., 1989) provides congruence data for two-point codes using MMPI-2 norms and the original test instrument norms in a sample of 232 male and 191 female psychiatric patients. These data indicate a congruence rate of approximately 70% for males and 65% for females when high points were defined as the most elevated clinical scale regardless of the magnitude of that elevation. Graham, Timbrook, Ben-Porath, and Butcher (1991) reexamined these data and report that when two-point codetype elevations were "well defined," as reflected in at least a five point T-score difference between the second and third most elevated scales in the clinical scale codetype, the congruence rate increased to 81.6% for males and 94.3% for females. In general, it is possible to conclude that although the MMPI and MMPI-2 are not psychometrically equivalent forms, the two instruments are likely to produce similar profiles, particularly when a two-point codetype represents a well defined configural pattern. Further, these general conclusions appear applicable to codetype congruence issues centered on adolescent assessment and the relationship between profiles produced by the MMPI-A and the original MMPI.

Table 5.2 provides data from the MMPI-A manual (Butcher et al., 1992) on the congruence rate between profiles generated by normal adolescents, based on the Marks and Briggs (1972) original norms, and on the MMPI-A adolescent norm set. Table 5.2 also provides similar data, comparing MMPI and MMPI-A profile characteristics, for a group of adolescents in psychiatric treatment settings. Table 5.2 indicates that the overall congruence rate between profiles generated from the original test instrument and the MMPI-A is 67.8% for boys and 55.8% for girls, with the congruence rate increasing to 95.2% for boys and 81.8% for girls when the criterion for two-point codetype definition requires at least a five-point T-score difference between the second and third most elevated scale. In the clinical sample of adolescents, the overall congruence rate is 69.5% for boys and 67.2% for girls, and reaches 95% for boys and 91% for girls employing well defined codetype classification procedures. Table 5.2 also shows the very dramatic reductions that occur in the number of profiles classified into two-point codetypes when the five-point level of definition is required. These estimates for MMPI and MMPI-A congruence for adolescent samples are comparable to the

TABLE 5.2
Two-point Codetype Congruence Rates as a Function of Codetype Definition
for Profiles Scored on the MMPI-A Norms and the Marks, Seeman, and
Haller (1974) Adolescent Norms

Definition[a]	Boys		Girls	
	N	%	N	%
	Normal Sample			
0	805	67.8	815	55.8
1	692	71.7	703	57.8
2	518	81.1	521	64.1
3	384	87.8	379	70.4
4	288	92.4	277	76.9
5	208	95.2	203	81.8
6	152	94.7	125	88.0
7	116	95.7	89	88.8
8	81	97.5	63	90.5
9	63	96.8	41	90.2
10	43	100.0	23	95.7
	Psychiatric Sample			
0	420	69.5	293	67.2
1	368	72.6	266	70.7
2	294	82.0	213	75.6
3	223	89.2	169	81.1
4	175	93.7	134	87.3
5	141	95.0	100	91.0
6	105	94.3	80	93.8
7	85	96.5	56	92.9
8	65	96.9	41	95.1
9	45	100.0	27	92.6
10	32	100.0	22	95.5

Note. From Butcher, Williams, Graham, Archer, Tellegen, Ben-Porath, and Kaemmer (1992). Copyright (c) 1992 by the Regents of the University of Minnesota. Reprinted by permission.

[a] = T-score difference between the second and third most elevated clinical scales in the MMPI codetype (using the Marks et al. norms).

congruence agreement rates reported for adults on the MMPI and MMPI-2 (Butcher et al., 1989; Graham et al., 1991). Thus, it seems reasonable to assume that much of the MMPI clinical research literature for adolescent samples may be generalized to the MMPI-A, but it is erroneous to assume that all adolescent patients will produce equivalent or congruent profiles across the two test instruments.

At present, many clinicians who are beginning to use the MMPI-A may feel more comfortable creating adolescent profiles based on MMPI-A norms as well as T-score values that are generated using the original Marks and Briggs (1972) adolescent norms. The MMPI-A manual (Butcher et al., 1992) contains T-score conversions for MMPI-A basic scales that provide estimates of the T score that would have been derived using the Marks and Briggs adolescent norms. This table is also reprinted in Appendix E in this text. Clinicians who employ the option of scoring the MMPI-A on both the original adolescent norms and the MMPI-A norms will be able to examine the ways in which these profiles are comparable or divergent for a specific adolescent respondent. This comparison process, in turn, may contribute to the clinician's knowledge of the new test instrument. Thus, this approach permits the interpretation of the MMPI-A profiles with an awareness of the degree of comparability or congruence that occurs in reference to the original test instrument. Other clinicians and researchers may, however, prefer to interpret the MMPI-A exclusively through the use of the MMPI-A adolescent norms, believing this strategy enhances their adaptation to the new instrument. At this point in our knowledge concerning the MMPI-A, both approaches appear reasonable and defensible as a means of interpreting MMPI-A profiles. Table 5.3 provides data on the frequency of profile assignments to two-point codes as reported in the MMPI-A manual (Butcher et al., 1992) for samples of normal adolescents and psychiatric patients scored on the MMPI-A adolescent norms.

Table 5.4 provides data from Archer, Gordon, and Klinefelter (1991) on 1,762 adolescent inpatients and outpatients scored on the Marks and Briggs norms, and rescored on MMPI-A norms, presented separately by gender. The adolescents used in these analyses were 12 to 18 years old ($M = 16.19$ years; $SD = 1.51$) who completed the group booklet form of the MMPI, produced F scores of $T < 100$ on the Marks and Briggs norms, and omitted less than 30 responses. The data sources include psychiatric settings in Missouri, Minnesota, and Texas and are described in Archer and Klinefelter (1991). Table 5.4 shows codetype frequency data for 45 codetype combinations and for *no-code* profiles. A no-code profile was defined as a profile containing no clinical scale value ≥ 65 T for the Marks and Briggs norms, and no clinical scale T-score value ≥ 60 for MMPI-A norms.

THE CODETYPE INTERPRETATION APPROACH

As noted by Graham (1990), configural approaches to the interpretation of the MMPI have been viewed as the potentially richest source of diagnostic and descriptive information that may be derived from this test instrument. The early writings on the MMPI (Meehl, 1951, 1956; Meehl & Dahlstrom, 1960) emphasized the interpretation of codetype information, and several of the early MMPI validity studies were

TABLE 5.3
Frequency Distribution of MMPI-A Codetypes With No Definition

Codetype	Normative Boys N=805	Normative Girls N=815	Clinical Boys N=420	Clinical Girls N=293
1-2/2-1	21	26	3	4
1-3/3-1	51	60	4	8
1-4/4-1	16	6	7	2
1-6/6-1	16	12	0	2
1-7/7-1	23	12	3	3
1-8/8-1	6	11	2	3
1-9/9-1	23	24	3	4
2-3/3-2	69	43	18	20
2-4/4-2	21	36	50	44
2-6/6-2	16	25	6	7
2-7/7-2	35	39	9	14
2-8/8-2	7	13	0	1
2-9/9-2	16	12	4	0
3-4/4-3	27	27	35	43
3-6/6-3	27	47	6	4
3-7/7-3	6	3	1	2
3-8/8-3	5	4	1	3
3-9/9-3	32	30	13	2
4-6/6-4	25	19	35	25
4-7/7-4	11	18	27	9
4-8/8-4	13	14	9	8
4-9/9-4	48	42	87	37
6-7/7-6	14	21	10	2
6-8/8-6	23	17	4	4
6-9/9-6	29	37	9	3
7-8/8-7	36	30	14	3
7-9/9-7	45	23	6	3
8-9/9-8	24	36	7	3

Note. From Butcher, Williams, Graham, Archer, Tellegen, Ben-Porath, and Kaemmer (1992). Copyright (c) 1992 by the Regents of the University of Minnesota. Reprinted by permission.

focused on identifying reliable clinical correlates of MMPI two-point codetypes (e.g., Meehl, 1951).

A high-point codetype is usually referred to by the numerical designation of the two scales that are most elevated in that profile, with convention dictating that the most elevated scale be designated first in the codetype sequence. Thus, if an adolescent produces his or her highest T-score elevations on scales *Pd* and *Ma* (in that order), the profile would result in classification as a 4-9 codetype. Throughout this text, individual MMPI scales have often been referred to by their names or alphabetic abbreviations rather than numerical designations. This pro-

TABLE 5.4
A Comparison of MMPI-A and MMPI Codetype Frequencies for 1,762 Adolescents Receiving Mental Health Services

| | MMPI-A | | | | MMPI | | | |
| | Males | | Females | | Males | | Females | |
Codetype	N	%	N	%	N	%	N	%
1-2/2-1	9	0.9%	16	2.2%	14	1.4%	25	3.4%
1-3/3-1	23	2.2%	44	6.0%	33	3.2%	38	5.2%
1-4/4-1	16	1.5%	2	0.3%	21	2.0%	7	1.0%
1-5/5-1	4	0.4%	5	0.7%	12	1.2%	2	0.3%
1-6/6-1	12	1.2%	3	0.4%	14	1.4%	2	0.3%
1-7/7-1	7	0.7%	2	0.3%	13	1.3%	4	0.5%
1-8/8-1	9	0.9%	6	0.8%	19	1.8%	24	3.3%
1-9/9-1	6	0.6%	6	0.8%	13	1.3%	12	1.6%
1-0/0-1	7	0.7%	2	0.3%	4	0.4%	1	0.1%
2-3/3-2	25	2.4%	30	4.1%	25	2.4%	22	3.0%
2-4/4-2	52	5.0%	24	3.3%	38	3.7%	50	6.9%
2-5/5-2	12	1.2%	9	1.2%	25	2.4%	3	0.4%
2-6/6-2	8	0.8%	5	0.7%	4	0.4%	7	1.0%
2-7/7-2	11	1.1%	6	0.8%	9	0.9%	16	2.2%
2-8/8-2	1	0.1%	2	0.3%	5	0.5%	7	1.0%
2-9/9-2	0	0.0%	0	0.0%	2	0.2%	5	0.7%
2-0/0-2	19	1.8%	28	3.8%	9	0.9%	13	1.8%
3-4/4-3	51	4.9%	26	3.6%	41	4.0%	20	2.7%
3-5/5-3	10	1.0%	22	3.0%	34	3.3%	5	0.7%
3-6/6-3	6	0.6%	10	1.4%	4	0.4%	5	0.7%
3-7/7-3	0	0.0%	4	0.5%	2	0.2%	3	0.4%
3-8/8-3	1	0.1%	5	0.7%	0	0.0%	4	0.5%
3-9/9-3	7	0.7%	6	0.8%	6	0.6%	15	2.1%
3-0/0-3	1	0.1%	3	0.4%	0	0.0%	1	0.1%
4-5/5-4	17	1.6%	28	3.8%	37	3.6%	8	1.1%
4-6/6-4	64	6.2%	29	4.0%	58	5.6%	33	4.5%
4-7/7-4	25	2.4%	9	1.2%	18	1.7%	12	1.6%
4-8/8-4	29	2.8%	15	2.1%	21	2.0%	31	4.3%
4-9/9-4	104	10.1%	29	4.0%	82	7.9%	63	8.6%
4-0/0-4	24	2.3%	15	2.1%	7	0.7%	5	0.7%
5-6/6-5	5	0.5%	8	1.1%	20	1.9%	0	0.0%
5-7/7-5	1	0.1%	1	0.1%	5	0.5%	1	0.1%
5-8/8-5	1	0.1%	5	0.7%	7	0.7%	3	0.4%
5-9/9-5	3	0.3%	19	2.6%	29	2.8%	9	1.2%
5-0/0-5	3	0.3%	8	1.1%	4	0.4%	0	0.0%
6-7/7-6	14	1.4%	4	0.5%	16	1.5%	1	0.1%
6-8/8-6	33	3.2%	25	3.4%	25	2.4%	21	2.9%
6-9/9-6	22	2.1%	12	1.6%	22	2.1%	17	2.3%
6-0/0-6	3	0.3%	2	0.3%	1	0.1%	1	0.1%
7-8/8-7	19	1.8%	14	1.9%	21	2.0%	17	2.3%
7-9/9-7	18	1.7%	5	0.7%	16	1.5%	10	1.4%
7-0/0-7	13	1.3%	9	1.2%	4	0.4%	2	0.3%
8-9/9-8	16	1.5%	7	1.0%	12	1.2%	18	2.5%
8-0/0-8	2	0.2%	7	1.0%	1	0.1%	0	0.0%
9-0/0-9	6	0.6%	0	0.0%	4	0.4%	0	0.0%
No Code	314	30.4%	212	29.1%	276	26.7%	186	25.5%
Total	1033		729		1033		729	

cedure has been followed to minimize confusion in scale delineations for the novice MMPI user. In discussing codetype classifications, however, MMPI scales are referred to in this chapter by their numerical designation in the manner consistent with the codetype literature. In addition to MMPI tradition, numerical designation of scales is the generally preferred practice among experienced MMPI users for a very important reason: The names that were originally given to clinical scales may be misleading and may serve as inadequate labels of what that scale is currently believed to measure. For example, the Psychasthenia scale was originally developed to measure symptomatology related to what was later referred to as obsessive-compulsive neuroses and now is termed obsessive-compulsive disorder. Psychasthenia is not a psychiatric label in common use today, and Graham (1990) noted that the *Pt* scale is currently thought of as a reliable index of psychological distress, turmoil, and discomfort, particularly related to symptoms of anxiety, tension, and apprehension.

Several codetype "cookbook" systems have been developed, such as those provided by Gilberstadt and Duker (1965) and Marks and Seeman (1963), which have employed very complex rules for classifying multiscale elevations. However, the more recent efforts regarding codetype descriptors have tended to employ much simpler two-point approaches to classify MMPI profiles. These systems, such as those exemplified in Graham (1990) and Greene (1991), have typically interpreted codetypes based on the two scales with the highest clinical-range elevation. Several investigations, such as research by Lewandowski and Graham (1972), demonstrated that reliable clinical correlates can be established for profiles that are classified based on the simpler two-point code systems. Recent data by Pancoast, Archer, and Gordon (1988) also indicate that assignments to simple codetype systems can be made with acceptable levels of reliability by independent raters. Additionally, diagnoses derived by the simpler MMPI classification systems provide comparable levels of agreement with clinicians' diagnoses as do those diagnoses derived from more complex methods of MMPI profile classification. The obvious advantage of using the two-point code system is that a much larger percentage of profiles can be classified in a typical clinical setting when numerous stringent criteria are not required for codetype assignments (Graham, 1990).

Of primary importance in employing codetype descriptors with any population is a clear understanding that the attribution of correlate descriptors to a particular client entails probability estimates. These estimates of accuracy may vary greatly based on the source of the descriptor statement (adequacy of research methodology, characteristics of the population sampled, statistical strength of findings) and the individual characteristics of the client being assessed (the base rate of the symptoms/diagnoses in the general psychiatric population). Additionally, it is likely that the accuracy of descriptor statements will vary based on the degree of elevation and definition exhibited by a codetype (i.e., the degree to which the two-point code is clinically elevated, and elevated substantially above the remainder of the clinical scale profile). Even under optimal conditions in which cross-validated research has led to the derivation of clinical correlates from MMPI profiles highly similar to that of the individual being evaluated, a specific clinical correlate may be found not to apply to a specific individual. Thus, as Greene (1991) noted, MMPI cookbooks, even within adult populations, "have not been the panacea that was originally thought" (p. 234). Nevertheless, they continue to serve as a valuable source of hypotheses concerning client characteristics when such cautions are borne in mind by the interpreter.

DERIVING A CODETYPE CLASSIFICATION FOR ADOLESCENTS

In the adult codetype information provided by such sources as Graham (1990) and Greene (1991), profiles are typically placed into two-point codetypes based on the two clinical scales that show the greatest degree of clinical-range elevation. In these and most other systems, few high-point codes are provided that involve scales 5 and 0, because these scales have often been excluded from designation as clinical scales. These scales were also frequently excluded in codetype research in early MMPI investigations (Graham, 1990).

In general, two-point codes are used interchangeably; for example, 2-7 codetypes are seen as equivalent to 7-2 codetypes, unless differences are specifically noted. Furthermore, the absolute elevation of two high-point scales within the profile is typically not considered beyond the assumption that such elevations occur within clinical ranges. The relative elevation of the two highest scales in relation to the remaining profile is also not typically considered or discussed in codetype narratives. As previously noted, however, the degree to which the two-point code is well defined appears to be related to the short-term stability of the codetype (i.e., the degree to which profile characteristics are subject to change over relatively brief periods of time), and the degree to which clinical correlate patterns will be applicable for a codetype configuration. In standard codetype interpretation practice, if a profile does not fit any of the two-point codetypes presented, the clinician is generally advised to employ an interpretation strategy based on clinical correlates found for the individual MMPI scales that are elevated.

Marks, Seeman, and Haller (1974) developed a classification system for adolescent MMPI profiles designed to increase the clinicians' flexibility in rendering codetype assignments. Once an adolescent's MMPI profile had been plotted, Marks et al. recommended that the resulting configuration be compared to the codetype profiles provided in their 1974 text in terms of the two highest elevations occurring within that particular profile. If the codetype for the individual adolescent corresponded to one of the two-digit codetypes presented by Marks et al., the clinician was referred to the codetype descriptors appropriate for that configuration. If the respondent's codetype was not classifiable, however, the authors recommended dropping the second high-point scale and substituting the third-highest scale to produce a new two-point code. If this procedure then resulted in a classifiable codetype, the clinician was encouraged to interpret that profile based on the clinical correlate information provided for that code. If the profile remained unclassifiable following this "substitution and reclassification" procedure, Marks et al. suggested that their actuarial interpretation system not be applied for that respondent. As in the adult literature, these authors encourage clinicians with unclassifiable profiles to employ a single-scale correlate interpretive strategy.

Alex Caldwell (as reported in Friedman, Webb, & Lewak, 1989) developed a productive system for classifying and interpreting profiles that, because of multiple-scale clinical-range elevations, do not fit cleanly into simple two-point codetypes. This system, which is referred to as the A-B-C-D Paradigm, divides the multiply-elevated clinical-scale profile into discrete two-point codetype entities, and builds the interpretive narrative based on clinical correlate descriptors that are commonly found across these two-point codes. Figure 5.6 provides an illustration of the Caldwell A-B-C-D Paradigm for an adolescent MMPI profile characterized by elevations on scales 4, 8, 2, and 6. This profile is used to demonstrate Caldwell's method of breaking down a multiply-elevated profile into more easily interpretable two-point codes.

As shown in this figure, the four most elevated clinical scales (elevated within clinical ranges) are assigned a corresponding letter of the alphabet in order of elevation magnitude. The profile is then divided into high-point pairs using the combinations A-B, A-C, A-D, B-C, B-D, and C-D. Descriptors commonly shared by these two-point codetype classifications emphasize an adolescent who might be described as impulsive, maladaptive, and antisocial, and whose interpersonal relationships are characterized by conflict. The interpretation would place more emphasis on codetype correlates for 4-8 and 4-2 given the relative prominence of these features within this MMPI profile, and place less emphasis on codetypes including 8-6/6-8 and 2-6/6-2 because of the

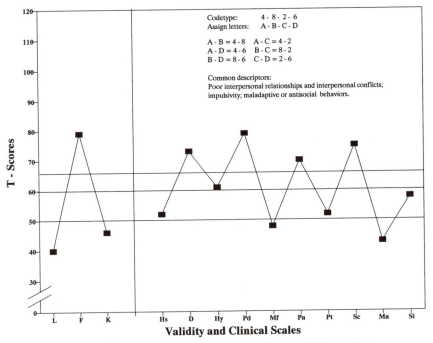

FIGURE 5.6   Illustration of the Caldwell A-B-C-D Paradigm.

relatively weaker elevations for these latter configural features. When contradictory descriptors are derived, emphasis will be placed on the primary codetype descriptors (e.g., A-B) rather than the secondary scale pairs (e.g., C-D).

In terms of recommendations for the clinician deriving codetype assignments, it appears most appropriate to employ a simple codetype strategy that seeks to place an individual profile into a codetype classification based on the highest two-point characteristics occurring within clinical ranges for that profile. The clinician should be mindful, however, that less elevated and less well-defined codetypes (the degree of elevation of the two-point code relative to the remainder of the profile) are likely to manifest fewer of the correlate features associated with that particular codetype. When classification does not result in a two-point codetype placement for which clinical correlate information is available from standard sources, it is suggested that the clinician interpret the profile based upon single-scale correlates. The substitution and reclassification procedure suggested by Marks et al. (1974) is *not* recommended. For clinical profiles that demonstrate more than two scales elevated within clinical ranges, the experienced interpreter may wish to consider use of the Caldwell A-B-C-D Paradigm in terms of an interpretive strategy.

SINGLE-SCALE AND TWO-POINT CODETYPES

A substantial research literature has developed on the clinical correlate patterns exhibited by adolescents on the basic MMPI scales. Hathaway and Monachesi (1963), for example, investigated high-point and low-point correlate patterns for approximately 15,000 ninth graders who were administered the MMPI in the Minnesota public school system during 1948 and 1954. Lachar and Wrobel (1990), and Wrobel and Lachar (1990) recently examined single-scale correlate patterns in a sample of adolescents from predominantly outpatient settings, with analyses conducted separately by gender. Information concerning the correlates of basic MMPI scales for inpatient adolescents was examined in research studies by Archer et al. (1985); Archer and Gordon (1988); Archer, Gordon, Giannetti, and Singles (1988); Ball, Archer, Struve, Hunter, and Gordon (1987); and by Williams and Butcher (1989a). Single-scale correlates for the MMPI-A basic clinical scales were reported in the manual for this instrument by Butcher et al. (1992). Additionally, information concerning correlate patterns for various codetype configurations was presented by Archer (1987), Archer and Klinefelter (1992), Marks et al. (1974), and by Williams and Butcher (1989b). These research investigations serve as the primary sources of single-scale and codetype correlate data presented in this chapter.

In deriving the following codetype descriptors for adolescents, the 29 codetypes reported by Archer (1987) were selected for presentation. In general, the core of this clinical correlate information is based on the Marks et al. (1974) data reported for high-point codetypes occurring within clinical ranges. This information was then supplemented with adult correlate information for these 29 high-point pairs from Friedman et al. (1989), Graham (1990), Greene (1991), and Lachar (1974). The typical narrative created by this method begins with statements found to be common across both the adolescent and adult descriptors for a particular MMPI configuration, based upon the observations by Archer (1987) and Archer et al. (1988) that MMPI scale descriptors found in studies of adolescents have typically been consistent with those found in adult studies. Further, when sources of adult correlate data were not available for a particular codetype, a relatively rare occurrence, this is noted in the first few sentences of the narrative. When marked or important differences occur between descriptors derived from adolescent and adult clinical populations, the interpretive implications of these discrepancies are presented. Finally, codetype frequency data for adolescents is based on our analyses of the codetype classification data for 1,762 adolescent patients shown in Table 5.4, as scored on MMPI-A norms.

In addition to the 29 codetype narratives, the following sections also contain information concerning characteristics of each of the 10 clinical MMPI scales. High and low single-scale correlates are suggested based upon findings reported in studies of adolescent samples in normal and/or psychiatric settings. In the case of single-scale high-point correlates, this description is enriched by the MMPI-A correlate research reported in the test manual (Butcher et al., 1992). Much of the codetype correlate information provided in the following sections is based on research conducted with the original form of the MMPI utilizing the traditional adolescent norms as derived by Marks and Briggs (1972). This approach is similar to that taken by Graham (1990), Greene (1991), and by Butcher (1990) in the generation of codetype findings for the MMPI-2. The generalization of MMPI findings to the MMPI-A appears supported in that the MMPI-A clinical scales (except *Mf* and *Si*) have retained basically the same items as their counterparts in the original instrument. Further, as previously discussed in this chapter, the codetype congruence data for the MMPI and MMPI-A indicate that these instruments will produce similar or equivalent profiles in a majority of cases. Empirical research findings are needed, however, concerning the degree to which codetype correlates found for adolescents on the original test instrument may be validly generalized to the MMPI-A.

Scale 1 (*Hs*: Hypochondriasis) Codetypes

Scale 1 originally consisted of 33 items developed to identify respondents who manifested a history of symptomatology associated with hypochondriasis. These symptoms include vague physical complaints and ailments and a preoccupation with bodily functioning, illness, and disease. One item was dropped from the original scale in the creation of the MMPI-A due to objectionable content, resulting in a revised scale length of 32 items. Graham (1990) reported that scale 1 appears to be the most unidimensional and homogeneous MMPI clinical basic scale in terms of item composition and content. All of the items on scale 1 relate to somatic concerns and complaints. Literature in adult samples has established that individuals who score high on scale 1 typically report many somatic symptoms and exaggerated complaints regarding physical functioning. Additionally, Graham (1990) noted that adults who produce elevated scale 1 MMPI profiles are not psychologically minded and often use physical complaints as a means of controlling or manipulating significant others in their environment.

Reports concerning physical functioning on scale 1 would also be expected to be influenced by the individual's actual physical condition—respondents with physical illness typically produce moderate subclinical elevations on this measure. For example, Ball et al. (1987) found subtle but detectable neurological differences between adolescent psychiatric inpatients with and without marked scale 1 elevations. MMPI profiles with scale 1 elevations have also been reported for adolescents with medical problems, including epilepsy (Dodrill & Clemmons, 1984), muscular dystrophy (Harper, 1983), nonprogressive physical impairments (Harper & Richman, 1978), Gilles de la Tourette Syndrome (Grossman, Mostofsky, & Harrison, 1986), sleep disorders (Monroe & Marks, 1977), surreptitious insulin administration among insulin-dependent diabetics (Orr, Eccles, Lawlor, & Golden, 1986), and rheumatic fever (Stehbens, Ehmke, & Wilson, 1982). Colligan and Osborne (1977) investigated the MMPI response features of 659 female and 534 male adolescents (ages 15 through 19) who presented at the Mayo Clinic for medical evaluation, and found these adolescents produced higher scores on the neurotic triad, which consists of scales 1, 2, and 3. Profiles with elevations on scale 1 were unusual in the normal adolescent data collected by Hathaway and Monachesi (1963), although a larger number of these profiles were classified as producing the lowest value on this scale.

High Scores on Scale 1

The following is a summary of descriptors for high scale 1 scores (T ≥ 60):

- Excessive somatic and bodily concerns that are likely to be vague in nature.
- Likely to display somatic responses to stress, which may include eating problems.
- Increased likelihood of problems related to neurotic diagnoses.
- Likely to be seen by others as self-centered, pessimistic, dissatisfied, and cynical.
- Demanding, critical, selfish, and whining in interpersonal relationships.
- Likely to display little insight in psychotherapy.
- Less likely to engage in delinquent behaviors.
- Likely to report school problems including academic and adjustment difficulties.

Low Scores on Scale 1

Low Scale 1 scores have been associated with the following characteristics (T ≤ 40):

- Few physical symptoms and freedom from somatic preoccupation.
- Higher scores on tests of intelligence.
- More likely to come from urban than rural settings.
- Greater psychological sophistication and insight.

1-2/2-1 Codetype

Adolescent and adult clients with this codetype frequently complain of physical symptoms including weakness, fatigue, and tiredness. These individuals often show a consistent pattern of somatic preoccupation and overreactions to minor physical dysfunction. Marked affective distress appears to be associated with the 1-2/2-1 codetype and these individuals are often described as ruminative, tense, anxious, and insecure. There are also frequent reports of depression, social withdrawal, and isolation.

In both the adult and adolescent literatures, the 1-2/2-1 codetype has been associated with a very low probability of the use of acting out as a primary defense mechanism. There are often marked interpersonal concerns and unmet needs for attention and approval by others. Thus, individuals who produce this codetype have been described as fearful and hypersensitive in their interactions with others, and often as dependent and indecisive.

The 1-2/2-1 codetype occurred with a frequency of 0.9% for males and 2.2% for females in our sample of adolescent psychiatric patients scored on MMPI-A norms. Marks et al. (1974) reported that obsession and compulsion are the primary mechanisms of defense employed by adolescents with the 1-2/2-1 codetype. Adolescents with this codetype in the Marks et al. sample often complained of being teased by others during their childhood and indicated that they were afraid of making mistakes. They appeared to be quiet, depressed teenagers who established very few friendships and often manifested obsessional defenses. Although Graham (1990) reported that adults with the 1-2/2-1 profile often display excessive use of alcohol, the adolescents in the Marks et al. study with this codetype did not manifest significant drug or alcohol involvements. Finally, Marks and his colleagues noted that adolescents often had histories that included parental separation and divorce, academic problems including several cases of social phobias, and delayed academic progress.

1-3/3-1 Codetype

Both adult and adolescent sources of clinical correlate data indicate that individuals with the *1-3/3-1* codetype typically present themselves as physically or organically ill. Indeed, when scales *1* and *3* are greater than a T-score value of 65, and both of these scales exceed the T-score value for scale *2* by at least 10 points, this profile may be described as a classic *conversion V*. The types of physical complaints that have been noted in the general literature for the *1-3/3-1* include headaches, dizziness, chest pain, abdominal pain, insomnia, blurred vision, nausea, and anorexia. It would be expected that these physical symptoms would increase in times of psychological stress, and the clinician might be advised to attempt to identify secondary gain characteristics associated with this symptomatology.

In the adult and adolescent literatures, the *1-3/3-1* codetype is associated more with neurotic and psychophysiological symptomatology rather than diagnoses related to psychoses. These respondents are frequently perceived as insecure and attention-seeking. Behaving in socially acceptable ways appears important to the *1-3/3-1* person. For the adult and adolescent *1-3/3-1*, there are problems in successfully establishing relationships with members of the opposite sex. Often, these problems are related to the lack of development of appropriate skills in these interpersonal areas. Primary defense mechanisms for this codetype consist of somatization, denial, and externalization.

As shown in Table 5.4, 2.2% of male and 6.0% of female adolescents in psychiatric settings produce the *1-3/3-1* codetype. Data unique to adolescent clinical sources for this profile indicate that the *1-3/3-1* teenagers are more frequently referred for treatment because of problems or concerns in their academic settings. The majority of adolescents in the Marks et al. (1974) sample indicated that they were afraid of receiving poor grades; a fear that appeared to be realistic in that 44% of this sample were a year behind their age-appropriate academic placement. In general, Marks et al. noted that adolescents with this codetype often displayed "diagnostic insight" into the descriptive features of their psychological problems. They were able to talk superficially about conflicts and were not evasive in psychotherapy. These features are in contrast to the descriptors in the adult literature indicating that *1-3/3-1* individuals typically display little willingness to acknowledge psychological factors in their life problems and little insight into their problems. Of the 20 patients in the Marks et al. (1974) 1970-1973 sample who produced a *1-3/3-1* codetype, over two-thirds had no history of drug abuse or drug involvement.

1-4/4-1 Codetype

The *1-4/4-1* codetype is relatively rare among adults, and it is found in approximately 1.5% of male and 0.3% of female adolescents in psychiatric settings. In both the adult and adolescent sources of clinical correlate information, the *1-4/4-1* individual appears to be defensive, negativistic, resentful, pessimistic, and cynical. Furthermore, research findings suggest these individuals may be described as self-centered and immature. The use of somatic complaints is a primary defense mechanism for both adolescents and adults, although this feature is more prevalent among adolescents producing a higher elevation on scale *1* in contrast to scale *4*.

In addition to these features, derived from the combined literature, a number of characteristics appear to be uniquely related to the adolescents' *1-4/4-1* codetypes. Specifically, more scale *4* features are reported as descriptive of adolescents with this codetype, including defiance, disobedience, and provocative behaviors. These problem areas are most likely to be manifested in the relationship between the adolescent and his or her parents. In the psychotherapy relationship, adolescents with this codetype have been described as superficial, cognitively disorganized, and moderately impaired in judgment. Therapists in the Marks et al. (1974) study rated adolescents with a *1-4/4-1* profile as manifesting an overall degree of psychiatric disturbance that was mild to moderate for most cases. In addition to the somatization, adolescents with this codetype often manifest acting out as their primary defense mechanism. Therapists describe adolescent patients with this codetype as aggressive, outspoken, resentful, headstrong, and egocentric. Despite the use of acting out as a primary defense mechanism, adolescents with the *1-4/4-1* codetype in the Marks et al. sample were typically not found to be substance abusers.

1-5/5-1 Codetype

The *1-5/5-1* is a relatively infrequent codetype among adults, and is found for less than 1% of male and female adolescents in psychiatric treatment. In both the adult and adolescent literatures, the *1-5/5-1* is often accompanied by somatic complaints of a hypochondriacal nature and patients with this codetype often present as physically ill. Additionally, these individuals are often seen as passive, and the adolescent data indicates that teenagers with this codetype are unlikely to enter into open conflict or disagreement with their parents.

Teenagers with this codetype are often referred for treatment by parents and by school officials. Primary therapists view these adolescents as displaying mildly inappropriate affect, and compulsion appeared to be a primary defense mechanism distinctive to this codetype. Interestingly, many of these teenagers in the Marks et al. (1974) sample actually had experienced serious physical illnesses as children. Therapists described 1-5/5-1 adolescent patients as having difficulty in discussing their problems and conflict areas, and these teenagers were seen as unreliable in terms of the information they provided to their therapists. They were not generally liked by others and had difficulty in forming close relationships. Finally, teenage males with this profile type were described as effeminate.

1-6/6-1 Codetype

Of the adult sources reviewed, only Greene (1980, 1991) and Friedman et al. (1989) provide descriptive summaries for the 1-6/6-1 profile. Greene's brief description of this codetype emphasizes the occurrence of hypochondriacal symptomatology combined with hostile and suspicious traits related to elevations on scale 6. Additionally, he noted that the personality structure of the adult 1-6/6-1 appeared resistant to change as a result of psychotherapy. In contrast, the results of investigation of adolescent 1-6/6-1 codetypes by Marks et al. (1974) produced a quite different descriptive picture. Confidence in any codetype descriptors for this configuration must be tempered, however, by awareness-that little research has been done in adult settings and that the 1-6/6-1 codetype reported by Marks et al. was based on a very small sample size (N = 11). Among adolescent psychiatric patients, only 1.2% of males and 0.4% of females produced 1-6/6-1 codetypes (see Table 5.4).

Hypochondriacal tendencies and somatic complaints do not appear to be characteristics of adolescents with the 1-6/6-1 codetype. Rather, these adolescents were primarily referred for psychotherapy because of excessive emotional control. Therapists viewed these teenagers as evasive, defensive, and fearful of emotional involvement with others. More than half of these adolescents lived with their mothers in father-absent homes. When fathers were present in the family of these teenagers, their attitude toward the adolescent was reported to be rejecting. The 1-6/6-1 adolescent was viewed as egocentric and prone to rationalization as a defense mechanism. Data from the Marks et al. 1970-1973 sample indicated some drug abuse involvement for this codetype, but it was not widespread or particularly characteristic of this code. Intense anger directed at parents was frequent for this group, including occasional violent outbursts. Suicidal attempts, perhaps representing an internalization of rage and anger, were also characteristic of the *1-6/6-1* 1970-1973 adolescent sample.

1-8/8-1 Codetype

Common features across the adolescent and adult literatures for the *1-8/8-1* codetype emphasize correlates commonly associated with both scales *1* and *8*. Patients with this profile type frequently present somatic concerns such as headaches and insomnia, and often perceive themselves as physically ill. There are additional data from adolescent sources to suggest that teenagers with this codetype were, in fact, often ill with serious health problems during their childhood. These adolescents also frequently reported histories of poor social adjustment and social inadequacy. Further, individuals with the *1-8/8-1* profile appear to have difficulty in forming and maintaining interpersonal relationships. There is evidence across the adolescent and adult literatures that the *1-8/8-1* codetype is often associated with delusional or disordered thinking, including symptoms related to difficulty in concentration and thought processes. Adolescents with the *1-8/8-1* codetype often described themselves as distractable and forgetful.

Approximately 0.9% of male and 0.8% female adolescents in psychiatric settings produce the *1-8/8-1* codetype. Several clinical descriptors are uniquely available for this codetype classification from the Marks et al. (1974) study. These adolescents frequently reported problems during childhood involving being teased and harassed by peers, and often had difficulty in academic performance, including reading. Overall, their adjustment appeared to be problematic both in and outside of school settings, and they experienced substantial difficulty in making friends. Nearly one-half of the *1-8/8-1* teenagers in the Marks et al. sample were a grade behind their expected academic placement.

Unique among the two-point codetypes involving scale *1*, the *1-8/8-1* adolescents in the Marks et al. data were likely to be involved in drug abuse, and over 50% of the sample reported a drug use history. Data from Archer and Klinefelter (1992) also indicate adolescents with this codetype frequently exhibit elevated values on the MacAndrew Alcoholism scale. Additionally, attempted suicides frequently occurred among these adolescents, with 65% of adolescents with this codetype attempting to take their own lives. Finally, intense family conflict was present for a very high percentage of the *1-8/8-1* teenagers, which often involved fighting or overt conflict with their parents. Two-thirds of these adolescents were from families in which their parents were divorced.

Scale 2 (*D*: Depression) Codetypes

Scale 2 (Depression) originally consisted of 60 items, of which 57 were retained in the MMPI-A scale 2. The essential characteristics of this MMPI dimension include poor morale, lack of hope for the future, and general dissatisfaction with one's life status and situation (Hathaway & McKinley, 1942). The major content areas involved in this scale include lack of interest in activities or general apathy, physical symptoms such as sleep disturbances and gastrointestinal complaints, and excessive social sensitivity and social withdrawal. Graham (1990) described scale 2 as a sensitive measure of the respondent's life discomfort and dissatisfaction. He noted that although very elevated values on this scale are suggestive of clinical depression, more moderate scores have generally been seen as reflective of a life attitude or lifestyle characterized by apathy and poor morale. The subscales derived by Harris and Lingoes (1955) for scale 2 include item groupings labeled *Subjective Depression* (D_1), *Psychomotor Retardation* (D_2), *Physical Malfunctioning* (D_3), *Mental Dullness* (D_4), *and Brooding* (D_5).

Scale 2 high points were very infrequent among adolescents in the Hathaway and Monachesi (1963) Minnesota sample. Profiles containing their lowest values on scale 2, however, were relatively more common among these adolescents. Greene (1991) reported that adult psychiatric patients who produce elevations on scale 2 generally have characteristics of clinically depressed individuals including feelings of inadequacy, lack of self-confidence, guilt and pessimism, and self-depreciation. Greene also noted that individuals who produce spike 2 profiles tend to be good psychotherapy candidates, and often show significant improvement as a result of relatively brief psychiatric interventions. Consistent with this finding, Archer et al. (1988) found that high scale 2 inpatient adolescents were perceived by clinicians and psychiatric staff as more motivated to engage in psychotherapy and openly discuss their feelings and perceptions. They were also less likely than other adolescents to engage in rebellious, deceitful, manipulative, or hostile behaviors. In addition, Archer and his colleagues found that high scale 2 adolescents were described as more introspective, self-critical, guilty, ashamed, and more likely to have presenting problems involving suicidal thoughts or ideations. Butcher et al. (1992), based on analyses of MMPI-A data, found that adolescent inpatients with scale 2 elevations were more likely to be characterized as depressed and more likely to have problems related to suicidal ideations and/or gestures. Archer and Gordon (1988), however, found no evidence of a significant relationship between scale 2 elevations among adolescent inpatients and clinicians' use of depression-related diagnoses, including dysthymia and major depression. Research by Nelson (1987) suggested that scale 2 may more accurately identify clinically depressed individuals when only face-valid or obvious Depression scale items are employed.

Although clinical lore holds that scale 2 results may be predictive of suicide attempts, the empirical literature does not appear to support this assumption. Marks and Haller (1977) examined groups of male and female adolescents who made suicide attempts in contrast with other emotionally disturbed adolescents without suicidal histories. The authors reported that MMPI scales 3 and 5 were significantly higher for male attempters, whereas scale 9 elevations were associated with suicide attempts among females. Spirito, Faust, Myers, and Bechtel (1988) found no significant differences in scale 2 mean elevations between female adolescent suicide attempters and a control group of female adolescents initially hospitalized for medical problems and referred for psychiatric consultation. Based upon very similar profiles produced by these two groups, in conjunction with the largely negative findings in the adult literature, Spirito et al. (1988) concluded that, "primary reliance on the MMPI alone to determine suicidal risk seems nonjudicious" (p. 210).

High Scores on Scale 2

The following is a summary of descriptors for high scale 2 scores $(T \geq 60)$:

- Feelings of dissatisfaction, hopelessness, and unhappiness.
- General apathy and lack of interest in activities.
- Presence of guilt feelings, shame, and self-criticism.
- Lack of self-confidence and a sense of inadequacy and pessimism.
- Social withdrawal and social isolation.
- A degree of emotional distress that may serve as a positive motivator for psychotherapy efforts.

Low Scores on Scale 2

The following are characteristics that have been associated with low scale 2 scores $(T \leq 40)$:

- Higher levels of intelligence and academic performance.
- Freedom from depression, anxiety, and guilt.
- Self-confidence and emotional stability.

- The ability to function effectively across a variety of situations.
- Alert, active, and competitive.
- Rebellious, argumentative, irresponsible, and manipulative when found for adolescent psychiatric patients.

2-3/3-2 Codetype

There is substantial overlap in the correlates of the 2-3/3-2 codetype for adolescent and adult psychiatric patients. They are characteristically described as emotionally overcontrolled, and unlikely to employ acting out as a primary defense mechanism. They typically have histories that reflect a lack of involvement or interest in relationships with others, and when relationships are established they tend to have dependent characteristics. Adjectives such as *passive, docile,* and *dependent* are frequently applied to individuals with the 2-3/3-2 profile, and they are often described as unassertive, inhibited, insecure, and self-doubting. Both adolescents and adults with the 2-3/3-2 code are very achievement oriented and set high goals for their own performance. These aspirations are often unrealistic and appear to be a contributor to their sense of inferiority and depression. Antisocial personality or psychopathic diagnoses are extremely rare for adolescents and adults who produce the 2-3/3-2 code. There is also little evidence of thought disorder or the presence of schizophrenic or psychotic diagnoses among these individuals. Defense mechanisms involving somatization and hypochondriasis appear to be central to the 2-3/3-2 code. In particular, weakness, fatigue, and dizziness appear to be common physical symptoms.

Among adolescent patients, the 2-3/3-2 codetype is relatively common and found in 2.4% of males and 4.1% of females (see Table 5.4). Data unique to the adolescent findings for the 2-3/3-2 code indicate that the majority of these adolescents were referred for treatment because of poor peer relationships. These adolescents were seen as socially isolated and lonely individuals. They have few friends inside the school environment and are loners outside of academic settings. The 2-3/3-2 adolescent reported a relatively passive, compliant and obedient childhood that often involved an under-involved father in a professional occupation and a mother who may have been over-involved with these children. Sexual acting out and drug abuse do not appear to be high-frequency problem areas for these adolescents, and 76% of the teenagers in the Marks et al. 1970-1973 sample reported no history of drug abuse. In research by Archer and Klinefelter (1992), the *MAC* scale raw scores for these adolescents were typically quite low. In the adult literature, the 2-3/3-2 codetype is more prevalent among female patients, and the majority of patients with this codetype are seen as psychoneurotic or reactive depressive.

2-4/4-2 Codetype

Among teenagers and adults, high-point codes involving scales 2 and 4 are typically produced by individuals who have difficulty with impulse control and often act without sufficient deliberation. They exhibit a marked disregard for accepted social standards, and problems with authority figures are manifested by inappropriate or antisocial behaviors and actions. Hypochondriacal and somatic defense mechanisms are not typically displayed by these individuals. Acting out, displacement, and externalization appear to be primary defense mechanisms. There is often a history of legal violations, including incidents of arrest, legal convictions, and court actions. Indeed, one-half of the adolescents in the Marks et al. (1974) sample had been placed on probation or held in detention.

In the adult and adolescent literatures there are also frequent references to substance abuse and alcohol problems associated with this codetype. In the adult literature, the 2-4 profile is often the mean profile produced by samples of alcoholics (Greene & Garvin, 1988; Sutker & Archer, 1979). Marks et al. (1974) also noted that adolescents with the 2-4/4-2 codetype reported a wide variety of drug use, which included all pharmacological categories except narcotics. Indeed, Marks et al. found patterns indicating drug addiction, as well as drug abuse, among their 2-4/4-2 sample of adolescents. The 2-4/4-2 codetype was a very frequent codetype in the findings shown in Table 5.4, found for 5.0% of males and 3.3% of females in this sample. In hospital settings, adolescents with the 2-4/4-2 profile were often found to be elopement risks. They also had frequent histories of promiscuous sexual behavior, truancy, and running away from home. In general, the 2-4/4-2 adolescents indicated that much of their antisocial behaviors were attempts to escape or run away from what they perceived to be intolerable or highly conflicted home situations. In the adult literature, the 2-4/4-2 has been associated with a relatively poor prognosis for change. The major difficulty in treatment of adult psychiatric patients with this codetype is their tendency to terminate psychotherapy prematurely when situational stress has been reduced, but before actual attitudinal or behavioral change has occurred. Adolescents with this codetype are frequently referred for treatment because of difficulty with concentration. Further, these adolescents often perceive their parents as unaffectionate and inconsistent. The majority of adolescents in the Marks et al. (1974) sample stated that they had no one in their family with whom to discuss their personal concerns, feelings, and thoughts. Williams and Butcher (1989b) found that 2-4/4-2 adolescents were frequently described as depressed.

2-5/5-2 Codetype

The *2-5/5-2* codetype is quite rare among adults, and is found for 1.2% of male and 1.2% of female adolescents in psychiatric settings. Among the commonly used MMPI sources, Greene (1980, 1991) and Friedman et al. (1989) report information concerning this codetype. Greene noted, based on findings from King and Kelley (1977), that male college students in outpatient psychotherapy who produced a *2-5/5-2* codetype were anxious, disoriented, and withdrawn and often had a history of somatic complaints. Further, the *2-5/5-2* college students displayed relatively poor heterosexual adjustment and dated infrequently.

Adolescents with this codetype were typically referred for treatment because of poor sibling relationships, indecisiveness, shyness, extreme negativism, hypersensitivity, and suspiciousness (Marks et al., 1974). As a group, these adolescents were seen to be quite vulnerable to stress, anxious, guilt-ridden, self-condemning, and self-accusatory. Similar to findings in the adult literature, these adolescents appeared to be quite anxious and indecisive and to have substantial difficulty in committing themselves to a definite course of action. The *2-5/5-2* adolescents typically displayed defense mechanisms involving obsession, manifested in perfectionistic and meticulous concerns, and intellectualization. They were described as depressed, socially awkward, and showed evidence of poor heterosexual adjustment. Individuals with the *2-5/5-2* profile were not described as athletic, and they performed poorly in sports. Males with this codetype were described as not masculine.

In general, teenagers with this codetype were interpersonally shy, passive, and unassertive. Unsurprisingly, drug use and abuse was not found to be associated with adolescents who produced this codetype. MacAndrew Alcoholism scale (*MAC*) raw scores for males with this codetype are typically below critical elevation levels (Archer & Klinefelter, 1992). Although many of these adolescents were seen to be intellectually and academically achieving at high levels, one-third of them were teased by their peers in school settings (Marks et al., 1974).

2-7/7-2 Codetype

The *2-7/7-2* codetype occurs with a relatively high frequency in adult psychiatric patients, and appears to be less prevalent among adolescents in psychiatric settings, where it was found for only 1.1% of males and 0.8% of females. The adjectives and description for the *2-7/7-2* codetype, however, are quite consistent across both populations. Individuals with this profile type are anxious, tense, depressed, and highly intropunitive. They are often self-preoccupied and rigidly focused on their personal deficiencies and inadequacies. The adolescents in the Marks et al. (1974)

group consistently employed negative adjectives in their self-descriptions.

Individuals with the 2-7/7-2 codetype tend to employ obsessive-compulsive defenses. They typically do not come into conflict with others, and when interpersonal conflicts or difficulties do arise they are handled by the 2-7/7-2 in a self-punitive and self-accusatory manner. These individuals are rigid in their thinking, and tend to be meticulous and perfectionistic in their everyday lives. They are seen by psychotherapists as self-defeating and behaviorally passive. Strong feelings of depression and anxiety frequently co-occur for these individuals, and there is often a history of overreaction or overresponse to minor life stress events. These individuals are frequently described as overcontrolled and unable to deal with or express their feelings in an open manner. In interpersonal relationships there is often a pattern of dependency, passivity, and lack of assertiveness. Adolescents with a 2-7/7-2 codetype appear to have the capacity to form deep emotional ties with others, and typically report close relationships with family members. The primary reasons for referral among adolescents includes tearfulness, restlessness, anxiety, excessive worry, and nervousness. Acting out behaviors such as drug use or school truancy were markedly low-frequency events for these teenagers. Roughly 40% of the adolescents in the Marks et al. (1974) sample with this codetype admitted or expressed suicidal thoughts. Roughly one out of four 2-7/7-2 teenagers were characterized as exhibiting severe depression.

2-8/8-2 Codetype

Both teenagers and adults with the 2-8/8-2 codetype are characterized by fearfulness, timidity, anxiety, and social awkwardness. This codetype appears with a frequency of less than 1% for males and for females in our clinical sample of adolescents. These teenagers appear to prefer a large degree of emotional distance from others, and are fearful and anxious concerning interpersonal relationships. Among adolescents, isolation and repression have been reported as primary defense mechanisms. Impaired self-concept and poor self-esteem are also associated with the 2-8/8-2 codetype. Kelley and King (1979) found that 2-8/8-2 female college outpatients were described with features related to affective distress and schizophrenic symptomatology, whereas 2-8/8-2 males were withdrawn and displayed flat or blunted affect. In the adult literature, individuals with a 2-8/8-2 codetype are often described as fearful of losing control, whereas the adolescent literature describes these individuals as highly emotional and characterized by deficits in the ability to moderate or modulate emotional expression. Further, adolescents with this codetype describe themselves as awkward and fearful of making mistakes. A high percentage of 2-8/8-2 adolescents in the Marks et al. (1974) study (44%) presented histories involving active suicide attempts. In the adult literature, the 2-8/8-2 codetype is associated with suicidal preoccupation, and Graham (1990) noted that adults with this codetype frequently have suicidal thoughts that are accompanied by specific plans for suicidal actions.

For adolescents and adults, the 2-8/8-2 codetype is also frequently associated with more profound psychiatric symptomatology, particularly when marked elevations occur on these two scales. Schizophrenic, schizoaffective, and manic depressive diagnoses are often attributed to adults with this codetype, and adolescents with these profile features have been found to display a higher than average frequency of such symptoms as hallucinations, preoccupation with bizarre or unusual concerns, and unusual sexual beliefs and practices. In the Marks et al. (1974) sample, over 25% of the 2-8/8-2 codetype adolescents were found to have vague and nonlocalized organic deficits such as minimal brain damage, or a history of seizure disorders, including epilepsy.

2-0/0-2 Codetype

Among both teenagers and adults, the 2-0/0-2 high-point code has been associated with symptomatology including depression, feelings of inferiority, anxiety, social introversion, and withdrawal. These individuals are typically described as conforming, passive persons who are highly unlikely to engage in antisocial or delinquent behavior. Many 2-0/0-2 individuals show areas of social ineptitude and a general lack of social skills. Greene (1991) noted that social skills and assertiveness training may be particularly beneficial in helping individuals with this codetype.

The 2-0/0-2 codetype is found for 1.8% of male and 3.8% of female adolescents in psychiatric treatment settings (see Table 5.4), and occurs more frequently for adolescents on the MMPI-A, in contrast to the original test instrument. Adolescents with this codetype were typically referred for psychiatric treatment with presenting problems including tension and anxiety, apathy, shyness, lethargy, and excessive interpersonal sensitivity. As both children and adolescents, teenagers with the 2-0/0-2 codetype appear to be meek, socially isolated loners who conform to parental demands and who do not engage in alcohol or drug abuse. They typically expressed concerns to their therapists regarding feelings of inferiority, social rejection, and a self-perception of unattractiveness. They describe themselves as awkward, dull, gloomy, cowardly, shy, silent, and meek. Primary defense mechanisms include social withdrawal, denial, and obsessive-compulsive mechanisms. Psychotherapists in the Marks et al. (1974) study tended to view adolescents with a 2-0/0-2 codetype as schizoid, and individuals with this profile configuration produced a very low frequency of drug or alcohol abuse. Based on findings from the Marks et al. 1970-1973 sample, teenage girls with this profile reported that they wished to appear younger and less mature than their actual chronological age. Both boys and girls were seen as socially awkward, unpopular, and maintaining few significant friendships.

Scale 3 (*Hy*: Hysteria) Codetypes

The MMPI-A scale 3 (Hysteria) consists of 60 items originally selected to identify individuals who utilize hysterical reactions to stressful situations. No items were deleted from this scale in the creation of the MMPI-A. The hysterical syndrome, as reflected in the item pool for scale 3, includes specific somatic concerns as well as items related to the presentation of self as well-socialized and well-adjusted. Greene (1991) noted that although these two areas of item content are often unrelated or even negatively correlated in well-adjusted individuals, they tend to be positively correlated and closely associated for individuals with hysterical features. Graham (1990) noted that it is not possible to obtain a clinically-elevated T-score value on scale 3 without endorsing a substantial number of items in both content areas.

The subscales derived by Harris and Lingoes (1955) for scale 3 include Denial of Social Anxiety (Hy_1), Need for Affection (Hy_2), Lassitude Malaise (Hy_3), Somatic Complaints (Hy_4), and Inhibition of Aggression (Hy_5). In the adult literature, marked elevations on scale 3 are typically associated with pathological conditions of hysteria. More moderate elevations have been found to be associated with a number of characteristics that include social extroversion, superficial relationships, exhibitionistic behaviors, and self-centeredness, but do not necessarily involve the classic hysterical syndrome.

Hathaway and Monachesi (1963) found that scale 3 profile high points (i.e., the highest elevation among the clinical scales) tended to occur with a greater frequency among Minnesota normal adolescents than scale 1 or scale 2 high points. They speculated that children who employ somatic complaints or "play sick" as a way of avoiding school and manipulating their parents would be expected to show elevations on scale 3. Further, these authors noted that moderate elevations on this scale might be expected among well-behaved and intelligent children who expressed what the authors referred to as "middle-class social conformity." In fact, Hathaway and Monachesi found that high scale 3 profiles were related to higher levels of intelligence and achievement and that these children often had parents in the professions. In contrast, scale 3 low point profiles (i.e., the lowest clinical scale value) among normal adolescents were associated with lower academic achievement and lower socioeconomic background than high scale 3 adolescents.

Among adolescent psychiatric patients, Archer et al. (1988) found that high scale 3 adolescent inpatients were perceived by psychiatric staff as dependent, non-assertive, and prone to quickly modify their behaviors in order to meet social expectations and demands. Additionally, high scale 3 adolescents were described by treatment staff as more likely to express anxiety or stress through somatization and physical symptoms. Butcher et al. (1992) found that female adolescent patients with elevations on MMPI-A scale 3 tended to manifest somatic complaints and concerns.

High Scores on Scale 3

The following is a summary of characteristics associated with high scale 3 profiles (T ≥ 60):

- Somatic concerns and preoccupations.
- Achievement oriented, socially involved, friendly.
- Patterns of overreaction to stress often involving development of physical symptoms.
- Self-centered, egocentric, and immature.
- Higher levels of educational achievement.
- Strong needs for affection, attention, and approval.
- Often from families of higher socioeconomic status.
- Psychologically naive with little insight into problem areas.

Low scores on Scale 3

The following are characteristics of individuals who produce low scores on Scale 3 (T ≤ 40):

- Narrow range of interests.
- Limited social involvement and avoidance of leadership roles.
- Unfriendly, tough minded, realistic.
- School underachievement and lower socioeconomic status.
- Unadventurous and unindustrious.

3-4/4-3 Codetype

There appear to be at least three common features among adolescents and adults who exhibit the 3-4/4-3 codetype. First, these individuals often present hypochondriacal or somatic complaints, including symptoms of weakness, fatigue, loss of appetite, and headaches. Second, both teenagers and adults with 3-4/4-3 code tend not to perceive themselves as emotionally distressed, although they are often perceived as such by their therapists. Finally, individuals with this codetype in both age groups tend to manifest problems with impulse control and often report histories that include both antisocial behaviors and suicide attempts.

These problems in impulse control are often manifested in several ways. Sexual promiscuity appears to be relatively common among females with this codetype during adolescence and adulthood, and problems with substance abuse and dependence also appear prevalent. Adolescents with this codetype frequently have a history of theft, school truancy, and running away from home. As psychiatric inpatients, 3-4/4-3 adolescents often pose an elopement risk for the hospital unit. Drug use is also associated with this codetype, particularly among the adolescent sample. In the Marks et al. (1974) study, 63% of adolescents with this codetype reported a drug use history. Further, roughly one-third of these adolescents had made suicide attempts, a finding also characteristic of adults with 3-4/4-3 codes.

In the adult literature, the 3-4/4-3 individual is typically described as chronically angry, and harboring hostile and aggressive impulses. Particularly when scale 4 is higher than scale 3, overcontrolled hostility may be manifested by episodic outbursts that could take the form of aggressive or violent behavior. Graham (1990) noted that prisoners with the 4-3 codetype frequently have histories of assaultive and violent crimes.

The 3-4/4-3 codetype is relatively common among adolescents, and was found for 4.9% of male and 3.6% of female adolescent patients (see Table 5.4). The 3-4/4-3 teenager is typically referred to treatment for sleep difficulties and for suicidal thoughts. They are often known as "roughnecks" in school, and their main problems and concerns relate to conflicts with their parents. Therapists of these teenagers frequently describe them as depressed, although also finding adequate ego strength among these teenagers. As Marks et al. (1974) noted however, several of the descriptors associated with the 3-4/4-3 codetypes for adults may not apply to adolescents. The overcontrolled hostility syndrome that has been associated with the 3-4/4-3 codetype among adults, for example, does not appear to be applicable to teenagers with these MMPI features. In support of this observation, Truscott (1990) also reported that elevations on the Overcontrolled Hostility (O-H) MMPI special scale do not appear to be associated with the overcontrolled hostility syndrome for adolescents because adolescents do not typically employ repression or overcontrol as a defense mechanism.

3-5/5-3 Codetype

This profile is extremely rare in the adult literature, and Greene (1991) stated, "There is little information on the 3-5/5-3 codetypes. College-educated males with histrionic features would be expected to achieve this codetype" (p. 272). No discussion of this codetype is available in either Graham (1990) or Lachar (1974), although Friedman et al. (1989) did briefly review it.

Among adolescents, this codetype was produced by 1.0% of males and 3.0% of females in psychiatric treatment (Archer, Gordon, & Klinefelter, 1991). Marks et al. (1974) was able to identify only 13 individuals who produced this codetype, all of whom were male. Among adolescents, the 3-5/5-3 codetype has many features that would be associated with individual scale high points for scales 3 and 5. None of the adolescents in the Marks et al. 3-5/5-3 codetype were referred to treatment by court agencies or authorities, an unusual finding in adolescent psychiatric populations. Many of the teenagers with this codetype came from homes in which moral and religious values were firmly and perhaps rigidly enforced, and the teenagers in this sample viewed the moral and ethical judgments of their parents as highly predictable. 3-5/5-3 adolescents were seen by their therapists as moderately depressed. Perhaps consistent with the scale 3 utilization of denial, however, several of these adolescents described themselves as elated. A major symptom pattern connected with this codetype was one of withdrawal and inhibition. Although these adolescents were perceived as basically insecure and having strong needs for attention, they were also perceived as shy, anxious, inhibited, and socially uncomfortable. These teenagers were often found to be affectively shallow and their rate of speech was described as rapid. They did not employ acting out as a primary defense mechanism, and, in fact, tended to overcontrol their impulses. When adolescents with this codetype were involved with drug abuse, the substances employed were alcohol, marijuana, amphetamines, and sopors. Interestingly, 43% of the teenagers in the Marks et al. (1974) sample were found to have weight problems, including obesity and anorexia.

3-6/6-3 Codetype

There are a variety of characteristics commonly displayed by adolescents and adults who produce a 3-6/6-3 profile type. They tend to be generally suspicious and distrustful individuals who manifest poor interpersonal relationships and have substantial difficulty in acknowledging the presence of psychological problems and conflicts. In general, both teenagers and adults with this codetype utilize defenses of rationalization and projection, and often have difficulty in understanding why others are concerned about their behavior. Among adolescents, descriptors associated with suspicion and paranoia were often used to characterize these 3-6/6-3 teenagers. In general, individuals with this codetype appear difficult to get along with, self-centered, and distrustful and resentful of others. They maintain an egocentric and guarded stance concerning the world around them.

The 3-6/6-3 codetype was found among 0.6% of male and 1.4% of female adolescents receiving psychiatric services. Among adolescents, the most distinctive characteristic of this group was a relatively high incidence of suicide attempts, and one-third of adolescents in the Marks et al. (1974) study were seen for psychotherapy following such behaviors. In the Marks et al. 1970-1973 sample, this profile was associated with substance abuse, but not as extensively as other adolescent codetypes. In this sample, roughly 50% of these adolescents acknowledged drug involvement. Interestingly, 40% of this 3-6/6-3 codetype group were academically superior students.

Scale 4 (Pd: Psychopathic Deviate) Codetypes

This MMPI-A scale consists of 49 items, with one item deleted from the original Pd scale due to inappropriate content. Scale 4 was originally designed to identify or diagnose the psychopathic personality, now referred to under the *DSM-III-R* as *antisocial personality disorder*. As described by Dahlstrom, Welsh, and Dahlstrom (1972), the criterion group for scale 4 consisted largely of individuals who were court referred for psychiatric evaluation because of delinquent actions including lying, stealing, truancy, sexual promiscuity, alcohol abuse, and forgery. The 49 items in the MMPI-A Pd scale cover a diverse array of content areas including family conflicts, problems with authority figures, social isolation, delinquency, and absence of satisfaction in everyday life. Scale 4 has a substantial degree of item overlap with many of the validity and clinical scales, and it contains an almost equal number of true and false responses that are keyed in the critical direction.

In the adult literature, individuals who score high on scale 4 are typically described in pejorative or unfavorable terms that include strong features of anger, impulsivity, interpersonal and emotional shallowness, interpersonal manipulativeness, and unpredictability. Thus, a marked elevation on scale 4 often indicates the presence of antisocial beliefs and attitudes, although Greene (1991) noted that such elevations do not necessarily imply that these traits will be expressed overtly. The degree to which antisocial behaviors are manifested is typically seen as related to the individual's standing on additional MMPI scales, including scales 9 and 0. Higher scale 9 and lower scale 0 values, in combination with an elevated scale 4, increase the likelihood for the overt behavioral expression of antisocial attitudes, beliefs, and cognitions. Harris and Lingoes (1955) identified five content subscales within scale 4, which are labeled *Familial Discord (Pd$_1$), Authority Problems (Pd$_2$), Social Imperturbability (Pd$_3$), Social Alienation (Pd$_4$), and Self-Alienation (Pd$_5$)*.

Scores on scale 4 have been identified as varying in relationship to the respondent's age and race. Colligan, Osborne, Swenson, and Offord (1983) provided data from cross-sectional studies of 18- to 70-year-old adults that indicated that scale 4 values tend to decrease with age for both males and females. There is quite clear evidence that scale 4 values also differ as a function of adolescence versus adulthood in both normal and clinical populations (Archer, 1984). It has also been reported that Black subjects may score higher on scale 4 in contrast to White subject groups (Graham, 1990), but findings have been mixed on this issue.

In normal samples, adolescents tend to endorse more scale 4 items in the critical direction than do adult respondents, and the mean scale 4 value for the MMPI-A sample would produce a T-score value of approximately 55 if scored using MMPI-2 norms. Research by Pancoast and Archer (1988) indicated that adolescents, in contrast to adults, are particularly likely to endorse items in the scale 4 content area labeled by Harris and Lingoes (1955) as Familial Discord (Pd$_1$). Hathaway and Monachesi (1963) found that scale 4 was the most frequent high point for normal adolescents in the Minnesota statewide sample, with the highest frequency of scale 4 elevations found for girls and for adolescents from urban settings. The Minnesota data also indicated that scale 4 elevations increased as a function of severity of delinquent behavior. Further, high scale 4 profiles for both boys and girls were associated with higher rates of broken homes.

Within clinical samples, although codetypes involving scale 4 are relatively frequent in adult populations, they could be described as ubiquitous in adolescent settings. Nine of the 29 codetypes reported for adolescents by Marks et al. (1974) involved a scale 4 two-point code (that is, scale 4 was one of the two scales most elevated in the profile), and nearly one-half of their clinical cases involved a high-point code that included scale 4. Similarly, in our analysis of MMPI profiles produced by adolescents in clinical settings, roughly 48% involved two-point codetypes that included scale 4 (Archer, Gordon, & Klinefelter, 1991).

Archer et al. (1988) found that adolescent inpatients who produced elevations on scale 4 were described by psychiatric staff members as evasive and unmotivated in psychotherapy. These adolescents were also found to be rebellious, hostile, and incapable of profiting from prior mistakes. Additionally, these adolescents had a high frequency of presenting problems involving drug and alcohol abuse, and nearly half received conduct disorder diagnoses. In the research by Archer and Klinefelter (1992), adolescent codetypes that involved scale 4 often produced substantially elevated mean raw score values on the MacAndrew Alcoholism scale. Butcher et al. (1992) found that adolescent boys and girls in their clinical sample with elevations on MMPI-A scale 4 were more likely to be described as delinquent and prone to exhibiting acting out or externalizing behaviors. In addition, girls who produced elevations on scale 4 were more likely to engage in sexual activity, and boys were more likely to exhibit incidents of running away.

High scores on Scale 4

The following is a summary of characteristics for high scale 4 profiles (T ≥ 60):

- Poor school adjustment and problems in school conduct.
- Increased probability of delinquent, externalizing, and aggressive behaviors.
- Increased probability of a family history involving parental separation and divorce.
- Higher frequency of urban backgrounds.
- Difficulty incorporating or internalizing the values and standards of society.
- Rebelliousness and hostility toward authority figures.
- Increased likelihood of diagnoses involving conduct disorder.
- Inability to delay gratification.
- Poor planning ability and impulsivity.
- Low tolerance for frustration and boredom.
- Reliance on acting out as a primary defense mechanism.
- Increased probability of parent-adolescent conflicts and familial discord.
- Risk taking and sensation-seeking behaviors, including use of drugs and alcohol.
- Selfishness, self-centeredness, and egocentricity.
- Ability to create a favorable first impression.
- Extroverted, outgoing interpersonal style.
- Relative freedom from guilt and remorse.
- Relatively little evidence of emotional/affective distress.

Low Scores on Scale 4

The following features have been associated with individuals who score low on scale 4 (T ≤ 40):

- Conventional, conforming, and compliant with authority.
- Lower probability of delinquency.
- Concerns involving status and security rather than competition and dominance.
- Accepting, passive, and trusting in interpersonal styles.
- Lower likelihood of delinquent behaviors.

4-5/5-4 Codetype

The adult and adolescent literatures for the 4-5/5-4 profile codetype are substantially discrepant. Adults with these profile characteristics are typically discussed in terms of immaturity, emotional passivity, and conflicts centered around dependency. Greene (1991) noted that this codetype among adults is almost exclusively produced by male respondents as a result of the infrequency with which scale 5 is clinically elevated among females. Adults with this codetype are frequently rebellious in relation to social convention and norms, and this nonconformity is often passively expressed through selection of dress, speech, and social behavior. Although these individuals appear to have strong dependency needs, there are also conflicts created by their fear of domination by others. This latter pattern appears most marked in the relationships of males, with 4-5/5-4 men often entering into heavily conflicted relationships with females.

Although adults with these codetypes typically display adequate control, there are also indications that these individuals are subject to brief periods of aggressive or antisocial acting out. Sutker, Allain, and Geyer (1980) reported that the 4-5/5-4 codetype is found among 23% of women convicted of murder. Among male college students, King and Kelley (1977) related this codetype to passivity, heterosexual adjustment problems, and both transient and chronic interpersonal difficulties. This sample did not display significant evidence of personality disorders, nor was homosexuality apparently characteristic of this group. Greene (1991) recommended that detection of homosexual drive or behavior in adults with this codetype is most effectively achieved when the clinician directly raises this issue with the respondent in the clinical interview.

As shown in Table 5.4, the 4-5/5-4 codetype is found among 1.6% of male and 3.8% of female adolescents in psychiatric treatment settings. Marks et al. (1974) indicated that teenagers with this codetype appear to get along well with their peer group, and are gregarious and extroverted in their social interactions. In contrast to teenagers with other co-detypes, the 4-5/5-4 adolescents were described by their therapists as better adjusted, easier to establish rapport with, and as demonstrating greater ego strength. Further, therapists felt that teenagers with this codetype typically displayed relatively effective defenses in terms of protection of the adolescent from conscious awareness of depression or anxiety. The typical defense mechanisms utilized by these adolescents included acting out and rationalization. In contrast to 5-4s, 4-5 adolescents appeared to have greater difficulty in controlling their tempers, and they described themselves as argumentative, opinionated, and defensive. Over half of the adolescents in the 4-5 codetype were rated by their therapists as having a good prognosis. In contrast to the adult literature, over 80% of the 4-5/5-4 adolescents in the Marks et al. study were engaged in heterosexual dating, a figure substantially higher than the base rate for other adolescent codetype groups.

Respondents with the 4-5/5-4 configuration in the Marks et al. 1970-1973 sample reported a relatively high frequency (i.e., 72%) of drug abuse history. The drug use patterns found for these teenagers appeared to involve a broad variety of substances. In addition, adolescents in this sample had a high rate of antisocial behaviors, including shoplifting, auto theft, breaking and entering, and drug dealing. As a group, they were described as emotionally reactive and prone to temper tantrums and violent outbursts. Finally, teenagers in this sample also evidenced significant problems in school adjustment, including histories of truancy, school suspension, and failing academic grades.

4-6/6-4 Codetype

A relatively consistent picture emerges from the adolescent and adult literatures for individuals with the 4-6/6-4 codetype. They are uniformly described as angry, resentful, and argumentative. Adolescents with this codetype who are referred for treatment typically present symptoma-tology involving defiance, disobedience, and negativism. Treatment referrals for 4-6/6-4 adolescents are often made from court agencies.

4-6/6-4 individuals typically make excessive demands on others for attention and sympathy, but are resentful of even mild demands that may be placed on them in interpersonal relationships. They are gener-ally suspicious of the motives of others, and characteristically avoid deep emotional attachments. Adolescents with this codetype appear to be aware of deficits in their interpersonal relationships and often reported that they were disliked by others. For both adults and teenagers, however, there is very little insight displayed into the origins or nature of their psychological problems. Individuals with this co-detype tend to deny serious psychological problems, and they ratio-nalize and transfer the blame for their life problems onto others. In short, they characteristically do not accept responsibility for their behavior and are not receptive to psychotherapy efforts. Although adolescents with this codetype are rated by others as aggressive, bitter, deceitful, hostile, and quarrelsome, they often appear to view them-selves as attractive, confident, and jolly.

The 4-6/6-4 codetype is relatively common among adolescents and is found for 6.2% of male and 4.0% of female adolescents in psychiatric treatment settings (see Table 5.4). Among adolescents, the 4-6/6-4 codetype is almost inevitably associated with child-parent conflicts, which often take the form of chronic, intense struggles. These adoles-cents typically undercontrol their impulses and act without thought or deliberation. Williams and Butcher (1989b) found adolescents with this codetype were more likely to engage in acting out behaviors, which included sexual acting out. Marks et al. (1974) reported that the 4-6/6-4 adolescent typically encountered problems with authority figures. Nar-cissistic and self-indulgent features appear prevalent in this codetype for both adolescents and adults. Therapists in the Marks et al. study described the 4-6/6-4 adolescent as provocative, and indicated that major defense mechanisms included acting out and projection. About half of the adolescents with this codetype in the Marks et al. sample reported a history of drug abuse, most frequently involving the use of alcohol.

4-7/7-4 Codetype

The 4-7/7-4 codetype appears to be characteristic of adolescents and adults who employ acting out as their primary defense mechanism, but experience substantial feelings of guilt, shame, and remorse concerning the consequences of their behavior. Thus, they tend to alternate between behaviors that show a disregard for social norms and stan-dards, and excessive and neurotic concerns regarding the effects of their actions. Underlying impulse control problems and tendencies to behave in a provocative and antisocial manner, these individuals appear to be insecure and dependent. They have strong needs for reassurance and attention.

The 4-7/7-4 codetype occurs in 2.4% of male and 1.2% of female adolescent psychiatric evaluations. In the Marks et al. (1974) research, the 4-7/7-4 teenager was described by therapists as impulsive, provoc-ative, flippant, and resentful. At the same time, they demonstrated evidence of substantial conflicts concerning emotional dependency and sexuality. The majority of these adolescents exhibited substantial feelings of guilt and shame and were viewed by their therapists as guilt-ridden and self-condemning. Williams and Butcher (1989b) found that adolescents with the 4-7/7-4 codetype presented a mixed picture of internalizing and externalizing behaviors, and concluded that tension/ nervousness, substance abuse, and acting out behaviors were associated with this profile.

4-8/8-4 Codetype

The 4-8/8-4 codetype is associated with marginal social adjustments for both adolescents and adults. Marks et al. (1974) described the 4-8/8-4 adolescent as "one of the most miserable groups of adolescents we studied" (p. 218). They were frequently perceived as angry, odd, peculiar, and immature individuals who displayed impulse control problems and often exhibited chronic interpersonal conflicts. Only 16% of teenagers with this codetype were rated as showing a definite improvement as a result of psychotherapy, and only 9% were rated as showing a good prognosis for future adjustment. Adolescents with this codetype were often evasive in psychotherapy, and frequently attempted to handle their problems by denying the presence of any difficulties.

The 4-8/8-4 codetype is found with a frequency of 2.8% among male and 2.1% among female adolescent psychiatric patients. Teenagers with this profile typically display patterns of very poor academic achievement, and were often seen in psychotherapy as frequently as three times a week. Their family lives were described as chaotic, and unusual symptomatology such as anorexia, encopresis, enuresis, and hyperkinesis were often noted. Although excessive drinking and drug abuse are common among adults with this codetype, the 4-8/8-4 teenagers do not appear to be among the heavier drug abuser groups. Although the 8-4 adolescents were described as more regressed than the 4-8s, the 4-8 adolescent was also noted to display thought patterns that were unusual and sometimes delusional. Thus, individuals with this codetype display antisocial features related to elevations on scale 4 in combination with schizoid or schizophrenic symptomatology characteristic of elevations on scale 8. Williams and Butcher (1989b) reported that the 4-8/8-4 adolescents were more likely than other teenagers to have a history of sexual abuse.

4-9/9-4 Codetype

A striking degree of similarity exists in the description of both teenagers and adults who produce a 4-9/9-4 codetype. These individuals almost always display a disregard for social standards and are likely to have difficulties in terms of acting out and impulsivity. They are characteristically described as egocentric, narcissistic, selfish, and self-indulgent and are often unwilling to accept responsibility for their own behavior. They are seen as high sensation-seekers who have a markedly low frustration tolerance and are easily bored. In social situations, the 4-9/9-4s are often extroverted and make a positive first impression. They also, however, appear to manifest chronic difficulties in establishing close and enduring interpersonal relationships, and are highly manipulative and shallow in dealing with others. Classic features of the antisocial personality type are clearly relevant for adults with this codetype and adolescents with the 4-9/9-4 code often receive conduct disorder diagnoses.

The 4-9/9-4 is a very frequently occurring codetype among adolescent psychiatric patients, and shows a substantial gender difference on the MMPI-A. Specifically, 10.1% of males and 4.0% of females produce this codetype, as shown in Table 5.4, when scored on MMPI-A norms. Huesmann, Lefkowitz, and Eron (1978) reported findings indicating that the summation of T-score values on scales F, 4, and 9 serve as a viable predictor of aggression in older adolescents. In the Marks et al. (1974) research, the 4-9/9-4 adolescent was invariably referred for treatment because of defiance, disobedience, impulsivity, provocative behaviors, and truancy from school. In most cases, there were constant conflicts between the adolescents and their parents resulting from their history of misbehaviors. Intriguingly, fewer adolescents in the Marks et al. 4-9/9-4 codetype were raised in their natural homes than youngsters from any other codetype grouping. Specifically, 17% of adolescents with this codetype grew up in foster or adoptive homes, and 20% did not reside with their parents at the time of their evaluations in this study. As a group, these adolescents appeared to be socially extroverted and reported an earlier age of dating than other teenagers. Williams and Butcher (1989b) reported 4-9/9-4 teenagers were more sexually active than other adolescents. Nearly 50% of the subjects with this codetype in the Marks et al. study had a history of illegal behaviors that resulted in placements in detention or on probation. Ninety-three percent of these teenagers employed acting out as their primary defense mechanism, and problems with affective distress such as anxiety or feelings of inadequacy were not found for these teenagers.

Therapists described adolescents with this codetype as resentful of authority figures, socially extroverted, narcissistic, egocentric, selfish, self-centered, and demanding. Further, this group was noted to be impatient, impulsive, pleasure-seeking, restless, and emotionally and behaviorally undercontrolled. Sixty-one percent of the adolescents with this codetype in the Marks et al. 1970-1973 sample reported a history of drug abuse. These teenagers, however, appeared to be selective in the substances they used and tended to avoid drugs such as hallucinogens or opiates. Archer and Klinefelter (1992) found that the 4-9/9-4 adolescents produced higher mean *MAC* scores than any other codetype group. This finding probably reflected the influence of a variety of factors, including the degree of item overlap between scales 4 and 9 and *MAC*, and the degree to which both the 4-9/9-4 codetype and the *MAC* scale commonly measure an extroverted, high sensation-seeking, risk-taking lifestyle. In the Marks et al. (1974) study, 83% of the 4-9/9-4s were either chronically truant from school, had run away from home, or had run away from treatment settings. Many of these adolescents had engaged in all three of these activities. Marks et al. described these adolescents as provocative and seductive problem children with histories of lying, stealing, and other antisocial behaviors. These authors used the phrase "disobedient beauties" in reference to the 4-9/9-4 codetype. In the adult literature, these MMPI features have been repeatedly related to a poor prognosis for personality or behavioral change as a result of psychotherapy. It should be remembered, however, that adolescents who produce this codetype are likely to show substantially greater capacity for change and benefit from treatment than adults. In comparison to 4-9/9-4 features in adults, this personality structure is not as firmly entrenched and solidified during adolescence.

4-0/0-4 Codetype

As noted by Greene (1991), the 4-0/0-4 codetype is extremely rare in adults and there is little empirical data upon which to describe these individuals. Conceptually, there is an inherent conflict presented by high-point elevations on both scales 4 and 0. Whereas individuals who score high on scale 4 tend to be relatively comfortable around others and often show extroverted traits, high scale 0 respondents are often socially uncomfortable and introverted. Thus, codetype elevations involving both scales would be an infrequent occurrence. Among adolescents in psychiatric settings, 2.3% of males and 2.1% of females produced the 4-0/0-4 codetype based on MMPI-A norms (Archer, Gordon, & Klinefelter, 1991). Marks et al. (1974) were able to identify 22 adolescents who produced the 4-0/0-4 codetype, evenly divided between high- and low-point codes.

Surprisingly, 4-0/0-4 adolescents appeared to display more features related to elevations on scale 6 than they did characteristics related to elevations on either scale 4 or scale 0. They were described as suspicious and distrustful by their therapists. Additionally, they frequently expressed grandiose ideas and their main defense mechanism consisted of projection. These individuals were often resentful and argumentative adolescents who perceived themselves as shy and socially uncomfortable. Therapists described the 4-0/0-4 adolescent as quiet, passively resistant, and relatively underinvolved in activities around them. They had few close friends, and establishing friendships tended to be one of their primary problem areas. Furthermore, they were judged to display moderate ego strength, and to demonstrate a pattern of overreaction to minor stressors.

Scale 5 (Mf: Masculinity-Femininity) Codetypes

Sixteen items were eliminated from the original MMPI Mf scale in the creation of the 44-item MMPI-A Mf scale. The content areas of scale 5 are heterogeneous, and include work and recreational interests, family relationships, and items related to fears and sensitivity. This scale was originally developed by Hathaway and McKinley to identify homosexual males, but the authors encountered difficulty in identifying or defining a clear diagnostic grouping to create a single criterion group. The primary criterion group eventually selected consisted of 13 homosexual males who were relatively free from neurotic, psychotic, or psychopathic tendencies. Items were assigned to the Mf scale, however, if they differentiated between high- and low-scoring men on an attitude interest test, or if the item showed a significant difference in endorsement between males and females. Dahlstrom, Welsh, and Dahlstrom (1972) noted that an unsuccessful attempt was made by Hathaway and McKinley to develop a corresponding scale to identify female "sexual inversion," that is, an Fm scale.

Forty-one of the 44 items in scale 5 are keyed in the same direction for both sexes. The 3 remaining items, which deal with overt sexual material, were keyed in opposite directions for males and females. T-score conversions are reversed for males and females so that a high raw score value for boys results in a high T-score placement, whereas a high raw score value for girls is converted to a low T-score value. Thus, the Mf scale represents a bipolar measure of gender role identification. The Mf scale and scale 0 constitute the two basic scales for which linear T-score conversions were retained in the MMPI-A, rather than the uniform T-score procedures utilized for the remaining eight standard clinical scales. Linear T scores were employed for Mf and Si because the distributions for these scales were different than the remaining basic scales, and more closely approximated a normal distribution.

Serkownek used item-factor loading patterns to construct six subscales for the Mf scale (Schuerger, Foerstner, Serkownek, & Ritz, 1987). The Serkownek subscales for Mf are Mf_1 (Narcissism-Hypersensivity),

Mf_2 (Stereotypic Feminine Interest), Mf_3 (Denial of Stereotypic Masculine Interests), Mf_4 (Heterosexual Discomfort-Passivity), Mf_5 (Introspective-Critical), and Mf_6 (Socially Retiring). Attempts to create a factor-analytically-derived set of subscales for Mf were unsuccessful in the MMPI-2 Restandardization Project, and a similar attempt was not undertaken in the development of the MMPI-A.

Substantial controversy and debate has surrounded the meaning and interpretation of scale 5, particularly in recent years. Graham (1990) noted that scores on scale 5 have been related to intelligence, education, and socioeconomic level. As suggested by Greene (1991), the usefulness of scale 5 in identifying homosexuality appears to be substantially limited because elevations on this scale may reflect the influence of a variety of factors in addition to sexual identification and orientation. Further, in the creation of both the MMPI-A and the MMPI-2, items directly related to sexual preferences were deleted, thereby essentially eliminating the usefulness of this scale as a measure of homosexuality. Greene (1991) noted that when scale 5 is the only clinical-range elevation in an MMPI profile, those individuals are unlikely to be diagnosed as manifesting a psychiatric disorder. Mid-range elevations ($T \geq 40$ and $T \leq 60$) on the Mf scale have been difficult to interpret due to the variety of item endorsement patterns that may create this range of scores (e.g., a balance between masculine and feminine characteristics versus low endorsement of both content areas may result in mid-range values).

Markedly low T scores on the Mf scale for women appear to indicate a substantial identification with traditional feminine roles, which may include passivity, submissiveness, and the adaptation of many aspects of traditional femininity. Todd and Gynther (1988) found that low Mf females described themselves as tender and emotional. Low-scoring males have been described by Greene as displaying an "almost compulsive masculinity" in an inflexible and rigid manner (1991, p. 158). Todd and Gynther found low Mf males described themselves as domineering and impersonal. T scores of 60 or more on the Mf scale appear to be associated with women who are not interested in a traditional feminine role, and moderate elevations for men have been related to aesthetic interests. Todd and Gynther found high Mf females describe themselves as self-confident and exploitive, and were rated by their peers as unsympathetic and bold. High Mf scores for males in this study were related to the perception of self as undemanding and shy. Clinical-range elevations on scale 5 have also been related to passivity for males.

On the original form of the MMPI, there was relatively little difference in the mean Mf raw score values found between normal male adolescents and adults, but there was a tendency for female adolescents to produce raw score values two to three points lower than adult females (Archer, 1987). Data from Hathaway and Monachesi (1963) indicated that the boys in their Minnesota normal sample who produced their highest values on scale 5 tended to be of higher socioeconomic status, with parents from professional and semi-professional occupations. These adolescents tended to have higher intelligence scores and academic grades. They also exhibited a lower frequency of delinquent and antisocial behaviors. In contrast, boys with low scale 5 scores tended to display patterns of school underachievement and delinquency, and produced lower intelligence test scores than high scale 5 boys. Similarly, female adolescents from the Minnesota normal sample who scored low on scale 5 were higher in terms of intelligence scores and displayed evidence of higher levels of academic achievement. Female adolescents scoring high on scale 5 were less clearly defined, but appeared to come from rural environments and did less well in school. Wrobel and Lachar (1990) found that male adolescents who scored high on scale 5 were more frequently described by their parents as fearful, and high scale 5 females were more frequently rated as aggressive. Williams and Butcher (1989a) reported that they were unable to find clinically relevant descriptors for scale 5 in their study of adolescent inpatients. In a reanalysis of these data for MMPI-A scales, however, Butcher et al. (1992) found high scores related to the occurrence of behavior problems for girls and fewer legal actions for boys.

High Scores on Scale 5

The following is a summary of descriptors for high scale 5 males (T ≥ 60):

- Intelligent, aesthetic interests, higher levels of academic achievement.
- Possible areas of insecurity or conflict regarding sexual identity.
- Emotional and comfortable in expressing feelings and emotions with others.
- Passive and submissive in interpersonal relationships.
- Lower likelihood of antisocial or delinquent behaviors.

The following is a summary of high scale 5 characteristics for females (T ≥ 60):

- Vigorous and assertive.
- Competitive, aggressive, tough minded.
- Greater problems in terms of school conduct.

- Increased frequency of behavioral problems.
- Possibility of "masculine" interests in academic areas and sports.

Low Scores on Scale 5

The following is a summary of low scale 5 characteristics for males (T ≤ 40):

- Presentation of self with extremely masculine emphasis.
- Higher frequency of delinquency and school conduct problems.
- Overemphasis on strength, often accompanied by crude and coarse behaviors.
- Lower intellectual ability and academic achievement.
- Relatively narrow range of interests defined by traditional masculine role.

The following is a summary of low scale 5 characteristics for females (T ≤ 40):

- Presentation of self in stereotyped female role.
- Passive, yielding, and submissive in interpersonal relationships.
- Lower socioeconomic background.
- Higher levels of academic performance.
- Lower incidence of learning disabilities.

5-6/6-5 Codetype

Friedman et al. (1989) and Greene (1991) provide the only available information concerning the 5-6/6-5 codetype among the commonly used guides to interpretation of adult profiles. Both sources indicate that little is known concerning this codetype among adults. The 5-6/6-5 codetype is found with a frequency of only 0.5% for males and 1.1% for females in treatment settings for adolescents (see Table 5.4). Marks et al. (1974) presented the 5-6/6-5 codetype based on findings from 11 adolescents. Thus, the 5-6/6-5 is a relatively rare codetype and very limited data is available concerning the characteristics of individuals who produce this MMPI configuration.

Most of the descriptors identified by Marks et al. (1974) for adolescents with the 5-6/6-5 profile appear to be related to the scale 6 elevation. Although teenagers with this codetype were able to acknowledge psychological problems with their therapists, they were often hesitant to establish deep or frequent contacts with them. In general, they were seen as fearful of emotional involvement with others. Of this group, 30.6% were given a good prognosis by their therapists, a percentage that is roughly three times higher than that found by Marks et al. for therapists' ratings for other codetypes. The 5-6/6-5 adolescents were described as resentful and insecure, and acting out was their primary defense mechanism.

The majority of teenagers in this small codetype grouping had a history of drug abuse, which entailed a variety of psychoactive drug classes. Additionally, a history of violent actions appeared to be associated with the 5-6/6-5 adolescent. Legal actions and arrests were reported for such offenses as assault and battery, and assault with a deadly weapon. Marks et al. (1974) described this group as preoccupied with themes of death, murder, and brutality.

5-9/9-5 Codetype

Like the previous codetype, the 5-9/9-5 profile has received little research attention in the adult literature. A summary of the literature on this configuration may be found in Friedman et al. (1989) and in Greene (1991). This codetype is found with a frequency of only 0.3% for male and 2.6% for female adolescent psychiatric patients (Archer, Gordon, & Klinefelter, 1991). Marks et al. (1974) identified 10 teenagers with the 5-9 code and 10 teenagers with the 9-5 code in their clinical samples used to develop codetype descriptors.

In general, teenagers who produced the 5-9/9-5 code appeared to display substantially less psychopathology than adolescents from other codetype groups. Their overall degree of disturbance was typically judged to be mild to moderate. Primary defense mechanisms for this code appear to be rationalization for the 5-9 group, and denial for the 9-5 codetype. Psychotherapists found that conflicts regarding emotional dependency and assertiveness were primary problems among these adolescents. One-third of the adolescents in the Marks et al. (1974) sample reported that they were raised by their mothers in a single-parent household.

A slight majority of 5-9/9-5 adolescents (56%) were found to have a history of drug abuse in the 1970-1973 Marks et al. sample. In contrast to adolescents from other codetype groups, members of the 5-9/9-5 group typically did well in school. None of these teenagers had been suspended or expelled from school, and in general they appeared to value academic achievement and emphasize aesthetic interests. Nevertheless, the parents of the teenagers with this codetype reported that they were unmanageable and rebellious. Family conflicts, rather than peer conflicts, appear to be most characteristic of this group.

5-0/0-5 Codetype

Consistent with the other high-point codes involving scale 5, little information is available on adults with the 5-0/0-5 codetype and what data is available is summarized in Friedman et al. (1989) and in Greene (1991). This configuration is found in 0.3% of male and 1.1% of female adolescents evaluated in clinical settings. The Marks et al. (1974) 5-0/0-5 codetype was created based on a sample of only 11 adolescents.

Consistent with the elevations on scales 5 and 0, adolescents with the 5-0/0-5 codetype in the Marks et al. (1974) study were seen as cautious, anxious, and inhibited teenagers who were fearful of emotional involvement with others. They did not employ acting out as a defense mechanism, generally exhibited few problems in impulse control, and did not report histories of antisocial behaviors. In fact, teenagers with this codetype typically exhibit overcontrol and are ruminative and overideational. Slightly more than one-third of the teenagers in the 5-0/0-5 codetype were involved in special education classroom settings, including classes for emotionally disturbed children.

The majority of adolescents with the 5-0/0-5 codetype perceive their major problems as social awkwardness and difficulty in forming friendships. In general, they describe themselves as awkward, shy, timid, inhibited, cautious, and submissive. Therapists tended to view these adolescents as manifesting severe anxiety. Major conflicts for these adolescents typically involve sexuality and difficulties in assertive behavior. The general picture that emerges for this codetype group is that of adolescents who retreat into personal isolation rather than reaching out to others in interpersonal relationships.

Scale 6 (Pa: Paranoia) Codetypes

Scale 6, in both the MMPI and the MMPI-A, consists of 40 items that were created to assess an individual's standing in relation to symptomatology involving ideas of reference, suspiciousness, feelings of persecution, moral self-righteousness, and rigidity. Although many of the items in scale 6 deal with overt psychotic symptoms such as ideas of reference and delusions of persecution, there are also large groups of items dealing with interpersonal sensitivity, cynicism, and rigidity that are not necessarily psychotic markers or symptoms. Further, Graham (1990) noted that it is possible to achieve an elevated T-score value on scale 6 without endorsing overtly or blatantly psychotic symptomatology. Harris and Lingoes (1955) identified three subscale areas for scale 6 that include *Persecutory Ideas (Pa₁), Poignancy (Pa₂), and Naivete (Pa₃).*

Although individuals who produce marked clinical elevations on scale

6 usually present paranoid symptomatology, some paranoid patients are able to achieve within–normal–limits values on this scale. Greene (1991), for example, noted that normal-range T-score values on scale 6 are typically produced by individuals in two categories: First, respondents without paranoid symptomatology, and, second, individuals who have well-established paranoid symptomatology but maintain sufficient reality contact to avoid critically endorsing obvious items on this dimension. Unfortunately, little research has been focused on this latter group, and most of the information concerning these individuals is based on MMPI clinical lore.

Extreme elevations on MMPI-A scale 6 (T-score values above 70) typically identify persons with a psychotic degree of paranoid symptomatology such as paranoid schizophrenics and individuals manifesting paranoid states. Moderate elevations in the range of T scores of 60 to 70 are often produced by individuals who are relatively free of psychotic symptomatology. They may be characterized, however, by excessive sensitivity to the opinions and actions of others, a suspicious or guarded approach to interpersonal exchanges, and the use of rationalization and projection as primary defense mechanisms. They frequently present as suspicious, resentful, hostile, and argumentative individuals who are rigid and inflexible. Mild elevations on scale 6, which would be within a T-score range of 55 to 59 on the MMPI-A, are often seen as a positive sign when the respondent is not in a psychiatric setting. Individuals within this elevation range are frequently described as sensitive to the needs of others, and trusting and frank in interpersonal relationships. Graham (1990) noted that individuals within this range on scale 6 may be submissive and dependent in interpersonal relationships and describe themselves as prone to worry and anxiety. Greene (1991) noted that mental health workers frequently score within a moderate range of T-score values on scale 6, perhaps reflective of interpersonal sensitivity.

Adolescents have traditionally scored somewhat higher on scale 6 than adults on the original form of the MMPI (Archer, 1987). Pancoast and Archer (1988) found that normal adolescents (in contrast to adults) endorsed more scale 6 items related to the Harris–Lingoes Pa_1 (Persecutory Ideas) content area, reflecting the belief that one is misunderstood and unjustly punished or blamed by others. Data from Hathaway and Monachesi (1963), based on Minnesota normal adolescents, indicated that boys who scored high on scale 6 are more likely to drop out of school, perhaps as a function of their interpersonal sensitivity in the school environment. In contrast, girls who scored high on scale 6 in this sample tended to have higher IQ scores and better academic grade averages, and were considered well-adjusted by others. Hathaway and Monachesi observed that moderate elevations on scale 6 appear to be an academic and social asset for girls, whereas boys with elevations on scale 6 tended to get into greater academic and social difficulties, perhaps reflecting increased aggressiveness for the males. Hathaway, Monachesi, and Salasin (1970) reported, in a follow-up study of the Hathaway and Monachesi (1963) sample, that elevations on scales 6 and 8 were associated with poor academic and social outcomes primarily among adolescents with average or lower levels of intelligence. Lachar and Wrobel (1990) found that outpatient adolescent males who produced high scale 6 scores were more likely to be described as distrustful and suspicious, and more likely to manifest delusions of persecution or paranoia. Butcher et al. (1992) found scale 6 elevations related to neurotic/dependent and hostile/withdrawn behaviors for male adolescent inpatients. Overall, it appears that clinically relevant scale 6 descriptor patterns for female adolescents have been difficult to identify in these research investigations, and that more is known concerning the correlate patterns for teenage boys.

High Scores on Scale 6

The following is a summary of characteristics for individuals who produced marked elevations on scale 6 (T ≥ 70):

- Anger, resentment, hostility.
- Use of projection as primary defense mechanism.
- Disturbances in reality testing.
- Delusions of persecution or grandeur.
- Ideas of reference.
- Diagnoses often associated with the manifestation of thought disorder as exhibited in psychosis or schizophrenia.
- Social withdrawal.

The following are features usually associated with moderate elevations on scale 6 (T = 60 to 69):

- Marked interpersonal sensitivity.
- Suspicion and distrust in interpersonal relationships.
- Tendencies toward hostility, suspiciousness, resentfulness, and argumentativeness.
- Problems in school adjustment.
- Increased disagreements with parents.
- Difficulty in establishing therapeutic relationships due to interpersonal guardedness.

Low Scores on Scale 6

The following are associated with low scale 6 features (T ≤ 40):

- Lower levels of intelligence and academic achievement.
- Presentation of self as cheerful and balanced.
- Cautious and conventional.
- Interpersonally insensitive, unaware of the feelings and motives of others.
- If psychiatric patient, possibility of overcompensation for paranoid symptoms.

6-8/8-6 Codetype

The 6-8/8-6 codetype is indicative of serious psychopathology for both teenagers and adults. This codetype has clearly been associated with paranoid symptomatology, including delusions of grandeur, feelings of persecution, hallucinations, and outbursts of hostility. Individuals with this codetype appear to be socially isolated and withdrawn, and their behavior is frequently unpredictable and inappropriate. Difficulties in thought processes are often apparent, ranging from deficits in concentration to bizarre and schizophrenic ideation. It would appear that the 6-8/8-6 individual frequently has difficulty in differentiating between fantasy and reality, and will often withdraw into autistic fantasy in response to stressful events.

The 6-8/8-6 codetype occurs with a frequency of 3.2% for male and 3.4% for female adolescents in psychiatric settings (see Table 5.4). Adolescents with this codetype are typically referred for treatment in response to the occurrence of bizarre behaviors or excessive fantasy. As children, this group appears to have been subjected to physical punishment as a primary form of discipline. Nearly half of the adolescents with this codetype in the Marks et al. (1974) sample had received beatings as punishment for misbehaviors. Additionally, the majority of these adolescents had fathers who had committed either minor or major legal offenses, and 30% of these teenagers had attended five or more school settings within their elementary education years.

The 6-8/8-6 adolescents often have a violent temper and when angry these teenagers may express their feelings directly (e.g., hitting others or throwing objects). They are not liked by their peers and they often perceive their peer group as "picking on" them or teasing them. In general, these adolescents were preoccupied with their physical appearance, and ratings by their psychotherapists indicated that they were, indeed, below average in appearance. The predominant affective distress for these teenagers included moderate depression and feelings of guilt and shame. Adolescents with this codetype were frequently delusional and displayed grandiose ideas. In the Marks et al. 1970-1973 sample, slightly over half of these teenagers had used drugs, although much of their drug use was connected with suicide attempts. As might be expected for a group of adolescents who produced this codetype, these teenagers typically displayed little or no insight into their psychological problems.

Scale 7 (*Pt*: Psychasthenia) Codetypes

Scale 7, in both the MMPI and MMPI-A, consists of 48 items designed to measure psychasthenia, a neurotic syndrome that was later conceptualized as obsessive-compulsive neurosis and most recently labeled obsessive-compulsive disorder. Such individuals are characterized by excessive doubts, compulsions, obsessions, and high levels of tension and anxiety. Because this symptom pattern is more typically found among outpatients, the original criterion group employed by McKinley and Hathaway in the development of this scale was restricted to a relatively small group of 20 inpatients with this condition. McKinley and Hathaway were reluctant to use outpatients in their criterion groups because of their inability to confirm diagnoses for patients in this setting (Greene, 1991). The content areas of scale 7 cover a wide array of symptomatology including unhappiness, physical complaints, deficits in concentration, obsessive thoughts, anxiety, and feelings of inferiority and inadequacy. Harris and Lingoes (1955) did not identify subscales for scale 7, perhaps reflective of the relatively high degree of internal consistency (as reflected in Cronbach Coefficient Alpha) typically found for this MMPI basic scale.

In general, those who score high on scale 7 have been described as anxious, tense, and indecisive individuals who are very self-critical and perfectionistic. At extreme elevations, there are often patterns of intense ruminations and obsessions constituting disabling symptomatology. Low scores on this scale are frequently indicative of self-confident, secure, and emotionally stable individuals who are achievement and success oriented. Greene (1980) noted that females typically endorse more scale 7 items than men. Data from normal adolescents as reported by Hathaway and Monachesi (1963) showed that scale 7 high-point elevations were more common in adult than adolescent profiles, although scale 7 was the most frequently elevated neurotic scale in adolescent MMPI profiles. Scale 7 has also been reported to be a relatively rare high point among adolescent profiles in clinical settings (Archer, 1989). Data for adolescent outpatients, reported by Lachar and

Wrobel (1990), indicated that high scale 7 males and females were described as overly self-critical, anxious, tense, nervous, and restless. Wrobel and Lachar (1990) reported that high scale 7 scores for male and female adolescents were related to an increased frequency of nightmares. Butcher et al. (1992) found that a clinical sample of girls who produced elevations on MMPI-A scale 7 were more likely to be described as depressed and to report an increase in disagreements with their parents.

High Scores on Scale 7

The following is a summary of characteristics associated with high scale 7 scores (T ≥ 60):

- Anxious, tense, and apprehensive.
- Self-critical, perfectionistic approach to life.
- Feelings of insecurity, inadequacy, and inferiority.
- Emotionally overcontrolled and uncomfortable with feelings.
- Introspective and ruminative.
- Lacking in self-confidence and ambivalent in decision-making situations.
- Rigid, moralistic, conscientious.
- At marked elevations, obsessive thought patterns and compulsive behaviors.

Low Scores on Scale 7

The following are features associated with low scale 7 scores (T ≤ 40):

- Lack of emotional distress and freedom from anxiety and tension.
- Capable and self-confident in approach to problems.
- Perceived as warm, cheerful, and relaxed.
- Flexible, efficient, and adaptable.

7-8/8-7 Codetype

The 7-8/8-7 profile appears to be related to the occurrence of inadequate defenses and poor stress tolerance for both adults and adolescents. These individuals are frequently described as socially isolated, withdrawn, anxious, and depressed. There is also evidence that individuals with the 7-8/8-7 codetype feel insecure and inadequate. They have substantial difficulty in modulating their feelings and expressing their emotions in appropriate ways.

The *7-8/8-7* codetype is found among 1.8% of male and 1.9% of female adolescents in psychiatric settings (Archer, Gordon, & Klinefelter, 1991). Among adolescents, this profile configuration appears to be related to the presence of substantial tension resulting from failing defenses. These adolescents were typically described as anxious and depressed. They were also inhibited and conflicted in terms of their interpersonal relationships, particularly those involving aspects of emotional dependency. Many of these teenagers expressed fears of failure in school, and Marks et al. (1974) reported that roughly one-half of this sample had failed at least one academic grade.

In the adult literature, the relationship in elevation between scales *7* and *8* is frequently cited as a highly significant factor in interpretation of this profile. Scale *7* is seen as a suppressor of scale *8* symptomatology such that profiles displaying higher elevations on scale *7* (relative to scale *8*) are seen as more neurotic, whereas profiles containing higher elevations on scale *8* (relative to scale *7*) are frequently seen as indicative of more schizophrenic symptomatology. Marks et al. (1974) noted that there is no evidence of this phenomenon among the adolescents in their *7-8/8-7* codetype. Specifically, based on their data from the 1970-1973 sample, they observed that *7-8s* and *8-7s* were both quite deviant in thought and behavior, and nearly one-half of these adolescents had experienced either auditory or visual hallucinations.

7-9/9-7 Codetype

Across both adult and adolescent respondents, the *7-9/9-7* codetype appears to be associated with tension, anxiety, and rumination. Over three fourths of the adolescents with this codetype were characterized by their therapists as worriers who were vulnerable to both real and unrealistic threats and fears. For adults with this codetype, Greene (1991) recommended that the possibility of manic features be investigated and that psychopharmacological medications be considered for the reduction of the very high levels of anxiety and tension.

Among adolescents in clinical settings, the *7-9/9-7* codetype occurs with a frequency of 1.7% for males and 0.7% for females (Archer, Gordon, & Klinefelter, 1991). Adolescents with this codetype were described by Marks et al. as insecure. These adolescents also tended to have strong needs for attention, conflicts involving emotional dependency issues, and fears of losing control. They were tense and had difficulty "letting go," but did not show evidence of scale *9* manic characteristics such as elation. In general, these teenagers appeared to be defensive when discussing their psychological problems, and very sensitive to demands placed on them by others. Within the adolescent sample, scale 7 correlates were more predominant for this codetype than scale 9 characteristics.

7-0/0-7 Codetype

The 7-0/0-7 codetype appears to be rare among adults, and is found with a frequency of 1.3% for male and 1.2% for female adolescents in clinical settings (Archer, Gordon, & Klinefelter, 1991). Marks et al. (1974) were able to identify only 11 adolescents with this codetype in their research sample. For both adolescents and adults, this codetype appears related to the presence of neurotic symptomatology, including excessive anxiety, tension, social introversion, and shyness.

The predominant presenting problems for the 7-0/0-7 adolescents consisted of shyness and extreme sensitivity. Although defiant and disobedient behaviors were relatively common for this group, these characteristics tended to occur with a base rate frequency that was lower than that of many other adolescent codetype groups. Interestingly, almost one half of these adolescents had family members with a history of psychiatric disorder. Psychotherapists responded positively to adolescents with the 7-0/0-7 codetype and indicated that they displayed moderate motivation for treatment, good treatment prognosis, and good cognitive-verbal insight. These teenagers performed well in academic settings and maintained high needs for achievement. Reaction formation and isolation appear to be the predominant defense mechanisms for the 7-0/0-7 adolescent. These individuals become intropunitive in response to stress or frustration, and have a decided tendency toward emotional overcontrol. Marks et al. (1974) noted that these adolescents are basically insecure and tend to have conflicts regarding emotional dependency and assertion.

Scale 8 (Sc: Schizophrenia) Codetypes

Scale 8 consists of 77 items and constitutes the largest scale in the MMPI-A. One item, related to sexuality, was deleted from the original scale 8 in the modification of this measure for the MMPI-A. Scale 8 was developed to identify patients with schizophrenia, and deals with content areas involving bizarre thought processes, peculiar thoughts, social isolation, difficulties in concentration and impulse control, and disturbances in mood and behavior. Harris and Lingoes (1955) identified six subscales within the schizophrenia scale: Social Alienation (Sc_1); Emotional Alienation (Sc_2); Lack of Ego Mastery, Cognitive (Sc_3); Lack of

Ego Mastery, Conative (Sc_4); Lack of Ego Mastery, Defective Inhibition (Sc_5); and Bizarre Sensory Experiences (Sc_6).

Individuals who score high on scale *8* are typically described as alienated, confused, and delusional. They often display psychotic features, and are socially isolated, withdrawn, shy, and apathetic. Extreme elevations on scale *8*, particularly T-score values in excess of 100 for adults and 90 for adolescents, are typically produced by clients who are not schizophrenic but are experiencing intense, acute situational distress. Greene (1980) noted that an adolescent undergoing a severe identity crisis may frequently score in this extreme range. Individuals who score markedly low in scale *8* have typically been described as conventional, cautious, compliant persons who may be overly accepting of authority and who place a premium on practical and concrete thinking. Comprehensive reviews of the MMPI literature on schizophrenia in adult populations were provided by Walters (1983, 1988).

Research on scale *8* has shown a large degree of difference in the mean raw score endorsement patterns between adolescent and adult normals, with adolescents typically endorsing substantially more scale *8* items than their adult counterparts (Archer, 1984, 1987; Pancoast & Archer, 1988). Hathaway and Monachesi (1963) found that boys were more likely than girls to have profiles that exhibited scale *8* as the highest point. Further, both male and female adolescents who produced high scale *8* scores were likely to be lower in intelligence and in academic achievement than other adolescents. High scale *8* girls were also more likely to drop out of school. Archer et al. (1988) found that high scale *8* adolescent inpatients were described as mistrustful, vulnerable to stress, interpersonally isolated, and socially withdrawn. Often, these adolescents had presenting problems that included impaired reality testing. Archer and Gordon (1988) found that scale *8* scores were significantly associated with schizophrenic diagnoses in an adolescent inpatient sample. Employing a criterion of a T-score value of ≥75 to identify schizophrenia, an overall hit rate of 76% was obtained. This result is comparable to Hathaway's (1956) original finding for this scale in adult samples. Butcher et al. (1992) found MMPI-A scale *8* elevations to be associated with higher levels of acting out, schizoid, and psychotic behaviors among adolescent male inpatients. They also reported an association between scale *8* elevations and histories of sexual abuse for both male and female inpatients. In addition to schizophrenia, adolescent scale *8* elevations may reflect a teenager's drug use history, particularly previous experiences with hallucinatory drugs (Archer, 1989). Interpretation of elevated scale *8* values, therefore, require the clinician's awareness of the adolescent's drug-taking history and behaviors. Review of critical item endorsements and Harris-Lingoes subscales may often be used as a vehicle through which to determine whether an adolescent's scale *8* elevation represents a result of drug-taking experiences or actual schizophrenic symptomatology. Finally, Lachar and Wrobel (1990) found high scale *8* scores among adolescent inpatients to be related to frequent experiences of frustration, and Wrobel and Lachar (1990) found high scale *8* adolescents were often rejected and teased by other children.

High scores on Scale *8*

The following are characteristics associated with high scale *8* scores (T ≥ 60):

- Withdrawn, seclusive, and socially isolated.
- Confused and disorganized.
- Presence of schizoid features.
- Feelings of inferiority, incompetence, low self-esteem, and dissatisfaction.
- Feelings of frustration and unhappiness.
- Rejection and teasing by peers.
- Poor school adjustment and performance.
- Vulnerable and easily upset.
- Reluctance to engage in interpersonal relationships, including psychotherapy relationships.
- Nonconforming, unconventional, and socially deviant.
- Poor reality testing.
- At marked elevations, associated with delusions, hallucinations, and other schizophrenic symptoms.

Low Scores on Scale *8*

The following are characteristics of low scale *8* scores (T ≤ 40):

- Conforming, conventional, and conservative.
- Logical, practical, and achievement oriented.
- Unimaginative and cautious in approaches to problem solving.
- Responsible, cooperative, and dependable.

8-9/9-8 Codetype

The occurrence of an *8-9/9-8* codetype in either adolescence or adulthood appears to be related to the presence of serious psychopathology. Individuals who produce this MMPI configuration have been referred to as immature, self-centered, argumentative, and demanding. Although these individuals seek a great deal of attention, they are resentful and hostile in interpersonal relationships and display little capacity to form close relationships with others. Acting out, often of an unpredictable nature, is a salient defense mechanism for this codetype.

As shown in Table 5.4, the *8-9/9-8* codetype is found for 1.5% of male and 1.0% of female adolescents in psychiatric settings. Many of the respondents with this codetype display evidence of thought disorder, including grandiose ideas, as well as evidence of hyperactivity and a very rapid personal tempo. Marks et al. (1974) noted that adolescents with a *9-8* codetype appear to "think, talk, and move, at an unusually fast pace" (p. 239). For both adolescents and adults, this codetype has been associated with the presence of both schizophrenic and paranoid symptomatology. Within the Marks et al. 1970-1973 sample, this co-detype was not particularly associated with substance abuse or addic-tion. In the Archer and Klinefelter (1992) study, however, the *8-9/9-8* code was related to significantly higher *MAC* scale elevations for female adolescent psychiatric patients.

Scale 9 (*Ma*: Hypomania) Codetypes

Scale 9, in both the original MMPI and the MMPI-A, consists of 46 items developed to identify patients manifesting hypomanic symptomatology. The content areas covered in this scale are relatively broad and include grandiosity, egocentricity, irritability, elevated mood, and cognitive and behavioral overactivity. Harris and Lingoes (1955) identified four con-tent subscales contained within the hypomania scale: *Amorality (Ma₁)*, *Psychomotor Acceleration (Ma₂)*, *Imperturbability (Ma₃)*, and *Ego Inflation (Ma₄)*.

Greene (1991) noted that scale 9 elevations are often difficult to interpret in isolation. In this sense, elevations on scale 9 are often seen as facilitating or moderating the expression of qualities or characteristics identified by elevations on other clinical scales, particularly scales *D* and *Pd*. High scores on scale 9 have been related to impulsivity, excessive activity, narcissism, social extroversion, and a preference for action in contrast to thought and reflection. In addition, individuals who score high on this scale may display manic features such as flight of ideas, delusions of grandeur, and hyperactivity. Lumry, Gottesman, and Tuason (1982), however, demonstrated that individuals with bipolar manic-depressive disorder provide very different MMPI profiles de-pending on the phase of the disorder during which the patient is assessed. For example, patients in the depressed phase produced a profile characterized by elevations on scales 2 and 7, whereas patients assessed during the manic phase produced spike 9 profiles. These findings indicate that the accurate diagnosis of bipolar disorder may require a longitudinal series of MMPI administrations because of the state dependency nature of MMPI assessment. Markedly low scores on scale 9 (T-score values below 40) have been related to lethargy, apathy, listlessness, and decreased motivational states. Additionally, low scores on scale 9 have often been related to the presence of serious depressive symptomatology, including vegetative signs (Greene, 1991).

Normal adolescents typically endorse substantially more scale 9 items than do adults (Archer, 1984, 1987). Pancoast and Archer (1988) showed that adolescents are particularly likely to endorse scale 9 items related to the Harris–Lingoes content area of Psychomotor Acceleration, which measures feelings of restlessness and the need to engage in activity. Hathaway and Monachesi (1963) found low scores on scale 9 in their sample of normal adolescents to be associated with lower rates of delinquency. In general, the teenagers who scored low on this scale in the Minnesota sample were well behaved and conforming, and demonstrated high levels of achievement in the academic setting.

In adolescent psychiatric outpatient samples, Lachar and Wrobel (1990) reported that elevations on scale 9 are related to the occurrence of temper tantrums. Boys who score high on scale 9 were described as hostile or argumentative, and girls were found to display rapid mood shifts and a tendency not to complete tasks that they undertake. Archer et al. (1988) reported that high scale 9 adolescent inpatients were described as impulsive, insensitive to criticism, and unrealistically optimistic in terms of their goal setting and aspirations. Archer and Klinefelter (1992) found that elevations on scale 9 were associated with higher scores on the *MAC* scale. Butcher et al. (1992) found high MMPI-A scale 9 scores among adolescents in inpatient settings to be associated with amphetamine abuse for boys and more frequent school suspensions for girls.

High Scores on Scale 9

The following features are associated with high-point elevations on scale 9 (T ≥ 60):

- Accelerated personal tempo and excessive activity.
- Preference for action rather than thought and reflection.
- Impulsivity, restlessness, and distractibility.
- Lack of realism, and grandiosity in goal setting and aspirations.
- Outgoing, socially extroverted, and gregarious.

- Talkative and energetic.
- Egocentric, self-centered, insensitive, self-indulgent.
- Greater likelihood of school conduct problems and delinquent behaviors.
- Emotionally labile.
- Flight of ideas, euphoric mood, grandiose self-perceptions.

Low Scores on Scale 9

The following are characteristics or features associated with low scale 9 scores (T ≤ 40):

- Low energy level.
- Quiet, seclusive, withdrawn, depressed.
- Overcontrolled, inhibited, overly responsible.
- Decreased probability of acting out or delinquent behaviors.
- Depressed, lethargic, and apathetic.

Scale 0 (Si: Social Introversion) Codetypes

The MMPI-A Si scale consists of 62 items, reflecting the deletion of eight items from the original Si scale. Additionally, two items retained on the MMPI-A Si scale are keyed in the opposite direction from traditional scoring for this scale. These items are:

No. 308 Sometimes some unimportant thought will run through my mind and bother me for days. (Scored in *true* direction on MMPI-A, *false* direction on original MMPI.)

No. 334 I have often found people jealous of my good ideas, just because they had not thought of them first. (Scored in *true* direction on MMPI-A, *false* direction on original MMPI.)

The scoring direction of these items was modified for the MMPI-A because of the belief that the original scoring was counterintuitive and incorrect. The Si scale was originally developed by Drake (1946) based on the responses of college students who produced extreme scores on a social introversion/extroversion measure. Elevated T scores on the Si scale reflect greater degrees of social introversion. Although Harris and Lingoes did not attempt to create specific subscales for the social introversion scale, three Si subscales were created for the MMPI-2 and the MMPI-A based on a factor analytic approach. The MMPI-A Si subscales are discussed in the next chapter of this text. Graham (1990) indicated that the Si scale contains two broad clusters of items. These groups consist of items related to social participation and items related to neurotic maladjustment and self-depreciation. Graham noted that high scores on scale *0* can occur by the endorsement of either, or both, of these content areas.

Individuals who produce elevated scores on scale *0* are likely to be socially introverted, insecure, and markedly uncomfortable in social situations. They tend to be shy, timid, submissive, and lacking in self-confidence. When high scores occur for scale *0*, the potential for impulsive behaviors and acting out is decreased, and the likelihood of neurotic rumination and introspection is increased. Individuals who produce low scores on the *Si* scale are described as socially extroverted, gregarious, friendly, and outgoing. These individuals appear to have strong affiliation needs and are interested in social status, acceptance, and recognition. Low scorers may be subject to impulse control problems, and their relations with others may be more superficial than sincere and long enduring.

Greene (1991) noted that adolescents and college students typically scored toward the extroverted pole of the *Si* scale. Hathaway and Monachesi (1963) found an interesting pattern of correlates for scale *0* scores in their sample of Minnesota normal adolescents. Social introversion was a relatively frequent finding among boys and girls from rural farm settings, whereas social extroversion was characteristic of adolescents from families with parents in professional occupations. Intriguingly, low scale *0* profiles were found for children with higher intelligence levels but with spotty records of academic achievement. Hathaway and Monachesi interpreted these findings as indicating that there was a potential conflict between an adolescent's social interest and success, and his or her academic achievement.

Among psychiatrically disturbed adolescents, Lachar and Wrobel (1990) found that outpatients who produce high values on scale *0* are described as having few or no friends, and as being very shy. These teenagers often avoided calling attention to themselves and they did not initiate relationships with other adolescents. Butcher et al. (1992) found adolescent inpatients with elevations on scale *0* were described as socially withdrawn and manifesting low self-esteem. In addition, female adolescents with elevated scale *0* scores had lower levels of delinquency, acting out, and drug or alcohol use.

High Scores on Scale *0*

The following are features that have been associated with adolescents who score high on scale *0* (T $\geq$ 60):

- Social introversion and social discomfort.
- Low self-esteem.
- Reserved, timid, socially retiring.
- Decreased probability of delinquent or acting out behaviors.
- Submissive, compliant, accepting of authority.
- Insecure and lacking in self-confidence.
- Overcontrolled, difficult to get to know, interpersonally hypersensitive.
- Reliable, dependable, cautious.
- Lacking in social skills.

Low Scores on Scale 0

The following are features associated with adolescents who score low on scale 0 (T $\leq$ 40):

- Sociable, extroverted, gregarious.
- Intelligent, with a possible history of academic underachievement.
- Active, energetic, talkative.
- Interested in social influence, power, recognition.
- Socially confident and competent.

FACTORS POTENTIALLY AFFECTING CODETYPE INTERPRETATION

A substantial amount of research literature has established that demographic variables such as race, gender, and age *may* significantly influence the MMPI profiles of adult respondents (Dahlstrom, Welsh, & Dahlstrom, 1975). Before leaving the topic of codetype interpretation for adolescent profiles, each of these areas is examined in terms of the probable effects of these variables on codetype interpretation practices for the MMPI-A.

Race/Ethnic Factors

Gynther (1972) reviewed the literature on the influence of race on adults' MMPI scores and concluded that distinctive racial differences reliably occur that reflect variations in respective cultural and environmental backgrounds of Black and White respondents. In particular, Gynther interpreted findings from the analyses of item differences as indicating that the high scores for Blacks on scales *F*, *Sc*, and *Ma* reflected differences in perceptions, expectations, and values rather than differ-ential levels of psychological adjustment. He called for the development of MMPI norms for Black respondents in order to allow for more accurate assessment of psychopathology in Black populations. Gynther (1989) recently reevaluated the literature on comparisons of MMPI profiles from Blacks and Whites and concluded that, in the absence of studies employing unbiased criterion measures to evaluate potential racial differences, "definite conclusions to the racial bias question may be exceptionally difficult to reach" (p. 878).

The early studies that investigated the variable of subject race within adolescent populations appeared to support Gynther's (1972) position regarding the presence of racial differences in MMPI scale values. Ball (1960) examined MMPI scale elevations for a group of 31 Black and 161 White ninth graders and found that Black males tended to score higher on scale Hs than White male students, and that Black female students produced significantly higher elevations on scales F, Sc, and Si than did White females. Similarly, McDonald and Gynther (1962) examined the MMPI response patterns of Black and White students within segregated high school settings. These findings indicated that Black students produced higher scores than their White counterparts on scales L, F, K, Hs, D, and Ma. Further, Black female students had significantly higher scores on all MMPI scales, with the exception of K and Sc, than did White female students.

More recently, research results have suggested that when Blacks and Whites have experienced common cultural influences and socioeconomic backgrounds, racial differences are less likely to be found in MMPI profile elevations. Klinge and Strauss (1976) and Lachar, Klinge, and Grissell (1976) reported no significant MMPI differences between samples of Black and White adolescents. These results were attributable to the ob-servation that the Black and White respondents in these investigations had been raised and educated in similar or equivalent environments. Bertelson, Marks, and May (1982) matched 462 psychiatric inpatients(of whom 144 were adolescents) on variables such as gender, age, residence, education, employment, and socioeconomic status. No significant MMPI differences were found for the matched racial samples in this study. Archer (1987) reported evidence of minimal racial differences between groups of Black and White male and female adolescents from a predom-inantly middle-class public high school setting.

Marks et al. (1974) included 61 Black subjects in the clinical population they used to derive correlate descriptors of adolescent codetype profiles. These subjects were part of their Ohio State University Health Center sample. The authors found few Black-White differences among the descriptors generated for their adolescent codetypes, and statements regarding race of subject are seldom made in the Marks et al. (1974) text. Green and Kelley (1988) investigated the relationship between MMPI scores and external behavioral and interview criteria in 333 White and 107 Black male juvenile delinquents. They reported that as the apparent objectivity of the criterion increased, evidence of racial bias decreased (i.e., the predictability of the criteria did not differ as a function of race).

Figures 5.7 and 5.8 show the MMPI-A profile findings for Black, White, and other male respondents in the normative sample for this instrument, and Figs. 5.9 and 5.10 show comparable data for females. These profiles show racial or ethnic differences of about three to five T-score points across MMPI-A clinical scales *L, F, 4, 6, 7, 8,* and *9.* Demographic data for this sample, however, indicates a significant socioeconomic difference between these three ethnic groupings as reflected in adolescents' reports of parental occupation and socioeconomic status. Thus, the relatively limited profile differences found between these groups reflect both ethnic and socioeconomic effects.

Greene (1980, 1987) surveyed the literature on the issue of racial differences in MMPI response patterns. His review of studies examining

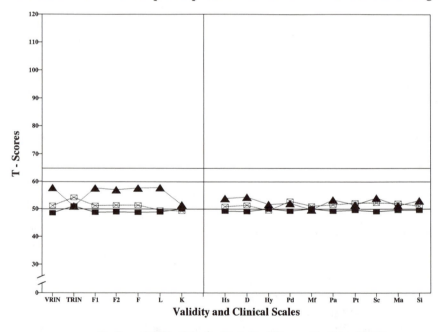

FIGURE 5.7   MMPI-A basic scale profiles produced by males from varying ethnic groups in the MMPI-A normative sample. *Note. TRIN* T-score values were calculated for this profile based on conversions from the mean raw score value for each sample.

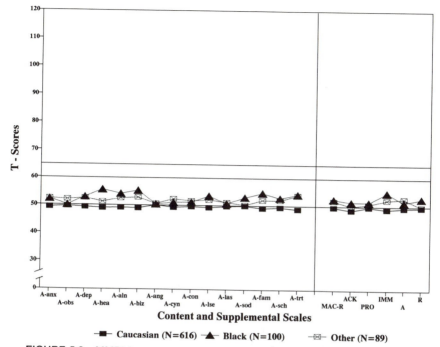

FIGURE 5.8   MMPI-A content and supplementary scale profile produced by males from varying ethnic groups in the MMPI-A normative sample.

Black-White differences within normal samples failed to reveal any MMPI scale that consistently demonstrated racial differences across 10 independent investigations. A similar conclusion has also been reached in a review by Pritchard and Rosenblatt (1980). Greene noted that scales *F* and *Ma* were most frequently affected by race, but that significant differences were not found for scale *Sc*, which had been reported by Gynther (1972) as one of the scales typically elevated among Black populations. Further, Greene noted that the actual mean differences in studies reporting significant differences between Black and White respondents typically were ≤5 T-score points, a range comparable to the largest racial differences found for the MMPI-A normative sample. Dahlstrom, Lachar, and Dahlstrom (1986) provided a comprehensive review of the relationship between ethnic status and MMPI response patterns that included data from both adolescent and adult samples. These authors concluded that this literature supports the use of the MMPI in the assessment of psychological functioning for Black clients, "since the relative accuracy of these scores were as good or better for this ethnic minority as it was for white clients" (p. 205).

In summary, the literature on ethnic or racial effects on the MMPI has

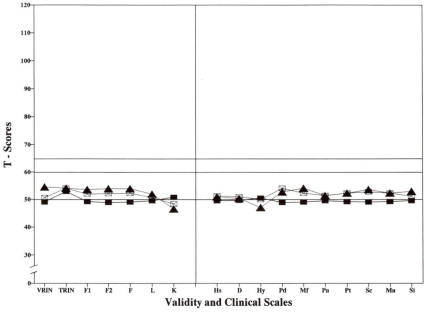

FIGURE 5.9 MMPI-A basic scale profiles produced by females from varying ethnic groups in the MMPI-A normative sample. *Note. TRIN* T-score values were calculated for this profile based on conversions from the mean raw score value for each sample.

provided mixed findings, and does not permit for firm conclusions. If ethnic differences, independent of socioeconomic factors, do occur on MMPI profiles, however, it appears likely that the interpretive significance of such differences are relatively limited in terms of the standard or basic clinical profile. As is discussed in the following chapter covering supplementary scales, there is evidence that the *MAC* (MacAndrew, 1965) and *MAC-R* scales may be less useful with Black populations (i.e., produces more false positive errors) than with White respondents.

Gender

Hathaway and Monachesi (1963), in their Minnesota statewide sample, identified gender differences in item endorsement patterns, and in the frequency of occurrence of high-point codetypes. The authors identified the presence of 63 items in which the difference in percentage of *true* endorsement by boys and girls was 25 points or more. Regarding this pattern of item endorsement differences, Hathaway and Monachesi

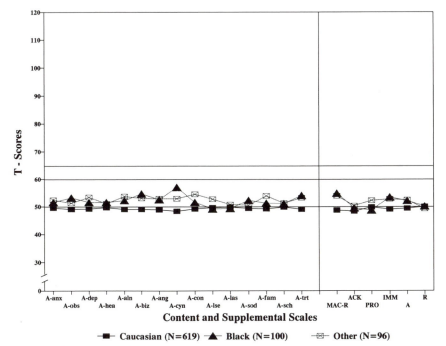

FIGURE 5.10   MMPI-A content and supplementary scale profile produced by females from varying ethnic groups in the MMPI-A normative sample.

(1963) stated, "It is informative to employ generalized adjectives like 'sensitive' or 'fearful' or 'candid.' Such adjectives organize the pattern of correlated items expressing the feminine role, while 'inquisitive' or 'desirous of active outdoor activities' or 'aggressive' may better characterize the male role" (p. 41). Table 5.5 provides the MMPI-A items that show the largest degree of difference in percentage of *true* responses by boys and girls in the normative sample. In general, this pattern of gender-related item differences is consistent with those found by Hathaway and Monachesi for the original form of the MMPI. In total, roughly 100 items showed an endorsement rate difference of at least 10% in the MMPI-A normative sample when data were analyzed separately by gender. Additionally, significant gender differences have traditionally been found in the number of items omitted on the original form of the MMPI by adolescent respondents. Although religion and sex were the content areas of items most frequently omitted by both boys and girls, items related to sex were more often left unanswered by female than male respondents (Archer, 1987).

In terms of codetype profiles on the original form of the MMPI, girls more frequently displayed peak elevations on scale *Si* whereas boys were

TABLE 5.5

Fifteen MMPI-A Items Showing the Greatest Gender Differences in Percent of Endorsement as True

MMPI-A Item Number	Content	Male % True	Female % True
61	I enjoy reading love stories.	19.0	77.8
131	I keep a diary.	19.3	73.5
59	I have often wished I were a girl. (Or if you are a girl) I have never been sorry that I am a girl.	9.3	60.5
139	I cry easily.	16.9	55.5
254	There never was a time in my life when I liked to play with dolls.	53.5	16.0
21	At times I have fits of laughing and crying that I cannot control.	30.2	63.8
64	I like poetry.	37.6	70.1
1	I like mechanics magazines.	34.5	4.0
114	I like collecting flowers or growing house plants.	15.2	43.2
121	Criticism or scolding hurts me terribly.	34.5	61.3
60	My feelings are not easily hurt.	49.6	23.4
190	I very much like hunting.	32.0	7.1
241	If I were a reporter I would very much like to report sporting news.	55.2	31.4
319	I love to go to dances.	47.5	69.9
19	At times I have very much wanted to leave home.	47.3	69.6

Note. Items reproduced from the MMPI-A by permission. Copyright (c) 1992 by the Regents of the University of Minnesota.

more likely to have high scale *Sc*. Hathaway and Monachesi (1963) noted that these gender differences were likely to be more marked when adolescents were viewed against the backdrop of adolescent norms in contrast to adult norms. Interactional effects between gender of respondent and type of norms utilized to score the profile (adolescent versus adult) on the original form of the MMPI were also reported by Ehrenworth (1984), Klinge and Strauss (1976), and by Lachar et al. (1976). The direction and meaning of these interactional findings, however, have been very complex and inconsistent. In the study by Ehrenworth, for example, T-score values for male adolescent inpatients on scales *F*, *Pt*, and *Sc* were significantly higher than female values when adult norms were employed, but nonsignificant when adolescent norms were used. In contrast, females produced higher *Si* T scores than males using adolescent norms, with a less marked scale difference using adult norms.

Moore and Handal (1980) examined the MMPI profile elevations of 16- and 17-year-old male and female volunteers from school settings in the

St. Louis area. These data were analyzed by sex of respondent using adult K-corrected T scores. They reported substantial evidence that males tended to score significantly higher than females on scales *F*, *Pd*, *Mf*, *Pt*, *Sc*, and *Ma*. MMPI gender differences were more prevalent in this sample than racial differences, with males producing MMPI profiles suggestive of greater impulsivity, problems with authority, identity confusion, and rebelliousness than their female counterparts. Similarly, Ehrenworth and Archer (1985) examined the MMPI profiles of adolescents in psychiatric treatment and found that males produced higher T-score elevations than females on several scales when adult norms were employed. Differences in profile elevations by gender were minimal, however, when adolescent norms were used in this sample. Equivalent profiles for males and females were also reported by Archer (1984) for inpatient samples employing adolescent norms. When the data presented in Table 5.4 for MMPI-A codetype frequencies were analyzed separately by gender, the *4-9/9-4* and the *2-4/4-2* codetypes were the most frequent for males, whereas the *2-3/3-2* codetype was most frequent for females.

On the two-point codetype level, Marks et al. (1974) stated they found no significant differences between males and females relative to clinical correlates of codetype descriptors. The Marks et al. text, therefore, provided codetype narratives that were not differentiated by gender. Williams and Butcher (1989a) analyzed correlate data for individual scales separately by gender and concluded that: "Our results, in most respects, show a rather limited impact of gender on MMPI descriptors for adolescents from clinical settings when using established procedures for determining MMPI behavioral correlates. Further research, especially studies using T scores, could combine male and female subjects when sample size is a critical issue and when studying adolescents in treatment settings" (p. 259). In contrast, Wrobel and Lachar (1990) and Lachar and Wrobel (1990), in their studies of adolescent outpatients, found substantial evidence of gender-related differences in single-scale correlates. Their findings indicated that the majority of significant correlates were gender specific, and indicated that gender may play an important role as a moderator variable in the interpretation of MMPI findings from adolescents.

In summary, it is clear that significant gender differences occur in item endorsement patterns for adolescent respondents, and that these differences are reflected in the need for the development of separate T-score conversions for male and female respondents in both adolescent and adult MMPI norms. Significant gender differences in mean raw score values can also be shown for MMPI-A special scales. For example, boys produce higher mean values than girls on the *MAC-R* and *IMM* scales.

The degree to which gender differences occur following T-score conversions, however, is currently unclear. Most importantly, the research by Lachar and Wrobel (1990) and Wrobel and Lachar (1990) suggest that significant gender-related differences in correlate patterns for MMPI scales may exist, and certainly underscore this area as one in crucial need of future, systematic research. Until such research is completed, however, firm conclusions cannot be drawn concerning the degree to which reliable gender differences occur in the correlate patterns of adolescents.

Age

Differences between adult and adolescent MMPI response patterns were briefly discussed in the first chapter of this book. It was evident that numerous items show dramatic differences in endorsement frequency as a function of whether the respondent is an adolescent versus an adult. Further, on the item level, Hathaway and Monachesi (1963) identified 24 items that showed more than 39% instability in the direction of item endorsement from the time of assessment in the ninth grade to reevaluation during the senior year of high school. Additionally, 29 items for boys and 30 items for girls were identified as showing more than 17% change in endorsement direction between the 9th- and 12th-grade assessments. The authors noted that these item endorsement shifts may be the result of item instability as well as true changes in personality that occurred across this 3-year period of adolescent development. Finally, these changes in item endorsement were found to be specifically related to the gender of the respondent, that is, no common items appeared on the lists for both males and females. In general, those items that were most likely to shift in endorsement direction tended to involve personal attitudes or perceptions rather than biographical information.

A central question concerns the degree to which MMPI scale values are related to the age of the adolescent respondent. McFarland and Sparks (1985), for example, showed that the internal consistency of a variety of personality measures is related to age and educational level in a sample of adolescents and young adults ranging in age from 13 to 25. The traditional adolescent norms created by Marks et al. (1974) provided separate adolescent T-score conversions for age groupings of 17, 16, 15, and 14 and below, suggesting that age-related raw score differences might affect adolescents' response patterns. In contrast, Colligan and Offord (1989) found little evidence of age-related effects on MMPI raw score values in their sample of 1,315 adolescents between the ages of 13 and 17, inclusive. Based on this observation, these authors produced a contemporary set of adolescent norms for the original form of the MMPI that collapsed across age groupings. In the development of the MMPI-A, there was evidence that adolescents under the age of 14 produced response patterns that differed significantly from adolescents within the age grouping of 14 through 18. Based on concerns regarding these differences, the MMPI-A norms were collapsed across ages 14 through 18, and excluded 12- and 13-year-old adolescents from the normative sample. Thus, the age differences that occurred in MMPI-A basic scale raw score values were primarily manifested in the comparison of younger adolescents (ages 12 and 13) versus adolescents 14 years of age and older.

A final question concerns the degree to which MMPI profiles of adolescents at different age groups yield differences in interpretive accuracy and validity. Three studies have produced findings relevant to this issue. Findings by Lachar, Klinge, and Grissell (1976), Ehrenworth and Archer (1985), and Wimbish (1984) indicated no evidence of significant age effects for clinical accuracy ratings of narrative MMPI reports for adolescents. Lachar et al. (1976) did find, however, significant age differences when comparing accuracy ratings produced from MMPI profiles using adolescent norms versus adult K-corrected norms. Specifically, the authors found that interpretations of profiles from adolescent norms produced more accurate ratings than statements for adult norms for adolescents in the 12- to 13-year-old age group. These norm-related differences were not significant for accuracy ratings for adolescents in the mid- and later-adolescent groupings. Examination of mean values show that although accuracy ratings remain relatively constant for adolescent norms across the three age groups (12 to 13, 14 to 15, and 16 to 17), ratings for profiles based on adult norms were substantially more inaccurate for the 12- to 13-year-old period than for the other two age groupings.

In summary, there are known and substantial differences in item endorsement patterns as a function of age when the responses of adults are contrasted with those of adolescents on the MMPI. Within adolescent age groups, however, the developers of adolescent norms have dealt with possible age-related differences in a variety of ways. In terms of the MMPI-A, norms were based on the responses produced by adolescents in the 14- to 18-year-old age group. Thus far, findings suggest that the accuracy of MMPI correlate statements based on profiles using adolescent norms tend to be relatively unaffected by the age of the adolescent.

REFERENCES

Archer, R. P. (1984). Use of the MMPI with adolescents: A review of salient issues. *Clinical Psychology Review, 4,* 241–251.

Archer, R. P. (1987). *Using the MMPI with adolescents.* Hillsdale, NJ: Lawrence Erlbaum Associates.

Archer, R. P. (1989). MMPI assessment of adolescent clients. *Clinical Notes on the MMPI, No. 12.* Minneapolis: National Computer Systems.

Archer, R. P. (in press). Review of the Minnesota Multiphasic Personality Inventory-2 (MMPI-2). In *The Tenth Mental Measurements Yearbook.* Lincoln, NE: The Buros Institute of Mental Measurements.

Archer, R. P., Ball, J. D., & Hunter, J. A. (1985). MMPI characteristics of borderline psychopathology in adolescent inpatients. *Journal of Personality Assessment, 49,* 47–55.

Archer, R. P., & Gordon, R. A. (1988). MMPI and Rorschach indices of schizophrenic and depressive diagnoses among adolescent inpatients. *Journal of Personality Assessment, 52,* 276–287.

Archer, R. P., Gordon, R. A., Giannetti, R. A., & Singles, J. M. (1988). MMPI scale clinical correlates for adolescent inpatients. *Journal of Personality Assessment, 52,* 707–721.

Archer, R. P., Gordon, R. A., & Klinefelter, D. (1991). [*Analyses of the frequency of MMPI and MMPI-A profile assignments for 1762 adolescent patients*]. Unpublished raw data.

Archer, R. P., & Klinefelter, D. (1991). MMPI factor analytic findings for adolescents: Item- and scale-level factor structures. *Journal of Personality Assessment, 57,* 356–367.

Archer, R. P., & Klinefelter, D. (1992). Relationships between MMPI codetypes and *MAC* scale elevations in adolescent psychiatric samples. *Journal of Personality Assessment, 58,* 149–159.

Archer, R. P., Pancoast, D. L., & Klinefelter, D. (1989). A comparison of MMPI code types produced by traditional and recent adolescent norms. *Psychological Assessment: A Journal of Consulting and Clinical Psychology, 1,* 23–29.

Archer, R. P., Stolberg, A. L., Gordon, R. A., & Goldman, W. R. (1986). Parent and child MMPI responses: Characteristics among families with adolescents in inpatient and outpatient settings. *Journal of Abnormal Child Psychology, 14,* 181–190.

Ball, J. C. (1960). Comparison of MMPI profile differences among Negro-white adolescents. *Journal of Clinical Psychology, 16,* 304–307.

Ball, J. D., Archer, R. P., Struve, F. A., Hunter, J. A., & Gordon, R. A. (1987). MMPI correlates of a controversial EEG pattern among adolescent psychiatric patients. *Journal of Clinical Psychology, 43,* 708–714.

Ben-Porath, Y. S. (1990). MMPI-2 items. In J. N. Butcher (Ed.), *MMPI-2 news and profiles: A newsletter of the MMPI-2 workshops and symposia* (Vol. 1, No. 1, pp. 8–9). Department of Psychology, University of Minnesota, Minneapolis, MN.

Bertelson, A. D., Marks, P. A., & May, G. D. (1982). MMPI and race: A controlled study. *Journal of Consulting and Clinical Psychology, 50,* 316–318.

Butcher, J. N. (1990). *MMPI-2 in psychological treatment.* New York: Oxford University Press.

Butcher, J. N., Dahlstrom, W. G., Graham, J. R., Tellegen, A., & Kaemmer, B. (1989). *Minnesota Multiphasic Personality Inventory-2 (MMPI-2): Manual for administration and scoring.* Minneapolis: University of Minnesota Press.

Butcher, J. N., Williams, C. L., Graham, J. R., Archer, R. P., Tellegen, A., Ben-Porath, Y. S., & Kaemmer, B. (1992). *MMPI-A (Minnesota Multiphasic Personality Inventory— Adolescent): Manual for administration, scoring, and interpretation.* Minneapolis: University of Minnesota Press.

Colligan, R. C., & Offord, K. P. (1989). The aging MMPI: Contemporary norms for contemporary teenagers. *Mayo Clinic Proceedings, 64,* 3–27.

Colligan, R. C., & Osborne, D. (1977). MMPI profiles from adolescent medical patients. *Journal of Clinical Psychology, 33*, 186–189.

Colligan, R. C., Osborne, D., & Offord, K. P. (1980). Linear transformation and the interpretation of MMPI T-scores. *Journal of Clinical Psychology, 36*, 162–165.

Colligan, R. C., Osborne, D., & Offord, K. P. (1984). Normalized transformations and the interpretation of MMPI T-scores: A reply to Hsu. *Journal of Consulting and Clinical Psychology, 52*, 824–826.

Colligan, R. C., Osborne, D., Swenson, W. M., & Offord, K. P. (1983). *The MMPI: A contemporary normative study.* New York: Praeger.

Dahlstrom, W. G., Lachar, D., & Dahlstrom, L. E. (1986). *MMPI patterns of American minorities.* Minneapolis: University of Minnesota Press.

Dahlstrom, W. G., Welsh, G. S., & Dahlstrom, L. E. (1972). *An MMPI handbook: Vol. I. Clinical interpretation* (rev. ed.). Minneapolis: University of Minnesota Press.

Dahlstrom, W. G., Welsh, G. S., & Dahlstrom, L. E. (1975). *An MMPI handbook: Vol. II. Research applications* (rev. ed.). Minneapolis: University of Minnesota Press.

Dodrill, C. B., & Clemmons, D. (1984). Use of neuropsychological tests to identify high school students with epilepsy who later demonstrate inadequate performances in life. *Journal of Consulting and Clinical Psychology, 52*, 520–527.

Drake, L. E. (1946). A social I.E. scale for the Minnesota Multiphasic Personality Inventory. *Journal of Applied Psychology, 30*, 51–54.

Ehrenworth, N. V. (1984). *A comparison of the utility of interpretive approaches with adolescent MMPI profiles.* Unpublished doctoral dissertation, Virginia Consortium for Professional Psychology, Norfolk, VA.

Ehrenworth, N. V., & Archer, R. P. (1985). A comparison of clinical accuracy ratings of interpretive approaches for adolescent MMPI responses. *Journal of Personality Assessment, 49*, 413–421.

Friedman, A. F., Webb, J. T., & Lewak, R. (1989). *Psychological assessment with the MMPI.* Hillsdale, NJ: Lawrence Erlbaum Associates.

Gilberstadt, H., & Duker, J. (1965). *A handbook for clinical and actuarial MMPI interpretation.* Philadelphia: Saunders.

Graham, J. R. (1990). *MMPI-2: Assessing personality and psychopathology.* New York: Oxford University Press.

Graham, J. R., Timbrook, R. E., Ben-Porath, Y. S., & Butcher, J. N. (1991). Code-type congruence between MMPI and MMPI-2: Separating fact from artifact. *Journal of Personality Assessment, 57*, 205–215.

Green, S. B., & Kelley, C. K. (1988). Racial bias in prediction with the MMPI for a juvenile delinquent population. *Journal of Personality Assessment, 52*, 263–275.

Greene, R. L. (1980). *The MMPI: An interpretive manual.* Boston: Allyn and Bacon.

Greene, R. L. (1987). Ethnicity and MMPI performance: A review. *Journal of Consulting and Clinical Psychology, 55*, 497–512.

Greene, R. L. (1991). *The MMPI-2/MMPI: An interpretive manual.* Boston: Allyn & Bacon.

Greene, R. L., & Garvin, R. D. (1988). Substance abuse/dependence. In R. L. Greene (Ed.), *The MMPI: Use in specific populations* (pp. 157–197). San Antonio: Grune & Stratton.

Grossman, H. Y., Mostofsky, D. I., & Harrison, R. H. (1986). Psychological aspects of Gilles de la Tourette Syndrome. *Journal of Clinical Psychology, 42*, 228–235.

Gynther, M. D. (1972). White norms and black MMPIs: A prescription for discrimination? *Psychological Bulletin, 78*, 386–402.

Gynther, M. D. (1989). MMPI comparisons of blacks and whites: A review and commentary. *Journal of Clinical Psychology, 45*, 878–883.

Harper, D. C. (1983). Personality correlates and degree of impairment in male adolescents with progressive and nonprogressive physical disorders. *Journal of Clinical Psychology,* *39,* 859–867.

Harper, D. C., & Richman, L. C. (1978). Personality profiles of physically impaired adolescents. *Journal of Clinical Psychology, 34,* 636–642.

Harris, R. E., & Lingoes, J. C. (1955). *Subscales for the MMPI: An aid to profile interpretation.* Department of Psychiatry, University of California School of Medicine and the Langley Porter Clinic, mimeographed materials.

Hathaway, S. R. (1956). Scales 5 (Masculinity-Femininity), 6 (Paranoia), and 8 (Schizophrenia). In G. S. Welsh & W. G. Dahlstrom (Eds.), *Basic readings on the MMPI in psychology and medicine* (pp. 104–111). Minneapolis: University of Minnesota Press.

Hathaway, S. R., & McKinley, J. C. (1942). A multiphasic personality schedule (Minnesota): III. The measurement of symptomatic depression. *Journal of Psychology, 14,* 73–84.

Hathaway, S. R., & Monachesi, E. D. (1963). *Adolescent personality and behavior: MMPI patterns of normal, delinquent, dropout, and other outcomes.* Minneapolis: University of Minnesota Press.

Hathaway, S. R., Monachesi, E. D., & Salasin, S. (1970). A follow-up study of MMPI high 8, schizoid children. In M. Roff & D. F. Ricks (Eds.), *Life history research in psychopathology* (pp. 171–188). Minneapolis: University of Minnesota Press.

Huesmann, L. R., Lefkowitz, M. M., & Eron, L. D. (1978). Sum of MMPI scales F, 4, and 9 as a measure of aggression. *Journal of Consulting and Clinical Psychology, 46,* 1071–1078.

Kelley, C. K., & King, G. D. (1979). Cross-validation of the 2-8/8-2 MMPI code type for young adult psychiatric outpatients. *Journal of Personality Assessment, 43,* 143–149.

King, G. D., & Kelley, C. K. (1977). MMPI behavioral correlates of spike-5 and two-point codetypes with Scale 5 as one elevation. *Journal of Clinical Psychology, 33,* 180–185.

Klinge, V., & Strauss, M. E. (1976). Effects of scoring norms on adolescent psychiatric patients' MMPI profiles. *Journal of Personality Assessment, 40,* 13–17.

Lachar, D. (1974). *The MMPI: Clinical assessment and automated interpretation.* Los Angeles: Western Psychological Services.

Lachar, D., Klinge, V., & Grissell, J. L. (1976). Relative accuracy of automated MMPI narratives generated from adult norm and adolescent norm profiles. *Journal of Consulting and Clinical Psychology, 44,* 20–24.

Lachar, D., & Wrobel, N. H. (1990, August). Predicting adolescent MMPI correlates: Comparative efficacy of self-report and other-informant assessment. In R. C. Colligan (Chair), *The MMPI and adolescents: Historical perspective, current research, and future developments.* Symposium conducted at the Annual Convention of the American Psychological Association, Boston, MA.

Lewandowski, D., & Graham, J. R. (1972). Empirical correlates of frequently occurring two-point code types: A replicated study. *Journal of Consulting and Clinical Psychology, 39,* 467–472.

Lumry, A. E., Gottesman, I. I., & Tuason, V. B. (1982). MMPI state dependency during the course of bipolar psychosis. *Psychiatric Research, 7,* 59–67.

MacAndrew, C. (1965). The differentiation of male alcoholic outpatients from nonalcoholic psychiatric outpatients by means of the MMPI. *Quarterly Journal of Studies on Alcohol, 26,* 238–246.

Marks, P., & Briggs, P. (1972). Adolescent norm tables for the MMPI. In W. G. Dahlstrom, G. S. Welsh, & L. E. Dahlstrom, *An MMPI handbook: Vol. I. Clinical interpretation* (rev. ed., pp. 388–399). Minneapolis: University of Minnesota Press.

Marks, P. A., & Haller, D. L. (1977). Now I lay me down for keeps: A study of adolescent suicide attempts. *Journal of Clinical Psychology, 33,* 390–400.

Marks, P. A., & Seeman, W. (1963). *The actuarial description of personality: An atlas for use with the MMPI.* Baltimore: Williams & Wilkins.

Marks, P. A., Seeman, W., & Haller, D. L. (1974). *The actuarial use of the MMPI with adolescents and adults.* New York: Oxford University Press.

McDonald, R. L., & Gynther, M. D. (1962). MMPI norms for southern adolescent Negroes. *Journal of Social Psychology, 58,* 277–282.

McFarland, S. G., & Sparks, C. M. (1985). Age, education, and the internal consistency of personality scales. *Journal of Personality and Social Psychology, 49,* 1692–1702.

Meehl, P. E. (1951). *Research results for counselors.* St. Paul, MN: State Department of Education.

Meehl, P. E. (1956). Wanted—a good cookbook. *American Psychologist, 11,* 263–272.

Meehl, P. E., & Dahlstrom, W. G. (1960). Objective configural rules for discriminating psychotic from neurotic MMPI profiles. *Journal of Consulting Psychology, 24,* 375–387.

Monroe, L. J., & Marks, P. A. (1977). MMPI differences between adolescent poor and good sleepers. *Journal of Consulting and Clinical Psychology, 45,* 151–152.

Moore, C. D., & Handal, P. J. (1980). Adolescents' MMPI performance, cynicism, estrangement, and personal adjustment as a function of race and sex. *Journal of Clinical Psychology, 36,* 932–936.

Nelson, L. D. (1987). Measuring depression in a clinical population using the MMPI. *Journal of Consulting and Clinical Psychology, 55,* 788–790.

Orr, D. P., Eccles, T., Lawlor, R., & Golden, M. (1986). Surreptitious insulin administration in adolescents with insulin-dependent diabetes mellitus. *Journal of the American Medical Association, 256,* 3227–3230.

Pancoast, D. L., & Archer, R. P. (1988). MMPI adolescent norms: Patterns and trends across 4 decades. *Journal of Personality Assessment, 52,* 691–706.

Pancoast, D. L., Archer, R. P., & Gordon, R. A. (1988). The MMPI and clinical diagnosis: A comparison of classification system outcomes with discharge diagnoses. *Journal of Personality Assessment, 52,* 81–90.

Pritchard, D. A., & Rosenblatt, A. (1980). Racial bias in the MMPI: A methodological review. *Journal of Consulting and Clinical Psychology, 48,* 263–267.

Schuerger, J. M., Foerstner, S. B., Serkownek, K., & Ritz, G. (1987). History and validities of the Serkownek subscales for MMPI Scales 5 and 0. *Psychological Reports, 61,* 227–235.

Spirito, A., Faust, D., Myers, B., & Bechtel, D. (1988). Clinical utility of the MMPI in the evaluation of adolescent suicide attempters. *Journal of Personality Assessment, 52,* 204–211.

Stehbens, J. A., Ehmke, D. A., & Wilson, B. K. (1982). MMPI profiles of rheumatic fever adolescents and adults. *Journal of Clinical Psychology, 38,* 592–596.

Sutker, P. B., Allain, A. N., & Geyer, S. (1980). Female criminal violence and differential MMPI characteristics. *Journal of Consulting and Clinical Psychology, 46,* 1141–1143.

Sutker, P. B., & Archer, R. P. (1979). MMPI characteristics of opiate addicts, alcoholics, and other drug abusers. In C. S. Newmark (Ed.), *MMPI clinical and research trends* (pp. 105–148). New York: Praeger.

Todd, A. L., & Gynther, M. D. (1988). Have MMPI Mf scale correlates changed in the past 30 years? *Journal of Clinical Psychology, 44,* 505–510.

Truscott, D. (1990). Assessment of overcontrolled hostility in adolescence. *Psychological Assessment: A Journal of Consulting and Clinical Psychology, 2,* 145–148.

Walters, G. D. (1983). The MMPI and schizophrenia: A review. *Schizophrenia Bulletin, 9,* 226–246.

Walters, G. D. (1988). Schizophrenia. In R. L. Greene (Ed.). *The MMPI: Use in specific populations* (pp. 50–73). San Antonio: Grune & Stratton.

Williams, C. L., & Butcher, J. N. (1989a). An MMPI study of adolescents: I. Empirical validity of standard scales. *Psychological Assessment: A Journal of Consulting and Clinical Psychology, 1,* 251–259.

Williams, C. L., & Butcher, J. N. (1989b). An MMPI study of adolescents: II. Verification and limitations of code type classification. *Psychological Assessment: A Journal of Consulting and Clinical Psychology, 1,* 260–265.

Wimbish, L. G. (1984). *The importance of appropriate norms for the computerized interpretations of adolescent MMPI profiles.* Unpublished doctoral dissertation, Ohio State University, Columbus, Ohio.

Wrobel, N. H., & Lachar, D. (1990, August). Refining adolescent MMPI interpretation: Is sex a moderator variable? In R. C. Colligan (Chair), *The MMPI and adolescents: Historical perspective, current research, and future developments.* Symposium conducted at the Annual Convention of the American Psychological Association, Boston, MA.

CONTENT AND SUPPLEMENTARY SCALE INTERPRETATION

In addition to the standard or basic validity and clinical scales, many supplementary or special scales have been created for the MMPI. Dahlstrom, Welsh, and Dahlstrom (1972, 1975), for example, noted that more than 450 supplementary scales have been developed for the test instrument. Butcher and Tellegen (1978) observed that there may be more MMPI special scales than there are statements in the MMPI item pool! Clopton (1978, 1979, 1982) and Butcher and Tellegen (1978) provided a critical review of the methodological problems encountered in the construction of MMPI special scales. Two recent texts have been published specifically in the area of MMPI special scale use with the original instrument. Caldwell (1988) provided interpretive information on 104 supplementary scales based on his extensive clinical experience with these measures. Levitt (1989) provided an overview of special scale interpretation that included discussion of the Wiggins (1966) content scales and the Harris-Lingoes subscales (1955).

Although some MMPI special scales, in particular the *MAC* scale (MacAndrew, 1965), have received substantial research attention in both adult and adolescent populations, most MMPI special scales have received relatively little research attention. The interpretive recommendations for these scales are typically based on clinical experience rather than empirical data. Gottesman, Hanson, Kroeker, and Briggs (1987) provided adolescent norms for the original form of the MMPI for a variety of special scales, including Welsh's Anxiety and Repression scales, MacAndrew's Alcoholism scale, the Wiggins content scales, and the Wiener-Harmon Subtle and Obvious subscales.

The MMPI-A special scales appear on two separate profile sheets. Fifteen content scales and six supplementary scales are placed on the

Profile for Content and Supplementary scales, as shown for females in Fig. 6.1. In addition, 28 Harris-Lingoes subscales and three *Si* subscales appear on the Profile for Harris-Lingoes and *Si* subscales, shown for males in Fig. 6.2. The purpose of this chapter is to review these MMPI-A special scales, beginning with the supplementary scales.

SUPPLEMENTARY SCALES

The supplementary scales consist of a set of six measures created by a variety of researchers. Three of the supplementary scales were adopted from the original MMPI with relatively limited modification and were also included in the MMPI-2 (Butcher et al., 1989). These measures include Welsh's (1956) Anxiety and Repression scales, and the MacAndrew Alcoholism scale (MacAndrew, 1965), denoted the *MAC-R* in the MMPI-A. In addition, the Immaturity (*IMM*) scale, the Alcohol/Drug Problem Acknowledgment (*ACK*) scale, and the Alcohol/Drug Problem Proneness (*PRO*) scale are measures created especially for the MMPI-A.

Three general statements may be offered concerning the MMPI-A supplementary scales:

1. The raw score totals for all supplementary scales are converted to T-score values based on linear T-score transformation procedures. Identical to the MMPI-A basic scales and content scales, however, a gray or shaded zone denoting marginal-range elevations for supplementary scales occurs between T scores 60 through 65, inclusive.
2. Although some of the supplementary scales (i.e., Welsh's *A* and *R* scales) may be scored within Stage 1, or the first 350 items of the MMPI-A booklet, most require the administration of the full test booklet.
3. Supplementary scale results should be used to refine, but not replace, the interpretation of the MMPI-A basic scales.

The following section provides a brief overview of each of the MMPI-A supplementary scales. Table 6.1 provides the intercorrelations of the supplementary scales, and Tables 6.2 and 6.3 show the correlations of these measures with the MMPI-A basic scales.

MacAndrew Alcoholism Scale—Revised (*MAC-R*)

The MacAndrew Alcoholism scale (*MAC*) was originally created by MacAndrew in 1965 by contrasting the item responses of 300 male

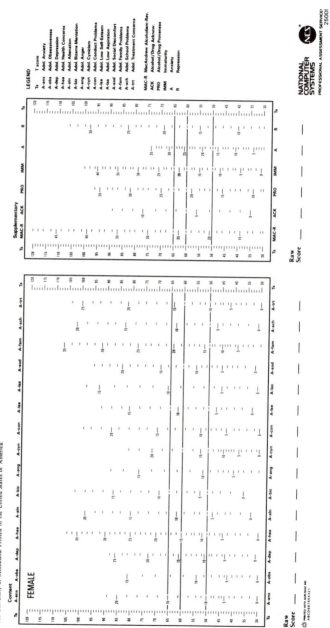

FIGURE 6.1 Profile for content and supplementary scales (female). (Profile form reproduced by permission. Copyright (c) 1992 by the Regents of the University of Minnesota).

221

FIGURE 6.2 Profile for Harris–Lingoes and Si subscales (male). (Profile form reproduced by permission. Copyright

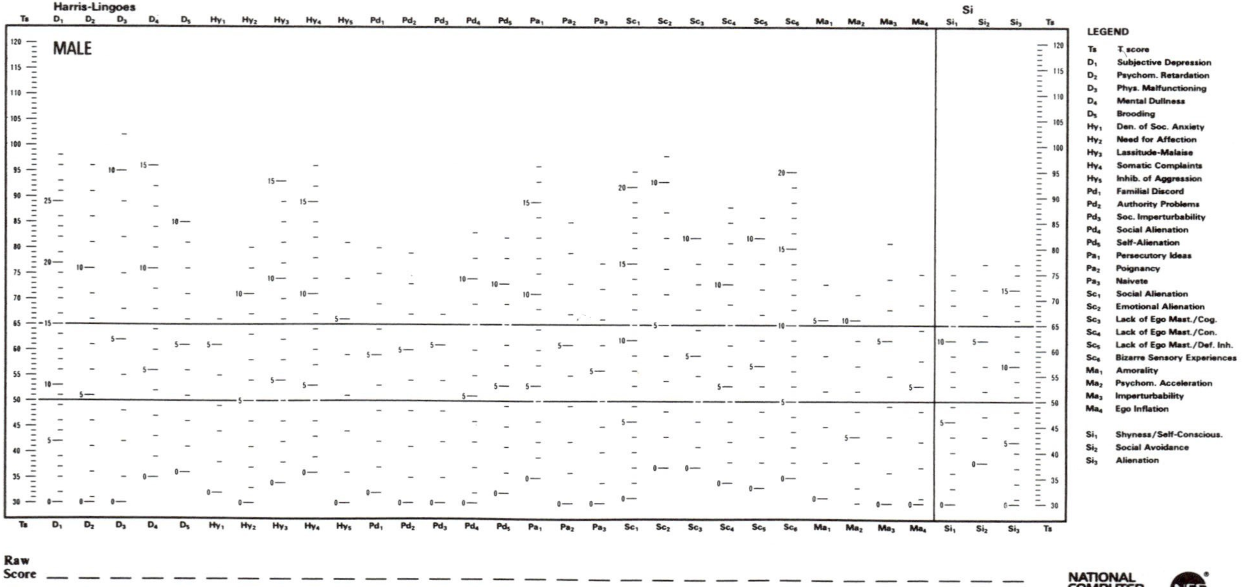

222

TABLE 6.1

Raw Score Intercorrelations of the MMPI-A Supplementary Scales for Male and Female Adolescents in the MMPI-A Normative Sample

	Scales	MAC-R	ACK	PRO	IMM	A	R
				Females			
M	MAC-R		.56	.45	.43	.22	-.38
a	ACK	.57		.57	.64	.38	-.12
l	PRO	.45	.60		.54	.30	-.07
e	IMM	.40	.62	.54		.53	.05
s	A	.23	.41	.33	.58		-.22
	R	-.26	-.09	-.05	.05	-.24	

TABLE 6.2

Raw Score Intercorrelations of the MMPI-A Supplementary and Basic Scales for Female Adolescents in the MMPI-A Normative Sample

Scale	MAC-R	ACK	PRO	IMM	A	R
F_1	.49	.59	.45	.68	.34	.17
F_2	.46	.56	.35	.72	.40	.19
F	.50	.61	.41	.75	.40	.19
L	-.01	-.15	-.25	-.03	-.27	.39
K	-.22	-.30	-.22	-.43	-.73	.37
Hs	.26	.36	.29	.48	.54	.07
D	.02	.24	.22	.43	.54	.32
Hy	.05	.14	.20	.13	.16	.21
Pd	.43	.54	.53	.57	.55	-.02
Mf	-.32	-.23	-.13	-.35	.07	-.32
Pa	.35	.42	.30	.48	.54	.06
Pt	.26	.46	.36	.62	.90	-.17
Sc	.42	.58	.44	.73	.79	-.09
Ma	.52	.48	.41	.40	.43	-.39
Si	-.06	.20	.12	.52	.68	.18

alcoholics with those of 300 male psychiatric patients. Items selected for the *MAC* scale showed the greatest endorsement differences between these two groups (excluding two items directly related to alcohol consumption). The final 49 items selected by these procedures correctly classified 81.5% of subjects in the cross-validation sample of male alcoholic and non-alcoholic psychiatric outpatients (MacAndrew, 1965). Based on their review of the MMPI literature in the substance abuse area, Sutker and Archer (1979) concluded that research findings on the *MAC* scale supported the view that it was "the most promising of current MMPI-derived alcoholism scales" (p. 127).

The *MAC* scale is the only MMPI special scale that has received substantial empirical investigation with adolescents (Archer, 1987b).

TABLE 6.3
Raw Score Intercorrelations of the MMPI-A Supplementary and Basic Scales
for Male Adolescents in the MMPI-A Normative Sample

Scale	MAC-R	ACK	PRO	IMM	A	R
F_1	.35	.61	.47	.70	.29	.22
F_2	.33	.57	.40	.70	.34	.20
F	.36	.62	.45	.74	.34	.22
L	-.06	-.04	-.11	.07	-.30	.47
K	-.24	-.20	-.13	-.30	-.70	.52
Hs	.12	.33	.29	.48	.40	.23
D	-.17	.13	.14	.32	.36	.48
Hy	-.12	.14	.19	.15	-.02	.46
Pd	.33	.54	.55	.58	.46	.05
Mf	-.29	-.08	-.03	-.12	.23	.13
Pa	.27	.48	.33	.54	.46	.17
Pt	.22	.41	.35	.58	.88	-.16
Sc	.30	.58	.46	.74	.74	-.06
Ma	.54	.50	.42	.40	.43	-.47
Si	-.09	.14	.06	.47	.67	.20

This literature has shown MAC scale scores to be related to substance abuse among adolescents in public school settings, and in hospital and residential psychiatric and drug treatment programs. Recommended adolescent MAC raw score cutoff values across assessment settings have ranged from Wolfson and Erbaugh's (1984) cutoff of 24 for females and 26 for males to Archer's (1987b) recommended cutoff of 28 for both male and female adolescents. Recent findings by Gantner, Graham, and Archer (in press) indicate a raw-score cutoff value of 28 for males and 27 for females provided maximum accurate classification of substance abusers from psychiatric inpatients, whereas values of 26 for males and 25 for females provided optimal discrimination of substance abusers from a sample of normal high school students. Further, as shown in Tables 6.4 and 6.5, findings by Archer and Klinefelter (1992) indicate that the probability of obtaining an elevated MAC scale score is associated with the type of basic scale MMPI codetype produced by an adolescent. Adolescents producing the 4-9/9-4 code, for example, were much more likely to produce elevated MAC scores, whereas adolescents producing the 2-3/3-2 code were more likely to produce lower-range MAC scale scores.

Similar to findings in adult populations, high MAC scores among adolescents appear to be related to the abuse of a variety of drugs in addition to alcohol. Andrucci, Archer, Pancoast, and Gordon (1989), for example, found high MAC scores related to abuse of amphetamines, barbiturates, cocaine, hallucinogens, and marijuana. In addition to indicating the possibility of substance abuse problems, elevated MAC

TABLE 6.4
MMPI Codetype Classification and MAC Scale Elevations at Two Criterion
Levels for Male Adolescent Psychiatric Patients

Codetype	MAC Cutoff Scores				MAC Mean	MAC S.D.
	<24	≥24	<28	≥28		
3	8(47%)	9 (53%)	15(88%)	2(12%)	23.7	4.7
4	4 (8%)	44 (92%)	17(35%)	31(65%)	28.8	4.0
5	10(36%)	18 (64%)	20(71%)	8(29%)	24.7	4.0
9	3(11%)	24 (89%)	8(30%)	19(70%)	29.3	4.6
13-31	10(43%)	13 (57%)	15(65%)	8(35%)	24.3	5.9
14-41	1 (6%)	15 (94%)	5(31%)	11(69%)	29.3	4.2
15-51	1 (9%)	10 (91%)	6(55%)	5(45%)	27.7	4.9
17-71	0 (0%)	12(100%)	9(75%)	3(25%)	26.4	2.4
18-81	0 (0%)	15(100%)	6(40%)	9(60%)	29.4	3.7
23-32	9(64%)	5 (36%)*[a]	13(93%)	1 (7%)	20.6	5.4
24-42	7(25%)	21 (75%)	20(71%)	8(29%)	25.3	4.0
25-52	11(79%)	3 (21%)*[a]	12(86%)	2(14%)	21.6	4.5
34-43	3(14%)	18 (86%)	9(43%)	12(57%)	26.9	4.3
35-53	2(20%)	8 (80%)	5(50%)	5(50%)	27.4	3.6
45-54	9(38%)	15 (62%)	15(63%)	9(37%)	25.3	5.0
46-64	1 (2%)	42 (98%)*[a]	9(21%)	34(79%)*[b]	30.1	3.6
47-74	0 (0%)	11(100%)	2(18%)	9(82%)	30.1	3.0
48-84	3(19%)	13 (81%)	9(56%)	7(44%)	27.4	4.3
49-94	1 (3%)	38 (97%)*[a]	8(21%)	31(79%)*[b]	31.5	4.2
56-65	3(25%)	9 (75%)	7(58%)	5(42%)	25.6	5.1
67-76	2(20%)	8 (80%)	5(50%)	5(50%)	27.4	4.9
68-86	5(36%)	9 (64%)	8(57%)	6(43%)	26.3	5.4
69-96	1 (7%)	14 (93%)	3(20%)	12(80%)	31.5	5.9
78-87	3(17%)	15 (83%)	6(33%)	12(67%)	28.8	5.0
No Code	70(31%)	153 (69%)	141(63%)	82(37%)*[b]	26.1	4.5
Other Codes	32(27%)	88(73%)	64(53%)	56(47%)	26.8	5.4
Total	199(24%)	630(76%)	437(53%)	392(47%)	27.0	5.0

Note. From Archer and Klinefelter (1992). Copyright (c) 1992 by Lawrence Erlbaum Associates, Inc. Reprinted by permission. Values within parentheses indicate percent of cases occurring at varying MAC scale values within specific codetypes.
   * = p<.002; [a] = Significant MAC elevation frequency difference found for codetype comparisons using MAC ≥24 criterion; [b] = Significant MAC elevation frequency difference found for codetype comparisons using MAC ≥28 criterion.

scale scores have also been associated with a variety of personality characteristics. For example, Archer et al. (1989) found high MAC adolescents to be described as assertive, independent, self-indulgent, undercontrolled, and much more likely to have an arrest record and to receive conduct disorder diagnoses. These findings are consistent with earlier reports by Rathus, Fox, and Ortins (1980), who found that MAC

TABLE 6.5
MMPI Codetype Classification and MAC Scale Elevations at Two Criterion
Levels for Female Adolescent Psychiatric Patients

Codetype	MAC Cutoff Scores				MAC Mean	MAC S.D.
	<24	≥24	<28	≥28		
4	8(31%)	18 (69%)	17(65%)	9(35%)	25.5	4.4
9	6(29%)	15 (71%)	18(86%)	3(14%)	24.6	3.5
12–21	14(74%)	5 (26%)	15(79%)	4(21%)	22.9	4.5
13–31	7(41%)	10 (59%)	12(71%)	5(19%)	24.1	4.2
18–81	7(41%)	10 (59%)	11(65%)	6(35%)	24.9	5.1
23–32	12(86%)	2 (14%)[*a]	14(100%)	0 (0%)	19.3	3.6
24–42	15(44%)	19 (56%)	28(82%)	6(18%)	23.3	4.6
46–64	11(50%)	11 (50%)	14(64%)	8(36%)	25.3	4.8
48–84	8(36%)	14 (64%)	15(68%)	7(32%)	25.0	4.7
49–94	3(10%)	27 (90%)[*a]	11(37%)	19(63%)[*b]	8.3	3.5
69–96	0 (0%)	10(100%)	3(30%)	7(70%)[*b]	30.2	4.0
78–87	3(25%)	9 (75%)	9(75%)	3(25%)	24.8	3.3
89–98	0 (0%)	11(100%)	2(18%)	9(82%)[*b]	30.1	2.8
No Code Other	65(48%)	70 (52%)	13(84%)	22(16%)	23.1	4.4
Codes	69(54%)	59 (46%)	105(82%)	23(18%)	23.2	4.7
Total	228(44%)	290 (56%)	387(75%)	131(25%)	24.1	4.8

Note. From Archer and Klinefelter (1992). Copyright (c) 1992 by Lawrence Erlbaum Associates, Inc. Reprinted by permission. Values within parentheses indicate percent of cases occurring at varying MAC scale values within specific codetypes.
* = p<.004; [a] = Significant MAC elevation frequency difference found for codetype comparisons using MAC ≥24 criterion; [b] = Significant MAC elevation frequency difference found for codetype comparisons using MAC ≥28 criterion.

scale scores were related to delinquent behaviors, as well as results by Wisniewski, Glenwick, and Graham (1985) who found that high MAC scores in a high school sample were related to a higher number of disciplinary incidents and lower grade point averages. MacAndrew (1981) described individuals who produce elevations on MAC as pursuing a bold, impulsive lifestyle, with little concern for the consequences of behaviors.

The MAC scale has probably received extensive attention in the adolescent MMPI literature because of the importance many clinicians and researchers have placed on drug and alcohol problems within this age group. Although the MAC scale holds substantial potential as a useful screening device for substance abuse among adolescents, several cautions appear appropriate regarding its use. Archer (1987b), for example, observed that the findings in adult samples suggest that the MAC scale may have little diagnostic utility among Black respondents, and that substantial caution should be used when interpreting the MAC in non-White populations. According to Greene (1991), accuracy hit rates are probably too low to justify the use of the *MAC* as a screening device to detect substance abuse problems among patients in medical treatment settings. Additionally, Gottesman and Prescott (1989) observed that lower-range cutting scores, such as a value of 24 or above, which has frequently been employed for adults, would misclassify a very high percentage of normal adolescents as a result of false positive errors. For example, the *MAC-R* scale mean value for adolescents in the MMPI-A sample was 21.07 for males and 19.73 for females (Butcher et al., 1992). Both Gottesman and Prescott and Greene (1988) noted the critical effects of substance abuse base rates on the clinical usefulness of the *MAC* scale. Many studies have examined the validity of the *MAC* scale based on equal, or nearly equal, samples of substance abuse and non-substance abuse groups. These studies have often yielded impressive rates of accurate classification of approximately 80% (e.g., MacAndrew, 1979). However, when hit rates are recalculated using more realistic estimates of the base rate of substance abuse, substantially less impressive accuracy is often obtained (e.g., Gantner et al., in press; Gottesman & Prescott, 1989).

In the creation of the MMPI-A, a revised form of the *MAC* scale (i.e., the *MAC-R* scale) was developed. The MMPI-A *MAC-R* scale contains 49 items and is identical in length to the original *MAC* scale. Forty-five of the original *MAC* items were retained in the *MAC-R* scale, with four *MAC-R* items added. These latter items were used to replace the four items deleted from the original *MAC* scale in the formation of the MMPI-A. Table 6.6 provides examples of *MAC-R* items. Thus far, there have been no studies on the comparability of the *MAC* and *MAC-R* scales for the MMPI-A. Research by Greene, Arredondo, and Davis (1990), however, indicates that the original *MAC* scale and the *MAC-R* scale of the MMPI-2 appear to produce comparable scores and may be used in a similar manner by clinicians. In general, it is expected that the following correlates would be related to raw score values of 28 or greater on the *MAC-R* scale of the MMPI-A:

- Increased likelihood of alcohol or drug abuse problems.
- Interpersonally assertive and dominant.
- Self-indulgent and egocentric.
- Unconventional and impulsive.
- Greater likelihood of conduct disorder diagnoses.
- Greater likelihood of legal involvement and violation of social norms.

In addition, individuals who produce low-range scores on the *MAC-R* might be expected to be dependent, conservative, indecisive, overcon-

TABLE 6.6
Items From the MMPI-A MacAndrew Alcoholism Scale—Revised (MAC-R)

Examples of items scored if true

7.   I like to read newspaper articles on crime.

46.   I am a very sociable person.

80.   I have been suspended from school one or more times for bad behavior.

99.   I enjoy a race or game more when I bet on it.

177.*   I sometimes think about killing myself.

342.*   I can express my true feelings only when I drink.

407.   The person to whom I have been most attached and whom I have most admired is a woman (mother, sister, aunt, or other woman).

429.*   I have some habits that are really harmful.

Examples of items scored if false

70.   I am certainly lacking in self-confidence.

153.   I like school.

159.   I am worried about sex.

305.   I have more trouble concentrating than others seem to have.

Note. Items reproduced from the MMPI-A by permission. Copyright (c) 1992 by the Regents of the University of Minnesota.

* Denotes a new item added to the original MAC scale.

trolled, and sensation-avoidant. As noted by MacAndrew (1981), individuals who abuse alcohol but produce low *MAC* scores (false negatives) are likely to be neurotic individuals who may use alcohol to self-medicate their affective distress.

The Alcohol/Drug Problem Acknowledgment (*ACK*) Scale

The Alcohol/Drug Problem Acknowledgment (*ACK*) scale was developed for the MMPI-A to assess an adolescent's willingness to acknowledge alcohol or drug use-related symptoms, attitudes, or beliefs (Butcher et al., 1992). The *ACK* scale consists of 13 items initially selected based on the rational judgment that item content was relevant to drug use, and further refined based on statistical criteria, including item correlations. Table 6.7 provides examples of items found on the Alcohol/Drug Problem Acknowledgment scale. Elevations on the *ACK* scale indicate the extent to which an adolescent acknowledged or admitted alcohol and/or drug problems in their MMPI-A self-description. It should be noted, however, that not all items on the *ACK* scale directly involve an acknowledgment of drug use. Some items, for example items 81 and 249, deal with attitudes, beliefs, or behaviors that may be associated with drug use, but do not directly indicate the presence or absence of alcohol or drug use behaviors. For both boys and girls in the

TABLE 6.7
Items From the Alcohol/Drug Problem Acknowledgment (ACK) Scale

Examples of items scored if true
81.   At times I have a strong urge to do something harmful or shocking.
144.   I have a problem with alcohol or drugs.
247.   I have used alcohol excessively.
342.   I can express my true feelings only when I drink.
467.   I enjoy using marijuana.
Examples of items scored if false
249.   I have never been in trouble with the law.
431.   Talking over problems and worries with someone is often more helpful than taking drugs or medicines.

Note. Items reproduced from the MMPI-A by permission. Copyright (c) 1992 by the Regents of the University of Minnesota.

MMPI-A sample, the mean raw score for *ACK* was approximately 4, and a raw score total of 9 or greater converts to T-score values that exceed T = 70.

The Alcohol/Drug Problem Proneness (*PRO*) Scale

The Alcohol/Drug Problem Proneness (*PRO*) scale consists of 36 items. These items were empirically selected based on item endorsement differences found between adolescents in alcohol and drug treatment programs and adolescents receiving inpatient psychiatric services (Butcher et al., 1992). Thus, the scale construction method used for *PRO* is similar to that employed in the development of the *MAC* scale. Based on cross-validated research findings noted in the MMPI-A manual (Butcher et al., 1992), T-score values of 65 and greater are associated with an increased potential for the development of alcohol and drug problems. The 36 items in the *PRO* scale cover a wide variety of content including familial characteristics, peer group features, antisocial behaviors and beliefs, and academic interests and behaviors. Table 6.8 provides illustrations of *PRO* scale items.

The Immaturity (*IMM*) Scale

The Immaturity (*IMM*) scale was developed by Archer, Pancoast, and Gordon (1991) as a supplementary scale for the MMPI-A. The *IMM* scale assesses psychological maturation during adolescence using Loevinger's (1976) concept of ego development as a conceptual focus. Items for the *IMM* scale were selected based on a multistage procedure involving both rational and statistical criteria. In the initial stage, MMPI-TX item correlations were computed with scores derived from the Holt (1980)

TABLE 6.8

Items From the Alcohol/Drug Problem Proneness (PRO) Scale

Examples of items scored if true

32.   I have sometimes stolen things.

57.   My parents do not like my friends.

101.   In school I have sometimes been sent to the principal for bad behavior.

191.   My parents often object to the kind of people I go around with.

381.   One or more members of my family are very nervous.

462.   I often have to lie in order to get by.

476.   I have a close friend whom I can share secrets with.

Examples of items scored if false

40.   My judgment is better than it ever was.

153.   I like school.

188.   I like science.

410.   I spend most of my spare time by myself.

424.   I am not feeling much stress these days.

451.   We don't have trouble talking to each other in my family.

463.   I have no close friends.

Note. Items reproduced from the MMPI-A by permission. Copyright (c) 1992 by the Regents of the University of Minnesota.

Short-Form adaptation of the Loevinger and Wessler (1970) Sentence Completion Test of ego development in a sample of 222 normal adolescents. Preliminary items were selected for the *IMM* scale based on the occurrence of correlation coefficients achieving a significance level of ≤.01. In the second stage of scale construction, raters independently evaluated the degree to which preliminary items were related to Loevinger's concept of ego development. Items were retained in the preliminary *IMM* scale if at least four of the six raters were in agreement on the appropriateness of the item to the ego development construct. In the third stage, preliminary *IMM* scale items were eliminated if the removal of the item increased the scale's internal reliability (alpha coefficient value) in either the normal sample of 222 adolescents or in a sample of 122 adolescent inpatients who had completed the MMPI-TX. Finally, each of the 704 items in the experimental MMPI-TX Form were examined in terms of their correlations with the *IMM* scale. New items were added to the *IMM* scale if items demonstrated both a conceptual and statistical relationship to the ego development construct. The final form of the *IMM* scale consists of 43 items. Examples of these items are shown in Table 6.9. The alpha coefficient value for the *IMM* scale in the MMPI-A normative sample was .83 for females and .80 for males. As expected, *IMM* mean raw score values were significantly higher for males than for females in both the clinical sample (18.69 versus 14.88) and the MMPI-A normative sample (13.47 versus 11.75). This gender-related difference in *IMM* mean scores is consistent with conclusions

TABLE 6.9
Items From the MMPI-A Immaturity (IMM) Scale

Examples of items scored if true

16.   I am sure I get a raw deal from life.
20.   No one seems to understand me.
63.   It would be better if almost all laws were thrown away.
307. Bad words, often terrible words, come into my mind and I cannot get rid of them.
351. The only interesting part of newspapers is the comic strips.
358. I do not feel I can plan my own future.
405. I hate my whole family.
425. I think my teachers at school are stupid.
453. Others say I throw temper tantrums to get my way.

Examples of items scored if false

153. I like school.
322. I enjoy children.
336. I do not mind meeting strangers.
419. My main goals in life are within my reach.
431. Talking over problems and worries with someone is often more helpful than taking drugs or medicines.
436. I want to go to college.
448. Most people think they can depend on me.
476. I have a close friend whom I can share secrets with.

Note. Items reproduced from the MMPI-A by permission. Copyright (c) 1992 by the Regents of the University of Minnesota.

from a recent review (Cohn, 1991) of results from 63 studies using the Sentence Completion Test. Cohn reported that females consistently showed higher developmental levels than males during adolescence.

The 43 items in the *IMM* scale concern aspects of personality including lack of self-confidence, externalization of blame, lack of insight and introspection, interpersonal and social discomfort and alienation, "living for the present" without concern for future consequences, the occurrence of hostile and antisocial attitudes, and egocentricity and self-centeredness. High scores on the *IMM* scale would be expected to be associated with impulsive adolescents who have a limited capacity for self-awareness. Their egocentricity is likely to impair their ability to engage in reciprocal and mutually satisfying interpersonal relationships, and their cognitive processes could be characterized as concrete and simplistic. Within Loevinger's model of ego development, individuals producing elevated *IMM* scores are likely to reflect a *preconformist* stage of development. Interpersonal relationships during the preconformist stage have been described as opportunistic, demanding, and exploitive (Loevinger, 1976).

Preliminary data on the *IMM* scale (Archer, Pancoast, & Gordon, 1991) from both normal and clinical samples indicate that adolescents who produced high scores on this measure had a higher incidence of school difficulties and problems. Additionally, data analyses from the inpatient sample suggest the following correlates may be applied to adolescents who produce high *IMM* scores:

- Easily frustrated and quick to anger.
- Impatient, loud, and boisterous.
- Tends to tease or bully others.
- Not trustworthy or dependable.
- Likely to have a history of academic and social difficulties.
- Defiant and resistant.

Additionally, adolescents who produce low scores on the *IMM* scale are likely to be described as controlled, stable, patient, cooperative, and predictable.

Welsh's Anxiety (*A*) and Repression (*R*) Scales

As noted by Graham (1990), a large volume of factor analytic literature on the MMPI scale data has typically found two basic MMPI dimensions or factors accounting for a majority of basic scale score variance. The first factor has been assigned a variety of labels, including *general maladjustment* and *lack of ego resiliency* and the second factor has been referred to as *ego control* or *inhibition*. Welsh (1956) developed the Anxiety (*A*) and Repression (*R*) scales to assess the respondent's standing along these first and second dimensions, respectively.

The Anxiety scale was originally created as a 39-item scale keyed in such a manner that higher scores on the *A* scale were associated with a greater degree of psychopathology. High scores have been described as reflective of individuals who are maladjusted, anxious, depressed, pessimistic, inhibited, and uncomfortable (Graham, 1990). Although these adjectives are largely negative in tone, it has also been noted that high scores on the *A* scale are associated with substantial emotional distress that may serve as a motivator for positive change in the psychotherapeutic process. In contrast, low scores on the *A* scale have been related to a preference for activity, freedom from anxiety and discomfort, sociability, manipulativeness, and impulsivity (Graham, 1990). Archer, Gordon, Anderson, and Giannetti (1989) examined special scale correlates in a sample of 68 adolescent inpatients. These authors reported that the high-*A* adolescent could be described as fearful, anxious, guilt-prone, overwhelmed, and self-critical. High *A* adolescents also tended to be viewed by both self (on other self-report instruments) and others, including family members and treatment staff, as significantly more maladjusted than other adolescent inpatients. MMPI scale *A* and basic scale *Pt* were highly correlated ($r = .90$) in this sample, and a higher incidence of presenting problems related to suicide attempts, thoughts, and ideations were related to elevations on the *A* scale.

In the MMPI-A, Welsh's *A* scale has been reduced to 35 items. Table 6.10 provides examples of these items, including two examples of items deleted from the *A* scale.

In general, the following correlates are associated with elevations on scale *A*:

- Tense and anxious.
- Fearful and ruminative.
- Maladjusted and ineffective.
- Self-critical and guilty.
- Overwhelmed.

The Repression scale originally consisted of 40 items developed by Welsh (1956) to assess the second dimension that emerges when the standard MMPI scales are subjected to factor analysis. Like the *A* scale, the *R* scale appears in the original version of the MMPI, the MMPI-2, and in the MMPI-A. In the MMPI-A, the *R* scale has been reduced to 33

TABLE 6.10
Items From the MMPI-A Anxiety (A) Scale

Examples of items scored if true

28.   I find it hard to keep my mind on a task or job.
35.   I have had periods of days, weeks, or months when I couldn't take care of things because I couldn't "get going."
53.   I wish I could be as happy as others seem to be.
62.   Most of the time I feel blue.
121. Criticism or scolding hurts me terribly.
129. I have often lost out on things because I couldn't make up my mind soon enough.
203. I brood a great deal.
255. Life is a strain for me much of the time.
270. I am easily embarrassed.

All items scored if false

360. I very seldom have spells of the blues.

Examples of MMPI items deleted from the MMPI-A A scale

I have several times had a change of heart about my life work (MMPI Item 465).
I feel tired a good deal of the time (MMPI Item 544).

Note. Items reproduced from the MMPI and MMPI-A by permission. Copyright (c) by the Regents of the University of Minnesota.

items, all of which are scored in the *false* direction. Table 6.11 provides examples of items retained and deleted in the MMPI-A *R* scale. In research by Archer et al. (1989), *R* scale scores were found to be negatively correlated with scale *9* and *MAC* scale values, and positively correlated with several scales, including *L*, *K*, and the neurotic triad (scales *Hs*, *D*, and *Hy*). This finding is consistent with expectations based on the loading patterns reported for the second factor of the MMPI. This factor typically shows positive loadings on the neurotic triad and a negative loading on scale *9* (Graham, 1990; Greene, 1991). Significant correlates for the high *R* scale adolescent in the Archer et al. study included the following:

- Overcontrolled.
- Shows little feeling.
- Inhibited and constricted.
- Pessimistic and defeated.

In contrast, adolescents who produced low scores on *R* were described as talkative, spontaneous, and optimistic. Archer (1987b) also noted, however, that low *R* scores among adolescent psychiatric patients are related to aggressiveness, impulsivity, argumentativeness, and a tendency to employ acting-out defense mechanisms.

TABLE 6.11
Items From the MMPI-A Repression (R) Scale

Examples of items scored if true
    None
Examples of items scored if false
1.   I like mechanics magazines.
10.   I am about as able to work as I ever was.
34.   At times I feel like smashing things.
112.   I do not worry about catching diseases.
115.   I frequently find it necessary to stand up for what I think is right.
180.   I like to flirt.
277.   My mother or father often make me obey even when I think it is unreasonable.
289.   At times I am all full of energy.
329.   If given the chance I would make a good leader of people.
335.   I enjoy the excitement of a crowd.
348.   I would like to wear expensive clothes.
Examples of MMPI items deleted from the MMPI-A R Scale
I am often inclined to go out of my way to win a point with someone who has opposed me (MMPI Item 447).
I like repairing a door latch (MMPI Item 550).

Note. Items reproduced from the MMPI and MMPI-A by permission. Copyright (c) 1992 by the Regents of the University of Minnesota.

CONTENT SCALES

As noted by Butcher, Graham, Williams, and Ben-Porath (1990), several approaches have been taken to the analysis of the content of MMPI responses. On the individual item level, a variety of "critical item" lists have been constructed that are composed of items believed to have a special significance in the task of clinical assessment. Grayson (1951), for example, employed a rational construction strategy to identify 38 items believed to serve as markers of significant symptomatology. Other critical item lists have also been constructed to analyze individual item responses, including those by Caldwell (1969), Koss and Butcher (1973), and Lachar and Wrobel (1979). The 99 Lachar and Wrobel critical items that appear in the MMPI-A, and the 12 deleted items, are shown in Appendix F.

A second approach to content analysis is exemplified by the work of Harris and Lingoes (1955). Since most of the MMPI basic scales contain a variety of content areas (i.e., the scales are heterogeneous), it is often difficult to infer what area of scale content was actually endorsed by a respondent in the production of a particular T-score elevation. This issue is particularly pronounced for T scores representing marginal clinical-range elevations. To deal with this problem, Harris and Lingoes developed subscales for basic scales 2, 3, 4, 6, 8, and 9 by rationally grouping similar items into homogeneous content areas for each of these scales. The resulting 28 subscales have been carried over into the MMPI-2 and the MMPI-A. In addition, three subscales for the *Si* scale are available for the MMPI-A, based on the work of Ben-Porath, Hostetler, Butcher, and Graham (1989).

On a separate and third level of content analysis, the MMPI may be discussed and interpreted in relation to a number of content dimensions represented by the total item pool. Because Hathaway and McKinley utilized external criterion groups to create the original MMPI basic scales, these clinical groups served to define the measurement focus of the inventory. Such a development method, however, made no effort to use the full item pool in deriving the maximum number of meaningful dimensions of psychopathology in construction of clinical scales. Indeed, the basic MMPI scales utilized only about half of the total item pool (Nichols, 1987). Wiggins (1966) offered an approach to MMPI scale construction and measurement that was based on a more complete utilization of this item pool. Beginning with the 26 content categories described by Hathaway and McKinley (see Chapter 1 for a description) to classify the total content array of all MMPI items, Wiggins derived 13 homogeneous content scales using a combination of rational and statistical scale construction methods. Nichols provided a 1987 monograph concerning the use of the Wiggins content scales in clinical interpretation of the original MMPI. Correlate patterns for the Wiggins content scales in adolescent samples were reported by Archer and Gordon (1991), Wrobel (1991), and Wrobel and Gdowski (1989). Based on a recognition of the usefulness of the Wiggins scales, content scales were developed for the MMPI-2 by Butcher, Graham, Williams, and Ben-Porath (1990) and for the MMPI-A by Williams, Butcher, Ben-Porath, and Graham (in press). The following section examines the analysis of content in the MMPI-A, as represented by the MMPI-A content scales, and by the Harris-Lingoes and *Si* subscales.

MMPI-A Content Scales

The 15 MMPI-A content scales exhibit a substantial degree of overlap with many of the MMPI-2 content scales, as well as several of the Wiggins content scales. As described in the MMPI-A manual (Butcher et al., 1992), the MMPI-A content scales were created in a series of five stages: The first stage involved an initial identification of those MMPI-2 content scales (and items within MMPI-2 content scales) that were appropriate for adaptation to the MMPI-A. Stage two of the development process involved the refinement of MMPI-A content scales by the addition or deletion of specific items designed to improve the psychometric properties, including reliability and validity coefficients, of these scales. The third stage included a rational review and examination of scale content in order to evaluate item relevance in terms of the target construct. Stage four involved further statistical refinement of the scales, including the elimination of items that showed higher correlations with content scales other than the content scale on which the item was scored. The final stage involved the selection of narrative descriptors for each content scale utilizing a combination of empirical findings and logical inferences based on the item content of the scale. In addition to the MMPI-A normative sample, Williams et al. utilized a clinical sample of 420 boys and 293 girls from Minneapolis treatment facilities to refine the MMPI-A content scales and to identify correlate patterns for these measures.

Several general statements may be made concerning the MMPI-A content scales. These points may be listed as follows:

1. The interpretation of MMPI-A content scales requires the administration of all 478 items in the MMPI-A booklet. The administration of the first stage of the MMPI-A booklet (i.e., the first 350 items) will not be sufficient to score the content scales.

2. Most of the MMPI-A content scales are predominantly composed of items from the original MMPI instrument. The School Problems (*A-sch*) scale and the Negative Treatment Indicators (*A-trt*) scale, however, consist primarily of items that do not appear on the original test instrument. In contrast, the Cynicism (*A-cyn*) scale consists entirely of items derived from the original form of the MMPI.

3. Eleven of the 15 MMPI-A content scales are heavily overlapping with MMPI-2 content scales in terms of item membership and the constructs that are the focus of measurement. The content scales unique to the MMPI-A form are Alienation (*A-aln*), Low Aspiration (*A-las*), School Problems (*A-sch*), and Conduct Problems (*A-con*).

4. Uniform T-score transformation procedures are consistently used in converting MMPI-A content scale raw score totals to T-score values. Thus, the content scales and eight basic clinical scales (*1, 2, 3, 4, 6, 7, 8,* and *9*) were the only MMPI-A scales to receive uniform T scores.

5. The *true* response is typically the deviant endorsement direction for MMPI-A content scales, with the exception of Health Concerns (*A-hea*) and Low Aspirations (*A-las*). The MMPI-A Obsessiveness (*A-obs*) and Cynicism (*A-cyn*) content scales, for example, consist entirely of items scored in the *true* direction, and the Bizarre Mentation (*A-biz*) and Anger (*A-ang*) scales each contain only one item scored in the *false* direction. Most MMPI-A content scales, therefore, involve the affirmation of the occurrence or presence of various psychiatric symptoms.

6. MMPI-A content scales, similar to the MMPI-2 and the Wiggins content scales, are composed of items that are face-valid and obvious in terms of their relevancy to psychopathology. The MMPI-A content scales, therefore, are easily influenced by an adolescent's tendency to underreport or overreport symptomatology. The MMPI-A interpreter should carefully evaluate the validity of the adolescent's responses, particularly the accuracy component of technical validity, prior to interpreting MMPI-A content scales.

7. The MMPI-A content scales, like their counterparts on the MMPI-2, exhibit relatively high internal reliability as reflected in alpha coefficient values (range .55 to .83). This characteristic might be expected given the scale construction method employed to develop these measures. Nevertheless, it is likely that many of the MMPI-A content scales contain several content dimensions or subcomponents and it should be possible to develop content component scales (i.e., subscales) for these scales in a manner similar to that used by Ben-Porath and Sherwood (in press) for the content scales of the MMPI-2.

8. MMPI-A content scale results may be used by interpreters to supplement, augment, and refine the interpretation of the MMPI-A basic clinical scales. Until much more research is available for these

measures, however, MMPI-A content scales should *not* be used independently of the basic scale profile.

Relatively limited information is available concerning the interpretation of the MMPI-A content scales. Empirically derived content scale descriptors are reported by Williams et al. (in press) for a clinical sample of 420 male and 293 female adolescents and by Archer and Gordon (1991) in an independent sample of 64 male and 58 female adolescent psychiatric inpatients. In addition, the examination of item content within the MMPI-A content scales can offer some inferences concerning the characteristics of individuals who produce elevated scores on these measures. As with all other MMPI-A scales, T scores >65 may be regarded as high scores and T-score values between 60 and 65, inclusive, may be described as marginally elevated. As additional research is conducted with the content scales, it should become possible to provide fuller descriptions of the clinical correlate patterns for these measures. Such research may also lead to an understanding of the ways in which the content scales interrelate, and interact with other MMPI-A scales including the basic or standard scales. Table 6.12 provides the intercorrelations for MMPI-A content scales in the normative sample, and Tables 6.13, 6.14, 6.15, and 6.16 provide the correlational values of these measures with the MMPI-A basic scales and the Wiggins content scales, respectively. As shown in Tables 6.15 and 6.16, there is a very high degree of interrelationship between eight of the Wiggins content scales and seven counterparts on the MMPI-A. Specifically, the following Wiggins scale—MMPI-A content scale pairs produced correlations of $r =$ .79 or greater for both genders: Depression and *A-dep*; Poor Health and *A-hea*; Organic Symptoms and *A-hea*; Family Problems and *A-fam*; Authority Conflict and *A-cyn*; Hostility and *A-ang*; Psychoticism and *A-biz*; and Social Maladjustment and *A-sod*. Two of the Wiggins content scales, however, including Feminine Interests and Religious Fundamentalism, produced consistently low correlations with MMPI-A content scales, and three other Wiggins scales (Poor Morale, Phobias, and Hypomania) produced moderate to high correlations involving several MMPI-A scales. Appendix G of this text provides a list of the Wiggins scale items retained in the MMPI-A. With the exception of the Religious Fundamentalism scale, the Wiggins content scales have retained a majority of scale items in the MMPI-A, with seven scales maintaining over 80% of their item pools. Table 6.17 provides an overview of the status of the Wiggins content scales within the structure of the MMPI-A.

Adolescent-Anxiety (A-anx) Scale. The MMPI-A Anxiety content scale consists of 21 items, 20 of which also appear on the MMPI-2 Anxiety

TABLE 6.12

Raw Score Intercorrelations of MMPI-A Content Scales for 815 Females and 805 Males in the MMPI-A Normative Sample

Females (above diagonal); Males (below diagonal)

Scale	A-anx	A-obs	A-dep	A-hea	A-aln	A-biz	A-ang	A-cyn	A-con	A-lse	A-las	A-sod	A-fam	A-sch	A-trt
A-anx		.69	.74	.56	.61	.56	.51	.54	.41	.62	.32	.31	.53	.41	.62
A-obs	.66		.61	.42	.48	.51	.54	.60	.44	.57	.31	.24	.44	.39	.64
A-dep	.73	.55		.53	.70	.56	.43	.50	.47	.74	.42	.42	.57	.50	.71
A-hea	.50	.27	.48		.50	.56	.33	.34	.37	.46	.26	.29	.41	.45	.48
A-aln	.62	.46	.69	.47		.55	.38	.42	.50	.63	.37	.54	.61	.52	.74
A-biz	.54	.45	.56	.53	.53		.44	.49	.52	.48	.24	.26	.45	.44	.53
A-ang	.50	.52	.41	.23	.40	.36		.52	.54	.38	.27	.15	.47	.43	.49
A-cyn	.43	.57	.37	.07	.54	.37	.51		.52	.45	.22	.23	.46	.40	.61
A-con	.36	.44	.40	.22	.38	.41	.50	.47		.45	.37	.17	.53	.58	.56
A-lse	.60	.55	.68	.47	.62	.53	.36	.35	.37		.49	.48	.48	.51	.69
A-las	.36	.22	.39	.39	.39	.32	.16	.10	.30	.45		.31	.35	.53	.48
A-sod	.43	.26	.47	.35	.55	.33	.14	.14	.03	.49	.33		.28	.30	.47
A-fam	.53	.43	.59	.48	.61	.51	.44	.35	.50	.51	.41	.28		.52	.58
A-sch	.46	.40	.53	.48	.53	.50	.40	.31	.56	.52	.48	.29	.60		.58
A-trt	.60	.58	.64	.42	.67	.56	.43	.49	.48	.67	.48	.45	.56	.58	

TABLE 6.13

Raw Score Intercorrelations of the Content and Basic Scales for Female Adolescents in the MMPI-A Normative Sample

	A-anx	A-obs	A-dep	A-hea	A-aln	A-biz	A-ang	A-cyn	A-con	A-lse	A-las	A-sod	A-fam	A-sch	A-trt
									Content Scales						
F₁	.36	.27	.50	.54	.59	.60	.29	.30	.54	.47	.37	.35	.55	.61	.54
F₂	.41	.32	.54	.55	.60	.63	.34	.31	.49	.54	.38	.46	.51	.56	.60
F	.42	.32	.55	.58	.64	.65	.34	.32	.54	.54	.40	.44	.56	.61	.61
L	-.19	-.30	-.14	.06	.01	-.02	-.31	-.19	-.25	-.12	-.10	.14	-.11	-.10	-.08
K	-.62	-.68	-.53	-.31	-.50	-.41	-.62	-.70	-.40	-.48	-.23	-.29	-.46	-.35	-.55
Hs	.62	.44	.59	.91	.48	.50	.33	.36	.33	.49	.29	.29	.40	.42	.46
D	.60	.33	.68	.51	.53	.34	.13	.22	.17	.57	.35	.47	.37	.31	.47
Hy	.33	.03	.34	.56	.15	.20	-.03	-.12	.03	.19	.14	-.02	.17	.16	.08
Pd	.59	.41	.68	.49	.59	.51	.39	.40	.50	.49	.31	.19	.68	.46	.51
Mf	.07	.05	.04	-.13	-.11	-.20	-.07	-.16	-.28	-.06	-.10	-.06	-.09	-.21	-.16
Pa	.56	.41	.63	.54	.55	.60	.28	.15	.38	.49	.23	.27	.42	.38	.47
Pt	.84	.78	.81	.58	.63	.62	.58	.57	.49	.73	.42	.39	.53	.50	.69
Sc	.76	.67	.79	.68	.71	.78	.54	.56	.60	.69	.44	.41	.66	.56	.74
Ma	.43	.48	.36	.36	.33	.52	.46	.51	.57	.26	.11	-.11	.47	.36	.36
Si	.54	.51	.59	.38	.60	.34	.31	.44	.24	.67	.47	.77	.37	.38	.62

Note. From Butcher, Williams, Graham, Archer, Tellegen, Ben-Porath, and Kaemmer (1992). Copyright (c) 1992 by the Regents of the University of Minnesota. Reproduced by permission.

240

TABLE 6.14

Raw Score Intercorrelations of the Content and Basic Scales for Male Adolescents in the MMPI-A Normative Sample

	A-anx	A-obs	A-dep	A-hea	A-aln	A-biz	A-ang	A-cyn	A-con	A-lse	A-las	A-sod	A-fam	A-sch	A-trt
									Content Scales						
F₁	.39	.21	.52	.63	.55	.64	.25	.11	.39	.47	.42	.34	.59	.64	.50
F₂	.42	.26	.53	.61	.56	.68	.24	.14	.35	.55	.45	.40	.56	.60	.58
F	.43	.25	.55	.65	.59	.70	.26	.13	.38	.54	.46	.40	.61	.65	.58
L	-.15	-.35	-.08	.28	.02	.06	-.33	-.39	-.29	-.02	.12	.14	-.01	.02	-.06
K	-.56	-.66	-.44	-.06	-.40	-.33	-.61	-.72	-.37	-.39	-.07	.22	-.33	-.26	-.44
Hs	.54	.27	.50	.90	.46	.47	.23	.09	.18	.44	.37	.35	.45	.40	.37
D	.50	.14	.54	.55	.43	.27	-.02	-.10	-.05	.45	.36	.46	.29	.24	.29
Hy	.21	-.15	.26	.63	.15	.16	-.14	-.39	-.09	.12	.24	.11	.20	.15	-.01
Pd	.54	.33	.64	.49	.57	.46	.33	.23	.43	.42	.38	.21	.67	.51	.43
Mf	.27	.14	.20	.11	.11	.04	.00	-.13	-.14	.16	.02	.20	.09	-.11	-.01
Pa	.53	.34	.62	.58	.56	.64	.24	.05	.25	.47	.35	.35	.50	.44	.45
Pt	.83	.76	.79	.48	.64	.60	.54	.50	.43	.69	.38	.46	.56	.52	.63
Sc	.74	.58	.79	.64	.73	.77	.49	.43	.50	.66	.46	.47	.72	.63	.69
Ma	.37	.50	.32	.18	.29	.44	.50	.54	.59	.25	-.09	.07	.46	.38	.37
Si	.58	.48	.58	.40	.61	.38	.26	.31	.13	.63	.42	.81	.39	.34	.57

Note. From Butcher, Williams, Graham, Archer, Tellegen, Ben-Porath, and Kaemmer (1992). Copyright (c) 1992 by the Regents of the University of Minnesota. Reproduced by permission.

TABLE 6.15

Raw Score Intercorrelations of the MMPI-A Content Scales and the MMPI Wiggins Content Scales for 58 Females in an Adolescent Inpatient Sample

	A-anx	A-obs	A-dep	A-hea	A-aln	A-biz	A-ang	A-cyn	A-con	A-lse	A-las	A-sod	A-fam	A-sch	A-trt
							MMPI-A Content Scales								
HEA	.54	.38	.44	.84	.42	.39	.15	.26	.33	.51	.23	.51	.17	.21	.44
DEP	.87	.81	.92	.61	.69	.43	.42	.53	.37	.85	.64	.54	.50	.47	.72
ORG	.77	.64	.60	.90	.50	.57	.38	.41	.44	.62	.35	.50	.29	.54	.53
FAM	.35	.44	.46	.22	.61	.28	.43	.46	.54	.44	.42	.11	.94	.35	.56
AUT	.42	.49	.38	.32	.45	.43	.50	.86	.70	.47	.39	.15	.47	.50	.57
FEM	-.10	-.11	-.11	.05	-.11	-.12	-.14	-.33	-.35	-.20	-.13	-.05	-.12	-.17	-.26
REL	.02	-.14	-.04	.18	-.08	.00	-.25	-.18	-.24	.02	-.18	.01	-.44	-.28	-.15
HOS	.54	.71	.45	.45	.44	.55	.83	.63	.72	.43	.41	.14	.52	.72	.58
MOR	.80	.74	.85	.53	.64	.35	.33	.54	.29	.88	.53	.58	.38	.36	.65
PHO	.57	.52	.38	.54	.35	.41	.32	.21	.29	.42	.15	.45	.23	.36	.32
PSY	.65	.58	.57	.62	.62	.86	.54	.53	.62	.56	.35	.34	.47	.59	.58
HYP	.34	.44	.16	.24	.15	.42	.65	.58	.58	.15	.14	-.13	.31	.50	.28
SOC	.50	.39	.55	.45	.46	.07	-.09	.22	-.02	.62	.36	.93	.08	.12	.46

W i g g i n s   S c a l e s

TABLE 6.16

Raw Score Intercorrelations of the MMPI-A Content Scales and the MMPI Wiggins Content Scales for 64 Males in an Adolescent Inpatient Sample

							MMPI-A Content Scales								
	A-anx	A-obs	A-dep	A-hea	A-aln	A-biz	A-ang	A-cyn	A-con	A-lse	A-las	A-sod	A-fam	A-sch	A-trt
W HEA	.46	.39	.56	.86	.46	.42	.02	-.11	-.14	.42	.09	.41	-.09	.14	.30
i DEP	.78	.73	.90	.68	.66	.55	.16	.19	-.03	.66	.23	.50	.05	.30	.59
g ORG	.57	.53	.65	.90	.54	.51	.01	-.10	-.06	.54	.11	.55	-.09	.23	.42
g FAM	.19	.25	.08	.02	.18	.13	.47	.31	.26	.10	.21	-.06	.82	.27	.19
i AUT	.03	.24	-.06	-.28	.15	.09	.61	.88	.65	.12	.29	-.05	.38	.39	.31
n FEM	.24	.12	.12	.24	.03	.22	-.04	-.19	-.01	.05	-.02	.15	-.00	.03	-.08
s REL	-.03	.19	-.00	.12	.11	.11	.08	-.07	.06	.08	-.24	.10	-.01	.06	.08
S HOS	.34	.54	.18	.15	.27	.30	.79	.73	.59	.18	.27	.08	.45	.56	.42
c MOR	.78	.83	.73	.55	.56	.47	.29	.39	-.02	.76	.20	.49	.02	.32	.59
a PHO	.33	.33	.37	.62	.46	.55	.13	.00	.08	.32	.06	.47	-.12	.26	.36
l PSY	.49	.61	.67	.63	.70	.89	.32	.29	.30	.64	.28	.59	.22	.47	.66
e HYP	.38	.57	.04	.05	.14	.09	.72	.68	.40	.16	.06	-.04	.23	.34	.36
s SOC	.39	.31	.41	.55	.47	.43	-.11	-.06	-.19	.46	.11	.86	-.04	.13	.43

TABLE 6.17
Wiggins Content Scale Items Retained in the MMPI-A

Wiggins Content Scale	Items on MMPI	Number (and Percent) of Items Retained on MMPI-A	
Social Maladjustment (SOC)	27	22	(81.5%)
Depression (DEP)	33	31	(93.9%)
Feminine Interests (FEM)	30	16	(53.3%)
Poor Morale (MOR)	23	20	(87.0%)
Religious Fundamentalism (REL)	12	1	(8.3%)
Authority Conflict (AUT)	20	20	(100.0%)
Psychoticism (PSY)	48	40	(83.3%)
Organic Symptoms (ORG)	36	31	(86.1%)
Family Problems (FAM)	16	16	(100.0%)
Manifest Hostility (HOS)	27	18	(66.7%)
Phobias (PHO)	27	15	(55.5%)
Hypomania (HYP)	25	18	(72.0%)
Poor Health (HEA)	28	17	(60.7%)

scale. Adolescents who score high on this measure report symptoms of anxiety, including tension, apprehension, and rumination, and the self-perception of being overwhelmed by stress. Most *A-anx* scale items involve cognitions and attitudes related to the experience of anxiety, with relatively few items related to physiological expression of anxiety symptoms. Table 6.18 provides examples of items from the *A-anx* scale. As shown in Tables 6.13 through 6.16, the *A-anx* scale is highly correlated with scale 7 of the basic profile, and also correlates highly with the Wiggins Depression (*DEP*) content scale.

TABLE 6.18
Items From the Anxiety (A-anx) Scale

Examples of A-anx items scored if true
14.   I work under a great deal of tension.
28.   I find it hard to keep my mind on a task or job.
36.   My sleep is fitful and disturbed.
163.   I am afraid of losing my mind.
279.   I cannot keep my mind on one thing.
377.   I am apt to take disappointments so keenly that I can't put them out of my mind.
383.   I worry quite a bit over possible misfortunes.
All A-anx items scored if false
134.   Most nights I go to sleep without thoughts or ideas bothering me.
196.   I hardly ever notice my heart pounding and I am seldom short of breath.
209.   I believe I am no more nervous than most others.
375.   I am usually calm and not easily upset.
424.   I am not feeling much stress these days.

Note. Items reproduced from the MMPI-A by permission. Copyright (c) 1992 by the Regents of the University of Minnesota.

Butcher et al. (1992) reported that the *A-anx* scale appears to measure general maladjustment as well as symptoms relating to depression and somatic complaints. Clinical correlates in the Archer and Gordon (1991) study were derived from staff ratings on the Devereux Adolescent Behavior (DAB) Rating Scale, parental reports on the Child Behavior Checklist (CBCL), and presenting problems as indicated in the adolescent's psychiatric records. These authors found that high *A-anx* scores for adolescent girls were related to low endurance and fatigue, domination by peers, obsessional thought processes, anxiety, and timidity, whereas high scores for males were related to problems in concentration, the occurrence of suicidal thoughts, and sadness and depression.

The following descriptors are applicable to adolescents who produce high scores on the *A-anx* scale:

- Anxious, tense, nervous, and ruminative.
- Problems in concentration.
- Low endurance and fatigability.
- Sadness and depression.
- Higher probability of suicidal thoughts and ideation.

Adolescent-Obsessiveness (A-obs) Scale. The *A-obs* scale consists of 15 items, 12 of which also appear on the MMPI-2 *OBS* scale. All of the items in the *A-obs* scale are scored in the *true* direction, and 13 of these items appear on the original form of the MMPI. The MMPI-A Obsessiveness scale contains items concerning ambivalence and difficulty in making decisions, excessive worry and rumination, and the occurrence of intrusive thoughts. In addition, adolescents who score high on the *A-obs* may also exhibit some compulsive behaviors. The *A-obs* scale is highly correlated with scale 7 of the basic profile, and negatively correlated with scale *K*. Table 6.19 provides an illustration of some of the items used in the *A-obs* scale.

Butcher et al. (1992) reported that high *A-obs* scores in a clinical sample were related to anxious and dependent behaviors in boys and to suicidal ideations or gestures in girls. A clear correlate pattern was not identified in the Archer and Gordon (1991) study.

The following are characteristics or correlates associated with high *A-obs* scores:

- Excessive worry and rumination.
- Difficulty in making decisions.
- The occurrence of intrusive thoughts and problems in concentration.

TABLE 6.19
Items From the Obsessiveness (A-obs) Scale

Examples of A-obs items scored if true

52. I sometimes keep on at a thing until others lose their patience with me.
83. I have met problems so full of possibilities that I have been unable to make up my mind about them.
129. I have often lost out on things because I couldn't make up my mind soon enough.
185. I frequently find myself worrying about something.
293. I have a habit of counting things that are not important such as bulbs on electrical signs, and so forth.
307. Bad words, often terrible words, come into my mind and I cannot get rid of them.
308. Sometimes some unimportant thought will run through my mind and bother me for days.
310. I usually have to stop and think before I act even in small matters.
370. My plans have frequently seemed so full of difficulties that I have had to give them up.
412. I have had periods in which I lost sleep over worry.
421. I feel helpless when I have to make some important decisions.
444. It bothers me greatly to think of making changes in my life.

Note. Items reproduced from the MMPI-A by permission. Copyright (c) 1992 by the Regents of the University of Minnesota.

Adolescent-Depression (A-dep) Scale. The A-dep scale consists of 26 items, of which 25 also appeared on the MMPI-2 Depression content scale. Further, 24 of the 26 items on the *A-dep* scale were derived from the original form of the MMPI. *A-dep* scale items appear to be related to depression and sadness, apathy, low energy, and poor morale. In the Archer and Gordon (1991) inpatient sample, *A-dep* scores were highly correlated with scores from the Wiggins Depression (*DEP*) content scale ($r = .92$ for females and $r = .90$ for males). *A-dep* scores were not highly correlated with scale 2, but were strongly associated with scores from basic scales 7 and 8 (see Tables 6.13 and 6.14). Table 6.20 shows examples of items from the *A-dep* scale. As shown in this table, several of the items on the *A-dep* scale involve feelings of pessimism and hopelessness. One *A-dep* scale item (Item No. 177) relates to the occurrence of suicidal ideation.

Butcher et al. (1992) reported that high *A-dep* scores for adolescents in clinical settings were associated with a variety of behaviors and symptoms related to depression and the occurrence of suicidal ideation and gestures. Archer and Gordon (1991) also found suicidal thoughts to be related to high *A-dep* scores for girls, whereas suicidal attempts were related to high *A-dep* scores for boys.

The following characteristics are associated with high *A-dep* scores:

TABLE 6.20
Items From the Depression (A-dep) Scale

Examples of A-dep items scored if true
49.   I have not lived the right kind of life.
53.   I wish I could be as happy as others seem to be.
62.   Most of the time I feel blue.
177. I sometimes think about killing myself.
372. Often, even though everything is going fine for me, I feel that I don't care about anything.
379. At times I think I am no good at all.
399. The future seems hopeless to me.
All A-dep items scored if false
3.   I wake up fresh and rested most mornings.
9.   My daily life is full of things that keep me interested.
71.   I usually feel that life is worthwhile.
91.   I am happy most of the time.
360. I very seldom have spells of the blues.

Note. Items reproduced from the MMPI-A by permission. Copyright (c) 1992 by the Regents of the University of Minnesota.

- Sadness, depression, and despondency.
- Fatigue and apathy.
- A pervasive sense of hopelessness that may include suicidal ideation.

Adolescent-Health Concerns (A-hea) Scale. The MMPI-A Health Concerns scale includes 37 items, of which 34 also appear on the MMPI-2 HEA scale. Thirty-four of the 37 items on the *A-hea* scale appeared on the original form of the MMPI. Twenty-three items on the *A-hea* scale also appear on scale *1* of the standard or basic MMPI-A clinical scales and scores from these two scales are highly correlated. The *A-hea* scale is one of only two MMPI-A content scales that contain a majority of items keyed in the *false* direction. Adolescents who produce elevated scores on the *A-hea* content scale are endorsing physical symptoms across a wide variety of areas including gastrointestinal, neurological, sensory, cardiovascular, and respiratory systems. These adolescents feel physically ill, and are worried about their health. Table 6.21 provides examples of items contained within the *A-hea* scale. In the Archer and Gordon (1991) inpatient sample, *A-hea* scale scores were also highly correlated ($r = .90$ for males and females) with scores from the Wiggins Organic Symptoms (*ORG*) content scale.

Williams et al. (in press) found high *A-hea* scores to be related to somatic complaints for adolescents in their clinical sample, and to misbehavior, school problems, and poor academic performance for normal adolescents. Archer and Gordon (1991) found high scores for

TABLE 6.21
Items From the Health Concerns (A-hea) Scale

Examples of A-hea items scored if true
11.   There seems to be a lump in my throat much of the time.
17.   I am troubled by attacks of nausea and vomiting.
56.   I am troubled by discomfort in the pit of my stomach every few days or oftener.
106.   I have a great deal of stomach trouble.
231.   I have numbness in one or more places on my skin.
443.   I have missed a lot of school in my life because of sickness.
470.   I have a cough most of the time.
Examples of A-hea items scored if false
87.   I have little or no trouble with my muscles twitching or jumping.
113.   I have never vomited blood or coughed up blood.
152.   I have never had a fainting spell.
239.   I do not often notice my ears ringing or buzzing.
374.   I have no trouble swallowing.

Note. Items reproduced from the MMPI-A by permission. Copyright (c) 1992 by the Regents of the University of Minnesota.

females to be associated with the occurrence of suicidal thoughts, tiredness, and fatigue, whereas high scoring boys were described as exhibiting poor reality testing, concentration difficulties, and somatic concerns. Future research should examine the extent to which poor physical health, including chronic medical conditions, affect *A-hea* scores.

The following descriptors are associated with elevated scores on *A-hea*:

- Physical symptoms and complaints.
- Tiredness and fatigue.

Adolescent-Alienation (A-aln) Scale.   The MMPI-A Alienation scale is 20 items in length and does not directly correspond to any of the MMPI-2 content scales. The *A-aln* scale is designed to identify adolescents who are interpersonally isolated and alienated, and feel pessimistic about social interactions. They tend not to believe that others understand or are sympathetic to them, and perceive their lives as being unfair or harsh. They may feel that they are unable to turn to, or depend on, anyone. These adolescents would be expected to have few or no close friends. Table 6.22 provides examples of *A-aln* scale items. The *A-aln* scale is most highly correlated with MMPI basic scale 8 ($r = .71$ for females and $r = .73$ for males). Data by Archer and Gordon (1991) indicate that this MMPI-A content scale is most highly correlated with

TABLE 6.22
Items From the Alienation (A-aln) Scale

Examples of A-aln items scored if true
16. I am sure I get a raw deal from life.
20. No one seems to understand me.
242. No one cares much what happens to you.
317. People often disappoint me.
369. I feel unable to tell anyone all about myself.
438. My parents do not understand me very well.
463. I have no close friends.

All A-aln items scored if false
74. I am liked by most people who know me.
104. Anyone who is able and willing to work hard has a good chance of succeeding.
260. I get all the sympathy I should.
448. Most people think they can depend on me.
450. I get along with most people.

Note. Items reproduced from the MMPI-A by permission. Copyright (c) 1992 by the Regents of the University of Minnesota.

the Wiggins Depression (*DEP*) content scale for females ($r = .69$) and with the Wiggins Psychoticism (*PSY*) scale for males ($r = .70$).

Williams et al. (in press) reported that the *A-aln* scale exhibited correlates in both the normative and clinical samples related to feeling emotionally distant from others. In the Archer and Gordon (1991) clinical sample, high scores among girls were related to withdrawal, lying, and irritability, whereas high scores for boys were related to provocativeness, excessive use of fantasy, and the occurrence of hallucinations and suicidal thoughts.

The following are characteristics associated with high *A-aln* scores:

• Sense of interpersonal isolation, alienation, and frustration.
• Social withdrawal.

Adolescent-Bizarre Mentation (A-biz) Scale. The *A-biz* scale consists of 19 items, of which 17 also appear on the MMPI-2 *BIZ* scale. Eleven of the 19 items on the *A-biz* scale also appear on the MMPI-A *F* scale. All but one of the *A-biz* scale items can be found in the original MMPI item pool. Adolescents who produce elevated scores on the *A-biz* scale are characterized by the occurrence of psychotic thought processes. They report strange and unusual experiences, which may include auditory, visual, or olfactory hallucinations. They may also have paranoid symptoms and delusions, including beliefs that they are being plotted against, or controlled by, others. *A-biz* scores are highly correlated with scales *F* and

8 from the basic MMPI-A profile in the normative sample (see Tables 6.13 and 6.14), and with the Wiggins Psychoticism (*PSY*) scale in the Archer and Gordon (1991) inpatient sample (see Tables 6.15 and 6.16). Table 6.23 provides examples of items from the *A-biz* scale.

Williams et al. (in press) reported that the *A-biz* scale appeared to measure general maladjustment among normal adolescents, and was associated in their clinical sample with the occurrence of bizarre sensory experiences and psychotic symptoms. Archer and Gordon (1991) found that high *A-biz* scores among female inpatients were related to hallucinations, poor emotional control, and poor reality testing, whereas high scores for males were associated with fighting, legal difficulties, the perpetration of sexual abuse, hallucinations, and poor reality testing.

The following characteristics are associated with elevated *A-biz* scale scores:

- Poor reality testing.
- Deficits in impulse control.
- The occurrence of a thought disorder or psychotic thought processes.
- Presence of paranoid symptomatology, including hallucinations and delusions.

Adolescent-Anger (A-ang) Scale.   The MMPI-A Anger scale consists of 17 items, of which 11 also appear on the MMPI-2 Anger scale. Twelve of the *A-ang* items appeared on the original form of the MMPI. Adolescents who score high on the *A-ang* scale may be described as irritable,

TABLE 6.23
Items From the Bizarre Mentation (A-biz) Scale

Example of A-biz items scored if true
22.   Evil spirits possess me at times.
29.   I have had very peculiar and strange experiences.
132.   I believe I am being plotted against.
155.   Someone has been trying to poison me.
250.   My soul sometimes leaves my body.
278.   Peculiar odors come to me at times.
291.   I often feel as if things are not real.
296.   I have strange and peculiar thoughts.
315.   Someone has control over my mind.
417.   Ghosts or spirits can influence people for good or bad.
433.   When I am with people, I am bothered by hearing very strange things.
All A-biz items scored if false
387.   I have never seen a vision.

Note. Items reproduced from the MMPI-A by permission. Copyright (c)1992 by the Regents of the University of Minnesota.

grouchy, and impatient. Problems with anger may include the potential of physical assaultiveness, and three of the items on the *A-ang* scale (Items 34, 128, and 445) specifically relate to the issue of physical aggression. Williams et al. (in press) found that high *A-ang* scores among adolescents in clinical settings were related to histories of assaultive behaviors. Table 6.24 provides examples of *A-ang* scale items. Like the other MMPI-A scales related to externalizing behaviors, *A-ang* scores are negatively and highly correlated with scale *K* in the normative sample. In addition, the *A-ang* scale was highly correlated ($r = .79$ for boys and $r = .83$ for girls) with scores from the Wiggins Hostility (*HOS*) scale in the Archer and Gordon (1991) inpatient sample. Additionally, these authors found high *A-ang* scores were associated with truancy, poor parental relationships, defiance and disobedience, anger, and assaultiveness for girls, and high heterosexual interest, drug abuse, hyperactivity, and threatened assaultiveness for boys.

The following features are associated with high *A-ang* scores:

- Anger and interpersonal hostility.
- Irritability, grouchiness, and impatience.
- Poor anger control and potential physical aggressiveness.

Adolescent-Cynicism (A-cyn) Scale. The *A-cyn* scale includes 22 items, 21 of which also appear on the MMPI-2 Cynicism scale. All of the *A-cyn* items are scored in the *true* direction and appeared on the original form

TABLE 6.24
Items From the Anger (A-ang) Scale

Examples of A-ang items scored if true
26.   At times I feel like swearing.
34.   At times I feel like smashing things.
128.   At times I feel like picking a fist fight with someone.
282.   I easily become impatient with people.
367.   I am often said to be hotheaded.
378.   I am often so annoyed when someone tries to get ahead of me in a line of people that I speak to that person about it.
382.   I have at times had to be rough with people who were rude or annoying.
401.   It makes me angry to have people hurry me.
416.   I am very stubborn.
445.   I often get into trouble for breaking and destroying things.
461.   I often have to yell to get my point across.
All A-ang items scored if false
355.   I am not easily angered.

Note. Items reproduced from the MMPI-A by permission. Copyright (c) 1992 by the Regents of the University of Minnesota.

of the MMPI. Adolescents who produce elevations on this MMPI-A content scale may be described as distrustful, cynical, and suspicious of the motives of others. They tend to believe that all individuals manipulate and use each other selfishly for personal gain. They assume that others behave in a manner that appears ethical or honest only because of the fear of being caught and punished for misbehavior. They expect others to lie, cheat, and steal in order to gain advantage. Table 6.25 provides examples of *A-cyn* scale items. The *A-cyn* scale correlates highly, and negatively, with scale *K* of the MMPI-A basic scale profile. Data from the Archer and Gordon (1991) adolescent inpatient sample indicate that the *A-cyn* scale correlates highly ($r = .86$ for females and .88 for males) with the Wiggins Authority Problems (*AUT*) content scale.

Williams et al. (in press) reported few meaningful external correlates for this scale in their investigation of MMPI-A normative and clinical samples. Archer and Gordon (1991) found that high *A-cyn* scores among female adolescents was related to the occurrence of sexual abuse and poor parental relationships as primary presenting problems, and to staff ratings of these adolescents as resistant and displaying a negative attitude. The *A-cyn* scale produced few correlates for male inpatient adolescents. Those correlates that were obtained involved the increased occurrence of hallucinations and the excessive use of fantasy.

TABLE 6.25
Items From the Cynicism (A-cyn) Scale

Examples of A-cyn items scored if true	
47.	I have often had to take orders from someone who did not know as much as I did.
72.	It takes a lot of argument to convince most people of the truth.
77.	I think most people would lie to get ahead.
100.	Most people are honest chiefly because they are afraid of being caught.
107.	Most people will use somewhat unfair means to get what they want.
211.	My way of doing things is apt to be misunderstood by others.
225.	It is safer to trust nobody.
238.	Most people make friends because friends are likely to be useful to them.
265.	I think nearly anyone would tell a lie to keep out of trouble.
267.	Most people inwardly dislike putting themselves out to help other people.
334.	I have often found people jealous of my good ideas, just because they had not thought of them first.
406.	A large number of people are guilty of bad sexual conduct.

Note. Items reproduced from the MMPI-A by permission. Copyright (c) 1992 by the Regents of the University of Minnesota.

Based on the item content of the *A-cyn* scale, the following descriptors may be associated with high scores on this measure:

• Guarded and suspicious of the motives of others.
• Unfriendly and hostile in relationships.

Adolescent-Conduct Problems (A-con) Scale. The MMPI-A Conduct Problems scale is composed of 23 items, of which 7 appear on the MMPI-2 Antisocial Practices scale. Twelve of the 23 items on the *A-con* scale were derived from the item pool of the original MMPI. The *A-con* scale was developed to identify adolescents who report problem behaviors, including impulsivity, risk-taking behaviors, and antisocial behaviors. Adolescents who produce elevations on this scale are likely to exhibit behaviors that may result in school suspensions and legal violations, and are more likely to receive conduct disorder diagnoses. In addition to behaviors and actions related to conduct problems, however, the *A-con* scale also measures attitudes and beliefs likely to be in conflict with societal norms and standards. Table 6.26 provides examples of items from the *A-con* scale. In the MMPI-A normative sample, the *A-con* scale produced substantial correlations ($r > .50$) with scales 8 and 9 of the basic scale profile for both genders, and was correlated ($r = .65$ for males and $r = .70$ for females) with the Wiggins Authority Problems (*AUT*) content scale in the inpatient sample.

TABLE 6.26
Items From the Conduct Problems (A-con) Scale

Examples of A-con items scored if true
32.   I have sometimes stolen things.
99.   I enjoy a race or game more when I bet on it.
117. If I could get into a movie without paying and be sure I was not seen, I would probably do it.
232. I do not blame a person for taking advantage of people who leave themselves open to it.
345. My friends are often in trouble.
445. I often get into trouble for breaking or destroying things.
455. I am often told that I do not show enough respect for people.
462. I often have to lie in order to get by.
477. My friends often talk me into doing things I know are wrong.
All A-con items scored if false
96.   I have never done anything dangerous for the thrill of it.
249. I have never been in trouble with the law.
465. I don't like having to get "rough" with people.

Note. Items reproduced from the MMPI-A by permission. Copyright (c) 1992 by the Regents of the University of Minnesota.

Williams et al. (in press) reported that high scores on *A-con* were associated with the occurrence of significant behavior problems. Archer and Gordon (1991) found high *A-con* scores among males to be associated with presenting problems including theft, truancy, drug abuse, legal difficulties, alcohol abuse, and assaultive behaviors. Among females, high *A-con* scores were related to truancy, defiance and disobedience, anger, and running away from home.

The following characteristics or correlates are associated with high *A-con* scores:

- Teenagers who are likely to be in trouble because of their behavior.
- Poor impulse control and antisocial behaviors.
- Attitudes and beliefs that conflict with societal norms and standards.
- Problems with authority figures.
- Increased likelihood of conduct disorder diagnoses.

Adolescent-Low Self-Esteem (A-lse) Scale. The *A-lse* scale consists of 18 items, all of which also appear on the MMPI-2 *LSE* content scale. The *A-lse* scale attempts to identify adolescents who have low self-esteem and little self-confidence. Adolescents who score high on this content scale often feel inadequate and useless, and not as capable and competent as others. They recognize many faults and flaws in themselves, both real and imagined, and feel unrespected or rejected by others. Table 6.27 presents examples of *A-lse* scale items. Among the basic

TABLE 6.27
Items From the Low Self-Esteem (A-lse) Scale

Examples of A-lse items scored if true
67.   I am easily downed in an argument.
70.   I am certainly lacking in self-confidence.
124.   I certainly feel useless at times.
358.   I do not feel I can plan my own future.
379.   At times I think I am no good at all.
385.   I am apt to pass up something I want to do because others feel that I am not going about it in the right way.
415.   I cannot do anything well.
441.   People do not find me attractive.
468.   I often get confused and forget what I want to say.
All A-lse items scored if false
58.   I am an important person.
74.   I am liked by most people who know me.
105.   I seem to be about as capable and smart as most others around me.

Note. Items reproduced from the MMPI-A by permission. Copyright (c) 1992 by the Regents of the University of Minnesota.

scales, A-lse produces the highest correlations with scales 7, 8 and 0 (see Tables 6.13 and 6.14). In addition, A-lse scores are highly correlated with scores from the Wiggins Poor Morale (MOR) scale (r = .76 for males and r = .88 for females).

Williams et al. (in press) reported that high scores on the A-lse scale are associated with negative self-view and poor school performance. Among girls in their clinical sample, high scores on this scale were also associated with the occurrence of depression. In the Archer and Gordon (1991) inpatient sample, high A-lse scores among girls were related to the occurrence of obsessive thoughts, social withdrawal, tiredness and fatigue, and suicidal thoughts. High scores among boys were related to suicidal thoughts, passivity, and self-blame or condemnation.

The following descriptors or correlates are associated with elevated scores on A-lse:

- Poor self-esteem or self-confidence.
- Feelings of inadequacy and incompetency.
- Interpersonal passivity, discomfort, and withdrawal.

Adolescent-Low Aspirations (A-las) Scale.   The MMPI-A Low Aspirations scale is composed of 16 items and does not have a direct counterpart among the MMPI-2 content scales. Like the A-hea scale, the majority of the items in the A-las content scale are scored in the *false* direction. Adolescents who score high on the A-las scale have few educational or life goals, and view themselves as unsuccessful. They do not apply themselves, tend to procrastinate, and give up quickly when faced with a frustrating or difficult challenge. Table 6.28 provides examples of A-las scale items. The A-las scale does not produce any correlations exceeding .50 with the MMPI-A basic scales, or with the Wiggins content scales (see Tables 6.13 through 6.16). Among supplementary scales, the A-las scale was most highly associated with the Immaturity (IMM) scale, reflected in a correlational value of r = .59 for the normative sample.

Williams et al. (in press) found A-las scores were related to poor achievement in school activities and to conduct-disordered behaviors including running away and truancy. In the Archer and Gordon (1991) inpatient sample, high A-las scores among boys were related to occurrence of arrests, legal difficulties, and suicidal threats. High scores for females were related to an inability to delay gratification, a defiant and resistant attitude, and frustration and anger in response to difficulties in learning or mastering new concepts and materials.

The following correlates are associated with elevated scores on the A-las scale:

TABLE 6.28
Items From the Low Aspirations (A-las) Scale

Examples of A-las items scored if true
27.   I shrink from facing a crisis or difficulty.
39.   If people had not had it in for me, I would be much more successful.
340. I feel like giving up quickly when things go wrong.
351. The only interesting part of newspapers is the comic strips.
430. When problems need to be solved, I usually let other people take charge.
464. Others tell me that I am lazy.
Examples of A-las items scored if false
170. I like to study and read about things that I am working at.
324. If given the chance I could do some things that would be of great benefit to the world.
397. I prefer work which requires close attention to work which allows me to be careless.
411. I like to attend lectures on serious subjects.
436. I want to go to college.
447. I usually expect to succeed in things I do.

Note. Items reproduced from the MMPI-A by permission. Copyright (c) 1992 by the Regents of the University of Minnesota.

- Poor academic achievement.
- Low frustration tolerance.
- Persistent pattern of underachievement.

Adolescent-Social Discomfort (A-sod) Scale. The MMPI-A Social Discomfort scale consists of 24 items, of which 21 also appear on the MMPI-2 Social Discomfort scale. Sixteen of the items on the *A-sod* scale also appear on the MMPI-A *Si* basic profile scale. Adolescents who produce elevated scores on the *A-sod* scale tend to be uncomfortable in social situations, and may be described as introverted and shy. They avoid social events, and find it difficult to interact with others. Table 6.29 provides examples of *A-sod* scale items. Among the basic MMPI-A scales, the *A-sod* is most highly correlated ($r > .75$) with *Si* scores (see Tables 6.13 and 6.14). The *A-sod* scale also produces a very high level of correlation ($r > .85$) with the Wiggins Social Maladjustment (*SOC*) scale, as shown in Tables 6.15 and 6.16.

William et al. (in press) found high *A-sod* scores to be associated with social withdrawal and discomfort for both boys and girls, and with depression and eating disorder problems for females. Archer and Gordon (1991) found high *A-sod* scores among inpatient girls to be related to social withdrawal, apathy, fatigue, shyness, and the avoidance of competition with peers. High *A-sod* scores among boys were related to an increased frequency of provocative behaviors, anxiety and nervousness, and suicidal thoughts.

TABLE 6.29
Items From the Social Discomfort (A-sod) Scale

Examples of A-sod items scored if true
160. I find it hard to make talk when I meet new people.
178. I wish I were not so shy.
264. I dislike having people around me.
304. Whenever possible I avoid being in a crowd.
328. I am never happier than when alone.
408. Some people think it's hard to get to know me.
Examples of A-sod items scored if false
46. I am a very sociable person.
262. I seem to make friends about as quickly as others do.
292. I like parties and socials.
319. I love to go to dances.
335. I enjoy the excitement of a crowd.
450. I get along with most people.

Note. Items reproduced from the MMPI-A by permission. Copyright (c) 1992 by the Regents of the University of Minnesota.

The following characteristics are associated with high *A-sod* scores:

- Social discomfort and withdrawal.
- Shyness and social introversion.

Adolescent-Family Problems (A-fam) Scale.   The MMPI-A Family Problems scale includes 35 items, of which 15 also appear on the MMPI-2 Family Problems content scale. Twenty-one of the items on the *A-fam* scale were derived from the original form of the MMPI. Adolescents producing elevations on the *A-fam* scale report the presence of substantial family conflict and discord. They are likely to have frequent quarrels with family members, and report little love or understanding within their families. They feel misunderstood and unjustly punished by family members, and may report being physically or emotionally abused. They may wish to run away or escape from their homes and families. Table 6.30 provides examples of items from the *A-fam* scale. Among the MMPI-A basic scales, *A-fam* is most highly correlated ($r > .65$) with scores from scales 4 and 8 (see Tables 6.13 and 6.14). Among the Wiggins content scales, *A-fam* scores are most highly correlated ($r > .80$) with the Wiggins Family Problems (*FAM*) scale (see Tables 6.15 and 6.16).

Williams et al. (in press) reported that high scores on the *A-fam* scale were associated with a variety of delinquent and neurotic symptoms and behaviors. Girls who produced high *A-fam* scores in the Archer and Gordon (1991) inpatient sample were found to have more problems with anger, to be loud and boisterous, and to have a higher frequency of

TABLE 6.30
Items From the Family Problems (A-fam) Scale

Examples of A-fam items scored if true

19.   At times I have very much wanted to leave home.
57.   My parents do not like my friends.
137.   I feel that I have often been punished without cause.
184.   There is very little love and companionship in my family as compared to other homes.
269.   My parents and family find more fault with me than they should.
344.   I cannot wait for the day when I can leave home for good.

Examples of A-fam items scored if false

6.   My father is a good man, or (if your father is dead) my father was a good man.
79.   I have very few quarrels with members of my family.
119.   I believe that my home life is as pleasant as that of most people I know.
365.   When things get really bad, I know I can count on my family for help.
398.   The members of my family and my close relatives get along quite well.
451.   We don't have trouble talking to each other in my family.

Note. Items reproduced from the MMPI-A by permission. Copyright (c) 1992 by the Regents of the University of Minnesota.

running away from home. Boys who scored high on this content scale were more likely to engage in drug and/or alcohol abuse, to have anger control problems, and to have a history of physical abuse.

The following characteristics are associated with high *A-fam* scores:

- Perception of family environment as unsupportive, hostile, unloving, or punitive.
- Increased probability of acting out, including running away from home.
- Resentment, anger, and hostility toward family members.

Adolescent-School Problems (A-sch) Scale. The MMPI-A School Problems scale consists of 20 items. This scale was created especially for the MMPI-A, and does not have a counterpart among the MMPI-2 scales. Only nine of the items that appear on the *A-sch* scale were derived from items appearing on the original instrument. Adolescents who score high on the *A-sch* scale do not like school, and are likely to encounter many behavioral and academic problems within the school setting. They may have developmental delays or learning disabilities, or may exhibit behavioral problems that have significantly interfered with academic achievement and their acquisition of academic skills. Table 6.31 provides examples of *A-sch* scale items. Among the MMPI-A basic scales, *A-sch* scores are most highly correlated with scales F ($r \geq .60$) and 8 ($r > .55$).

TABLE 6.31
Items From the School Problems (A-sch) Scale

Examples of A-sch items scored if true
12. My teachers have it in for me.
69. I think school is a waste of time.
101. In school I have sometimes been sent to the principal for bad behavior.
220. I am a slow learner in school.
364. I am often upset by things that happen in school.
380. Often I have not gone to school even when I should have.
425. I think my teachers at school are stupid.
464. Others tell me that I am lazy.
466. At school I am very often bored and sleepy.
All A-sch items scored if false
153. I like school.
166. I can read a long while without tiring my eyes.
459. My school grades are average or better.

Note. Items reproduced from the MMPI-A by permission. Copyright (c) 1992 by the Regents of the University of Minnesota.

The *A-sch* score is also correlated with the Wiggins Hostility (*HOS*) scale ($r > .50$) and with the Immaturity (*IMM*) supplementary scale ($r > .70$).

Williams et al. (in press) reported that high *A-sch* scores were related to the occurrence of academic and behavioral problems in the school environment and may also serve as a measure of general maladjustment. Archer and Gordon (1991) found that high scores on this MMPI-A content scale were related to the occurrence of academic decline and failure, truancy, and defiance among adolescent female inpatients. Among boys high scores were associated with legal difficulties, drug abuse, fighting, and intense interest in the opposite sex.

The following correlates or characteristics are associated with high *A-sch* scores:

- Negative attitude toward academic activities and achievement.
- Poor school performance, including behavioral and academic problems and deficits.
- Possibility of learning disabilities or significant developmental delays and learning problems.

Adolescent-Negative Treatment Indicators (A-trt) Scale. The MMPI-A Negative Treatment Indicator scale consists of 26 items, of which 21 also appeared on the MMPI-2 *TRT* scale. Only nine of the items in the *A-trt* scale are derived from the original MMPI instrument. Adolescents who produce elevations on the *A-trt* scale may present barriers to treatment stemming from apathy or despondency concerning their ability to change, or from suspiciousness and distrust of help offered by others (including mental health professionals). These adolescents may feel they are incapable of making significant changes in their lives, or that working with others in the change process is ineffective or a sign of weakness. Table 6.32 provides examples of A-trt scale items. The A-trt scale is most highly correlated ($r > .60$) with scales 7 and 8 among the MMPI-A basic scales (see Tables 6.13 and 6.14). The A-trt scale is also highly correlated ($r > .60$) with the Immaturity (IMM) supplementary scale, and the Wiggins Depression (DEP) and Psychoticism (PSY) content scales.

In the Archer and Gordon (1991) inpatient sample, high A-trt scores among boys were associated with interest in the opposite sex, poor sibling relationships, the excessive use of fantasy, and a tendency to physically threaten peers. Elevated A-trt scores for girls were associated with poor physical coordination and odd physical movements. Williams et al. (in press) also failed to find a clear pattern of clinical correlates for the A-trt scale.

Based upon the content of the A-trt scale, the following are correlates likely to be associated with high scores:

- Presence of negative attitudes or expectations concerning mental health treatment.
- Pessimism concerning one's ability to change.

TABLE 6.32
Items From the Negative Treatment Indicators (A-trt) Scale

Examples of A-trt items scored if true
20.   No one seems to understand me.
88.   I don't seem to care what happens to me.
256.   I am so touchy on some subjects that I can't talk about them.
356.   I have done some bad things in the past that I never tell anybody about.
357.   It makes me nervous when people ask me personal questions.
369.   I feel unable to tell anyone all about myself.
414.   I have one or more bad habits that are so strong it is no use fighting against them.
420.   Mental illness is a sign of weakness.
423.   I believe that people should keep personal problems to themselves.
434.   I hate going to doctors even when I'm sick.
All A-trt items scored if false
419.   My main goals in life are within my reach.
431.   Talking over problems and worries with someone is often more helpful than taking drugs or medicines.
437.   When I have a problem it helps to talk it over with someone.

Note. Items reproduced from the MMPI-A by permission. Copyright (c) 1992 by the Regents of the University of Minnesota.

- The belief that talking about problems with others is not helpful or useful, or is a sign of weakness.

THE HARRIS-LINGOES AND *Si* SUBSCALES

The Harris-Lingoes Subscales

As we have noted, the empirical keying method employed by Hathaway and McKinley resulted in the creation of basic scales that were heterogeneous in terms of content areas. In order to help clinicians in determining the content endorsement associated with MMPI basic scale elevations, Harris and Lingoes (1955) constructed subscales for six of the basic scales, using the following process:

> The items scored in each scale were examined, and those which seemed similar in content, or to reflect a single attitude or trait, were grouped into a subscale. In effect, the item correlations were estimated, purely subjectively. The items were grouped on the basis of these estimates, and then given a name which was thought to be descriptive of the inferred attitude underlying the sorting of the items in the scored direction. (1955, p. 1)

Harris and Lingoes used this method to develop 27 content subscales for 6 of the basic MMPI clinical scales, including 2, 3, 4, 6, 8, and 9. They did not attempt to restrict items to placement on only one subscale, and consequently there is substantial item overlap among the subscales and a high degree of subscale correlation. The authors did not develop content subscales for scales 1 or 7 because they considered these measures to be homogeneous (Graham, 1990), and they did not create subscales for 5 or 0 because these scales are often viewed as "nonclinical" scales or involving dimensions separate or apart from the standard "clinical" scales. Caldwell (1988) and Levitt (1989) reviewed the Harris-Lingoes subscales in their discussions of MMPI special scales, and a recent symposium was focused on these subscales (Colligan, 1988).

Relatively little research has been conducted on the Harris and Lingoes subscales in terms of the construct validity of these measures (Greene, 1991). Harris and Christiansen (1946) found significant differences on eight Harris-Lingoes subscales between patients judged successful versus unsuccessful in psychotherapy. Gocka and Holloway (1963) found few significant correlations between demographic variables and scores on the Harris-Lingoes subscales. Calvin (1975), however, empirically identified behavioral correlates for many of the Harris–Lingoes subscales, and these have been incorporated into the standard descriptions provided for these subscales in guides such as Graham's (1990) text.

No empirical research studies have been conducted on the Harris–Lingoes subscales in terms of the validity of these measures in adolescent populations. Pancoast and Archer (1988) showed that the standard adult norms produce marked elevations for normal adolescents on the Harris–Lingoes subscales, particularly for Pd_1 (Familial Discord), Pa_1 (Persecutory Ideas), several of the subscales related to scale 8, and Ma_2 (Psychomotor Acceleration). These findings support the belief that adult norms would tend to produce very substantial distortions in the interpretation of adolescents' MMPI profiles. Colligan and Offord (1989) provided a set of adolescent norms for the Harris–Lingoes subscales derived from their contemporary adolescent sample collected with the original MMPI instrument. The *MMPI Adolescent Interpretive System*, developed by Archer (1987a), and published by Psychological Assessment Resources, uses these Harris–Lingoes subscale T-score values in providing computer-based test interpretation for the *original* form of the MMPI.

The Harris–Lingoes subscales have been carried over into testing materials and scoring programs for the MMPI-2 and the MMPI-A. This was possible because very few standard scale items from scales 2, 3, 4, 6, 8, and 9 were deleted in the development of these instruments. A few Harris–Lingoes subscales have been slightly shortened in the revised instruments, however, because of item deletions. Because Harris and Lingoes apparently included some subscale items that were not scored on the corresponding basic scale (e.g., some items appear on *Pd* subscales that are not scored on the *Pd* scale), these items were also deleted from membership in the MMPI-A and MMPI-2 Harris–Lingoes subscales. Finally, the Harris–Lingoes subscales were renumbered in the MMPI-A and in the MMPI-2 to eliminate the lettered subscripts employed by Harris and Lingoes to delineate several of their subscales. The revised numbering system is designed to simplify the method used to denote specific subscales. Adolescent norms for the MMPI-A Harris–Lingoes subscales, based on the 1,620 boys and girls in the normative sample, are available in the test manual for this instrument (Butcher et al., 1992) and in Appendix D of this text.

Unlike the MMPI-A scales previously reviewed, the Harris–Lingoes subscales are not recommended for routine use if hand scoring procedures are used. This is because hand scoring of the Harris–Lingoes subscales is quite time consuming, and these data are primarily useful in supplementing basic scale profiles under certain conditions (i.e., in selective cases). For example, Graham (1990) recommends the use of the Harris–Lingoes subscales if, first, "a subject receives an elevated score on a clinical scale when that elevation was not expected from the history and other information available to the clinician" (p. 113); or second, when the clinician is interpreting basic scale elevations that occur within a marginally elevated range (corresponding to a T = 60 to 65 range on the MMPI-A). This latter recommendation implicitly recognizes that when basic scale elevations are within normal limits, or markedly elevated, Harris–Lingoes values are relatively less important. Additionally, Friedman, Webb, and Lewak (1989) raised several concerns and cautions regarding the use of the Harris–Lingoes subscales that appear to be well-founded. First, they noted that Harris and Lingoes made no attempts to cross-validate their subscales, and the external validity data concerning these measures is quite limited. In this regard, Friedman et al. cited the results of the investigation by Miller and Streiner (1985), in which independent judges were unable to accurately group items into the rational categories employed by Harris and Lingoes for the majority of these subscales. Friedman et al. also reviewed the recent factor analytic results by Foerstner (1986), which showed that several of the Harris–Lingoes subscales contained items that did not load on factors in a manner that might be expected, given the names attributed to these subscales. Further, Friedman et al. noticed that most of the Harris–Lingoes subscale items are obvious in nature and therefore susceptible to the effects of response set. Finally, the authors noted normative concerns about the Harris–Lingoes subscales, an issue that has certainly been evident in terms of the absence of adolescent norms for these measures on the original MMPI.

The descriptions that follow for elevations on the Harris–Lingoes subscales are based on the original descriptions provided by Harris and Lingoes (1955), a rational inspection of the item content within each subscale, and a review of the descriptions provided for the scales in standard guides (e.g., Graham, 1990; Greene, 1991) to the use of the MMPI with adults. It is emphasized, however, that the Harris–Lingoes subscales should only be used to supplement and refine interpretation derived from the standard validity and clinical scales. Further, given the lack of validity data on these measures, substantial caution should be employed in using the MMPI-A Harris–Lingoes subscales. The following are suggested interpretations for the MMPI-A Harris–Lingoes subscales, grouped by parent scale:

Scale 2 (Depression) Subscales

Subjective Depression (D_1). High scores on the D_1 subscale may be associated with the following characteristics:

- Feelings of depression and unhappiness.
- Lack of energy and interest in everyday activities.
- Deficits in concentration and attention.

Psychomotor Retardation (D_2).   High scores on the D_2 subscale may be associated with:

- Lack of energy or inability to mobilize resources.
- Social withdrawal and social avoidance.
- Denial of hostile or aggressive impulses.

Physical Malfunctioning (D_3).   High scores on the D_3 subscale may be associated with the following characteristics:

- Concerns and preoccupation with physical health.
- Reporting of a wide array of physical symptoms.

Mental Dullness (D_4).   High scores on the D_4 subscale may be associated with the following characteristics:

- Complaints of difficulties with memory, concentration, or judgment.
- Lack of energy.
- Poor self-concept and feelings of inferiority.

Brooding (D_5).   High scores on the D_5 subscale may be associated with the following characteristics:

- Lack of energy, apathy, and lethargy.
- Excessive sensitivity to criticism.
- Feelings of despondency and sadness.

Scale 3 (Hysteria) Subscales

Denial of Social Anxiety (Hy_1).   High scores on the Hy_1 subscale may be associated with the following characteristics:

- Social extroversion.
- Ease in talking to, and dealing with, others.

Need for Affection (Hy_2).   High scores on the Hy_2 subscale may be associated with the following characteristics:

- Strong needs for attention and affection.
- Optimistic and trusting in relationships.
- Denial of cynical, hostile, or negative feelings about others.

Lassitude-Malaise (Hy₃). High scores on the Hy_3 subscale may be associated with the following characteristics:

- Unhappiness and discomfort.
- Fatigue, physical problems, and the perception of poor physical health.
- Sadness and despondency.
- Poor appetite and sleep disturbance.

Somatic Complaints (Hy₄). High scores on the Hy_4 subscale may be associated with the following characteristics:

- Multiple somatic complaints and concerns.
- Head or chest pains.
- Fainting, dizziness, and problems with balance.
- Nausea, vomiting, and gastrointestinal disturbances.

Inhibition of Aggression (Hy₅). High scores on the Hy_5 subscale may be associated with the following characteristics:

- Denial of hostile or aggressive impulses.
- Self-perception as decisive.
- Self-perception as socially sensitive.

Scale 4 (Psychopathic Deviate) Subscales

Familial Discord (Pd₁). High scores on the Pd_1 subscale may be associated with the following characteristics:

- View of home and family as unpleasant, hostile, or rejecting.
- View of home situation as lacking in love, critical, and controlling.
- The occurrence of frequent quarrels and conflict within the family.

Authority Problems (Pd₂). High scores on the Pd_2 subscale may be associated with the following characteristics:

- History of legal violations and antisocial behaviors.
- History of conflicts with individuals in authority.
- Resentful of societal standards, customs, or norms.

Social Imperturbability (Pd₃). High scores on the Pd_3 subscale may be associated with the following characteristics:

- Denial of social anxiety and dependency needs.
- Social extroversion and social confidence.
- Tendency to hold strong opinions which are vigorously defended.

Social Alienation (Pd₄). High scores on the Pd_4 subscale may be associated with the following characteristics:

- Feeling misunderstood, alienated, and isolated.
- Feelings of loneliness, unhappiness, and estrangement from others.
- Tendency to blame others for problems or conflicts.
- Feelings of despondency and sadness.

Self-Alienation (Pd₅). High scores on the Pd_5 subscale may be associated with the following characteristics:

- Emotional discomfort and unhappiness.
- Problems in concentration and attention.
- Feelings of guilt, regret, and remorse.
- Possibility of excessive alcohol use.

Scale 6 (Paranoia) Subscales

Persecutory Ideas (Pa₁). High scores on the Pa_1 subscale may be associated with the following characteristics:

- A sense of being treated unfairly by others.
- Externalization of blame for problems and frustrations.
- Use of projection.
- Possible presence of persecutory ideas and delusions of persecution.

Poignancy (Pa₂). High scores on the Pa_2 subscale may be associated with the following characteristics:

- View of self as sensitive, high-strung, and easily hurt.
- Belief that one feels emotions more intensely than do others.
- Loneliness, sadness, and a sense of being misunderstood.
- Self-perception of uniqueness or specialness.

Naivete (Pa₃). High scores on the Pa_3 subscale may be associated with the following characteristics:

- Naively trusting and optimistic.
- Denial of hostile or cynical feelings or attitudes.
- Presentation of high moral or ethical standards.

Scale 8 (Schizophrenia) Subscales

Social Alienation (Sc₁). High scores on the Sc_1 subscale may be associated with the following characteristics:

- Lack of rapport with others.
- Avoidance of social situations and withdrawal from relationships.
- Sense of being misunderstood, unfairly criticized, or unjustly punished by others.
- Hostility or anger toward family members.

Emotional Alienation (Sc₂). High scores on the Sc_2 subscale may be associated with the following characteristics:

- Feelings of despondency, depression, and despair.
- Possibility of suicidal ideation.
- View of life as difficult or hopeless.
- Possibility of sadistic or masochistic experiences.

Lack of Ego Mastery–Cognitive (Sc₃). High scores on the Sc_3 subscale may be associated with the following characteristics:

- Admission of strange thought processes.
- Feelings of unreality.
- Problems in concentration and attention.

Lack of Ego Mastery–Conative (Sc₄). High scores on the Sc_4 subscale may be associated with the following characteristics:

- Feelings of psychological weakness and vulnerability.
- Problems in concentration and attention.
- Lack of energy and psychological inertia.
- Despondency, depression, and possible suicidal ideation.

Lack of Ego Mastery—Defective Inhibition (Sc₅).   High scores on the Sc_5 subscale may be associated with the following characteristics:

- Loss of control over emotions and impulses.
- Restlessness, irritability, and hyperactivity.
- Episodes of uncontrollable laughing or crying.
- Possible dissociative experiences or symptoms.

Bizarre Sensory Experiences (Sc₆).   High scores on the Sc_6 subscale may be associated with the following characteristics:

- Strange or unusual sensory experiences.
- Loss of emotional control.
- The occurrence of a variety of neurological symptoms including paralysis, loss of balance, or involuntary muscular movements.

Scale 9 (Hypomania) Subscales

Amorality (Ma₁).   High scores on the Ma_1 subscale may be associated with the following characteristics:

- A tendency to perceive others as motivated by selfishness and self-gain.
- Endorsement of antisocial or asocial attitudes, beliefs, or behaviors.

Psychomotor Acceleration (Ma₂).   High scores on the Ma_2 subscale may be associated with the following characteristics:

- Acceleration of thought or speech.
- Tension, restlessness, and hyperactivity.
- Need to seek out excitement and stimulation.
- Attraction to sensation-seeking and risk-taking behaviors.

Imperturbability (Ma₃).   High scores on the Ma_3 subscale may be associated with the following characteristics:

- Denial of social anxiety.
- Comfort and confidence in social situations.
- Freedom or independence from the influence of the opinions of others.

Ego Inflation (Ma₄).   High scores on the Ma_4 subscale may be associated with the following characteristics:

- Feelings of self-importance, possibly including grandiosity.
- Resentfulness of perceived demands from, or interference by, others.

Si Subscales

As previously noted, Harris and Lingoes did not attempt to develop subscales for the MMPI basic scales *1, 5, 7,* and *0.* Graham, Schroeder, and Lilly (1971) performed factor analyses of scales *5* and *0* based on the item-level responses of adults in normal and psychiatric settings. Serkownek (1975) utilized the findings from the Graham et al. factor analysis to develop subscales for scales *5* and *0.* The Serkownek subscales received relatively limited clinical attention with adolescents on the original form of the MMPI, and may not be applicable to the MMPI-A because of the extensive item deletions that occurred for scales *5* and *0.*

Ben-Porath, Hostetler, Butcher, and Graham (1989) developed *Si* scale subscales for the MMPI-2 based on their analyses of the responses of normal college men and women. After creating preliminary scales based on item-level factor analysis, three subscales were developed using procedures to maximize internal consistency (alpha coefficient values) while producing scales that were composed of non-overlapping or mutually exclusive items. The *Si* subscales developed by Ben-Porath et al. for the MMPI-2 were carried over to the MMPI-A without modification and are grouped with the Harris–Lingoes subscales on a single profile sheet.

Si_1 has been labeled *Shyness/Self-Consciousness* and Table 6.33 provides examples of the item content from this subscale. The following characteristics may be associated with elevations on the Si_1 subscale:

TABLE 6.33
Items From the Shyness/Self-Consciousness (Si_1) Subscale

Examples of items scored if true
160. I find it hard to make talk when I meet new people.
178. I wish I were not so shy.
270. I am easily embarrassed.
Examples of items scored if false
46.   I am a very sociable person.
336. I do not mind meeting strangers.

Note. Items reproduced from the MMPI-A by permission. Copyright (c) 1992 by the Regents of the University of Minnesota.

TABLE 6.34
Items From the Social Avoidance (Si₂) Subscale

Examples of items scored if true
304.   Whenever possible I avoid being in a crowd.
316.   At parties I am more likely to sit by myself or with just one other person than to join in with the crowd.
Examples of items scored if false
82.   I like to go to parties and other affairs where there is lots of loud fun.
319.   I love to go to dances.
335.   I enjoy the excitement of a crowd.

Note. Items reproduced from the MMPI-A by permission. Copyright (c) 1992 by the Regents of the University of Minnesota.

- Shy around others and easily embarrassed.
- Ill at ease in social situations.
- Uncomfortable in new situations.

Ben-Porath et al. (1989) labeled Si_2 as *Social Avoidance*. Table 6.34 shows examples of items from this subscale. The following characteristics or features are associated with elevations on this subscale:

- Dislike or avoidance of group activities.
- Avoidance of contact or involvement with others.

The Si_3 subscale was labeled *Alienation—Self and Others*. Table 6.35 provides examples of items from this subscale. This Si subscale appears to involve psychiatric symptomatology that interferes with the ability to

TABLE 6.35
Items From the Alienation-Self and Others (Si₃) Subscale

Examples of items scored if true
53.   I wish I could be as happy as others seem to be.
107.   Most people will use somewhat unfair means to gain what they want.
280.   I am apt to pass up something I want to do when others feel that it isn't worth doing.
282.   I easily become impatient with people.
288.   I forget right away what people say to me.
317.   People often disappoint me.
340.   I feel like giving up quickly when things go wrong.
Examples of items scored if false
    None

Note. Items reproduced from the MMPI-A by permission. Copyright (c) 1992 by the Regents of the University of Minnesota.

adaptively engage with, or relate to, others. The following are characteristics or features that may be associated with elevations on Si_3:

- Low self-esteem and self-concept.
- Self-critical and lack of confidence in judgment.
- Nervous, fearful, indecisive.
- Suspicious or fearful of others.

REFERENCES

Andrucci, G. L., Archer, R. P., Pancoast, D. L., & Gordon, R. A. (1989). The relationship of MMPI and sensation seeking scales to adolescent drug use. *Journal of Personality Assessment, 53*, 253–266.

Archer. R. P. (1987a). *MMPI adolescent interpretive system* [Computer program]. Odessa, FL: Psychological Assessment Resources, Inc.

Archer, R. P. (1987b). *Using the MMPI with adolescents.* Hillsdale, NJ: Lawrence Erlbaum Associates.

Archer, R. P., & Gordon, R. A. (1991, August). Use of content scales with adolescents: Past and future practices. In R. C. Colligan (Chair), *MMPI and MMPI-2 supplementary scales and profile interpretation—content scales revisited.* Symposium conducted at the Annual Convention of the American Psychological Association, San Francisco, CA.

Archer, R. P., Gordon, R. A., Anderson, G. L., & Giannetti, R. A. (1989). MMPI special scale clinical correlates for adolescent inpatients. *Journal of Personality Assessment, 53*, 654–664.

Archer, R. P., & Klinefelter, D. (1992). Relationships between MMPI codetypes and MAC scale elevations in adolescent psychiatric samples. *Journal of Personality Assessment, 58*, 149–159.

Archer, R. P., Pancoast, D. L., & Gordon, R. A. (1991). *The development of the MMPI-A Immaturity (IMM) scale: Findings for normal and clinical samples.* Manuscript in preparation.

Ben-Porath, Y. S., Hostetler, K., Butcher, J. N., & Graham, J. R. (1989). New subscales for the MMPI-2 Social Introversion (Si) scale. *Psychological Assessment: A Journal of Consulting and Clinical Psychology, 1*, 169–174.

Ben-Porath, Y. S., & Sherwood, N. E. (in press). *The MMPI-2 content component scales.* Minneapolis: University of Minnesota Press.

Butcher, J. N., Dahlstrom, W. G., Graham, J. R., Tellegen, A., & Kaemmer, B. (1989). *Minnesota Multiphasic Personality Inventory—2 (MMPI-2): Manual for administration and scoring.* Minneapolis: University of Minnesota Press.

Butcher, J. N., Graham, J. R., Williams, C. L., & Ben-Porath, Y. S. (1990). *Development and use of the MMPI-2 content scales.* Minneapolis: University of Minnesota Press.

Butcher, J. N., & Tellegen, A. (1978). Common methodological problems in MMPI research. *Journal of Consulting and Clinical Psychology, 46*, 620–628.

Butcher, J. N., Williams, C. L., Graham, J. R., Archer, R. P., Tellegen, A., Ben-Porath, Y. S., & Kaemmer, B. (1992). *MMPI-A (Minnesota Multiphasic Personality Inventory—Adolescent): Manual for administration, scoring, and interpretation.* Minneapolis: University of Minnesota Press.

Caldwell, A. B. (1969). *MMPI critical items.* Unpublished mimeograph. (Available from Caldwell Report, 1545 Sawtelle Boulevard, Ste. 14, Los Angeles, CA 90025).

Caldwell, A. B. (1988). *MMPI supplemental scale manual*. Los Angeles: Caldwell Report.

Calvin, J. (1975). *A replicated study of the concurrent validity of the Harris subscales for the MMPI*. Unpublished doctoral dissertation, Kent State University, Kent, Ohio.

Clopton, J. R. (1978). MMPI scale development methodology. *Journal of Personality Assessment, 42,* 148–151.

Clopton, J. R. (1979). Development of special MMPI scales. In C. S. Newmark (Ed.), *MMPI: Clinical and research trends* (pp. 354–372). New York: Praeger.

Clopton, J. R. (1982). MMPI scale development methodology reconsidered. *Journal of Personality Assessment, 46,* 143–146.

Cohn, L. D. (1991). Sex differences in the course of personality development: A meta-analysis. *Psychological Bulletin, 109,* 252–266.

Colligan, R. C. (Chair). (1988, August). *MMPI subscales and profile interpretation: Harris and Lingoes revisited*. Symposium conducted at the Annual Convention of the American Psychological Association, Atlanta, GA.

Colligan, R. C., & Offord, K. P. (1989). The aging MMPI: Contemporary norms for contemporary teenagers. *Mayo Clinic Proceedings, 64,* 3–27.

Dahlstrom, W. G., Welsh, G. S., & Dahlstrom, L. E. (1972). *An MMPI handbook: Vol. I. Clinical interpretation* (rev. ed.). Minneapolis: University of Minnesota Press.

Dahlstrom, W. G., Welsh, G. S., & Dahlstrom, L. E. (1975). *An MMPI handbook: Vol. II. Research applications* (rev. ed.). Minneapolis: University of Minnesota Press.

Foerstner, S. B. (1986). *The factor structure and factor stability of selected Minnesota Multiphasic Personality Inventory (MMPI) subscales: Harris and Lingoes subscales, Wiggins content scales, Wiener subscales, and Serkownek subscales*. Unpublished doctoral dissertation, University of Akron.

Friedman, A. F., Webb, J. T., & Lewak, R. (1989). *Psychological assessment with the MMPI*. Hillsdale, NJ: Lawrence Erlbaum Associates.

Gantner, A., Graham, J., & Archer, R. P. (in press). The usefulness of the MAC scale in differentiating adolescents in normal, psychiatric, and substance abuse settings. *Psychological Assessment: A Journal of Consulting and Clinical Psychology*.

Gocka, E. F., & Holloway, H. (1963). *Normative and predictive data on the Harris and Lingoes subscales for a neuropsychiatric population* (Report No. 7). American Lake, WA: Veterans Administration Hospital.

Gottesman, I. I., Hanson, D. R., Kroeker, T. A., & Briggs, P. F. (1987). New MMPI normative data and power-transformed T-score tables for the Hathaway-Monachesi Minnesota cohort of 14,019 15-year-olds and 3,674 18-year-olds. In R. P. Archer *Using the MMPI with adolescents* (pp. 241–297). Hillsdale, NJ: Lawrence Erlbaum Associates.

Gottesman, I. I., & Prescott, C. A. (1989). Abuses of the MacAndrew Alcoholism scale: A critical review. *Clinical Psychology Review, 9,* 223–242.

Graham, J. R. (1990). *MMPI-2: Assessing personality and psychopathology*. New York: Oxford University Press.

Graham, J. R., Schroeder, H. E., & Lilly, R. S. (1971). Factor analysis of items on the Social Introversion and Masculinity-Femininity scales of the MMPI. *Journal of Clinical Psychology, 27,* 367–370.

Grayson, H. M. (1951). *A psychological admissions testing program and manual*. Los Angeles: Veterans Administration Center, Neuropsychiatric Hospital.

Greene, R. L. (1988). Introduction. In R. L. Greene (Ed.), *The MMPI: Use with specific populations* (pp. 1–21). San Antonio: Grune & Stratton.

Greene, R. L. (1991). *The MMPI-2/MMPI: An interpretive manual*. Boston: Allyn & Bacon.

Greene, R. L., Arredondo, R., & Davis, H. G. (1990, August). *The comparability between the MacAndrew Alcoholism Scale-Revised (MMPI-2) and the MacAndrew Alcoholism Scale*

(MMPI). Paper presented at the Annual Meeting of the American Psychological Association, Boston, MA.

Harris, R. E., & Christiansen, C. (1946). Prediction of response to brief psychotherapy. *Journal of Psychology, 21,* 269–284.

Harris, R. E., & Lingoes, J. C. (1955). *Subscales for the MMPI: An aid to profile interpretation.* Department of Psychiatry, University of California School of Medicine and the Langley Porter Clinic, mimeographed materials.

Holt, R. R. (1980). Loevinger's measure of ego development: Reliability and national norms for male and female short forms. *Journal of Personality and Social Psychology, 39,* 909–920.

Koss, M. P., & Butcher, J. N. (1973). A comparison of psychiatric patients' self-report with other sources of clinical information. *Journal of Research in Personality, 7,* 225–236.

Lachar, D., & Wrobel, T. A. (1979). Validating clinicians' hunches: Construction of a new MMPI critical item set. *Journal of Consulting and Clinical Psychology, 47,* 277–284.

Levitt, E. E. (1989). *The clinical application of MMPI special scales.* Hillsdale, NJ: Lawrence Erlbaum Associates.

Loevinger, J. (1976). *Ego development: Conception and theories.* San Francisco: Jossey-Bass.

Loevinger, J., & Wessler, R. (1970). *Measuring ego development: Vol. I. Construction and use of a Sentence Completion Test.* San Francisco: Jossey-Bass.

MacAndrew, C. (1965). The differentiation of male alcoholic outpatients from non-alcoholic psychiatric outpatients by means of the MMPI. *Quarterly Journal of Studies on Alcohol, 26,* 238–246.

MacAndrew, C. (1979). On the possibility of psychometric detection of persons prone to the abuse of alcohol and other substances. *Addictive Behaviors, 4,* 11–20.

MacAndrew, C. (1981). What the MAC scale tells us about men alcoholics: An interpretive review. *Journal of Studies on Alcohol, 42,* 604–625.

Miller, H. R., & Streiner, D. L. (1985). The Harris–Lingoes subscales: Fact or fiction? *Journal of Clinical Psychology, 41,* 45–51.

Nichols, D. S. (1987). Interpreting the Wiggins MMPI content scales. *Clinical Notes on the MMPI, No. 10.* Minneapolis: National Computer Systems.

Pancoast, D. L., & Archer, R. P. (1988). MMPI adolescent norms: Patterns and trends across 4 decades. *Journal of Personality Assessment, 52,* 691–706.

Rathus, S. A., Fox, J. A., & Ortins, J. B. (1980). The MacAndrew scale as a measure of substance abuse in delinquency among adolescents. *Journal of Clinical Psychology, 36,* 579–583.

Serkownek, K. (1975). *Subscales for Scales 5 and 0 of the MMPI.* Unpublished manuscript.

Sutker, P. B., & Archer, R. P. (1979). MMPI characteristics of opiate addicts, alcoholics and other drug abusers. In C. S. Newmark (Ed.), *MMPI clinical and research trends* (pp. 105–148). New York: Praeger.

Welsh, G. S. (1956). Factor dimensions A and R. In G. S. Welsh & W. G. Dahlstrom (Eds.), *Basic readings on the MMPI in psychology and medicine* (pp. 264–281). Minneapolis: University of Minnesota Press.

Wiggins, J. S. (1966). Substantive dimensions of self-report in the MMPI item pool. *Psychological Monographs, 80* (22, Whole No. 630).

Williams, C. L., Butcher, J. N., Ben-Porath, Y. S., & Graham, J. R. (in press). *MMPI-A content scales: Assessing psychopathology in adolescents.* Minneapolis: University of Minnesota Press.

Wisniewski, N. M., Glenwick, D. S., & Graham, J. R. (1985). MacAndrew scale and sociodemographic correlates of alcohol and drug use. *Addictive Behaviors, 10,* 55–67.

Wolfson, K. P., & Erbaugh, S. E. (1984). Adolescent responses to the MacAndrew Alcoholism scale. *Journal of Consulting and Clinical Psychology, 52,* 625–630.

Wrobel, N. H. (1991, August). Utility of the Wiggins content scales with an adolescent sample. In R. C. Colligan (Chair), *MMPI and MMPI-2 supplementary scales and profile interpretation—content scales revisited*. Symposium conducted at the Annual Conference of the American Psychological Association, San Francisco, CA.

Wrobel, N. H., & Gdowski, C. L. (1989, August). *Validation of Wiggins content scales with an adolescent sample*. Paper presented at the Annual Convention of the American Psychological Association, New Orleans, LA.

INTERPRETIVE STRATEGIES

The MMPI-A, used in conjunction with data from other psychometric tests, psychosocial assessment results, and clinical interview findings, provides a rich source of information concerning a variety of respondent characteristics. MMPI-A findings include data concerning profile validity and the adolescent's test-taking attitude. Validity findings also encompass the degree to which the adolescent's responses were consistent and accurate, both of which bear on the technical validity of the responses. The MMPI-A profile also provides information concerning the presence or absence of psychiatric symptoms along a number of dimensions of psychopathology, as well as indicating the type, nature and extent of symptomatology. Further, review of the adolescent's MMPI-A results should allow for an overall estimate of the adolescent's adjustment level and maturation. The MMPI-A will also typically provide information concerning the adolescent's characteristic defense mechanisms, and the relative effectiveness of these defenses in protecting the adolescent from consciously perceived affective distress and ego threat. The test interpreter should also be able to form an impression concerning the adolescent's typical interpersonal relationships, including such issues as the need for dominance versus submissiveness, and the tendency to be involved with others versus socially withdrawn and isolated.

The use of the MMPI-A will often yield valuable diagnostic impressions and hypotheses for the treatment team of the adolescent patient. It is important to stress, however, that test instruments such as the MMPI-A are most productively used to generate a variety of diagnostic possibilities, rather than an exclusive and single diagnosis. Substantial research has shown that MMPI-derived diagnoses and clinician-derived diagnoses differ substantially in clinical studies of adult psychiatric patients (Graham, 1990) and adolescent patients (Archer & Gordon, 1988). Research has also indicated (Pancoast, Archer, & Gordon, 1988) that simple diagnostic systems for the MMPI appear to perform as well as more complex diagnostic classification systems developed for the MMPI by Goldberg (1965, 1972) and by Meehl and Dahlstrom (1960). Finally, and perhaps most importantly, the MMPI-A provides the clinician with important information concerning treatment considerations and options. These data may include the adolescent's level of motivation to engage in psychotherapy and openness to the therapeutic process. The clinician may also be able to derive information concerning the type of therapy, or combination of therapies, most likely to be effective with the adolescent (e.g., supportive psychotherapies, insight-oriented psychotherapies, behavioral psychotherapies, or psychopharmacological interventions). The MMPI-A results may also allow for inferences concerning the modalities of treatment that appear to be indicated, including individual, family, and group psychotherapies.

STEPS IN MMPI-A PROFILE INTERPRETATION

The ability to derive meaningful and useful information from the MMPI-A is a function of the overall interpretive process utilized with this instrument. Table 7.1 summarizes an interpretive approach for the MMPI-A.

The first two steps in this model emphasize the importance of consideration of the setting in which the MMPI-A is administered, and the history and background information available for the adolescent who is being evaluated. Interpretive hypotheses generated from MMPI-A findings should be carefully coordinated with what is known about the adolescent from extra-test sources. It is possible to usefully interpret an MMPI-A profile in a blind fashion without consideration of the patient's background and history or features of the administration setting. Indeed, these latter sources of information are typically not utilized in computerized interpretations of the MMPI. Nevertheless, demographic, psychosocial history, and psychiatric history information generally increase the accuracy and utility of inferences derived from the MMPI-A.

The third step shown in Table 7.1 concerns the evaluation of the technical validity of the MMPI-A profile. This process includes a review of the number of item omissions that occurred in the response process, and an evaluation of response consistency and response accuracy. Validity assessment approaches were presented in detail in Chapter 3 of

TABLE 7.1
Steps in MMPI-A Profile Interpretation

---

1. Setting in which the MMPI-A is administered
   a. Clinical/psychological/psychiatric
   b. School/academic evaluation
   c. Medical
   d. Neuropsychological
   e. Forensic
2. History and background of patient
   a. Cooperativeness/motivation for treatment or evaluation
   b. Cognitive ability
   c. History of psychological adjustment
   d. History of stress factors
   e. History of interpersonal relationships
   f. Family history, and characteristics
3. Validity
   a. Omissions
   b. Consistency
   c. Accuracy
4. Codetype (provides main features of interpretation)
   a. Degree of match with prototype
      (1) Degree of elevation
      (2) Degree of definition
      (3) Caldwell A-B-C-D Paradigm for multiple high-points
   b. Low-point scales
   c. Note elevation of scales 2 (*D*) and 7 (*Pt*)
5. Supplementary scales (supplement and confirm interpretation)
   a. Factor 1 and Factor 2 issues
      (1) Welsh *A* and *R*
   b. Substance abuse scales
      (1) *MAC-R* and *PRO*
      (2) *ACK*
   c. Psychological maturation
      (1) *IMM* scale
6. Content scales
   a. Supplement, refine, and confirm basic scale data
   b. Interpersonal functioning (*A-fam, A-cyn, A-aln*), treatment recommendations (*A-trt*), and academic difficulties (*A-sch* and *A-las*).
   c. Consider effects of overreporting/underreporting
7. Review of Harris-Lingoes subscales and critical item content
   a. Items endorsed can assist in understanding reasons for elevation of basic scales

---

this text, based on the work of Greene (1989a). As previously noted, response consistency may be evaluated using the MMPI-A Variable Response Inconsistency (*VRIN*) scale, and scores from the True Response Inconsistency (*TRIN*) scale may be used for assessing the presence of an acquiescence or "nay-saying" response style. Inferences concerning response consistency can also be derived by examining the

T-score elevation difference between the MMPI-A F_1 and F_2 subscales, and the overall elevation of F. As we have noted, consistency is a necessary, but not sufficient, condition for technical validity. The accuracy of the adolescent's response patterns may be evaluated using the traditional validity scales F, L, and K, with particular attention to the overall configuration of these three validity measures. In addition to issues of technical validity, however, the MMPI-A validity measures can provide valuable information concerning the adolescent's willingness to engage in the psychotherapeutic process. For example, an MMPI-A validity configuration may indicate a technically valid profile and also demonstrate a level of K scale elevation indicative of a teenager who is likely to underreport psychiatric symptoms and to be guarded and defensive in the psychotherapy process. Thus, MMPI-A validity scales provide information concerning technical validity *and* extra-test characteristics or correlates of the teenager that should be included in the overall interpretation of the adolescent's profile.

The fourth step in the interpretation of the MMPI-A profile involves an examination of the basic or standard scales, including an evaluation of the adolescent's codetype assignment based on his or her most elevated clinical scales. The process of evaluating the adolescent's MMPI codetype includes consideration of the degree of elevation manifested in the profile. The higher the adolescent's basic scale elevations, the more likely that adolescent is to display more of the symptoms or characteristics associated with a codetype classification. Additionally, the greater the degree to which the adolescent's specific MMPI profile corresponds to the prototypic profiles used in research investigations for that codetype, the more confidence we can place in the accuracy of the codetype correlates attributed to the obtained profile. The degree of correspondence between a particular MMPI codetype and the prototypic profile characteristics for a given codetype may be ascertained, for example, by visual inspection of the Marks, Seeman, and Haller (1974) modal profiles. In contrast, the MMPI-A Interpretive System software, distributed by Psychological Assessment Resources and written by Archer (1992), illustrates a statistical approach to this issue. Specifically, the program provides a correlation coefficient that expresses the degree of association between an adolescent's MMPI-A profile and the mean MMPI-A profile characteristics for adolescents classified in that codetype grouping. Further, this program calculates the definition of the codetype, expressed in T scores. The greater the degree to which the adolescent's codetype is clearly defined, that is, the two-point codetype demonstrates a substantial T-score elevation difference between the two most elevated scales and the third highest elevation, the more likely that the particular codetype descriptors will be found to be accurate. As noted in Chapter 5, Alex Caldwell's A-B-C-D Paradigm may prove useful in interpreting profiles with clinical-range elevations on several scales. In addition to high-point descriptors, it may also be useful to examine the low-point characteristics of the adolescent's MMPI-A profile. Chapter 5 of this text provided information concerning the correlates of scale values substantially below T = 50 for the basic MMPI-A scales. Finally, a specific review of MMPI-A scales 2 and 7 will provide information concerning the degree of affective distress currently experienced by the adolescent, permitting important inferences concerning the adolescent's motivation to engage in psychotherapy.

A review of MMPI-A supplementary scales (step 5 in Table 7.1) should provide substantial information to support and refine basic scale interpretation. Welsh's A and R scales indicate an overall level of maladjustment and the use of repression as a primary defense mechanism, respectively. Substance abuse screening information is available through the MMPI-A revision of the MacAndrew (1965) Alcoholism Scale (the MAC-R), as well as two new scales created for the MMPI-A (ACK and PRO) to evaluate alcohol and drug abuse problem areas. The adolescent's level of psychological maturity may be assessed through the use of the Immaturity (IMM) scale.

In addition to supplementary scales, there are 15 content scales on the MMPI-A that may also be used to improve profile interpretation (see step 6 in Table 7.1). Many of the MMPI-A content scales may be used to refine the interpretation of basic scales. For example, scale A-anx may be helpful in relation to scale Pt, scale A-biz may be useful in clarifying interpretations from scale Sc, and scales A-con and A-fam may be helpful in refining interpretations from MMPI scale Pd. Further, content scales such as A-trt may provide very important information concerning the adolescent's probable response to therapy, and A-sch and A-las may signal the presence of academic difficulties. Content scales including A-fam, A-cyn, and A-aln are relevant to descriptions of the adolescent's interpersonal functioning. In evaluating content scale data, however, it is important to consider the effects of overreporting or underreporting, that is, response accuracy, on content scale findings. Because content scales are constructed based on obvious items, adolescents may easily suppress content scale values when underreporting symptomatology, and grossly elevate content scale values when consciously or unconsciously overreporting symptomatology.

In the final stage (step 7) of profile analysis, the MMPI-A interpreter may wish to selectively examine the content of the adolescent's MMPI-A responses as manifested in the Harris–Lingoes (1955) subscales for the standard MMPI-A scales 2, 3, 4, 6, 8, and 9, and as exhibited in responses to "critical" or "follow-up" items. A content review may refine interpretive hypotheses generated from examination of the MMPI-A basic, supplementary, and content scales. This content information, however, should be used only as a means of refining or clarifying hypotheses generated based on results of the standard MMPI-A scales. For example, we have previously noted that Harris–Lingoes subscales should not be interpreted unless a clinical-range elevation has occurred on the corresponding MMPI-A basic scale. Further, since responses to any single MMPI-A item are highly unreliable, extreme caution should be employed in interpreting individual item responses.

CLINICAL CASE EXAMPLES

The purpose of this section is to provide five clinical case examples of MMPI-A findings and interpretations for adolescents in inpatient and outpatient psychiatric settings. These clinical cases were selected from assessment records to illustrate a variety of interpretive issues found in adolescent psychiatric populations. Specifically, these cases illustrate major principles related to determining profile validity, dealing with multiple high-point codetypes, and interpreting supplementary scale and content scale data for adolescents. The MMPI-A interpretations provided for these cases are not exhaustive, and it is likely that the reader may observe additional characteristics or features highly relevant to the description or treatment of these adolescents. Clinical correlate statements are based on a combination of sources including both adolescent and adult correlate studies with the original MMPI as summarized in Chapter 5 of this text, and MMPI-A findings presented in the test manual (Butcher et al., 1992). Psychometric findings from other test instruments are occasionally included in the discussion of these clinical examples to provide additional relevant data and to offer a limited illustration of the ways in which results from other test instruments may enrich the interpretation of MMPI-A profiles. In these presentations, data from other test instruments are typically presented in a very abbreviated form, and the reader is referred to the basic source documents for these instruments to obtain more comprehensive information on their use. The clinical case presentations in this chapter include discussions of the standard or basic MMPI-A scales, the supplementary scales, and the content scales. Data from the Harris-Lingoes subscales are selectively integrated into test findings to illustrate specific points of interpretation.

Clinical Case Example I: 15-Year-Old Male Inpatient

James R. was a 15-year-old, White male from an upper-middle class background who was admitted to an acute adolescent inpatient unit. His presenting problems included the following: (a) increasing depression and suicidal ideation; (b) decreased appetite and hypersomnia; (c) increased communication problems with family members; and (d) self-injurious behaviors involving the use of pointed objects to inflict lacerations on forearm areas. Approximately one year prior to this hospitalization the patient had begun to experiment with the use of marijuana, alcohol, and amphetamines, and had been referred for outpatient counseling and evaluation. At the time of admission, this patient's Wechsler Intelligence Scale for Children—Revised (WISC-R) results produced a Full Scale IQ score of 118, a Performance IQ score of 120, and a Verbal IQ score of 112. Additionally, achievement test data consistently indicated academic skill levels one to two academic grades above age expectations. Data completed by the patient's mother on the Child Behavior Checklist (CBCL), described by Achenbach and Edelbrock (1983), indicated substantial elevations on the Somatic Complaints and Uncommunicative scales. These test findings also indicated an elevated score on the Hostile Withdrawal dimension of the CBCL. This patient's DSM-III-R admission diagnosis was major depression recurrent, unspecified (296.30) and parent-child problem (V Code 61.20).

Figure 7.1 presents James' admission MMPI-A basic scale profile scored on MMPI-A norms, and on adolescent norms for the original MMPI as derived by Marks and Briggs (1972) and provided in Appendix E of this text. Evaluating these findings using the validity assessment model proposed by Greene (1989a), we can note that item omissions (? = 3) and measures of response consistency ($VRIN$ = 3, T = 45, and $TRIN$ = 7, T = 62F) are both within acceptable ranges for James. There is, however, strong evidence that the accuracy of James' responses are unacceptable, with distortion occurring in the significant underreporting of symptomatology. Review of the basic scale profile reveals a validity scale configuration that should raise, even for the novice interpreter, serious concerns regarding profile validity. In particular, the "most closed" configuration formed by F_1, F_2, F, L, and K strongly suggests that this respondent, consciously or unconsciously, underreported symptomatology. In addition to validity scale data, this profile also meets the second criterion for underreporting discussed in Chapter 3, that is, all clinical scale values are within normal limits in an adolescent with known or established evidence of psychopathology. Thus, James' responses to the MMPI-A appear to be consistent, but not accurate.

In addition to the basic scale profile, Fig. 7.2 provides data on the MMPI-A content and supplementary scales. We review this figure to illustrate the effects of underreporting on MMPI-A special scales, but in clinical practice these measures should not be interpreted for invalid

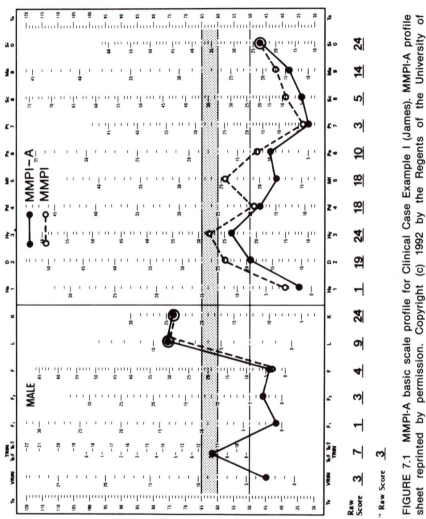

FIGURE 7.1 MMPI-A basic scale profile for Clinical Case Example I (James). MMPI-A profile sheet reprinted by permission. Copyright (c) 1992 by the Regents of the University of Minnesota.

282

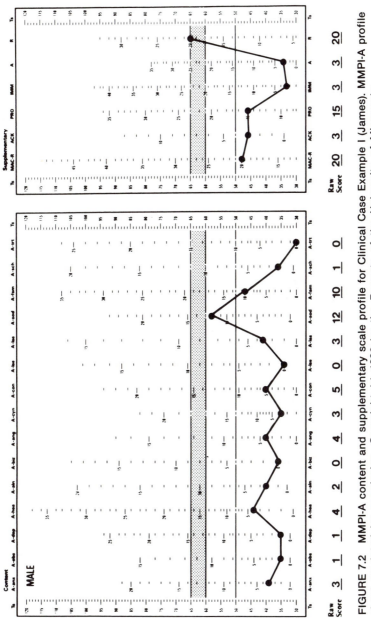

FIGURE 7.2 MMPI-A content and supplementary scale profile for Clinical Case Example I (James). MMPI-A profile sheet reprinted by permission. Copyright (c) 1992 by the Regents of the University of Minnesota.

profiles. MMPI-A content scales are all within normal limits, and might be described as "hyper-normal" in terms of the tendency for scores to occur below T-score values of 50. These low content scale values are related to the marked elevations on validity scales *L* and *K*, and show the degree to which content scale T-score values may be driven down by underreporting response sets because of the obvious nature of content scale items. It is crucial that the MMPI-A interpreter realize that in the present case a T-score value of 30 on the *A-trt* scale, for example, would *not* be related to an openness to engage in psychotherapy or a positive prognosis for therapy outcome. Further, review of the supplementary scales indicates a very low T-score value on Welsh's *A* (T = 34), consistent with James' underreporting of symptomatology and symptoms related to anxiety and maladjustment. His tendency to deny undesirable psychological traits or characteristics may also be seen in the relatively low T-score values obtained for the substance abuse scales *MAC-R, ACK,* and *PRO,* and the very low T-score value found for the Immaturity (*IMM*) scale. In contrast, Welsh's *R* scale shows a moderate level of elevation (T = 65), indicative of a tendency to employ repression as a primary defense mechanism.

Overall, the MMPI-A characteristics produced by James indicate an invalid profile that substantially underrepresents the adolescent's actual symptomatology. James' standard profile, and his content and supplementary scale profiles, are not subject to meaningful or valid interpretation. Further, it is unlikely that readministering the MMPI-A to James will result in a valid profile (Greene, 1989a). The data from James' MMPI-A, however, does provide a very valuable piece of information concerning this adolescent that should be summarized in the psychologist's report. Specifically, the defensive response set displayed by this adolescent indicates that he is probably unmotivated to seriously engage in psychotherapy, has little insight into his problems, and will be very guarded and defensive in the therapy process. This impression was confirmed by the adolescent's individual therapist, who described this adolescent as withdrawn, defensive, and resistant. Following 17 days of inpatient care, this adolescent was released to outpatient psychotherapy, including both individual and family treatment modalities. At the time of discharge, the therapy team rated this patient as minimally improved, and the patient was readmitted within 90 days to an acute adolescent inpatient unit with symptomatology very similar to the presentation for the first hospitalization.

Clinical Case Example II: 17-Year-Old Female Adolescent

Deborah was a 17-year-old, White female adolescent admitted to an acute inpatient adolescent unit within a psychiatric hospital. She had a history of legal violations involving petty larceny, loitering, vagrancy, possession of drugs, possession of drugs with intent to distribute, and psychiatric symptomatology including hostility, anger, and depression. At the time of her admission, the patient's diagnoses were dysthymic disorder (300.40); conduct disorder, undifferentiated type (312.90); and psychoactive substance abuse (305.90). The patient's substance abuse had included alcohol, hallucinogens, marijuana, cocaine, and barbiturates. Immediately prior to this hospitalization, this adolescent had experienced an unintentional drug overdose involving the combination of Valium and cocaine, which required emergency hospitalization.

The patient was an only child from an upper socioeconomic class background, and her father served as an executive vice president for a multinational corporation. His job responsibilities resulted in relocation of the family to Western European countries, and approximately one year prior to this hospitalization the patient had been arrested by British authorities for the possession and sale of narcotics. The patient's parents indicated a chronic history of difficulties in controlling their daughter's behavior, which included repeated episodes of running away from home and school truancy. The patient had a long history of academic underachievement with grades typically in the average to below-average range. The patient's parents also indicated suspicions and concerns regarding possible sexual promiscuity on the part of their daughter, including the possible use of prostitution as a means of acquiring and maintaining drug supplies.

Results of administration of the Wechsler Adult Intelligence Scale— Revised produced a Verbal IQ score of 110, a Performance IQ score of 124, and a Full Scale IQ score of 116. Results of the mother's responses to the Child Behavior Checklist (CBCL) produced marked elevations on the Delinquent and Hyperactive scales. Staff ratings on the Devereux Adolescent Behavior (DAB) Rating Scale, developed by Spivack, Haimes, and Spotts (1967), showed elevations on the Unethical and Defiant/Resistant behavior factors.

Deborah's MMPI-A basic scale profile is shown in Fig. 7.3. We might begin the evaluation of the technical validity of Deborah's profile by noting that she omitted only one item on the Cannot-Say scale, clearly well within acceptable limits for profile interpretation. The response consistency measures of VRIN (raw score = 2) and TRIN (raw score = 10) also produce T-score values (T = 43 and T = 54T, respectively) that are within acceptable standards based on guidelines provided in the MMPI-A manual (Butcher et al., 1992). Further, there is relatively little difference between the magnitude of elevation on scales F_1 (T = 66) and F_2 (T = 53), providing data that assists in ruling out the possibility that Deborah engaged in a random response pattern during the latter part of the test booklet. Also, the validity scale configuration created by scales

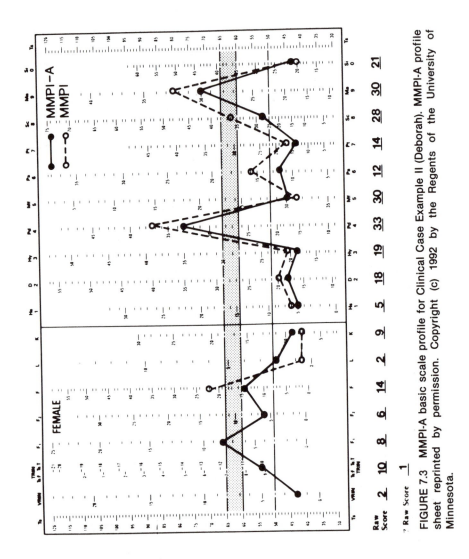

FIGURE 7.3 MMPI-A basic scale profile for Clinical Case Example II (Deborah). MMPI-A profile sheet reprinted by permission. Copyright (c) 1992 by the Regents of the University of Minnesota.

F, L, and *K* are within acceptable limits and consistent with meaningful interpretation of the MMPI-A clinical scale findings.

The basic scale profile produced by Deborah is a well-defined 4-9 codetype, with the term *definition* referring to a T-score difference between the second (scale *9*) and third (scale *8*) most elevated clinical scales. The 4-9 codetype is very commonly found among adolescents in clinical settings, on both the original MMPI and on the MMPI-A. In Marks, Seeman, and Haller's (1974) descriptions of two-point codetypes, the 4-9 code was found to be common among those adolescents referred for treatment because of disobedience, defiance, impulsivity, and school truancy. Marks et al. also observed that these adolescents were likely to be runaways who were described by their parents as difficult to control. Their chief defense mechanism was acting out, and therapists described these adolescents as insecure, resentful of authority figures, socially extroverted, and likely to initially arouse liking in others. Marks et al. noted that adolescents who produced the 4-9/9-4 codetype were often described as provocative, seductive, and handsome, and they referred to these adolescents as "disobedient beauties" (1974, p. 221). Congruent with this description, the correlate data from adult populations indicate that individuals with the 4-9/9-4 codetype are often in trouble with their environment because of antisocial behaviors. Terms including *selfish, self-indulgent,* and *impulsive* are frequently applied to adults with the 4-9 codetype, and a diagnosis of antisocial personality is often assigned to individuals with this code. Consistent with externalizing defenses and antisocial features, it is notable that Deborah's scores on MMPI-A scales *2* and *7*, measures of affective distress, are markedly low for an adolescent recently admitted to inpatient treatment. Indeed, her scores on these scales are below those found for the MMPI-A normative population. This absence of affective distress is a substantial, negative prognostic indicator in terms of the treatment of this adolescent because she may lack the necessary motivation to engage in a difficult therapeutic change process.

Deborah's MMPI-A content scale and supplementary scale profile are presented in Fig. 7.4. Consistent with the basic scale profile, this adolescent produced normal-range scores on measures of affective distress and internal symptoms, including *A-anx, A-obs, A-dep, A-hea,* and *A-biz.* Deborah produced high normal-range elevations on the *A-ang, A-cyn,* and *A-con* scales (T $\geq$ 55 and < 60), the latter indicative of some problem behaviors involving unlawful actions or behaviors that violate societal standards. Overall, this pattern suggests that Deborah is likely to use externalizing defenses and to be in interpersonal conflict as well as conflict with societal norms or expectations. In addition, Deborah produced clinically elevated scores on the *A-fam,*

288

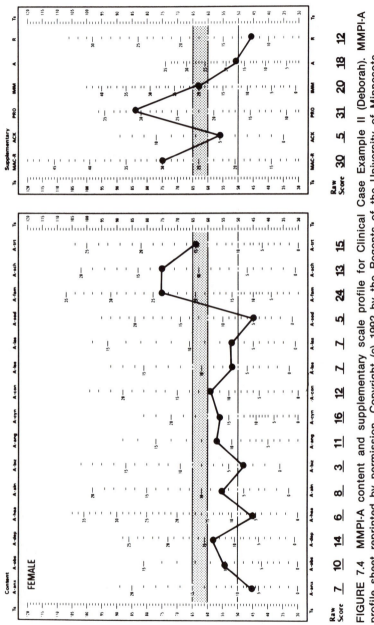

FIGURE 7.4 MMPI-A content and supplementary scale profile for Clinical Case Example II (Deborah). MMPI-A profile sheet reprinted by permission. Copyright (c) 1992 by the Regents of the University of Minnesota.

A-sch, and *A-trt* content scales. The *A-fam* score indicates the presence of substantial family conflict and discord, and the *A-sch* score accurately reflects Deborah's extensive problems in her academic environment involving marginal academic performance, extensive school truancy, and repeated suspensions and disciplinary actions. This adolescent's *A-trt* score probably reflects a negative attitude toward mental health treatment, and may also indicate doubts about her own capacity to change. The *A-trt* scale value underscores the difficulty involved in treating this conduct-disordered adolescent patient.

A survey of Deborah's supplementary scale scores also provides a number of interesting observations. Deborah's raw score value of 30 on the *MAC-R* would result in identification of this adolescent as a probable substance abuser, a finding that is consistent with her very elevated *PRO* scale score (T = 84). Additionally, adolescents with elevated *MAC-R* scores are more likely to receive conduct disorder diagnoses. In contrast, Deborah scores within normal limits on the *ACK* scale (T = 56), a measure of her willingness to acknowledge problematic alcohol or drug use and symptoms associated with such use. Deborah also shows a marginal clinical elevation on the Immaturity scale, a measure of problems and deficits in the area of ego maturation, self-awareness, and the ability to form meaningful relationships with others. Female adolescents producing elevations on this scale have been found to have poor relationships with their parents, and a history of school truancy (Archer, Pancoast, & Gordon, 1991). Deborah's *A* and *R* scale scores (T = 51 and T = 46, respectively) suggest that she was in relatively little general distress at the time of this MMPI-A assessment and that she did not tend to utilize repression as a primary defense mechanism. Such findings are generally consistent with the 4-9/9-4 codetype, in which acting out is a primary defense mechanism.

Following 27 days of intensive inpatient care, Deborah was discharged to outpatient care involving weekly individual, family, and group therapy sessions. This adolescent's prognosis was rated as guarded by treatment staff who believed that her low frustration tolerance, interpersonal manipulativeness, and relative absence of guilt or remorse remained largely unchanged by treatment efforts. Following Deborah's discharge from inpatient treatment, she dropped out of high school and within six months of her discharge was cohabiting with a 27-year-old male actively involved in the use and distribution of drugs. Approximately 18 months following her discharge from inpatient treatment, this adolescent was arrested on multiple counts of possession and distribution of drugs.

Unfortunately, negative treatment outcomes appear to be common for individuals producing the 4-9/9-4 codetype. The 4-9/9-4 codetype has been repeatedly identified as characteristic of adults who are unlikely to show basic personality structure change as a function of treatment (Lachar, 1974; Sutker, Archer, & Kilpatrick, 1981). Lachar, for example, reported that the 4-9/9-4 codetype is a very stable personality pattern among adults that carries a poor prognosis for behavioral improvement as a result of treatment. Further, he reported that roughly 80% of patients with an admission codetype of 4-9 were rated as demonstrating no change at the time of their discharge from treatment. Marks and Seeman (1963) found that adult psychiatric patients who produced a 4-9/9-4 profile at inpatient admission also produced a 4-9 mean profile at discharge.

Clinical Case Example III: 17-Year-Old Adolescent Female

Carolyn was a 17-year-old, Black adolescent female with presenting problems including suicidal ideation, decreased appetite and weight loss, difficulty in sleeping, lethargy, and despondency. The patient came from a lower middle-class background and had three younger siblings. Her mother and father had engaged in a series of escalating arguments and conflicts, resulting in the decision to seek a divorce and her father's departure from the family home. Carolyn's presenting symptoms appear to have originated following her parents' decision to divorce. Carolyn was in the 12th grade at the time of this assessment, with her grades typically in the average to above-average range. She had no history of disciplinary actions in school, and was described as a good and conscientious student. At the time of her admission to treatment, her primary diagnosis was dysthymic disorder (300.40). The patient had no history of substance abuse, nor was there any history of antisocial behaviors or legal infractions. The patient was described by her mother as very responsible, compliant, and cooperative.

Administration of the Wechsler Adult Intelligence Scale–Revised resulted in a Verbal IQ score of 84, Performance IQ score of 91, and a Full Scale IQ score of 86. Achievement test findings indicated reading ability at the 8.5 grade level, math skills at the 11.8 grade level, and written language skills at the 9.5 grade level. The Rorschach, scored using the Comprehensive System (Exner, 1986; Exner & Weiner, 1982), produced the following values: Texture = 0; FC:CF+C = 0:0; W:M = 9:1; Isolate/R = .24; C' = 3; FM = 5; and the Egocentricity Index = .24. These features suggest that Carolyn can be described as interpersonally guarded and isolated; emotionally constricted or overcontrolled; unrealistic in terms of aspirations and goal setting; affected by painful and unexpressed distress; and experiencing deficits in self-concept or self-evaluation. Major indices in the Comprehensive System, including the Depression Index (DEPI) and the Schizophrenia Index (SCZI), were within normal limits. Staff members' ratings of Carolyn on the Devereux Adolescent Behavior (DAB) Rating Scale produced elevations above one standard deviation on the Needs Approval/Dependency dimensions.

Carolyn's MMPI-A basic scale profile is shown in Fig. 7.5. This patient did not omit any items on the MMPI-A, and her $VRIN = 2$ (T = 43) and $TRIN = 8$ (T = 59F) scores are within acceptable limits for adequate response consistency. Further, her T scores on the F_1 (T = 46) and F_2 (T = 51) subscales show a minimal difference in elevation, indicative of a consistent response pattern throughout the entire length of the MMPI-A test booklet. Her validity scale configurations for F, L, and K demonstrate significant differences between MMPI-A norms and the Marks and Briggs (1972) adolescent norms created for the original form of the MMPI. Specifically, her T-score values are substantially higher on scale L, and substantially lower on scale F, when plotted using the MMPI-A normative set. These different patterns produced by the Marks and Briggs and MMPI-A norms probably reflect the relatively high socioeconomic background of the adolescents employed in the MMPI-A normative sample. Beyond this observation, this MMPI-A norm validity scale pattern suggests a relatively naive and unsophisticated adolescent with substantial concerns about "doing the right thing." She is also, however, relatively open and non-defensive in discussing psychiatric symptomatology, perhaps as a reflection of some impairment in self-esteem. Overall, the validity scale data indicate that Carolyn's MMPI-A clinical profile is likely to be valid and subject to meaningful interpretation.

The basic scale profile for this patient shows primary clinical-range elevations on scales *2-3-1*, with secondary clinical-range elevations on MMPI scales *0*, *7*, and *8*. The primary three-point codetype produced by this patient exceeds the available reference literature for the interpretation of adolescent profiles, which is based entirely on studies of single-scale and two-point elevation patterns. The interpretation of a three-point code may be undertaken using either, or both, of two methods. One approach would be to interpret this patient's primary codetype by combining the descriptors derived from the interpretation of the single-scale elevations for scales *1*, *2*, and *3*. Scale *1* correlates would emphasize excessive somatic and bodily concerns (Archer, 1987b; Butcher et al., 1992). It should be noted, however, that part of this patient's elevations on scale *1* may be related to the presence of a seizure disorder, and the scale *1* elevation should be interpreted in light of this factor. Correlates associated with scale *2* elevations involve dissatisfaction, unhappiness, apathy, guilt, pessimism, and possible suicidal ideation, and scale *3* elevations are likely to be related to somatic

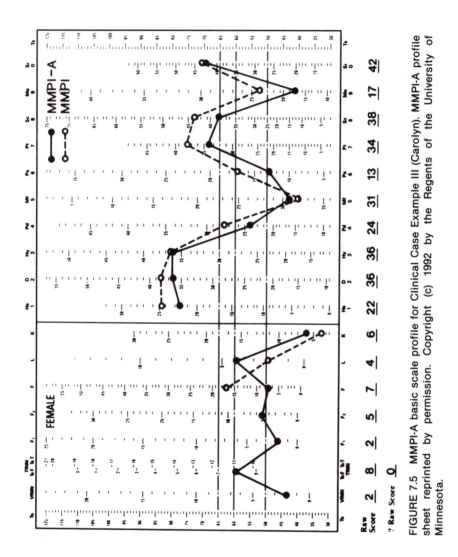

FIGURE 7.5 MMPI-A basic scale profile for Clinical Case Example III (Carolyn). MMPI-A profile sheet reprinted by permission. Copyright (c) 1992 by the Regents of the University of Minnesota.

complaints, emotional dependency, achievement orientation, and emotional lability (Archer, Gordon, Giannetti, & Singles, 1988; Butcher et al., 1992).

A second method for interpreting the primary elevations of this basic scale profile involve the use of Alex Caldwell's (1976) A-B-C-D Paradigm for interpreting multiscale elevations. Using this approach, we would interpret all codetype combinations involving scales *1*, *2*, and *3*, and emphasize correlate features commonly found among the codetype classifications. As noted in Chapter 5, the *1-2/2-1 (A-C/C-A)* codetype is frequently associated with physical symptoms and complaints among adolescents who are described as ruminative, tense, anxious, and insecure. Further, these adolescents are frequently described as depressed, socially withdrawn, and isolated. They often have marked interpersonal concerns and unmet needs for attention and approval by others. The *2-3/3-2 (A-B/B-A)* codetype is often found among adolescents who are emotionally overcontrolled, and unlikely to employ acting out as a primary defense mechanism. Their interpersonal relationships tend to have dependent characteristics, and these adolescents are often described as docile, passive, and unassertive. Further, it was noted in Chapter 5 that the *2-3/3-2* adolescent often has unrealistic aspirations that serve as a major contributor to their sense of inferiority and depression. They are socially isolated, and Marks et al. (1974) noted social histories related to this codetype including an underinvolved father and an overinvolved mother. Finally, the *1-3/3-1 (B-C/C-B)* codetype is also associated with physical symptoms and the use of somatization as a primary defense mechanism. Additional defense mechanisms associated with this codetype include denial and externalization. Taken together, the common features across these codetypes involve the presentation of an unassertive, dependent, and socially isolated adolescent who is very unlikely to engage in antisocial behaviors or to employ acting out as a primary defense mechanism. The use of somatization and denial is common across the codetypes, and the affective component of her profile includes feelings of depression, pessimism, and concerns about physical functioning. In Lachar's (1974) codetype classification system, all three of these codetypes are related to neurotic diagnoses in contrast to psychotic, characterological, or indeterminate classifications.

In addition to these primary codetype features, secondary, marginal-range clinical elevations occur on scales *7*, *8*, and *0*. Carolyn's scale *7* elevation may be associated with tension, apprehension, anxiety, and feelings of insecurity and inadequacy. This patient's *Si* scale elevation indicates a tendency toward social introversion and, potentially, social discomfort and low self-esteem (Butcher et al., 1992). Her values on the

Si subscales, which are plotted on the profile sheet with the Harris-Lingoes subscales, suggest a lack of self-confidence and symptoms of self-alienation that underscore this social introversion. Finally, her scale *8* elevation may involve feelings of inferiority, social withdrawal, and social alienation and could also extend to schizoid or schizophrenic symptoms. In the analyses of MMPI-A data from clinical settings, elevations on scale *8* were also associated with a history of sexual abuse for boys and girls (Butcher et al., 1992). A review of the Harris-Lingoes subscales for scale *8* (not shown in profile figures) indicates that the primary content areas endorsed by this adolescent involve social and emotional alienation and do *not* include psychotic or schizophrenic symptomatology.

Carolyn's content scale and supplementary scale profile is shown in Fig. 7.6. This adolescent demonstrated substantial elevations on four content scales: *A-anx, A-obs, A-dep,* and *A-hea.* These content scales are related to symptomatic behaviors, overall maladjustment, and affective distress. In contrast, this patient shows no elevations on the four content scales related to externalizing behaviors: *A-ang, A-cyn, A-aln,* and *A-con.* The relatively low T-score value for *A-biz* reinforces the view that Carolyn is relatively free from schizophrenic or psychotic symptomatology. Within the subset of content scales related to general problem areas, Carolyn shows a marked elevation on *A-sod,* which tends to underscore the *Si* scale finding that this adolescent is introverted, uneasy around others, and uncomfortable in social situations. Additionally, this adolescent produced an *A-trt* score that, in combination with her relatively low *K* scale value, underscores her potential openness to the psychotherapy process. Carolyn's high *A* supplementary scale score is congruent with elevations on basic scales 2 and 7 in revealing high levels of emotional distress. Supplementary scale values for Carolyn also indicate, consistent with her elevation on the neurotic triad (scales *1, 2,* and *3*), the utilization of repression as a primary defense mechanism (high *R* scale value).

Carolyn was discharged from acute inpatient treatment after seven days and transferred to 45 days of treatment in a day hospital program. Treatment modalities in the latter program included individual, group, and family psychotherapies. During a group psychotherapy session, this adolescent revealed the occurrence of sexual abuse, which then became a primary focus of treatment. Individual therapy emphasis was placed on helping Carolyn explore her mixture of feelings concerning the sexual abuse allegedly perpetrated by her father, as well as her feelings regarding her parents' divorce and her father's departure from their home. Family therapy was focused on assisting Carolyn and her mother in being able to openly discuss the incidents of sexual abuse,

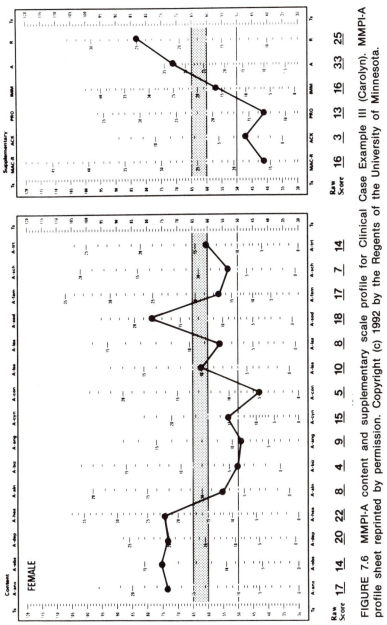

FIGURE 7.6 MMPI-A content and supplementary scale profile for Clinical Case Example III (Carolyn). MMPI-A profile sheet reprinted by permission. Copyright (c) 1992 by the Regents of the University of Minnesota.

295

which had previously been unknown to Carolyn's mother. The day treatment program staff felt Carolyn's progress and prognosis was good, and she was placed in outpatient treatment involving family and individual psychotherapy. Carolyn subsequently graduated from high school and enrolled in a technical college program.

Clinical Case Example IV: 17-Year-Old Female Adolescent

Denise was a 17-year-old, White female adolescent who was administered the MMPI-A as part of an outpatient psychological evaluation. Denise was referred for evaluation by her parents, who indicated presenting problems including running away from home for periods of up to 8 days, suspected alcohol and drug abuse, depression and feelings of dysphoria, and possible suicidal ideations. In a clinical interview, Denise acknowledged that she had abused hallucinogens, marijuana, and cocaine combined with alcohol or Valium. Her parents reported that she was often disrespectful and "talked back" to them, and that she had recently been suspended from school after drugs were found in her locker. Denise's parents, who were from a working-class background, indicated that their daughter's problems had been increasing in intensity over the past 12 months. Denise reported the following stress factors within the last 12 months: death of a close friend due to an accidental drowning, a date rape incident that Denise did not report to the police, and a school suspension related to the incidence of drug possession noted previously. The outpatient admission diagnoses included dysthymic disorder (300.40); conduct disorder, group type (312.20); psychoactive substance abuse (305.90); and a provision to rule out post-traumatic stress disorder (309.89) related to this adolescent's self-report concerning the occurrence of a rape.

In addition to the MMPI-A, this patient was administered the Wechsler Adult Intelligence Scale—Revised, which resulted in a Verbal IQ score of 88, a Performance IQ score of 90, and a Full Scale IQ score of 88. On a standardized achievement test, this patient produced reading skills at the eighth-grade second-month level, math skills at the seventh-year fourth-month level, and written language skills at the ninth-year level. Rorschach findings, as scored and evaluated using the Comprehensive System (Exner, 1986; Exner & Weiner, 1982), indicated a normal length record that included five white-space responses, a D score of -2, an FC:CF+C ratio of 1:4 (including two pure color responses), and a texture = 0 record. These results indicate that Denise may be described as oppositional and angry, impulsive, emotionally labile, and interpersonally guarded as reflected in her need to maintain substantial interpersonal distance.

Denise's MMPI-A basic scale profile is shown in Fig. 7.7. The contrast between this profile, scored using MMPI-A norms, and the Marks and Briggs (1972) traditional adolescent norms is most striking for scales 6, 7, 8, and 9. On these MMPI-A scales, the application of the contemporary norm set collected for this instrument produces T-score values approximately 10 points lower than the Marks and Briggs normative values. There are, however, relatively few interpretive differences between these two profiles, and both result in the classification of this adolescent with a 4-6 codetype. Analysis of the MMPI-A profile should begin at the level of validity assessment. Denise omitted only two items on the MMPI-A profile, well within acceptable limits for profile interpretation. Additionally, this adolescent's *VRIN* raw score of 2 and *TRIN* raw score of 10 (T = 43 and T = 54T, respectively) indicate sufficient response consistency to permit meaningful interpretation of her response patterns. Denise's basic validity scale configuration on F, L, and K indicate a valid protocol without evidence of substantial under or overreporting of symptomatology. There was relatively little difference between her T-score values on F_1 (T = 59) and F_2 (T = 49), and both were well within acceptable limits for profile interpretation. Therefore, validity indicators suggest that Denise's clinical scale profile is valid and interpretable.

This adolescent's two-point codetype (4-6) is among the codetypes more frequently encountered among adolescents receiving psychological evaluations. As noted in Chapter 5, adolescents who produce this codetype frequently report conflicts with their parents, and employ defense mechanisms involving acting out and projection. These adolescents are described as argumentative, angry, and resentful, and are often referred for treatment because of oppositionalism, defiance, and disobedience. Scale 6 elevations in the MMPI-A clinical sample were associated with hostile, dependent, and withdrawn behaviors for boys, while scale 4 elevations were associated with a variety of school and family conflicts and problems across genders (Butcher et al., 1992). Teenagers who produce a 4-6 codetype tend to be interpersonally distant and attempt to avoid forming emotional attachments. They are generally suspicious of the motives of others, and have little insight into the origin of their problems. They have been described as aggressive, bitter, hostile, and quarrelsome, and Marks et al. (1974) reported this codetype to be associated with drug abuse. Additional data available from this adolescent's basic scale profile suggests that her current defenses are effective in protecting her from feelings of affective distress, including depression (scale 2) or anxiety (scale 7), a factor that may be seen as a negative indicator for progress in psychotherapy. A

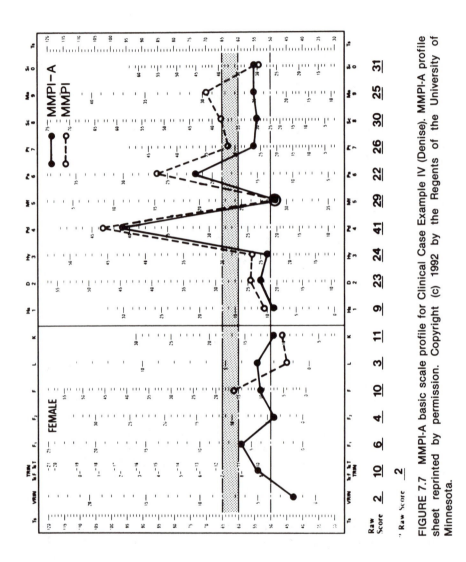

FIGURE 7.7 MMPI-A basic scale profile for Clinical Case Example IV (Denise). MMPI-A profile sheet reprinted by permission. Copyright (c) 1992 by the Regents of the University of Minnesota.

298

review of the Harris-Lingoes subscales for scales 4 and 6 (not shown on figures) indicates that scale 4 is heavily contributed to by responses to the content areas of Familial Discord (Pd_1), Authority Problems (Pd_2), and Self-alienation (Pd_4). Thus, Denise tends to view her family as unsupportive and non-empathetic. She is also in conflict with societal and parental standards, and is likely to feel alienated and estranged. Denise's elevation on the Pa scale is accounted for by a very elevated score on the Persecutory Ideas (Pa_1) subscale, reflecting her sense of being misunderstood and treated unfairly by others, as well as a perception of her environment as threatening or hostile.

In addition to the information derived from the MMPI-A basic scale profile, it is also possible to refine and supplement these interpretive hypotheses by integrating data from the content scales and supplementary scales. The content and supplementary scale profile for this adolescent is shown in Fig. 7.8. As shown in the content scale component of this profile, Denise's clinical-range elevations on scales *A-ang* and *A-fam* reinforce the 4-6 codetype findings by stressing the importance of anger (and anger-control problems), and family conflict and discord in the symptomatology of this adolescent. Comparable to the relative absence of affective distress as reflected on scales 2 and 7 of the basic profile, MMPI-A content scales related to symptomatic distress involving *A-anx*, *A-obs*, *A-hea*, and *A-biz* are all at expected values for normal adolescents. Denise does show, however, an elevation on the *A-dep* scale (T = 66), which stands in contrast to her normal-range score on scale 2 of the basic profile. Her *A-dep* score raises interpretive hypotheses concerning the degree to which Denise feels depressed, unsupported by others, and despondent. This perspective is further reinforced by Denise's low clinical-range score on *A-lse* (T = 65), combined with her marginal-range elevation on *A-aln* (T = 59). Among the more favorable prognostic indicators for this adolescent, Denise's score on *A-trt* (T = 50) is at the mean for normal female adolescents. This finding suggests that her anger and conflicts with authority may not necessarily extend to include inevitable struggles and defensiveness with her therapist. This possibility is further reinforced by Denise's relatively moderate score on scale *K* of the basic profile.

Inspection of Denise's supplementary scale results raise the possibility of alcohol and drug abuse as a significant problem area. Interpreted on a raw score basis, the *MAC-R* value of 26 falls into a "gray" area that would warrant further exploration of substance abuse problems with this adolescent. In contrast, both *ACK* (T = 72) and *PRO* (T = 70) produced T-score elevations within clinically elevated ranges. The *ACK* scale value indicates that this adolescent exhibited a willingness to acknowledge or discuss alcohol or drug use issues and problems.

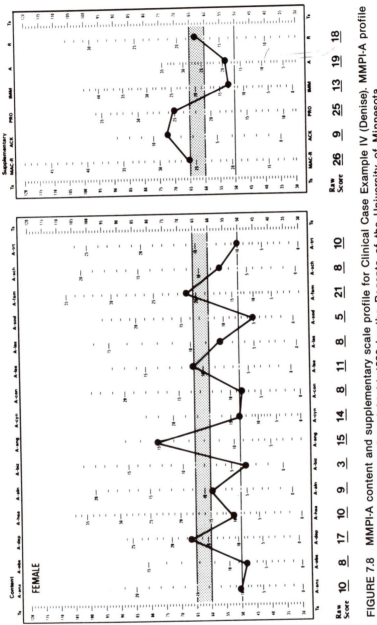

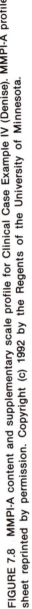

FIGURE 7.8 MMPI-A content and supplementary scale profile for Clinical Case Example IV (Denise). MMPI-A profile sheet reprinted by permission. Copyright (c) 1992 by the Regents of the University of Minnesota.

Another favorable sign for this adolescent is her relatively low value on the Immaturity scale (T = 52), suggesting the presence of age-appropriate psychological development, capacity to form reciprocal interpersonal relationships, and to engage in more complex cognitive operations. Denise's relatively low score on the A scale is consistent with the absence of reports of subjective distress on her basic profile, and her marginal-range elevation on the Repression scale indicates that this defense mechanism may also be employed by Denise in addition to her extensive use of acting out and externalization or projection.

Denise was referred for placement in individual and family psychotherapy, with these services offered by separate psychotherapists. Family therapy focused on Denise's sense of alienation from her family and challenged her perception that her parents were unwilling to respond in a nurturing or comforting manner to the traumatic events that had occurred to her in the past year. Emphasis was also placed on Denise's perception of herself as the "stupid" member of the family in contrast to her high-achieving and academically very successful siblings. Individual psychotherapy focused on Denise's sense of interpersonal loss and fragility following the death of her close friend and the alleged date rape. Individual psychotherapy followed an insight-oriented model in attempting to promote an awareness of the relationship between these feelings and this adolescent's use of projection and acting out as primary defense mechanisms. A major initial focus of individual psychotherapy with Denise also related to building a meaningful and trusting therapist-patient relationship. Denise's individual psychotherapist described her as experiencing problems in the appropriate expression of anger, persistent negativistic or oppositional behaviors, difficulties in frustration tolerance and impatience, and interpersonal manipulativeness. Additionally, Denise was described by her therapist as prone to maintaining a substantial interpersonal distance in her relationships with both peers and adults.

Clinical Case Example V: 16-Year-Old Male Adolescent

Charles was a 16-year-old, Hispanic male adolescent from a lower socioeconomic class family that included two younger sisters and one older brother. Charles was fluent in English and it was the primary language spoken in his home and educational settings. Charles was referred for psychological evaluation with presenting problems of severe depressive symptoms involving anhedonia, feelings of hopelessness, marked lassitude, psychomotor retardation, and sleep disturbance. Charles reported in a mental status examination the occurrence of suicidal ideation, but denied any intent or plan to harm himself. Over the past 2 years, Charles' school performance had deteriorated from As and Bs to marginal grades, including several course failures. Charles had no history of drug or alcohol abuse, nor was there any history of antisocial behaviors or illegal activities. Charles had been seen in outpatient individual therapy for approximately 3 months prior to this referral. The therapist referred this patient for evaluation with a request to provide clarification of the extent and possible etiology of Charles' depression. Charles' father completed the Child Behavior Checklist (CBCL), producing high-range scores for the patient on internalizing behavior problems, including the dimensions of Schizoid, Uncommunicative, and Somatic Complaints.

Charles' MMPI-A basic scale profile, scored on both MMPI-A and Marks and Briggs (1972) adolescent norms, is shown in Fig. 7.9. This adolescent's total item omissions (? = 1) is well within acceptable limits, and his scores on VRIN (raw score = 6, T = 54) and TRIN (raw score = 8, T = 57F) are indicative of a consistent response pattern. Further, the relative difference between this adolescent's T-score value on F_1 (T = 57) and F_2 (T = 52) is quite small, and also supports the conclusion of adequate response consistency for this teenager. Charles' validity scale configuration on scales F, L, and K indicate a valid profile, produced by an adolescent who may be somewhat rigid, guarded, and concerned with issues involving "right and wrong," as reflected in an elevation of the L scale. It should also be noted that some elevation on scale L is not uncommon among Hispanic males (Dahlstrom, Lachar, & Dahlstrom, 1986).

Charles' basic clinical scale profile is not adequately described in two- or three-point codetypes because of the extreme magnitude (over 30 T-score points) of difference between the first- and second-most elevated scales, and the poor definition between the second- and third-most elevated scales. Indeed, the second-most important scale in this basic profile may be the very low elevation on Ma. The high scale 2 score, combined with an extremely low scale 9 score, is indicative of severe depression that is likely to have a strong vegetative component, including sleep and appetite disturbance and psychomotor retardation. Greene (1980) suggested that extremely low scores on scale 9 are indicative of depression, regardless of the degree of elevation exhibited on scale 2. The level of depression, hopelessness, and despair being experienced by this adolescent is likely to be pervasive and overwhelming and should certainly serve as the immediate focus of treatment. Although it was noted in Chapter 5 that the use of the MMPI to determine suicidal risk has not proven productive in systematic research studies, the level of negative affect being reported by this adolescent is so overwhelming that inquiry into suicidal ideation and suicide intent

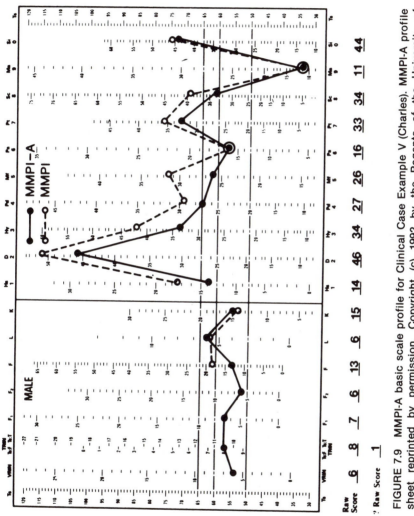

FIGURE 7.9 MMPI-A basic scale profile for Clinical Case Example V (Charles). MMPI-A profile sheet reprinted by permission. Copyright (c) 1992 by the Regents of the University of Minnesota.

303

would be strongly indicated. In the MMPI-A clinical sample, scale 2 elevations were associated with suicidal ideations and/or gestures for both genders (Butcher et al., 1992). In addition to depression, Charles indicated clinically significant levels of anxiety and apprehension as assessed by the *Pt* scale, and substantial somatic concerns and preoccupations as reflected in the scale *Hs* elevation. Additionally, Charles produced a clinical-range elevation on scale *Hy*, which is largely accounted for by a marked elevation on the Harris-Lingoes subscale of lassitude-malaise. This subscale (*Hy$_3$*) is described in the MMPI-A manual (Butcher et al., 1992) as reflecting feelings of discomfort and poor health, and related to weakness, fatigue, and difficulties in concentration and sleeping.

The MMPI-A content scale and supplementary scale profile for this adolescent patient is shown in Fig. 7.10. Charles' content scale results may be initially evaluated by examining elevations on scales related to symptomatic behaviors. Among these scales, Charles' profile shows clinical-range elevations on *A-anx*, *A-obs*, and *A-dep*. These scales, as measures of affective distress, are consistent with the basic scale profile elevations on scales 2 and 7. In contrast, Charles' scores on measures of externalizing behaviors (*A-ang*, *A-cyn*, and *A-con*) produced T-score values of less than 50. This configuration of content scales suggests that Charles is unlikely to be seen as hostile, abrasive, resentful, or angry. Further, his behavior is not likely to pose problems to others in terms of conflicts or violations of commonly accepted social norms and expectations. Unfortunately, this pattern may render Charles a more difficult child to identify in terms of his needs for psychological help. This is because he may "blend into the background" of his peers and his behaviors will not serve to draw attention to himself.

This adolescent's most elevated score occurs on the Low Self-Esteem (*A-lse*) scale, which probably reflects the degree to which Charles is overwhelmed by the number of problems and faults he finds within himself. Charles' profile also shows a secondary clinical-range elevation on *A-trt*, raising issues concerning this adolescent's unwillingness or reluctance to be self-disclosing in psychotherapy. Inspection of Charles' *A-trt* scale item endorsements indicated that this elevation was related to his perception that he could not be helped, that is, that his behaviors and mistakes were "unforgivable" and hopeless. Thus, Charles' elevation on this scale was a reflection of his despondency and depression, rather than cynicism or anger toward treatment providers.

The supplementary scale portion of the profile is shown in Fig. 7.10. All of Charles' T-scores on MMPI-A measures of alcohol and drug abuse (i.e., *MAC-R*, *ACK*, and *PRO*) were T ≤ 60, suggesting no significant problems in the area of alcohol or drug abuse. His score on the *IMM*

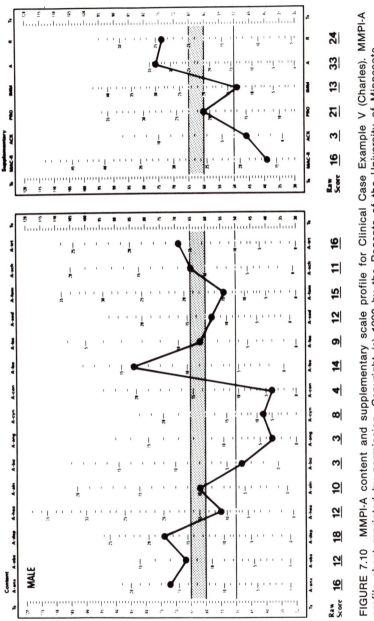

FIGURE 7.10 MMPI-A content and supplementary scale profile for Clinical Case Example V (Charles). MMPI-A profile sheet reprinted by permission. Copyright (c) 1992 by the Regents of the University of Minnesota.

scale (T = 49) indicates that this adolescent is capable of internalizing societal norms and standards, and forming meaningful relationships with others. He is unlikely to exhibit problems in impulse control or externalizing defense mechanisms. Charles does display marked elevations on both the Anxiety scale, a measure of general maladjustment, and the Repression scale. Welsh (1956) suggested that the combination of high scores on *A* and *R* is commonly associated with depressive diagnoses. On a descriptive level, such a pattern would also be consistent with the presence of defense mechanisms that are failing to protect the individual from substantial ego threats and distress.

The evaluation report sent to Charles' outpatient psychotherapist stressed the severity of this adolescent's current level of depression, including the need to evaluate the potential use of psychoactive medications or inpatient hospitalization in the treatment process. The MMPI-A findings, however, do not provide sufficient data to make inferences concerning whether the depressive features found in this testing were situational or more chronic, nor do these data necessarily allow for useful inferences concerning the etiology of these symptoms.

The assessment of adolescents for diagnostic and treatment-planning purposes is often enriched by the inclusion of MMPI or MMPI-2 findings from the adolescent's parents. This practice allows for the evaluation of individual parental features, as well as a potential understanding of family dynamics, in forming recommendations concerning adolescent patients. Although it is recognized that assessment procedures with parents are often difficult or challenging, Archer (1987b) noted that psychological assessment of both the adolescent and his or her parents is possible in the majority of families with adolescents receiving either inpatient or outpatient psychiatric services.

Archer (1987b, 1989); Archer, Stolberg, Gordon, and Goldman (1986); Marks (1961); Williams (1986), and others recommended that the MMPI be given to parents of adolescents to understand the ways in which parental features may interact or influence the presentation of adolescent symptomatology. Research reviews of the MMPI literature in the area of parental-offspring interrelationships have been provided by Archer (1987b); Hafner, Butcher, Hall, and Quast (1969); and Lachar and Sharp (1979). As noted by Archer (1987b), the concept that important and meaningful relationships occur between parental and adolescent personality functioning is congruent with the basic assumptions of numerous theoretical frameworks, including behavioral genetics, psychoanalytic/psychodynamic perspectives, family therapy systems approaches, and behavioral and social learning theory orientations. One of the clearest and most consistent findings in research on parents of psychiatrically disturbed children is that these adults typically display substantial features of psychological distress and maladjustment (Archer, 1987b). The involvement of parents in the assessment process for their teenagers, therefore, does not necessarily involve the assumption of a parental role in the etiology of the adolescent's disorder. Rather, such evaluation efforts are more parsimoniously based on the recognition of the substantial degree of psychological pain and disturbance commonly reported among parents of children experiencing psychological maladjustment and distress. In soliciting the cooperation of parents, Archer (1987b) recommended an approach in which the assessment of parental personality features is explicitly linked to the importance of parents in the treatment process for their teenagers. Thus, as part of their involvement in the treatment process, parents are routinely requested to participate in psychological assessment. Parental assessment results are confidential, and the MMPI or MMPI-2 findings for parents are not discussed in front of adolescents or other family members. Individual parental feedback, or feedback in a couples format, is provided based on parental preferences and psychotherapeutic indications.

In the case of Charles, it was possible to administer the MMPI-2 to both parents within 10 days of the adolescent's MMPI-A administration. Figure 7.11 provides the MMPI-2 profile of Charles' 37-year-old mother. Charles' mother had a substantial antisocial history involving a variety of minor legal violations including over 100 traffic violations, public intoxication charges, and shoplifting violations. There were also questions raised by social service agencies concerning the possibility that mother-son incest may have occurred, with Charles' mother acknowledging that this adolescent slept in the same bed with her until 3 months prior to this psychological evaluation. A review of Charles' mother's MMPI-2 profile indicates the presence of a *4-9-8* codetype, which is associated with impulsive, immature, and poorly thought out or controlled behaviors and actions. Antisocial personality characteristics associated with the *4-9* codetype are combined with aspects of alienation and possible schizophrenic symptomatology associated with elevations on scale *8*. Overall, Charles' mother's MMPI-2 profile indicated a collection of personality traits that would mitigate against this parent's capacity to offer consistent, nurturing parenting for this adolescent.

Charles' father was a 43-year-old factory worker with a history of treatment for chronic depression. Charles' therapist described this adolescent's father as chronically depressed, passive, and guilt ridden. Charles' father stated that he had continued to maintain a marital relationship because of his perception that a parental separation or divorce would do substantial damage to the children. Figure 7.12 provides the MMPI-2 basic scale profile for Charles' father. This MMPI-2

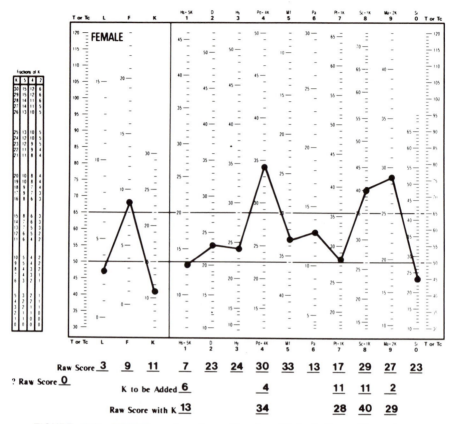

Raw Score __3__ __9__ __11__   __7__   __23__ __24__ __30__ __33__ __13__   __17__ __29__ __27__ __23__

? Raw Score __0__

K to be Added __6__   __4__   __11__   __11__   __2__

Raw Score with K __13__   __34__   __28__   __40__   __29__

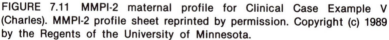

FIGURE 7.11 MMPI-2 maternal profile for Clinical Case Example V (Charles). MMPI-2 profile sheet reprinted by permission. Copyright (c) 1989 by the Regents of the University of Minnesota.

profile appears to be consistent with the impression that Charles' father is experiencing substantial depression, within clinically significant ranges. Review of the Harris and Lingoes (1955) subscales for scale 2 (not provided in figures) indicated that Charles' father produced elevations on subjective depression (D_1) indicative of feelings of unhappiness, depression, and despondency, as well as elevations on psychomotor retardation (D_2) reflective of low energy levels and difficulty in mobilizing energy to cope with the demands of everyday activities. Despite these characteristics, Charles' father had served as the primary parent and care giver for the three dependent children in this family. His continuation of the marital relationship despite his discomfort with his wife's antisocial behaviors may be at least partially attributed to his level of depression and apathy. This decision may also be affected by Charles' father's relatively high *Mf* score, which may reflect passivity and a

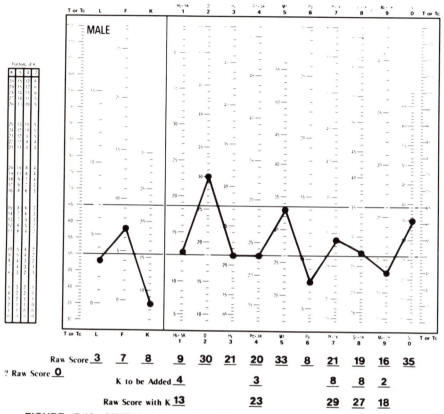

Raw Score 3   7   8   9   30   21   20   33   8   21   19   16   35
? Raw Score 0

K to be Added 4   3   8   8   2

Raw Score with K 13   23   29   27   18

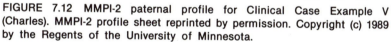

FIGURE 7.12 MMPI-2 paternal profile for Clinical Case Example V (Charles). MMPI-2 profile sheet reprinted by permission. Copyright (c) 1989 by the Regents of the University of Minnesota.

preference to work through problems in an indirect and nonconfrontational manner (Greene, 1980).

Overall, the results of Charles' MMPI-A evaluation, combined with the MMPI-2 assessment of his mother and father, indicated several important directions for intervention. First, it is apparent that individual and family treatment should be combined in providing comprehensive services to this adolescent. An ongoing treatment issue will be the capacity of Charles' mother and father, for differing reasons, to provide adequate guidance and care for this adolescent. Charles' mother, because of characterological and possible thought-disorder symptomatology, has exhibited, and is likely to continue to exhibit, substantial deficits in judgment. Issues related to possible incest require further exploration, and should be reported to Child Protective Services. Charles' father, although responsible, is sufficiently depressed and interpersonally passive to raise questions about his ability to take decisive and necessary actions in providing supervision and protection for his family. It is quite possible that Charles' current symptomatology may reflect a variety of familial influences. These factors could include a genetic predisposition to experience depressive affect, and his possible internalization of anger concerning the failure of his parents, particularly his mother, to provide reasonable and responsible care.

COMPUTER-BASED TEST INTERPRETATION (CBTI) SYSTEMS

The use of computer technology to assist in the administration, scoring, or interpretation of psychological tests is a rapidly developing and evolving area. Butcher (1987b) edited a text overviewing the use of CBTI technology in relationship to a broad variety of assessment measures and tasks, and Moreland (1990) examined the use of computer-assisted technology for adolescent and child personality assessment.

Butcher (1987a) noted that the MMPI served as the first subject of a computer scoring and interpretation system among psychological test instruments because of the extensive empirical literature available on the MMPI, and the strong conceptual basis for actuarial interpretation of MMPI test findings provided by Meehl (1954, 1956, 1986) and others. Further, the MMPI is also the most widely used objective measure of personality in both adult (Lubin, Larsen, & Matarazzo, 1984) and adolescent (Archer, Maruish, Imhof, & Piotrowski, 1991) settings. Thus, the MMPI provided sufficient commercial incentive to motivate individuals to develop CBTI packages for this instrument. The use of CBTI technology has spread far beyond the MMPI to include many diverse assessment instruments. Groth-Marnat and Schumaker (1989) reported that the Veterans Administration has computerized 62 psychological tests for general clinical use. These authors also noted that in a single 1987 edition of the American Psychological Association *Monitor* there were 18 advertisements for psychological test software involving a total of 71 instruments. Krug (1987) provided a sourcebook describing over 300 CBTI products involving various aspects of psychological assessment.

The first application of computer-based test interpretation to the MMPI was developed at the Mayo Clinic in Rochester, Minnesota (Rome et al., 1962; Swenson & Pearson, 1964). This computer-based system was designed to handle the large volume of patients seen at the Mayo Clinic. The first CBTI system to receive widespread professional use, however, was developed by Fowler (1964, 1985) and became operational in 1963. In 1965, the Roche Psychiatric Service Institute, a subdivision of

Roche Laboratories, made the Fowler system commercially available on a national basis. Fowler (1985) reported that over the 17-year period that the report was nationally marketed, one fourth of all clinical psychologists in the United States used this service and approximately 1.5 million MMPI computer-based reports were produced. Another widely used and popular MMPI interpretation system was developed by Alex Caldwell (1971) and is marketed as the *Caldwell Report*. In addition, James Butcher developed an interpretive system in the late 1970s, which was licensed in 1982 by the University of Minnesota to National Computer Systems as the *Minnesota Report* (Fowler, 1985). Both the *Caldwell Report* and the *Minnesota Report* are examples of narrative report services in which computer-based test interpretation software is not sold directly to the consumer. In contrast, Roger Greene, in collaboration with Psychological Assessment Resources, Inc., developed an unlimited-use software system for the interpretation of the MMPI, marketed in 1989 as the *MMPI Adult Interpretive System*. Examples of each of these three reports (i.e., Caldwell's, Butcher's, and Greene's) may be found in Friedman, Webb, and Lewak's (1989) text. Each of these reports were revised and updated to include output on the MMPI-2 following the release of that instrument in August, 1989.

At the time of this writing, CBTI interpretive systems for adolescents' MMPI profiles are available in the form of the *MMPI Adolescent Interpretive System*, developed by Archer (1987a) and marketed through Psychological Assessment Resources (PAR), and the *Marks Adolescent Clinical Report* developed by Phil Marks and Richard Lewak (1991) and distributed by Western Psychological Services. In addition, an MMPI-A interpretive report is scheduled for release in 1992 that was developed by Archer and will be distributed by PAR (the *MMPI-A Interpretive System*), and an MMPI-A report is also being developed by James Butcher and Carolyn Williams (in press), to be distributed through National Computer Systems (NCS). A preliminary (alpha) version of the PAR MMPI-A Adolescent Interpretive System, applied to the second clinical case example presented in this chapter (i.e., Deborah), is presented in the appendix immediately following this chapter.

The development of computer-based test interpretation systems for the MMPI, as well as for other psychometric instruments, has been accompanied by considerable controversy and debate. Automated CBTI reports are based on varying combinations of clinical experience and research findings, resulting in what has been described as an actuarial-clinical approach to test interpretation (Graham, 1987, 1990). For certain instruments, particularly the MMPI, a wide variety of CBTI reports are available, which vary greatly in quality and accuracy. Several MMPI CBTI systems have been written by individuals very knowledgeable in the use of this instrument who have augmented the available research literature with their expert judgment concerning test interpretation procedures. Unfortunately, other commercially available CBTI reports have been written by individuals less skilled in MMPI interpretation procedures, and less knowledgeable concerning the existing MMPI research. Matarazzo (1983, 1986) and Lanyon (1987) expressed concerns regarding the absence of validation studies on automated interpretations of the MMPI. Matarazzo further noted that CBTI programs may give the appearance of accuracy and that inexperienced clinicians may be unaware of the limitations and potential for misuse of these services. The American Psychological Association (APA) recently published a set of guidelines for the development and use of CBTI products (APA, 1986). These guidelines include the provision that professionals limit their use of CBTI products to those instruments with which they are familiar and competent, and that such reports only be used in conjunction with professional judgment. Butcher (1987b) noted that the advantages of computer-based test interpretation reports include the following:

1. *Objectivity.* CBTI products are not subject to interpreter bias, and test rules are automatically and consistently applied to the interpretation of cases.

2. *Use as an Outside Opinion.* CBTI products may serve as a source of second opinion for forensic or legal cases. The CBTI product is useful in this regard because test interpretation is not biased by subjective preconceptions of the interpreter concerning a specific client.

3. *Rapid Turnaround.* CBTI reports can typically be generated within a few minutes after data is entered in the system.

4. *Cost Effectiveness.* The cost of CBTI products varies widely depending on the test distributor, test authors, and nature of the service (e.g., software vs. test report service). Nevertheless, almost all forms of computer-based test interpretation reports compare favorably in terms of cost to clinician-generated reports.

5. *Reliability.* The reliability of a CBTI product should be invariant over repeated uses, in contrast to the errors and lapses in memory manifested by human beings.

In addition to these advantages, Butcher (1987a) also lists several disadvantages connected with CBTI products:

1. *The Question of Excessive Generality.* Computer-based reports are typically based on prototypic profiles, which may differ in many specifics from the individual patient who produced the MMPI profile

being interpreted. As noted by Butcher (1987a), "The most valid computerized reports are those that most closely match the researched prototype" (p. 5). In the worst cases, CBTI reports may include numerous statements that are highly generalizable and could apply to anyone. These types of reports, although appearing accurate to the novice test user, are of little use in attempting to identify the unique features of the individual.

2. *Potential for Misuse.* Because computerized reports are widely available and may be mass produced, the potential for abuse of this type of product may potentially be greater than that of clinically derived personality interpretation reports. This issue is also related to the need to establish that a computer-assisted test administration is equivalent to standard paper-and-pencil test administration procedures in terms of producing equivalent test results. Honaker (1988) noted that insufficient research attention has been directed to this equivalency issue and it remains unresolved at this time.

3. *Clinician Start-Up Time.* The use of computerized psychological testing requires a clinician to become familiar with various aspects of computer use. This task, depending on the degree of "user friendliness" of the CBTI product, may be accomplished quickly or be very time consuming and frustrating.

4. *Confusing Abundance of Packages.* Literally hundreds of CBTI products are currently available for clinician use, and it is becoming increasingly more difficult for clinicians to determine the optimal CBTI products for their applications and setting. Not only must clinicians determine the quality of CBTI products, but there is also the question of "fit" between their particular utilization of tests and various CBTI products that are designed for particular settings, use volume, and methods of scoring or data transfer.

Added to these cautions might be the recommendation that the clinician become aware of the limitations of CBTI reports. Moreland (1985a, 1985b) noted that CBTI programs should be used as only one element in the assessment process, and should never be employed as a substitute for professional judgment. Even the best CBTI programs for the MMPI produce descriptive statements that show only modest relationships, in terms of statement accuracy, to clinician descriptions of the patient (Graham, 1990). In choosing a CBTI product, the following five guidelines are offered to clinicians:

1. All CBTI products represent a combination or blending of the author's clinical judgment with research findings that have been established for a particular instrument. The potential test user, therefore,

should be aware of the identity and expertise of the individual or individuals who developed the CBTI package. In a very real sense, the clinician acquiring a CBTI product is purchasing/leasing the clinical and scientific judgment of the test developers.

2. Know how the CBTI report was written. Specifically, to what extent was the CBTI generated based on empirical findings, and how broad was the empirical base used for the development of the test instrument? The clinician should review the CBTI manual for this information prior to purchasing and using computerized reports.

3. To what degree does the company that markets the CBTI product support its use and application? Before purchasing a CBTI product it is reasonable for the consumer to request samples of interpretive output, and to check the history of the company in terms of customer satisfaction. Does the company have an 800 number available for product use support? Does the company provide a detailed and "user friendly" manual that contains sufficient detail to meaningfully assist the clinician in using the technical and clinical features of the product?

4. Is the CBTI product periodically revised or updated to reflect changes in interpretive practices based on new research findings? This point is particularly important for CBTI products related to the use of the MMPI-2 or the MMPI-A, for which empirical support is rapidly evolving.

5. To what extent has this CBTI product been subject to empirical validation? Moreland (1985b) noted that CBTI products have generated two basic types of research studies. These include consumer satisfaction studies in which CBTI users rate the degree of accuracy and usefulness of the CBTI, and external criterion studies in which comparisons are made between CBTI-based descriptors and patient ratings/descriptions made on the basis of external sources including, for example, psychiatric diagnoses, medical records, and clinician judgments. Based on findings for the original form of the MMPI, it would be anticipated that the accuracy of MMPI-2 and MMPI-A interpretive statements will be found to vary considerably from product to product. Further, Graham (1990) suggested that the accuracy of interpretive statements within a particular CBTI product may be found to vary from codetype to codetype. Also, Moreland (1984) noted that the accuracy of codetype descriptors for rare codetypes is likely to be less accurate than descriptors provided for commonly occurring codetypes that have received extensive research attention.

APPENDIX 7.1

***** MMPI-A INTERPRETIVE SYSTEM *****

developed by

Robert P. Archer, Ph.D.
and PAR Staff

-- CLIENT INFORMATION --

Client : Deborah Davis
Sex : Female
Date of Birth : 01/01/1975
Age : 17
Grade Level : 11
File Name : DAVIS
Test Date : 02/04/1992
Prepared For : ALPHA VERSION

The following MMPI-A interpretive information should be viewed as only one source of hypotheses about the adolescent being evaluated. No diagnostic or treatment decision should be based solely on these data. Instead, statements generated by this report should be integrated with other sources of information concerning this client, including additional psychometric test findings, mental status results, psychosocial history data, and individual and family interviews, to reach clinical decisions.

The information contained in this report represents combinations of actuarial data derived from major works in the adult and adolescent MMPI literatures. This report is confidential and intended for use by qualified professionals only. This report should not be released to the adolescent being evaluated or to his or her family members.

-- MMPI-A PROFILE FOR VALIDITY AND CLINICAL SCALES --

```
                                    Hs   D   Hy  Pd  Mf  Pa  Pt  Sc  Ma  Si
          Vr Tr F1 F2  F   L   K    1    2   3   4   5   6   7   8   9   0
   110- -- -- -- -- -- -- -- + --   --  --  --  --  --  --  --  --  -- -110
      -                     +                                            -
      -                     +                                            -
      -                     +                                            -
      -                     +                                           -100
   100-                     +                                            -
      -                     +                                            -
      -                     +                                            -
      -                     +                                            -
      -                     +                                           -90
    90-                     +                                            -
      -                     +                                            -
      -                     +                                            -
      -                     +                                            -
      -                     +                                           -80
    80-                     +                                            -
      -                     +                                            -
      -                     +           *                                -
      -                     +                                            -
      -                     +                                       * -70
    70-                     +                                            -
      -                     +                                            -
      - -- -- --*-- -- -- -- + --   --  --  --  --  --  --  --  --  -- -
      -                     +                                            -
      -                     +                                            -
    60- -- -- -- -- -- -- -- + --   --  --  --  --  --  --  --  -- -- -60
      -                     +                                            -
      -              *       +                                           -
      -                     +                                            -
      -     *                +                       *                   -
      -           *          +                                      -- -50
    50- -- -- -- -- -- -- -- + --   --  --  --  --  --  --   -- -- -50
      -                 *    +                                           -
      -                     +                   *                        -
      -               *   + *       *           *               * -
    40- *                  + *   *   *       *       *                  -40
      -                     +                                            -
      -                     +                                            -
      -                     +                                            -
      -                     +                                            -
    30- -- -- -- -- -- -- -- + --   --  --  --  --  --  --  --  -- -- -30
                                    Hs   D   Hy  Pd  Mf  Pa  Pt  Sc  Ma  Si
          Vr Tr F1 F2  F   L   K    1    2   3   4   5   6   7   8   9   0
   T-     43    66    59    44    42   45  42  77  45  47  42  52  71  43
   Scores    54    53    49
```

Unanswered (?) Items = 1   Welsh Code: 49'+-8/6<u>25</u> <u>0137</u>:   F/LK:

```
                -- MMPI-A PROFILE FOR CONTENT AND SUPPLEMENTARY SCALES --

                                                        M
         A   O   D   H   A   B   A   C   C   L   L   S   F   S   T   A   A   P   I
         n   b   e   e   l   i   n   y   o   s   a   o   a   c   r   C   C   R   M
         x   s   p   a   n   z   g   n   n   e   s   d   m   h   t   r   K   O   M   A   R
 110---  --  --  --  --  --  --  --  --  --  --  --  --  --  --  --  +   --  --  --  --  --  ---110
   -                                                                 +
   -                                                                 +
   -                                                                 +
 100-                                                                +                         -100
   -                                                                 +
   -                                                                 +
   -                                                                 +
   -                                                                 +
  90-                                                                +                         -90
   -                                                                 +
   -                                                                 +
   -                                                                 +               *         -
  80-                                                                +                         -80
   -                                                                 +
   -                                                                 +
   -                                               *   *           + *                         -
  70-                                                                +                         -70
   ---  --  --  --  --  --  --  --  --  --  --  --  --  --  --  --  + --  --  --  --  --  ---
   -                                                           *   +                           -
  60---  --  --  --  --  --  --  --  --  --  --  --  --  --  --  +  --  --  --  *   --  --  ---60
   -             *                                                   +                         -
   -                                   *                             +                         -
   -         *           *   *       *                               +           *             -
  50---  --  --  --  --  --  --  --  --  --  --  --  --  --  --  --  +  --  --  --  --  --*  ---50
   -                         *               *   *                   +                         -
   -   *           *                                   *             +               *-        -
  40-                                                                +                         -40
   -                                                                 +
   -                                                                 +
   -                                                                 +
  30---  --  --  --  --  --  --  --  --  --  --  --  --  --  --  --  +  --  --  --  --  --  ---30

         A   O   D   H   A   B   A   C   C   L   L   S   F   S   T   M   A   P   I
         n   b   e   e   l   i   n   y   o   s   a   o   a   c   r   A   C   R   M
         x   s   p   a   n   z   g   n   n   e   s   d   m   h   t   C   K   O   M   A   R
  T-  45      58      55      57      59      52      75      r   75      84      51
Scores   54      45      48      56      52      45      75          56      63      46
```

```
                   -- PROFILE MATCHES AND SCORES --


                                          Highest
                                Client    Scale        Best Fit
                       Scale    Profile   Codetype     Codetype
        -------------------------------------------------------------
        Codetype Match:                   4-9/9-4      4-9/9-4
        Coefficient of Fit:               0.95         0.95

        Scores:       F          59       58           58
                      L          49       50           50
                      K          44       50           50
                      Hs  (1)    42       50           50
                      D   (2)    45       50           50
                      Hy  (3)    42       53           53
                      Pd  (4)    77       71           71
                      Mf  (5)    45       49           49
                      Pa  (6)    47       55           55
                      Pt  (7)    42       52           52
                      Sc  (8)    52       54           54
                      Ma  (9)    71       70           70
                      Si  (0)    43       45           45
        -------------------------------------------------------------

        Codetype Definition:     19       15           15


        Mean Clinical
        Scale Elevation:         51       55           55


        Mean Excitatory
        Scale Elevation:         67       65           65

        Mean age-females:                 15.8         15.8
        Mean age-males:                   16.4         16.4

        % of Clinical Cases:              4.0          4.0

        -------------------------------------------------------------
```

Configural clinical scale interpretation is provided in the report for the following codetype(s):

```
                            4-9/9-4
```

```
        -------------------------------------------------------------
```

-- CONFIGURAL VALIDITY SCALE INTERPRETATION --

This adolescent has produced a consistent MMPI-A response pattern as reflected in acceptable values on validity scales VRIN and TRIN.

The F, L, and K pattern found for this profile is indicative of an adolescent who responded in a valid, accurate, and cooperative manner. This F, L, and K pattern is charachteristic of normal adolescents, and is unusual for teenagers in psychiatric settings.

Both F1 and F2 are below T-score values of 90 and within acceptable levels for MMPI-A profile interpretation.

-- VALIDITY SCALES --

Raw (?) = 1

There were a few items omitted in completing this MMPI-A. These omissions may represent areas of limitation in the adolescent's life experience which rendered certain items unanswerable, or limitations in the adolescent's reading ability. There is little probability of profile distortion as a result of these few item omissions.

VRIN T = 43

VRIN scores in this range suggest that the adolescent responded to test items with an acceptable level of consistency.

TRIN T = 54T

Scores in this range suggest that the adolescent responded to test items with an acceptable level of freedom from an acquiescence or "nay-saying" response style.

F1   T = 66

Scores in this range are elevated and suggest that this adolescent has endorsed a substantial number of psychiatric symptoms appearing in the first stage of the MMPI-A test booklet.

F2   T = 53

Scores in this range suggest that the adolescent has responded in a valid manner to items which appear in the latter stage of the MMPI-A test booklet.

F   T = 59

Scores in this range usually indicate that the respondent has answered the test items in a manner similar to most normal adolescents. While some clinical scale elevations may occur, this teenager has not reported many symptoms of highly deviant/unusual psychopathology.

L   T = 49

Scores in this range suggest an appropriate balance between the admission and denial of common social faults. These adolescents are often viewed as flexible and psychologically sophisticated.

K   T = 44

The majority of adolescents score in this range, which represents an appropriate balance between self-disclosure and guardedness. Prognosis for psychotherapy is often good in that such adolescents are open to discussion of life problems and symptoms.

-- CONFIGURAL CLINICAL SCALE INTERPRETATION --

4-9/9-4 Codetype

This MMPI-A profile is classified as a 4-9/9-4 codetype. It occurs more frequently among adolescents than adults, and is found in 10% or more adolescents evaluated in clinical settings.

Teenagers who obtain this profile type display a marked disregard for social standards and are likely to manifest problems related to acting-out and impulsivity. They are described as egocentric, narcissistic, selfish, and self-indulgent, and are often unwilling to accept responsibility for their behaviors. In social situations, these teenagers are extroverted and appear to make an excellent first impression. Their egocentric interpersonal style, however, typically results in chronic difficulties in establishing close and enduring relationships. They are usually referred for treatment because of defiance, disobedience, impulsivity, provocative behavior, and truancy in school. Many of the teenagers with this codetype will develop a history of repeated legal violations and court actions. Drug or alcohol use is also common among adolescents with this codetype. Findings from the supplementary scales MAC-R and PRO also indicate this adolescent has an increased probability of alcohol or drug abuse.

Adolescents who produce this codetype frequently receive Personality Disorder diagnoses (301.XX) and/or Conduct Disorder diagnoses (312.XX). Their primary defense mechanism consists of acting-out, and these teenagers often enter treatment settings without evidence of substantial emotional distress such as anxiety or depression. Therapists perceive these adolescents as resentful of authority figures, narcissistic, egocentric, socially extroverted, self-centered, selfish, and demanding. Adults with this codetype have a markedly poor prognosis for personality or behavior change as a result of psychotherapy. The prognosis for adolescents with this codetype probably is inversely related to the age at which psychotherapy is undertaken. The earlier the psychological intervention, the greater the probability of successful treatment. Examination of content scale A-trt results may assist in evaluating this adolescent's openess to the treatment process. Effective treatment efforts might be focused upon maintaining clear contingencies between the adolescent's behavior and the environmental consequences; i.e., holding the adolescent consistently responsible for their behaviors and setting appropriate limits and consequences for irresponsible or antisocial behaviors. In this latter regard, the use of carefully structured legal restrictions, such as clearly defined probation contingencies, are often useful for teenagers who have manifested repeated legal violations.

-- BASIC CLINICAL SCALES --

Hs (1) =   42

Individuals who score in this range are typically free from somatic preoccupations and report few physical symptoms. Among adolescents, scores in this range have been related to higher levels of intelligence, greater psychological sophistication, and urban rather than rural backgrounds.

D (2) =   45

Adolescents who score in this range often demonstrate higher levels of intelligence and academic achievement. They are self- confident, emotionally stable, and relatively free from feelings of depression and guilt. They are often perceived by others as being alert, competitive, and active. In addition, they usually have the capacity to function effectively across a variety of social situations. Among adolescent psychiatric patients, low scores on Scale 2 may also be related to manipulativeness, rebelliousness, and argumentativeness.

Hy (3) =   42

Scores in this range are frequently obtained by individuals who are perceived by others as unfriendly, tough-minded and realistic. They often have a narrow range of interests and limited social involvements, and avoid leadership roles. They are described by others as being unadventurous, lazy, and underachieving.

Pd (4) =   77

Scale 4 high points are very common among adolescents, particularly in psychiatric or criminal justice settings. Scores in this range are typical for adolescents who are characterized as rebellious, hostile toward authority figures, and defiant.   These adolescents often have histories of poor school adjustment and problems in school conduct. Higher scores on this scale present an increased probability of overtly delinquent behavior. These adolescents often show an inability to delay gratification and are described as being impulsive and having little tolerance for frustration and boredom. Primary defense mechanisms typically involve acting-out, and such behaviors may be unaccompanied by feelings of guilt or remorse. While these adolescents typically create a good first impression and maintain an extroverted and outgoing interpersonal style, their interpersonal relationships tend to be shallow and superficial. They are eventually viewed by others as selfish, self-centered, and egocentric. Review of MMPI-A scales IMM, A-con, A-fam, and A-sch may provide additional data on specific problem areas.

Mf (5) = 45

The obtained score is within normal or expected ranges and indicates
standard interest in traditional feminine activities.

Pa (6) = 47

The obtained score is within normal or expected ranges and items related to
paranoid ideation or excessive suspiciousness were not typically endorsed.

Pt (7) = 42

Scores in this range are frequently obtained by adolescents who are
perceived as self-confident, secure, and emotionally stable. They are
often capable and self-confident in their approach to problems and are
perceived by others as relaxed, warm, and cheerful.

Sc (8) = 52

The obtained score is within normal or expected ranges and suggests intact
reality testing and coherent thought processes.

Ma (9) = 71

Scores in this range are typically obtained by adolescents who are
described as overactive, impulsive, distractible, and restless. They
frequently prefer action to thought and reflection. They are often
unrealistic and grandiose in terms of goal setting. These adolescents have
a greater likelihood of school conduct problems and delinquent behaviors.
They are perceived by others as self-centered, egocentric, talkative, and
energetic. At marked elevations, scores in this range may reflect a
presence of symptoms related to mania such as flight of ideas, grandiose
self-perceptions, and euphoric mood. Review of the Harris-Lingoes
subscales may reveal a more specific view of the content areas endorsed by
this adolescent for scale 9.

Si (0) = 43

The obtained score is within normal or expected ranges and reflects a
balance between social introversion and extroversion in terms of attitude
and behavior patterns.

- CONTENT AND SUPPLEMENTARY SCALES -

Content Scales

Anxiety (A-anx) = 45

The obtained score on this content scale is within normal or expected
ranges.

Obsessiveness (A-obs) = 54

The obtained score on this content scale is within normal or expected ranges.

Depression (A-dep) = 58

The obtained score on this content scale is within normal or expected ranges.

Health Concerns (A-hea) = 45

The obtained score on this content scale is within normal or expected ranges.

Alienation (A-aln) = 55

The obtained score on this content scale is within normal or expected ranges.

Bizarre Mentation (A-biz) = 48

The obtained score on this content scale is within normal or expected ranges.

Anger (A-ang) = 57

The obtained score on this content scale is within normal or expected ranges.

Cynicism (A-cyn) = 56

The obtained score on this content scale is within normal or expected ranges.

Conduct Problems (A-con) = 59

The obtained score on this content scale is within normal or expected ranges.

Low Self-Esteem (A-lse) = 52

The obtained score on this content scale is within normal or expected ranges.

Low Aspirations (A-las) = 52

The obtained score on this content scale is within normal or expected ranges.

Social Discomfort (A-sod) = 45

The obtained score on this content scale is within normal or expected ranges.

Family Problems (A-fam) =   75

Scores in this range are produced by adolescents who have frequent quarrels with family members, and report little love or understanding within their families. They feel misunderstood or unjustly punished by their families. They may report being physically or emotionally abused. These adolescents are often angry, hostile, or frustrated with family members and may wish to leave their homes.

School Problems (A-sch) =   75

Scores in this range are produced by adolescents who are encountering significant behavioral and/or academic problems within the school setting. These adolescents often have developed a negative attitude toward academic achievement and activities. The possibility of learning disabilities or developmental delays should be evaluated.

Negative Treatment Indicators (A-trt) =   64

Scores in this range represent a marginal level of elevation on the A-trt Scale. Adolescents in this range may harbor some concerns regarding their ability to change their behaviors and perceptions, or may have doubts that talking to others is useful in the change process.

Supplementary Scales

MacAndrew Alcoholism (MAC-R) =   75

High scores for adolescents have been related to an increased probability of alcohol and substance abuse. Behaviorally, these adolescents typically appear to be extroverted, sensation seeking, and impulsive. They may have a higher incidence of conduct disorder diagnoses than other adolescents. The high probability of alcohol and drug taking problems would strongly suggest that this teenager be evaluated in terms of the need for substance abuse prevention or treatment interventions. Caution should be exercised in interpreting high MAC scores for minority group adolescents. It is probable that a high rate of false positive errors may occur for non-white respondents.

Alcohol-Drug Problem Acknowledgement (ACK) =   56

Scores in this range are within acceptable or normal limits on the ACK Scale. ACK scores reflect the degree to which an adolescent is prepared to acknowledge drug or alcohol use, which may differ from their actual use. Therefore scores from the MAC-R and PRO Scales should also be carefully reviewed to assist in screening for alcohol and drug related problems.

Alcohol-Drug Problem Proneness (PRO) =   84

Scores in this range are produced by adolescents who are at increased risk for drug and alcohol problems. Scores from the MAC-R and ACK Scales should also be carefully reviewed.

Immaturity (IMM) = 63

Scores in this range are produced by immature adolescents. These
adolescents are easily frustrated, impatient, defiant, and exploitative in
interpersonal relationships. They are likely to have histories of academic
and social difficulties. They are egocentric, tend to externalize blame,
and are simplistic and concrete in cognitive processes.

Anxiety (A) = 51

The obtained score is within normal or expected ranges and indicates
unremarkable levels of anxiety or discomfort.

Repression (R) = 46

The obtained score is within normal or expected ranges and this adolescent
appears to be capable of expressing or discussing problem areas and
negative feelings.

                  - HARRIS-LINGOES AND SI SUBSCALES -

Not selected for interpretation.

                         END OF REPORT
                         ****

REFERENCES

Achenbach, T. M., & Edelbrock, C. S. (1983). *Manual for the Child Behavior Checklist and revised child behavior profile*. Burlington, VT: University of Vermont.

American Psychological Association. (1986). Committee on psychological tests and assessment (CPTA). *Guidelines for computer-based tests and interpretations*. Washington, DC: Author.

Archer, R. P. (1987a). *MMPI adolescent interpretive system* [Computer program]. Odessa, FL: Psychological Assessment Resources, Inc.

Archer, R. P. (1987b). *Using the MMPI with adolescents*. Hillsdale, NJ: Lawrence Erlbaum Associates.

Archer, R. P. (1989). MMPI assessment of adolescent clients. *Clinical Notes on the MMPI, No. 12*. Minneapolis: National Computer Systems.

Archer, R. P. (1992). *MMPI-A interpretive system* [Computer program]. Odessa, FL: Psychological Assessment Resources, Inc.

Archer, R. P., & Gordon, R. A. (1988). MMPI and Rorschach indices of schizophrenic and depressive diagnoses among adolescent inpatients. *Journal of Personality Assessment, 52,* 276–287.

Archer, R. P., Gordon, R. A., Giannetti, R. A., & Singles, J. M. (1988). MMPI scale clinical correlates for adolescent inpatients. *Journal of Personality Assessment, 52,* 707–721.

Archer, R. P., Maruish, M., Imhof, E. A., & Piotrowski, C. (1991). Psychological test usage with adolescent clients: 1990 survey findings. *Professional Psychology: Research and Practice, 22,* 247–252.

Archer, R. P., Pancoast, D. L., & Gordon, R. A. (1991). *The development of the MMPI-A Immaturity (IMM) scale: Findings for normal and clinical samples*. Manuscript in preparation.

Archer, R. P., Stolberg, A. L., Gordon, R. A., & Goldman, W. R. (1986). Parent and child MMPI responses: Characteristics among families with adolescents in inpatient and outpatient settings. *Journal of Abnormal Child Psychology, 14,* 181–190.

Butcher, J. N. (Ed.). (1987a). Computerized clinical and personality assessment using the MMPI. In J. N. Butcher (Ed.), *Computerized psychological assessment: A practitioner's guide* (pp. 161–197). New York: Basic Books.

Butcher, J. N. (1987b). *Computerized psychological assessment: A practitioner's guide*. New York: Basic Books.

Butcher, J. N., Williams, C. L., Graham, J. R., Archer, R. P., Tellegen, A., Ben-Porath, Y. S., & Kaemmer, B. (1992). *MMPI-A (Minnesota Multiphasic Personality Inventory– Adolescent): Manual for administration, scoring, and interpretation*. Minneapolis: University of Minnesota Press.

Butcher, J. N., & Williams, C. L. (in press). *The Minnesota report: Adolescent interpretive system* [Computer program]. Minneapolis: National Computer Systems.

Caldwell, A. B. (1971, April). *Recent advances in automated interpretation of the MMPI*. Paper presented at the Sixth Annual MMPI Symposium, Minneapolis, MN.

Caldwell, A. B. (1976, January). *MMPI profile types*. Paper presented at The Eleventh Annual MMPI Workshop and Symposium, sponsored by the University of Minnesota Press, Minneapolis, MN.

Dahlstrom, W. G., Lachar, D., & Dahlstrom, L. E. (1986). *MMPI patterns of American minorities*. Minneapolis: University of Minnesota Press.

Exner, J. E., Jr. (1986). *The Rorschach: A comprehensive system: Vol. 1. Basic foundations* (2nd ed.). New York: Wiley.

Exner, J. E., Jr., & Weiner, I. B. (1982). *The Rorschach: A comprehensive system: Vol. 3. Assessment of children and adolescents*. New York: Wiley.

Fowler, R. D. (1964, September). *Computer processing and reporting of personality test data*.

Paper presented at the Annual Meeting of the American Psychological Association, Los Angeles, CA.

Fowler, R. D. (1985). Landmarks in computer-assisted psychological assessment. *Journal of Consulting and Clinical Psychology, 53*, 748–759.

Friedman, A. F., Webb, J. T., & Lewak, R. (1989). *Psychological assessment with the MMPI.* Hillsdale, NJ: Lawrence Erlbaum Associates.

Goldberg, L. R. (1965). Diagnosticians vs. diagnostic signs: The diagnosis of psychosis vs. neurosis from the MMPI. *Psychological Monographs, 79* (9, Whole No. 602).

Goldberg, L. R. (1972). Man vs. mean: The exploitation of group profiles for the construction of diagnostic classification systems. *Journal of Abnormal Psychology, 79*, 121–131.

Graham, J. R. (1987). *The MMPI: A practical guide* (2nd ed.). New York: Oxford University Press.

Graham, J. R. (1990). *MMPI-2: Assessing personality and psychopathology.* New York: Oxford University Press.

Greene, R. L. (1980). *The MMPI: An interpretive manual.* Boston: Allyn & Bacon.

Greene, R. L. (1989a). Assessing the validity of MMPI profiles in clinical settings. *Clinical Notes on the MMPI, No. 11.* Minneapolis: National Computer Systems.

Greene, R. L. (1989b). *MMPI adult interpretive system* [Computer program]. Odessa, FL: Psychological Assessment Resources, Inc.

Groth-Marnat, G., & Schumaker, J. (1989). Computer-based psychological testing: Issues and guidelines. *American Journal of Orthopsychiatry, 59*, 257–263.

Hafner, A. J., Butcher, J. N., Hall, M. D., & Quast, W. (1969). Parent personality and childhood disorders: A review of MMPI findings. In J. N. Butcher (Ed.), *MMPI: Research developments and clinical applications* (pp. 181–189). New York: McGraw-Hill.

Harris, R. E., & Lingoes, J. C. (1955). *Subscales for the MMPI: An aid to profile interpretation.* Department of Psychiatry, University of California School of Medicine and the Langley Porter Clinic, mimeographed materials.

Honaker, L. M. (1988). The equivalency of computerized and conventional MMPI administration: A critical review. *Clinical Psychology Review, 8*, 561–577.

Krug, S. E. (1987). *Psychware sourcebook: 1987–88 (2nd ed.).* Kansas City, MO: Test Corporation of America.

Lachar, D. (1974). *The MMPI: Clinical assessment and automated interpretation.* Los Angeles: Western Psychological Services.

Lachar, D., & Sharp, J. R. (1979). Use of parents' MMPIs in the research and evaluation of children: A review of the literature and some new data. In J. N. Butcher (Ed.), *New developments in the use of the MMPI* (pp. 203–240). Minneapolis: University of Minnesota Press.

Lanyon, R. I. (1987). The validity of computer-based personality assessment products: Recommendations for the future. *Computers in Human Behavior, 3*, 225–238.

Lubin, B., Larsen, R. M., & Matarazzo, J. D. (1984). Patterns of psychological test usage in the United States: 1935–1982. *American Psychologist, 39*, 451–454.

MacAndrew, C. (1965). The differentiation of male alcoholic outpatients from nonalcoholic psychiatric outpatients by means of the MMPI. *Quarterly Journal of Studies on Alcohol, 26*, 238–246.

Marks, P. A. (1961). An assessment of the diagnostic process in a child guidance setting. *Psychology Monographs, 75* (3, Whole No. 507).

Marks, P. A. (1991). *Marks adolescent clinical report* [Computer program]. Los Angeles: Western Psychological Services.

Marks, P. A., & Briggs, P. (1972). Adolescent norm tables for the MMPI. In W. G. Dahlstrom, G. S. Welsh, & L. E. Dahlstrom, *An MMPI handbook: Vol. 1. Clinical interpretation* (rev. ed., pp. 388–399). Minneapolis: University of Minnesota Press.

Marks, P. A., & Seeman, W. (1963). *The actuarial description of personality: An atlas for use with the MMPI.* Baltimore: Williams & Wilkins.

Marks, P. A., Seeman, W., & Haller, D. L. (1974). *The actuarial use of the MMPI with adolescents and adults.* New York: Oxford University Press.

Matarazzo, J. D. (1983). Computerized psychological testing. *Science, 221,* 323.

Matarazzo, J. D. (1986). Computerized clinical psychological test interpretations: Unvalidated plus all mean and no sigma. *American Psychologist, 41,* 14–24.

Meehl, P. E. (1954). *Clinical versus statistical prediction: A theoretical analysis and a review of the evidence.* Minneapolis: University of Minnesota Press.

Meehl, P. E. (1956). Wanted: A good cookbook. *American Psychologist, 11,* 263–272.

Meehl, P. E. (1986). Causes and effects of my disturbing little book. *Journal of Personality Assessment, 50,* 370–375.

Meehl, P. E., & Dahlstrom, W. G. (1960). Objective configural rules for discriminating psychotic from neurotic MMPI profiles. *Journal of Consulting Psychology, 24,* 375–387.

Moreland, K. L. (1984, Fall). Intelligent use of automated psychological reports. *Critical Items: A newsletter for the MMPI community, 1,* 4–6. (distributed by National Computer Systems, Minneapolis, MN).

Moreland, K. L. (1985a). Computer-assisted psychological assessment in 1986: A practical guide. *Computers in Human Behavior, 1,* 221–233.

Moreland, K. L. (1985b). Validation of computer-based test interpretations: Problems and prospects. *Journal of Consulting and Clinical Psychology, 53,* 816–825.

Moreland, K. L. (1990). Computer-assisted assessment of adolescent and child personality: What's available. In C. R. Reynolds & R. W. Kamphaus (Eds.), *Handbook of psychological and educational assessment of children: Personality, behavior, and context* (pp. 395–420). New York: Guilford.

Pancoast, D. L., Archer, R. P., & Gordon, R. A. (1988). The MMPI and clinical diagnosis: A comparison of classification system outcomes with discharge diagnoses. *Journal of Personality Assessment, 52,* 81–90.

Rome, H. P., Swenson, W. M., Mataya, P., McCarthy, C. E., Pearson, J. S., Keating, F. R., & Hathaway, S. R. (1962). Symposium on automation techniques in personality assessment. *Proceedings of the Staff Meetings of the Mayo Clinic, 37,* 61–82.

Spivack, G., Haimes, P. E., & Spotts, J. (1967). *Devereux Adolescent Behavior (DAB) Rating Scale manual.* Devon, PA: The Devereux Foundation.

Sutker, P. B., Archer, R. P., & Kilpatrick, D. G. (1981). Sociopathy and antisocial behavior: Theory and treatment. In S. M. Turner, K. S. Calhoun, & H. E. Adams (Eds.), *Handbook of clinical behavior therapy* (pp. 665–712). New York: Wiley.

Swenson, W. M., & Pearson, J. S. (1964). Automation techniques in personality assessment: A frontier in behavioral science and medicine. *Methods of Information in Medicine, 3,* 34–36.

Welsh, G. S. (1956). Factor dimensions A and R. In G. S. Welsh & W. G. Dahlstrom (Eds.), *Basic readings on the MMPI in psychology and medicine* (pp. 264–281). Minneapolis: University of Minnesota Press.

Williams, C. L. (1986). MMPI profiles from adolescents: Interpretive strategies and treatment considerations. *Journal of Child and Adolescent Psychotherapy, 3,* 179–193.

ADOLESCENT NORMS FOR THE ORIGINAL MMPI FOR MALES AND FEMALES FOR AGES 14 AND BELOW, 15, 16, AND 17

Philip A. Marks

Peter F. Briggs

Note. Published in Marks, P. A., Seeman, W., and Haller, D. L. (1974). *The actuarial use of the MMPI with adolescents and adults* (pp. 155-162). Baltimore, MD: William and Wilkins. Originally published in Dahlstrom, W. G., Welsh, G. S., and Dahlstrom, L. E. (1972). *An MMPI handbook: Vol. 1. Clinical interpretation* (pp. 388-398). Minneapolis: University of Minnesota Press. Reprinted by permission.

TABLE A-1

T-score Conversions for Basic Scales Without K-corrections for Adolescents Age 14 and Below

Males

Raw Score	?	L	F	K	1 (Hs)	2 (D)	3 (Hy)	4 (Pd)	5 (Mf)	6 (Pa)	7 (Pt)	8 (Sc)	9 (Ma)	0 (Si)
0	41	32	36	23	34	9	10	10	0	23	30	32	15	11
1		37	38	25	37	12	13	12	3	25	32	33	17	12
2		42	40	27	40	15	16	14	5	27	33	35	19	14
3		46	42	29	43	17	18	16	8	30	34	36	21	15
4		51	44	31	46	19	20	18	10	33	36	37	23	16
5		56	46	33	49	21	22	21	12	35	37	38	25	18
6		61	48	35	52	23	25	23	15	38	38	39	27	19
7		66	50	37	55	26	27	25	17	41	40	40	29	20
8		71	52	39	58	28	29	28	20	44	41	41	31	22
9		76	54	41	61	30	31	30	22	46	43	42	33	23
10	44	80	56	43	64	32	33	32	24	49	44	43	35	24
11		85	58	45	67	35	36	35	27	52	45	44	37	26
12		90	60	48	70	37	38	37	29	55	47	45	39	27
13		95	62	50	73	39	40	39	31	57	48	46	41	28
14		100	64	52	76	41	42	42	34	60	49	47	43	30
15		105	66	54	79	43	44	44	36	63	51	48	45	31
16			68	56	82	46	46	46	38	65	52	50	47	33
17			70	58	84	48	49	49	41	68	54	51	49	34
18			71	60	87	50	51	51	43	71	55	52	50	35
19			73	62	90	52	53	53	46	74	56	53	52	37
20	47		75	64	93	55	56	56	48	76	58	54	54	38
21			77	66	96	57	58	58	50	79	59	55	56	39
22			79	68	99	59	60	60	53	82	60	56	58	41

Females

?	L	F	K	1 (Hs)	2 (D)	3 (Hy)	4 (Pd)	5 (Mf)	6 (Pa)	7 (Pt)	8 (Sc)	9 (Ma)	0 (Si)	Raw Score
41	31	36	19	36	11	7	14	126	28	29	32	16	13	0
	36	39	22	39	13	9	16	124	30	30	34	18	15	1
	41	41	24	41	15	11	19	122	32	32	35	20	16	2
	46	44	27	44	17	13	21	120	34	33	36	22	18	3
	50	46	29	46	20	15	23	118	36	34	37	24	19	4
	55	49	31	49	22	18	25	115	38	36	38	26	20	5
	59	51	33	51	24	20	27	113	40	37	40	28	21	6
	64	54	35	54	26	22	29	111	43	39	41	30	23	7
	69	56	38	56	28	24	31	109	45	40	42	32	24	8
	73	59	40	59	30	27	34	107	47	42	43	35	25	9
44	78	61	42	61	32	29	36	104	49	43	45	37	26	10
	83	64	44	64	34	31	38	102	51	44	46	39	28	11
	87	66	47	66	36	33	40	100	54	46	47	41	29	12
	92	69	49	69	38	35	42	99	56	47	48	43	30	13
	97	71	51	71	41	38	44	97	58	49	49	45	32	14
	101	74	53	74	43	40	46	95	60	50	51	47	33	15
		76	56	76	45	42	49	92	62	52	52	49	34	16
		79	58	79	47	44	51	90	65	53	53	51	35	17
		81	60	81	49	46	53	88	67	54	54	54	37	18
		84	62	84	51	49	55	86	69	56	56	56	38	19
47		86	65	86	53	51	57	84	71	57	57	58	39	20
		89	67	89	55	53	59	81	73	59	58	60	40	21
		91	69	91	57	55	61	79	75	60	59	62	42	22

Males

Raw Score	?	L	F	K	1 (Hs)	2 (D)	3 (Hy)	4 (Pd)	5 (Mf)	6 (Pa)	7 (Pt)	8 (Sc)	9 (Ma)	0 (Si)
23			81	70	102	61	62	62	55	84	62	57	60	42
24			83	72	105	63	64	65	57	87	63	58	62	43
25			85	74	108	66	67	67	60	90	65	59	64	45
26			87	76	111	68	69	69	62	93	66	60	66	46
27			89	79	114	70	71	72	65	95	68	61	68	47
28			91	81	117	72	73	74	67	98	69	62	70	49
29			93	83	120	75	75	76	69	101	70	63	72	50
30	50		95	85	123	77	78	79	72	104	71	65	74	51
31			97		126	79	80	81	74	106	73	66	76	53
32			99		129	81	82	83	76	109	74	67	78	54
33			101		132	83	84	86	79	112	75	68	80	56
34			103			86	87	88	81	114	77	69	82	57
35			105			88	89	90	83	117	78	70	84	58
36			107			90	91	93	86	120	80	71	86	60
37			109			92	93	95	88	123	81	72	88	61
38			111			95	95	97	91	125	82	73	90	62
39			113			97	97	100	93	128	84	74	92	64
40	53		115			99	100	102	95	131	85	75	94	65
41			117			101	102	104	98		86	76	96	66
42			119			103	104	106	100		88	77	98	68
43			121			106	107	109	102		89	78	100	69
44			123			108	109	111	105		91	80	101	70
45			125			110	111	113	107		92	81	103	72

Females

Raw Score	?	L	F	K	1 (Hs)	2 (D)	3 (Hy)	4 (Pd)	5 (Mf)	6 (Pa)	7 (Pt)	8 (Sc)	9 (Ma)	0 (Si)
23			94	71	94	59	58	58	77	78	62	60	64	43
24			96	73	96	62	60	60	75	80	63	62	66	44
25			99	76	99	64	62	62	73	82	64	63	68	45
26			101	78	101	66	64	64	70	84	66	64	70	47
27			104	80	104	68	66	66	68	86	67	65	72	48
28			106	82	106	70	69	69	66	89	69	67	75	49
29			109	85	109	72	71	71	64	91	70	68	77	51
30			111	87	111	74	73	73	62	93	72	69	79	52
31			114		113	76	75	75	59	95	73	70	81	53
32			116		116	78	78	78	57	97	74	71	83	54
33			119		118	80	80	80	55	99	76	73	85	56
34			121			83	82	82	53	102	77	74	87	57
35			124			85	84	84	51	104	78	75	89	58
36			126			87	86	86	48	106	79	76	91	59
37			129			89	89	89	46	108	80	77	94	61
38			131			91	91	91	44	110	82	79	96	62
39			134			93	93	93	42	113	83	80	98	63
40			136			95	95	95	40	115	84	81	100	64
41			139			97	98	98	37		87	82	102	66
42			141			99	100	100	35		89	84	104	67
43			144			102	102	102	33		90	85	106	68
44			146			104	104	104	31		92	86	108	69
45			149			106	106	106	29		93	87	110	71

(Continued)

TABLE A-1 (Continued)

Males

Raw Score	?	L	F	K	1 (Hs)	2 (D)	3 (Hy)	4 (Pd)	5 (Mf)	6 (Pa)	7 (Pt)	8 (Sc)	9 (Ma)	0 (Si)
46				127		112	113	116	109		93	82	105	73
47				129		115	115	118	112		95	83		75
48				131		117	118	120	114		96	84		76
49				133		119	120	123	117			85		77
50	56			135		121	122	125	119			86		79
51				137		123	124		121			87		80
52				139		126	126		124			88		81
53				141		128	129		126			89		83
54				143		130	131		128			90		84
55				145		132	133		131			91		85
56				147		135	135		133			92		87
57				149		137	138		135			93		88
58				151		139	140		138			95		89
59				153		141	142		140			96		91
60	58			155		143	144		143			97		92
61				157								98		93
62				159								99		95
63				161								100		96
64				163								101		98
65												102		99

Females

1 (Hs)	2 (D)	3 (Hy)	4 (Pd)	5 (Mf)	6 (Pa)	7 (Pt)	8 (Sc)	9 (Ma)	0 (Si)	?	L	F	K	Raw Score
	108	109	113	26		94	88		72				152	46
	110	111	115	24		96	90	113	73				154	47
	112	113	117	22		97	91		75				156	48
	114	115	119	20			92		76				159	49
	116	118	122	18			93		77	56			161	50
	118	120		15			95		78				164	51
	120	122		13			96		80				166	52
	123	124		11			97		81				169	53
	125	126		9			98		82				172	54
	127	129		7			99		83				174	55
	129	131		4			101		85				177	56
	131	133		2			102		86				179	57
	133	135					103		87	58			182	58
	135	138					104		88				184	59
	137	140					106		90				187	60
							107		91				189	61
							108		92				192	62
							109		94				194	63
							110		95				197	64
							112		96					65

Males

Raw Score	?	L	F	K	1 (Hs)	2 (D)	3 (Hy)	4 (Pd)	5 (Mf)	6 (Pa)	7 (Pt)	8 (Sc)	9 (Ma)	0 (Si)
66												103		100
67												104		102
68												105		103
69												106		104
70	62											107		106
71												108		
72												110		
73												111		
74												112		
75												113		
76												114		
77												115		
78												116		

Females

Raw Score	?	L	F	K	1 (Hs)	2 (D)	3 (Hy)	4 (Pd)	5 (Mf)	6 (Pa)	7 (Pt)	8 (Sc)	9 (Ma)	0 (Si)
66												113		97
67												114		99
68												115		100
69												117		101
70												118		102
71												119		
72												120		
73												121		
74												123		
75												124		
76												125		
77												126		
78												128		

TABLE A-2

T-score Conversions for Basic Scales Without K-corrections for Adolescents Age 15

Males

Raw Score	?	L	F	K	1 (Hs)	2 (D)	3 (Hy)	4 (Pd)	5 (Mf)	6 (Pa)	7 (Pt)	8 (Sc)	9 (Ma)	0 (Si)
0	41	32	37	22	36	9	12	10	6	27	29	33	15	10
1		37	38	24	39	11	15	13	8	29	31	34	17	12
2		42	40	26	41	13	17	15	10	31	32	35	19	13
3		46	41	28	44	15	20	17	12	33	34	36	21	15
4		50	43	30	46	18	22	19	14	35	35	37	22	16
5		55	45	32	48	20	24	22	16	37	37	38	24	17
6		59	46	34	51	22	26	24	18	40	38	39	26	19
7		63	48	37	53	24	28	26	20	42	39	40	28	20
8		67	50	39	55	27	30	28	22	44	41	41	30	21
9		72	52	41	58	29	32	30	24	46	42	42	32	23
10	44	76	53	43	60	31	34	32	26	48	44	43	34	24
11		80	55	45	62	33	36	34	28	50	45	44	36	25
12		85	57	47	65	36	38	37	31	52	46	45	38	27
13		89	58	49	67	38	40	39	33	54	48	46	40	28
14		93	60	51	69	40	42	41	35	56	49	47	42	30
15		98	62	53	72	43	44	43	37	58	51	48	43	31
16			63	55	74	45	46	45	39	60	52	49	45	32
17			65	58	76	47	48	47	41	63	54	50	47	34
18			67	60	79	49	50	49	43	65	55	51	49	35
19			68	62	81	52	52	52	45	67	56	52	51	36
20	47		70	64	84	54	54	54	47	69	57	53	53	38
21			72	66	86	56	57	56	49	71	59	54	55	39
22			73	68	88	58	59	58	51	73	61	55	57	40

Females

Raw Score	1 (Hs)	2 (D)	3 (Hy)	4 (Pd)	5 (Mf)	6 (Pa)	7 (Pt)	8 (Sc)	9 (Ma)	0 (Si)	?	L	F	K
0	37	9	9	13	120	26	29	32	19	13	41	31	36	21
1	39	11	11	15	118	29	31	34	20	14		36	38	23
2	41	13	13	17	115	31	32	35	22	15		40	41	25
3	43	15	15	19	113	33	33	36	24	17		45	43	27
4	46	17	17	21	111	36	35	37	26	18		49	45	29
5	48	19	19	23	109	38	36	39	28	19		53	47	32
6	50	21	21	25	107	40	37	40	29	21		58	50	34
7	52	24	23	27	105	42	39	41	31	22		62	52	36
8	55	26	25	30	103	44	40	42	33	23		66	54	38
9	57	28	27	32	101	47	41	43	35	24		70	57	40
10	59	30	29	34	100	49	43	44	37	26	44	75	59	42
11	61	32	31	36	98	51	44	45	39	27		79	61	45
12	64	34	33	38	96	53	45	46	41	28		83	63	47
13	66	37	35	40	94	55	47	47	42	30		88	66	49
14	68	39	37	42	92	58	48	48	44	31		92	68	51
15	70	41	39	44	90	60	49	49	46	32		96	70	53
16	72	43	42	46	88	62	51	50	48	33			73	56
17	75	45	44	48	86	64	52	51	50	35			75	58
18	77	47	46	51	84	66	53	53	52	36			77	60
19	79	49	48	53	82	68	55	54	54	37			79	62
20	81	52	50	55	79	71	56	55	56	39	47		82	64
21	84	54	52	57	77	73	58	56	57	40			84	67
22	86	56	54	59	75	75	59	57	59	41			86	69

Males

Raw Score	?	L	F	K	1 (Hs)	2 (D)	3 (Hy)	4 (Pd)	5 (Mf)	6 (Pa)	7 (Pt)	8 (Sc)	9 (Ma)	0 (Si)
23			70	75	91	61	61	60	53	75	62	56	59	42
24			72	77	93	63	63	62	56	77	64	57	61	43
25			74	78	95	65	65	64	58	79	65	58	63	44
26			76	80	98	67	67	66	60	81	66	59	65	46
27			78	82	100	70	69	69	62	83	68	60	66	47
28			81	83	102	72	71	71	64	86	69	61	68	48
29			83	85	105	74	73	73	66	88	71	62	70	50
30	50		85	87	107	77	75	75	68	90	72	63	72	51
31				88	109	79	77	77	70	92	73	64	74	52
32				90	112	81	79	79	72	94	75	65	76	54
33				92	114	83	81	81	74	96	76	66	78	55
34				93		86	83	84	76	98	78	67	80	56
35				95		88	85	86	79	100	79	68	82	58
36				97		90	87	88	81	102	81	69	84	59
37				98		92	89	90	83	104	82	70	86	60
38				100		95	91	92	85	106	83	71	87	62
39				102		97	94	94	87	109	85	72	89	63
40	53			103		99	96	96	89	111	86	73	91	64
41				105		101	98	99	91		88	74	93	66
42				107		104	100	101	93		89	75	95	67
43				108		106	102	103			90	76	97	69
44				110		108	104	105			92	77	99	70
45				112		111	106	107			93	78	101	71

Females

Raw Score	?	L	F	K	1 (Hs)	2 (D)	3 (Hy)	4 (Pd)	5 (Mf)	6 (Pa)	7 (Pt)	8 (Sc)	9 (Ma)	0 (Si)
23			71	89	88	58	56	61	73	77	60	58	61	42
24			73	91	90	60	58	63	71	79	62	59	63	44
25			75	93	93	62	60	65	69	82	63	60	65	45
26			77	95	95	65	62	67	67	84	64	61	67	46
27			80	98	97	67	64	69	65	86	66	62	69	48
28			82	100	99	69	66	71	63	88	67	63	70	49
29			84	102	102	71	68	74	61	90	68	64	72	50
30	50		86	104	104	73	70	76	59	93	70	65	74	52
31				107	106	75	72	78	57	95	71	66	76	53
32				109	108	78	74	80	55	97	72	67	78	54
33				111	110	80	76	82	53	99	74	68	80	55
34				114		82	79	84	51	101	75	69	82	57
35				116		84	81	86	49	103	76	71	83	58
36				118		86	83	88	47	106	78	72	85	59
37				120		88	85	90	45	108	79	73	87	61
38				123		90	87	92	42	110	80	74	89	62
39				125		93	89	95	40	112	82	75	91	63
40	53			127		95	91	97	38	114	83	76	93	64
41				130		97	93	99	36		85	77	95	66
42				132		99	95	101	34		86	78	96	67
43				134		101	97	103	32		87	79	98	68
44				136		103	99	105	30		89	80	100	70
45				139		106	101	107	28		90	82	102	71

(Continued)

TABLE A-2 (Continued)

Males

Raw Score	?	L	F	K	1 (Hs)	2 (D)	3 (Hy)	4 (Pd)	5 (Mf)	6 (Pa)	7 (Pt)	8 (Sc)	9 (Ma)	0 (Si)
46			114			113	108	109	101		95	79	103	73
47			115			115	110	111	104		96	80		74
48			117			117	112	114	106		98	81		75
49			119			120	114	116	108			82		77
50	56		120			122	116	118	110			83		78
51			122			124	118		112			84		79
52			124			126	120		114			85		81
53			125			129	122		116			86		82
54			127			131	124		118			87		83
55			129			133	126		120			88		85
56			130			135	128		122			89		86
57			132			138	131		124			90		87
58			134			140	133		127			91		89
59			135			142	135		129			92		90
60	58		137			145	137		131			93		91
61			139									94		93
62			140									95		94
63			142									96		95
64			144									97		97
65												98		98

Females

Raw Score	?	L	F	K	1 (Hs)	2 (D)	3 (Hy)	4 (Pd)	5 (Mf)	6 (Pa)	7 (Pt)	8 (Sc)	9 (Ma)	0 (Si)
46			141			108	103	109	26		91	83	104	72
47			143			110	105	111	24		93	84		73
48			146			112	107	113	22		94	85		75
49			148			114	109	115	20			86		76
50			150			116	111	118	18			87		77
51	56		152			119	113		16			88		79
52			155			121	115		14			89		80
53			157			123	118		12			90		81
54			159			125	120		10			91		82
55			162			127	122		8			92		84
56			164			129	124		6			93		85
57			166			131	126		3			94		86
58			168			134	128		1			95		88
59	58		171			136	130					97		89
60			173			138	132					98		90
61			175									99		92
62			178									100		93
63			180									101		94
64			182									102		95
65												103		97

Males

Raw Score	?	L	F	K	1 (Hs)	2 (D)	3 (Hy)	4 (Pd)	5 (Mf)	6 (Pa)	7 (Pt)	8 (Sc)	9 (Ma)	0 (Si)
66												99		99
67												100		101
68												101		102
69												102		103
70	62											103		105
71												104		
72												105		
73												106		
74												107		
75												108		
76												109		
77												110		
78												111		

Females

Raw Score	?	L	F	K	1 (Hs)	2 (D)	3 (Hy)	4 (Pd)	5 (Mf)	6 (Pa)	7 (Pt)	8 (Sc)	9 (Ma)	0 (Si)
66												104		98
67												105		99
68												106		101
69	62											107		102
70												108		103
71												109		
72												110		
73												112		
74												113		
75												114		
76												115		
77												116		
78												117		

TABLE A-3
T-score Conversions for Basic Scales Without K-corrections for Adolescents Age 16

Males

Raw Score	?	L	F	K	1 (Hs)	2 (D)	3 (Hy)	4 (Pd)	5 (Mf)	6 (Pa)	7 (Pt)	8 (Sc)	9 (Ma)	0 (Si)
0	41	31	35	20	33	8	10	10	0	34	28	30	11	8
1		35	37	22	36	11	12	12	3	35	30	32	13	10
2		40	39	24	39	13	15	15	5	36	31	33	15	11
3		44	40	27	42	15	17	17	8	37	33	35	17	12
4		49	42	29	45	18	19	19	10	39	34	36	19	14
5		53	44	31	47	20	21	21	12	40	36	37	21	15
6		58	46	33	50	22	23	23	15	42	37	38	23	17
7		62	47	36	53	24	26	25	17	43	39	39	25	18
8		67	49	38	56	27	28	28	20	45	40	40	28	20
9		71	51	40	59	29	30	30	22	46	42	41	30	21
10	44	76	53	42	62	31	32	32	24	48	43	42	32	22
11		80	54	45	64	33	34	34	27	49	45	43	34	24
12		85	56	47	67	36	37	36	29	51	46	44	36	25
13		89	58	49	70	38	39	38	31	52	48	45	38	27
14		94	60	51	73	40	41	41	34	54	49	46	40	28
15		99	61	54	76	42	43	43	36	55	51	48	43	29
16			63	56	78	45	45	45	39	57	52	49	45	31
17			65	58	81	47	47	47	41	58	54	50	47	32
18			66	60	84	49	50	49	43	60	55	51	49	34
19			68	63	87	51	52	51	46	61	56	52	51	35
20	47		70	65	90	54	54	53	48	63	58	53	53	37
21			72	67	93	56	56	56	50	64	59	54	55	38
22			73	70	95	58	58	58	53	66	61	55	58	39

Females

Raw Score	?	L	F	K	1 (Hs)	2 (D)	3 (Hy)	4 (Pd)	5 (Mf)	6 (Pa)	7 (Pt)	8 (Sc)	9 (Ma)	0 (Si)
0	41	29	35	22	35	8	10	11	127	21	27	32	12	10
1		34	37	24	37	10	12	14	125	24	29	33	14	12
2		38	39	26	40	12	14	16	122	27	30	34	17	13
3		42	41	28	42	14	16	18	120	29	32	35	19	15
4		47	43	30	44	16	18	20	118	32	33	36	21	16
5		51	46	33	47	18	20	23	116	35	34	38	23	17
6		56	48	35	49	20	22	25	113	37	36	39	26	18
7		60	50	37	51	22	24	27	111	40	37	40	28	20
8		64	53	39	54	24	26	29	109	42	38	41	30	21
9		69	55	41	56	26	28	31	106	45	40	42	32	22
10	44	73	57	44	58	28	30	33	104	48	41	43	35	23
11		78	59	46	61	30	32	36	102	50	42	44	37	24
12		82	62	48	63	32	34	38	100	53	44	45	39	26
13		86	64	50	65	34	36	40	98	55	45	46	41	27
14		91	66	52	67	36	38	42	96	58	46	47	44	28
15		95	68	55	70	38	40	44	94	61	48	49	46	29
16			71	57	72	40	42	47	91	63	49	50	48	31
17			73	59	74	43	44	49	89	66	50	51	50	32
18			75	61	77	45	46	51	87	68	52	52	53	33
19			77	63	79	47	48	53	84	71	53	53	55	34
20	47		80	66	81	49	50	55	82	74	54	54	57	36
21			82	68	84	51	52	57	80	76	56	55	59	37
22			84	70	86	53	54	60	77	79	57	55	62	38

Males

Raw Score	?	L	F	K	1 (Hs)	2 (D)	3 (Hy)	4 (Pd)	5 (Mf)	6 (Pa)	7 (Pt)	8 (Sc)	9 (Ma)	0 (Si)
23			75	72	98	60	61	60	55	67	62	56	60	41
24			77	74	101	63	63	62	57	68	64	57	62	42
25			79	76	104	65	65	64	60	70	65	58	64	44
26			80	79	107	67	67	66	62	71	67	59	66	45
27			82	81	109	69	69	69	65	73	68	61	68	46
28			84	83	112	71	71	71	67	74	70	62	70	48
29			86	85	115	74	74	73	69	76	71	63	73	49
30	50		87	88	118	76	76	75	72	77	73	64	75	51
31			89		121	78	78	77	74	79	74	65	77	52
32			91		124	80	80	79	76	80	76	66	79	54
33			92		126	82	82	82	79	82	77	67	81	55
34			94			85	85	84	81	83	79	68	83	56
35			96			87	87	86	83	85	80	69	85	58
36			98			89	89	88	86	86	82	70	88	59
37			99			92	91	90	88	88	83	71	90	61
38			101			94	93	92	91	89	85	72	92	62
39			103			96	96	95	93	91	86	74	94	63
40	53		105			98	98	97	95	92	87	75	96	65
41			106			101	100	99	98	94	89	76	98	66
42			108			103	102	101	100	96	90	77	100	68
43			110			105	104	103	103		92	78	103	69
44			112			107	106	105	105		93	79	105	71
45			113			110	109	107	107		95	80	107	72

Females

1 (Hs)	2 (D)	3 (Hy)	4 (Pd)	5 (Mf)	6 (Pa)	7 (Pt)	8 (Sc)	9 (Ma)	0 (Si)	K	F	L	?	Raw Score
88	55	56	62	75	81	58	56	64	39	72	86			23
91	57	57	64	73	84	60	58	66	41	74	89			24
93	59	59	66	70	87	61	59	68	42	77	91			25
95	61	61	68	68	89	62	60	71	43	79	93			26
98	63	63	71	66	92	64	61	73	44	81	95			27
100	65	65	73	64	94	65	62	75	46	83	98			28
102	67	67	75	61	97	66	63	77	47	85	100			29
105	69	69	77	59	99	67	64	80	48	88	102		50	30
107	71	71	79	57	102	69	65	82	49		104			31
109	73	73	82	54	105	70	66	84	51		107			32
112	75	75	84	52	107	71	67	86	52		109			33
	77	77	86	50	110	73	68	89	53		111			34
	79	79	88	47	112	74	69	91	54		113			35
	81	81	90	45	115	75	70	93	55		116			36
	83	83	92	43	118	77	71	95	57		118			37
	85	85	95	40	120	78	72	98	58		120			38
	87	87	97	38	123	79	73	100	59		122			39
	89	89	99	36	125	81	74	102	60		125		53	40
	92	91	101	34		82	75	104	62		127			41
	94	93	103	31		83	77	106	63		129			42
	96	95	106	29		85	78	109	64		131			43
	98	97	108	27		86	79	111	65		134			44
	100	99	110	24		87	80	113	67		136			45

(Continued)

TABLE A-3 (Continued)

Males

Raw Score	?	L	F	K	1 (Hs)	2 (D)	3 (Hy)	4 (Pd)	5 (Mf)	6 (Pa)	7 (Pt)	8 (Sc)	9 (Ma)	0 (Si)
46		115				112	111	110	110		96	81	109	73
47		117				114	113	112	112		98	82		75
48		118				116	115	114	114		99	83		76
49		120				119	117	116	117			84		78
50	56	122				121	120	118	119			85		79
51		124				123	122		121			86		81
52		125				125	124		124			88		82
53		127				128	126		126			89		83
54		129				130	128		129			90		85
55		131				132	130		131			91		86
56		132				134	133		133			92		88
57		134				137	135		136			93		89
58		136				139	137		138			94		90
59		138				141	139		140			95		92
60	58	139				143	141		143			96		93
61		141										97		95
62		143										98		96
63		144										99		98
64		146										101		99
65												102		100

Females

Raw Score	?	L	F	K	1 (Hs)	2 (D)	3 (Hy)	4 (Pd)	5 (Mf)	6 (Pa)	7 (Pt)	8 (Sc)	9 (Ma)	0 (Si)
46			138			102	101	112	22		89	81	115	68
47			140			104	103	114	20		90	82		69
48			143			106	105	116	17		91	83		70
49			145			108	107	119	15			84		72
50	56		147			110	109	121	13			85		73
51			149			112	111		10			86		74
52			152			114	113		8			87		75
53			154			116	115		6			88		77
54			156			118	117		4			89		78
55			158			120	119		1			90		79
56			161			122	121					91		80
57			163			124	123					92		82
58			165			126	124					93		83
59			167			128	126					94		84
60	58		170			130	128					95		85
61			172									97		86
62			174									98		88
63			176									99		89
64			179									100		90
65												101		91

Males

Raw Score	?	L	F	K	1 (Hs)	2 (D)	3 (Hy)	4 (Pd)	5 (Mf)	6 (Pa)	7 (Pt)	8 (Sc)	9 (Ma)	0 (Si)
66												103		102
67												104		103
68												105		105
69												106		106
70		62										107		107
71												108		
72												109		
73												110		
74												111		
75												112		
76												114		
77												115		
78												116		

Females

?	L	F	K	1 (Hs)	2 (D)	3 (Hy)	4 (Pd)	5 (Mf)	6 (Pa)	7 (Pt)	8 (Sc)	9 (Ma)	0 (Si)	Raw Score
											102		93	66
											103		94	67
											104		95	68
											105		96	69
											106		98	70
											107			71
											108			72
											109			73
											110			74
											111			75
											112			76
											113			77
											114			78

TABLE A-4
T-score Conversions for Basic Scales Without K-corrections for Adolescents Age 17*

Males

Raw Score	?	L	F	K	1 (Hs)	2 (D)	3 (Hy)	4 (Pd)	5 (Mf)	6 (Pa)	7 (Pt)	8 (Sc)	9 (Ma)	0 (Si)
0	41	30	32	20	35	16	13	6	5	19	27	31	12	6
1		34	34	23	38	17	15	9	7	22	28	32	14	8
2		38	36	25	40	19	17	11	9	25	30	33	16	9
3		43	39	27	43	21	19	13	11	28	32	34	18	11
4		47	41	29	45	23	21	16	13	31	33	35	20	12
5		51	43	31	48	24	23	18	16	34	35	36	22	14
6		55	45	34	50	26	25	20	18	37	36	37	24	15
7		59	47	36	53	28	27	23	20	40	38	38	26	17
8		63	50	38	55	30	29	25	22	43	39	39	28	18
9		68	52	40	58	32	30	27	24	46	41	40	31	20
10	44	72	54	42	60	34	32	29	26	49	42	41	33	21
11		76	56	45	63	35	34	32	29	52	44	43	35	23
12		80	58	47	65	37	36	34	31	55	45	44	37	24
13		84	60	49	68	39	38	36	33	58	47	45	39	26
14		88	63	51	70	41	40	39	35	61	48	46	41	27
15		93	65	53	73	43	42	41	37	64	50	47	43	29
16			67	56	75	44	44	43	40	67	52	48	45	30
17			69	58	78	46	46	46	42	70	53	49	48	32
18			71	60	80	48	48	48	44	72	55	50	50	33
19			73	62	83	50	49	50	46	75	56	51	52	35
20	47		76	64	85	52	51	52	48	78	58	52	54	36
21			78	67	88	54	53	55	50	81	59	53	56	38
22			80	69	90	55	55	57	53	84	61	55	58	39

Females

0 (Si)	9 (Ma)	8 (Sc)	7 (Pt)	6 (Pa)	5 (Mf)	4 (Pd)	3 (Hy)	2 (D)	1 (Hs)	K	F	L	?	Raw Score
7	15	29	25	21	125	7	7	5	31	18	32	28	41	0
9	17	31	27	24	122	10	9	7	34	21	35	33		1
10	19	32	28	27	120	12	11	9	36	23	37	37		2
11	22	33	30	30	117	14	13	11	38	26	40	41		3
12	24	35	31	33	115	17	15	13	41	28	42	45		4
14	26	36	33	35	113	19	17	15	43	31	45	49		5
15	28	37	34	38	111	21	19	17	45	33	47	54		6
17	30	38	36	41	108	24	21	20	48	36	49	58		7
18	32	39	37	44	106	26	23	22	50	38	52	62		8
19	34	40	39	47	104	28	25	24	52	41	54	66		9
21	37	41	40	50	102	31	27	26	55	44	57	70	44	10
22	39	43	42	53	100	33	29	28	57	46	59	74		11
23	41	44	43	56	98	35	31	30	59	49	62	79		12
25	43	45	44	59	96	37	33	32	61	51	64	83		13
26	45	46	46	61	94	40	35	35	64	54	67	87		14
27	47	47	47	64	92	42	37	37	66	56	69	91		15
29	50	48	49	67	89	44	39	39	68	59	72			16
30	52	49	50	70	87	47	41	41	71	61	74			17
31	54	50	52	73	85	49	43	43	73	64	77			18
33	56	52	53	76	83	51	45	45	75	66	79			19
34	58	53	55	79	80	54	47	47	77	69	81		47	20
35	60	54	56	82	78	56	49	50	80	71	84			21
37	63	55	58	84	76	58	51	52	82	74	86			22

(Continued)

Females

Raw Score	?	L	F	K	1 (Hs)	2 (D)	3 (Hy)	4 (Pd)	5 (Mf)	6 (Pa)	7 (Pt)	8 (Sc)	9 (Ma)	0 (Si)
23			89	76	84	54	53	61	74	87	59	56	65	38
24			91	79	87	56	55	63	71	90	60	57	67	39
25			94	81	89	58	57	65	69	93	62	58	69	41
26			96	84	91	60	59	67	67	96	63	60	71	42
27			99	86	93	62	61	70	65	99	65	61	73	43
28			101	89	96	65	63	72	62	102	66	62	76	45
29			104	91	98	67	65	74	60	105	68	63	78	46
30	50		106	94	100	69	67	77	58	108	69	64	80	47
31			109		103	71	69	79	56	110	71	65	82	49
32			111		105	73	71	81	53	113	72	66	84	50
33			113		107	75	73	84	51	116	74	68	86	51
34			116			78	75	86	49	119	75	69	89	53
35			118			80	77	88	47	122	77	70	91	54
36			121			82	79	91	44	125	78	71	93	55
37			123			84	81	93	42	128	79	72	95	57
38			126			86	83	95	40	131	81	73	97	58
39			128			88	85	98	38	134	82	74	99	59
40	53		131			90	87	100	36	136	84	76	101	61
41			133			93	89	102	33		85	77	104	62
42			136			95	91	104	31		87	78	106	63
43			138			97	93	107	29		88	79	108	65
44			141			99	95	109	27		90	80	110	66
45			143			101	97	111	24		91	81	112	67

Males

Raw Score	?	L	F	K	1 (Hs)	2 (D)	3 (Hy)	4 (Pd)	5 (Mf)	6 (Pa)	7 (Pt)	8 (Sc)	9 (Ma)	0 (Si)
23			82	71	93	57	57	59	55	87	62	56	60	41
24			84	73	95	59	59	62	57	90	64	57	62	42
25			87	75	98	61	61	64	59	93	65	58	65	44
26			89	78	100	63	63	66	61	96	67	59	67	45
27			91	80	103	64	65	69	63	99	69	60	69	47
28			93	82	105	66	67	71	66	102	70	61	71	49
29			95	84	108	68	68	73	68	105	72	62	73	50
30	50		97	86	110	70	70	75	70	108	73	63	75	52
31			100		113	72	72	78	72	111	75	64	77	53
32			102		115	73	74	80	74	114	76	65	79	55
33			104		118	75	76	82	77	117	78	66	82	56
34			106			77	78	84	79	120	79	67	84	58
35			108			79	79	86	81	123	81	68	86	59
36			110			81	81	87	83	126	82	70	88	61
37			113			83	83	89	85	128	84	71	90	62
38			115			84	85	91	87	131	86	72	92	64
39			117			86	87	94	90	134	87	73	94	65
40	53		119			88	89	96	92	137	89	74	96	67
41			121			90	90	98	94		90	75	99	68
42			124			92	92	101	96		92	77	101	70
43			126			93	93	103	98		93	78	103	71
44			128			95	95	105	100		95	79	105	73
45			130			97	97	108	103		96	80	107	74

TABLE A-4 (Continued)

Males

Raw Score	?	L	F	K	1 (Hs)	2 (D)	3 (Hy)	4 (Pd)	5 (Mf)	6 (Pa)	7 (Pt)	8 (Sc)	9 (Ma)	0 (Si)
46			132			99	101	112	105		98	81	109	76
47			134			101	103	114	107		99	82		77
48			137			102	105	117	109		101	83		79
49			139			104	107	119	111			84		80
50	56		141			106	108	121	114			85		82
51			143			108	110		116			86		83
52			145			110	112		118			88		85
53			147			112	114		120			89		86
54			150			113	116		122			90		88
55			152			115	118		124			91		89
56			154			117	120		127			92		91
57			156			119	122		129			93		92
58			158			121	124		131			94		94
59			161			122	126		133			95		95
60	58		163			124	127		135			96		96
61			165									97		97
62			167									99		98
63			169									100		100
64			171									101		101
65												102		103

Females

Raw Score	?	L	F	K	1 (Hs)	2 (D)	3 (Hy)	4 (Pd)	5 (Mf)	6 (Pa)	7 (Pt)	8 (Sc)	9 (Ma)	0 (Si)
46			145			103	99	114	22		93	82	114	69
47			148			105	101	116	20		94	84		70
48			150			108	103	118	18		95	85		71
49			153			110	105	121	15			86		73
50	56		155			112	107	123	13			87		74
51			158			114	109		11			88		75
52			160			116	111		9			89		77
53			163			118	113		6			90		78
54			165			120	115		4			92		79
55			168			123	117		2			93		81
56			170			125	119					94		82
57			173			127	121					95		83
58			175			129	123					96		85
59			177			131	125					97		86
60	58		180			133	127					98		87
61			182									100		89
62			185									101		90
63			187									102		91
64			190									103		93
65												104		94

Females

Raw Score	?	L	F	K	1(Hs)	2(D)	3(Hy)	4(Pd)	5(Mf)	6(Pa)	7(Pt)	8(Sc)	9(Ma)	0(Si)
66												105		95
67												106		97
68												108		98
69												109		99
70	62											110		101
71												111		
72												112		
73												113		
74												114		
75												116		
76												117		
77												118		
78												119		

Males

Raw Score	?	L	F	K	1(Hs)	2(D)	3(Hy)	4(Pd)	5(Mf)	6(Pa)	7(Pt)	8(Sc)	9(Ma)	0(Si)
66												103		106
67												104		107
68												105		109
69												106		110
70	62											107		112
71												108		
72												109		
73												111		
74												112		
75												113		
76												114		
77												115		
78												116		

Note. *Approximately 10% of the 17-year-old sample was 18-year-olds. This sample was reported by Marks, Seeman, and Haller (1974) in their norm tables as "Ages 17 and 18."

ITEM COMPOSITION OF MMPI-A BASIC SCALES, HARRIS-LINGOES SUBSCALES, *Si* SUBSCALES, SUPPLEMENTARY SCALES, AND CONTENT SCALES

Note. Reprinted from Butcher, James N., Williams, Carolyn L., Graham, John R., Archer, Robert P., Tellegen, Auke, Ben-Porath, Yossef S., and Kaemmer, Beverly. *MMPI-A (Minnesota Multiphasic Personality Inventory—Adolescent): Manual for Administration, Scoring, and Interpretation.* Copyright © 1992 by the Regents of the University of Minnesota. Means and standard deviations for each scale are based on the contemporary adolescent normative sample of 805 boys and 815 girls.

TABLE B-1
Basic Scales

VRIN — Variable Response Inconsistency (50 item-response pairs)
  For each of the following response pairs add one point.

6T	-	86F	77F	-	107T	188T	-	403F
6F	-	86T	78F	-	90T	188F	-	403T
20T	-	211F	79F	-	119F	212T	-	298F
25T	-	106F	80T	-	101F	215T	-	405F
25F	-	106T	94F	-	469T	215F	-	405T
34F	-	81T	95F	-	132T	253T	-	266F
43T	-	248F	99T	-	323F	286F	-	314T
46F	-	475F	124F	-	379T	292F	-	331T
53F	-	62T	128F	-	465F	304F	-	335F
57T	-	191F	144T	-	247F	309T	-	402F
60T	-	121T	146T	-	167T	318F	-	370T
63T	-	120T	154T	-	178F	332T	-	337F
63F	-	120F	160F	-	227T	355T	-	375F
69T	-	452F	177F	-	283T	463T	-	476T
70T	-	223T	182T	-	258F	477T	-	478F
71F	-	91T	182F	-	258T	477F	-	478T
77T	-	107F	185F	-	383T			

Males: Mean 4.64; S.D. 3.40.   Females: Mean 3.86; S.D. 2.84

TRIN — True Response Inconsistency (24 item-response pairs)

1) For each of the following response pairs *add* one point:

14T	-	424T	70T	-	228T	242T	-	260T
37T	-	168T	71T	-	283T	264T	-	331T
60T	-	121T	95T	-	294T	304T	-	335T
62T	-	360T	119T	-	184T	355T	-	367T
63T	-	120T	146T	-	167T	463T	-	476T

2) For each of the following response pairs *substract* one point:

46F	-	475F	71F	-	283F	158F	-	288F
53F	-	91F	82F	-	316F	245F	-	257F
63F	-	120F	128F	-	465F	304F	-	335F

3) Then add 9 points to the total raw score.

Males: Mean 9.21; S.D. 1.79.   Females: Mean 9.40; S.D. 1.56.

F₁ — Infrequency 1 (33 items)

True

12	17	22	30	33	39	51	57	63	69	80	92	108
132	136	144	155	173	187	215	219	224	230	236		

False

6	74	86	98	104	120	182	193	198

Males: Mean 4.06; S.D. 3.95.   Females: Mean 3.13; S.D. 3.07.

F₂ — Infrequency 2 (33 items)

True

242	250	264	273	283	297	303	309	315	321	328	332	337
342	350	358	366	384	392	399	405	415	422	428	433	439
458	463	470										

False

258	289	374	447

Males: Mean 5.09; S.D. 4.98.   Females: Mean 4.57; S.D. 4.61.

F — Infrequency (66 items)

True

12	17	22	30	33	39	51	57	63	69	80	92	108
132	136	144	155	173	187	215	219	224	230	236	242	250
264	273	283	297	303	309	315	321	328	332	337	342	350
358	366	384	392	399	405	415	422	428	433	439	458	463
470												

False

6	74	86	98	104	120	182	193	198	258	289	374	447

Males: Mean 9.15; S.D. 8.44.   Females: Mean 7.70; S.D. 7.22.

L — Lie (14 items)

True
None.
False

15	26	38	48	73	89	98	103	117	133	147	176	192
243												

Males: Mean 2.94; S.D. 2.34.   Females: Mean 2.26; S.D. 1.92.

K — Correction (30 items)

True
79
False

26	34	55	72	107	111	116	121	124	130	142	150	151
160	164	185	201	227	265	271	289	298	317	318	320	325
327	333	341										

Males: Mean 12.70; S.D. 4.73.   Females: Mean 11.54; S.D. 4.39.

---

1 Hs — Hypochondriasis (32 items)

True

17	25	36	50	56	93	97	106	143	167	231

False

2	3	8	10	18	42	44	54	87	113	135	140	146
157	166	168	172	196	210	233	239					

Males: Mean 7.68; S.D. 4.66.   Females: Mean 9.28; S.D. 5.04.

---

2 D — Depression (57 items)

True

5	14	17	28	35	36	43	53	70	88	113	121	124
139	141	163	167	174	203	218						

False

2	4	9	10	18	26	34	40	42	46	52	65	71
72	91	105	112	128	134	135	138	140	142	158	171	179
180	200	208	209	212	222	229	232	243	289	298		

Males: Mean 18.95; S.D. 5.51.   Females: Mean 20.81; S.D. 5.45.

---

3 Hy — Conversion Hysteria (60 items)

True

11	17	28	36	37	41	62	97	159	165	167	205	216

False

2	3	7	8	9	10	13	23	26	42	44	55	72
77	87	91	94	107	110	111	118	119	123	129	135	142
145	146	150	152	154	157	160	166	168	172	178	183	196
201	210	225	227	233	237	246	248					

Males: Mean 20.94; S.D. 5.66.   Females: Mean 22.85; S.D. 5.12.

4 Pd — Psychopathic Deviate (49 items)

True

16	19	20	28	29	32	39	49	51	53	68	78	85
90	95	101	109	184	191	206	211	247	269	286		

False

9	31	67	75	79	91	116	119	123	140	150	151	153
160	164	178	197	202	204	212	227	244	246	249	298	

Males: Mean 19.48; S.D. 5.28.   Females: Mean 20.33; S.D. 5.50.

5 Mf-m — Masculinity-Femininity (Masculine) (44 items)

True

59	61	64	76	114	116	122	131	159	169	185	194	197
206	235	240	251	253								

False

1	23	24	60	65	66	72	82	99	100	103	115	126
127	156	183	186	188	190	217	220	221	223	238	241	254

Males: Mean 21.28; S.D. 3.98.

5 Mf-f — Masculinity-Femininity (Feminine) (44 items)

True

59	61	64	76	114	116	122	131	169	185	194	206	235
240	253											

False

1	23	24	60	65	66	72	82	99	100	103	115	126
127	156	159	183	186	188	190	197	217	220	221	223	238
241	251	254										

Females: Mean 28.24; S.D. 3.73.

6 Pa — Paranoia (40 items)

True

15	16	20	21	22	39	95	109	132	136	137	139	155
219	253	259	266	285	286	287	314	315	332	337	350	

False

77	91	94	96	100	107	228	239	249	263	265	267	277
294	295											

Males: Mean 12.60; S.D. 4.12.   Females: Mean 12.99; S.D. 4.15.

---

7 Pt—Psychasthenia (48 items)

True

11	15	21	28	35	53	62	70	78	85	90	124	141
163	167	185	205	226	255	257	259	266	270	281	282	284
288	290	293	296	297	300	305	306	307	308	309	310	311

False

3	4	9	105	134	158	170	274	301

Males: Mean 17.97; S.D. 7.60.   Females: Mean 20.79; S.D. 8.07.

---

8 Sc—Schizophrenia (72 items)

True

15	16	19	20	21	28	29	32	35	39	41	43	45
62	81	88	132	137	141	159	161	163	173	175	181	205
208	214	218	219	226	231	236	240	251	255	256	259	261
264	268	272	273	276	278	279	283	287	291	296	299	300
302	303	305	309	314	321	332						

False

6	9	31	86	87	102	158	169	172	182	198	239	258
260	262	271	275	322								

Males: Mean 21.98; S.D. 10.23.   Females: Mean 23.26; S.D. 10.62.

---

9 Ma—Hypomania (46 items)

True

14	19	21	47	52	58	81	83	94	109	116	125	137
149	161	162	175	181	189	194	195	199	200	205	207	213
214	222	226	228	232	234	237	252	313				

False

84	89	96	102	103	130	148	151	160	227	246

Males: Mean 21.14; S.D. 5.01.   Females: Mean 21.81; S.D. 4.81.

---

0 Si—Social Introversion (62 items)

True

27	28	53	67	96	100	107	121	129	151	154	160	178
203	227	235	248	257	265	270	276	280	282	288	304	306
308	316	317	326	327	330	334	340					

False

29	46	75	82	102	125	174	180	197	217	221	239	245
262	292	298	301	312	319	323	324	329	331	335	336	338
339	343											

Males: Mean 25.99; S.D. 7.84.   Females: Mean 26.97; S.D. 8.01.

TABLE B-2
Harris-Lingoes Subscales

D_1 — Subjective Depression (29 items)

True

28	35	36	43	53	70	88	121	124	139	141	163	167
203	218											

False

2	9	40	46	71	91	105	112	134	142	171	179	180
209												

Males: Mean 8.58; S.D. 4.25.   Females: Mean 9.87; S.D. 4.64.

D_2 — Psychomotor Retardation (14 items)

True

35	43	163	218

False

9	26	34	46	52	72	128	179	180	200

Males: Mean 4.80; S.D. 2.01.   Females: Mean 4.79; S.D. 1.84.

D_3 — Physical Malfunctioning (11 items)

True

17	113	167	174

False

2	18	42	135	138	140	142

Males: Mean 3.26; S.D. 1.49.   Females: Mean 3.70; S.D. 1.60.

D_4 — Mental Dullness (15 items)

True

14	28	35	70	88	141	163	218

False

9	10	40	71	105	158	179

Males: Mean 3.62; S.D. 2.48.   Females: Mean 3.90; S.D. 2.61.

D_5 — Brooding (10 items)

True

35	53	88	121	124	139	163	203

False

71	91

Males: Mean 2.78; S.D. 2.04.   Females: Mean 3.77; S.D. 2.15.

Hy_1 — *Denial of Social Anxiety (6 items)*

True
None
False
123   154   160   178   227   248
Males: Mean 3.13; S.D. 1.77.   Females: Mean 3.31; S.D. 1.77.

Hy_2 — *Need for Affection (12 items)*

True
216
False
23   55   72   77   94   107   118   145   201   225   246
Males: Mean 5.04; S.D. 2.33.   Females: Mean 4.88; S.D. 2.40.

Hy_3 — *Lassitude — Malaise (15 items)*

True
28   36   62   167   205
False
2   3   9   10   42   91   119   135   142   146
Males: Mean 4.00; S.D. 2.54.   Females: Mean 4.74; S.D. 2.79.

Hy_4 — *Somatic Complaints (17 items)*

True
11   17   37   41   97   165
False
8   44   87   152   157   166   168   172   196   210   233
Males: Mean 4.02; S.D. 2.85.   Females: Mean 4.95; S.D. 3.07.

Hy_5 — *Inhibition of Aggression (7 items)*

True
None
False
7   13   26   110   111   129   150
Males: Mean 2.86; S.D. 1.33.   Females: Mean 2.92; S.D. 1.30.

Pd₁—Familial Discord (9 items)

True
19   51   184   191   269
False
79   119   202   204
Males: Mean 3.41; S.D. 1.86.   Females: Mean 3.87; S.D. 1.93.

Pd₂—Authority Problems (8 items)

True
32   101
False
31   67   123   153   246   249
Males: Mean 3.37; S.D. 1.58.   Females: Mean 2.75; S.D. 1.47.

Pd₃—Social Imperturbability (6 items)

True
None
False
67   123   151   160   178   227
Males: Mean 3.33; S.D. 1.58.   Females: Mean 3.20; S.D. 1.63.

Pd₄—Social Alienation (12 items)

True
16   20   39   53   78   95   109   206   211   286
False
123   150
Males: Mean 4.83; S.D. 2.18.   Females: Mean 5.36; S.D. 2.25.

Pd₅—Self-Alienation (12 items)

True
28   29   49   53   68   78   85   90   109   247
False
9   91
Males: Mean 4.29; S.D. 2.43.   Females: Mean 4.74; S.D. 2.54.

Pa_1 — *Persecutory Ideas (17 items)*

True

16	20	39	95	109	132	136	137	155	219	285	286	314
315	332	337										

False

294

Males: Mean 4.10; S.D. 2.78.   Females: Mean 4.09; S.D. 2.71.

Pa_2 — *Poignancy (9 items)*

True

20	139	253	259	266	287	350

False

96	228

Males: Mean 3.22; S.D. 1.63.   Females: Mean 3.74; S.D. 1.89.

Pa_3 — *Naïveté (9 items)*

True

15

False

77	94	100	107	263	265	267	295

Males: Mean 3.93; S.D. 1.89.   Females: Mean 3.75; S.D. 1.97.

Sc_1 — *Social Alienation (21 items)*

True

16	19	20	39	43	132	137	181	208	240	259	264	272
300	302	314										

False

86	258	260	262	322

Males: Mean 6.17; S.D. 3.29.   Females: Mean 6.46; S.D. 3.24.

Sc_2 — *Emotional Alienation (11 items)*

True

62	88	219	255	283	303	309	321

False

9	198	271

Males: Mean 2.29; S.D. 1.81.   Females: Mean 2.29; S.D. 1.81.

Sc₃—Lack of Ego Mastery, Cognitive (10 items)

True
28   29   141   163   173   279   291   296   305
False
158
Males: Mean 2.94; S.D. 2.20.   Females: Mean 3.10; S.D. 2.29.

Sc₄—Lack of Ego Mastery, Conative (14 items)

True
28   35   45   62   88   218   219   255   279   283   305
False
9   198   271
Males: Mean 4.10; S.D. 2.57.   Females: Mean 4.35; S.D. 2.71.

Sc₅—Lack of Ego Mastery, Defective Inhibition (11 items)

True
21   81   161   175   205   226   256   273   300   309   332
False
None
Males: Mean 3.47; S.D. 2.07.   Females: Mean 4.20; S.D. 2.16.

Sc₆—Bizarre Sensory Experiences (20 items)

True
21   29   41   161   175   214   231   236   276   278   287   291   299
332
False
87   102   169   172   239   275
Males: Mean 5.01; S.D. 3.33.   Females: Mean 5.46; S.D. 3.45.

Ma₁—Amorality (6 items)

True
125   213   232   234   252
False
246
Males: Mean 2.71; S.D. 1.40.   Females: Mean 2.37; S.D. 1.30.

Ma$_2$—Psychomotor Acceleration (11 items)

True
14   81   83   116   162   195   205   226   228
False
96   102
Males: Mean 6.52; S.D. 2.13.   Females: Mean 7.13; S.D. 1.97.

Ma$_3$—Imperturbability (8 items)

True
149   189   207
False
89   130   151   160   227
Males: Mean 3.16; S.D. 1.59.   Females: Mean 2.94; S.D. 1.52.

Ma$_4$—Ego Inflation (9 items)

True
47   52   58   94   137   181   199   200   313
False
None
Males: Mean 4.45; S.D. 1.83.   Females: Mean 4.61; S.D. 1.74.

TABLE B-3
Si Subscales

Si₁ — Shyness/Self-Consciousness (14 items)

True
151   154   160   178   227   248   257   270
False
46   245   262   301   312   336
Males: Mean 6.21; S.D. 3.12.   Females: Mean 6.23; S.D. 3.28.

Si₂ — Social Avoidance (8 items)

True
304   316
False
82   292   319   331   335   339
Males: Mean 2.52; S.D. 2.03.   Females: Mean 1.90; S.D. 1.85.

Si₃ — Alienation — Self and Others (17 items)

True
27   28   53   100   107   129   265   280   282   288   306   308   317
326   327   334   340
False
None
Males: Mean 7.58; S.D. 3.43.   Females: Mean 8.22; S.D. 3.68.

TABLE B-4
Supplementary Scales

MAC-R — MacAndrew Alcoholism Scale — Revised (49 items)

True
7   22   46   49   66   78   80   99   101   109   110   122   161
165   177   191   202   210   214   222   241   250   262   269   312   323
342   348   376   380   382   386   392   393   395   407   429   470
False
70   103   113   131   153   159   235   249   268   279   305
Males: Mean 21.07; S.D. 4.44.   Females: Mean 19.73; S.D. 4.14.

ACK — Alcohol/Drug Problems Acknowledgment (13 items)

True
| 81 | 144 | 161 | 247 | 269 | 338 | 342 | 429 | 458 | 467 | 474 |

False
| 249 | 431 |

Males: Mean 3.90; S.D. 2.45.　　　Females: Mean 3.68; S.D. 2.38.

PRO — Alcohol/Drug Problems Proneness (36 items)

True
| 32 | 38 | 57 | 82 | 101 | 117 | 191 | 336 | 345 | 376 | 381 | 389 | 435 |
| 438 | 440 | 452 | 455 | 462 | 476 |

False
| 40 | 142 | 143 | 153 | 188 | 272 | 304 | 403 | 410 | 418 | 424 | 436 | 451 |
| 457 | 459 | 460 | 463 |

Males: Mean 16.55; S.D. 4.42.　　　Females: Mean 16.75; S.D. 4.17.

IMM — Immaturity (43 items)

True
16	20	24	45	63	72	94	101	128	218	224	269	307
351	354	358	362	371	389	400	405	418	423	425	426	441
444	452	453	466

False
| 64 | 71 | 105 | 120 | 153 | 170 | 322 | 336 | 419 | 431 | 436 | 448 | 476 |

Males: Mean 13.47; S.D. 6.29.　　　Females: Mean 11.75; S.D. 6.31.

A — Anxiety (35 items)

True
28	35	53	62	78	121	129	203	218	227	235	255	259
270	281	290	291	305	308	310	317	318	320	326	368	369
370	372	377	379	383	385	394	404

False
| 360 |

Males: Mean 14.59; S.D. 7.17.　　　Females: Mean 16.90; S.D. 7.68.

R — Repression (33 items)

True
None

False
1	7	10	13	34	42	66	112	115	122	128	138	161
171	180	186	188	232	239	240	277	289	325	329	331	335
339	341	348	386	388	390	396

Males: Mean 13.41; S.D. 4.38.　　　Females: Mean 13.33; S.D. 3.50.

TABLE B-5
Content Scales

A-anx — Adolescent-anxiety (21 items)

True

14	28	36	163	185	255	279	281	285	318	353	377	383
402	404	468										

False

134	196	209	375	424

Males: Mean 7.84; S.D. 4.09.   Females: Mean 9.03; S.D. 4.41.

A-obs — Adolescent-obsessiveness (15 items)

True

52	78	83	129	185	293	307	308	310	368	370	394	412
421	444											

False

None

Males: Mean 6.91; S.D. 3.32.   Females: Mean 7.88; S.D. 3.23.

A-dep — Adolescent-depression (26 items)

True

35	49	53	62	68	88	124	139	177	203	219	230	242
259	283	311	347	371	372	379	399					

False

3	9	71	91	360

Males: Mean 7.59; S.D. 5.57.   Females: Mean 9.17; S.D. 5.08.

A-hea — Adolescent-health concerns (37 items)

True

11	17	25	37	41	50	56	93	97	106	143	167	187
231	422	443	470									

False

18	42	44	54	87	112	113	135	138	152	157	168	172
174	193	210	233	239	275	374						

Males: Mean 7.88; S.D. 5.13.   Females: Mean 9.03; S.D. 5.53.

A-aln — Adolescent-alienation (20 items)

True

16	20	39	211	227	242	317	362	369	413	438	446	463
471	473											

False

74	104	260	448	450

Males: Mean 5.95; S.D. 3.36.   Females: Mean 5.62; S.D. 3.49.

A-biz — Adolescent-bizarre mentation (19 items)

True

22	29	92	132	155	173	250	278	291	296	299	314	315
332	417	428	433	439								

False

387

Males: Mean 4.00; S.D. 3.13.   Females: Mean 4.05; S.D. 3.09.

A-ang — Adolescent-anger (17 items)

True

26	34	111	128	201	282	367	378	382	388	401	416	445
453	458	461										

False

355

Males: Mean 7.94; S.D. 3.23.   Females: Mean 8.51; S.D. 3.09.

A-cyn — Adolescent-cynicism (22 items)

True

47	55	72	77	100	107	118	211	213	225	238	263	265
267	295	325	330	334	371	373	395	406				

False

None

Males: Mean 12.36; S.D. 4.51.   Females: Mean 12.34; S.D. 4.72.

A-con — Adolescent-conduct problems (23 items)

True

32	99	117	224	232	234	252	345	354	356	361	391	442
445	455	456	462	469	477	478						

False

96	249	465

Males: Mean 9.62; S.D. 4.02.   Females: Mean 8.16; S.D. 3.85.

A-lse — Adolescent-low self-esteem (18 items)

True

67	70	124	280	306	358	379	384	385	400	415	430	432
441	468											

False

58	74	105

Males: Mean 5.01; S.D. 3.22.   Females: Mean 5.83; S.D. 3.47.

A-las — Adolescent-low aspirations (16 items)

True
27   39   218   340   351   430   464
False
170   188   324   397   403   409   411   436   447
Males: Mean 5.85; S.D. 2.63.   Females: Mean 6.00; S.D. 2.72.

A-sod — Adolescent-social discomfort (24 items)

True
43   151   160   178   248   264   290   304   316   328   408   410   475
False
46   82   245   262   292   319   331   335   336   339   450
Males: Mean 8.33; S.D. 4.36.   Females: Mean 7.19; S.D. 4.31.

A-fam — Adolescent-family problems (35 items)

True
19   57   137   181   184   191   194   215   240   269   277   302   303
344   352   359   363   366   381   396   405   438   440   454
False
6   79   86   119   182   258   365   398   451   457   460
Males: Mean 11.37; S.D. 5.63.   Females: Mean 12.53; S.D. 5.67.

A-sch — Adolescent-school problems (20 items)

True
12   33   69   80   101   220   257   338   364   380   389   425   435
443   452   464   466
False
153   166   459
Males: Mean 6.32; S.D. 3.37.   Females: Mean 5.83; S.D. 3.15.

A-trt — Adolescent-negative treatment indicators (26 items)

True
20   27   88   242   256   340   356   357   358   369   371   414   418
420   421   423   426   427   432   434   444   449   472
False
419   431   437
Males: Mean 9.11; S.D. 4.21.   Females: Mean 9.30; S.D. 4.42.

MMPI-A BASIC SCALE, CONTENT SCALE, AND SUPPLEMENTARY SCALE NORMS FOR 13-YEAR-OLD BOYS AND GIRLS BASED ON LINEAR T-SCORE CONVERSIONS

Note. These norms are based on linear T-score transformations of raw score values for 81 13-year-old boys and 144 13-year-old girls meeting the validity criteria of ? scale ≤35, and raw score <25 on the *F* scale of the original form of the MMPI. Ethnic backgrounds of this sample were as follows: 50.1% White, 39.2% Black, 5.4% Asian, 3.2% Hispanic, and 2.4% other. Adolescents in this sample reported paternal educational levels distributed into the following categories: some high school (9.3%), high school graduate (27.3%), some college (19.9%), college graduate (28.7%), graduate school (9.7%), and unreported (5.1%). Maternal educational levels were distributed into the following categories: some high school (12.1%), high school graduate (29.6%), some college (17.1%), college graduate (32.4%), graduate school (7.4%), and unreported (1.4%).

TABLE C-1 (Basic Scales)

Linear T-score conversions for MMPI-A Validity and Clinical Scales for 13-year-old Males (N = 81)

Raw Score	VRIN	TRIN	F_1	F_2	F	L	K	Hs	D	Hy	Pd	Mf	Pa	Pt	Sc	Ma	Si	Raw Score
0	30	96 F	33	32	31	35	30	30	30	30	30	30	30	30	30	30	30	0
1	33	91 T	36	35	32	39	30	32	30	30	30	30	30	30	30	30	30	1
2	36	86 F	39	37	33	43	30	35	30	30	30	30	30	30	30	30	30	2
3	40	81 F	42	39	35	47	30	38	30	30	30	30	30	30	30	30	30	3
4	43	77 F	45	41	36	52	32	41	30	30	30	30	30	30	30	30	30	4
5	46	72 F	47	43	37	56	34	44	30	30	30	30	30	30	30	30	30	5
6	50	67 F	50	45	39	60	37	47	30	30	30	30	30	31	30	30	30	6
7	53	62 F	53	47	40	64	39	50	30	30	30	30	32	32	30	30	30	7
8	56	58 F	56	49	42	68	41	53	30	30	30	30	34	33	30	30	30	8
9	60	53 F	59	52	43	72	44	56	30	30	30	30	37	35	30	30	30	9
10	63	52 F	61	54	44	76	46	59	31	32	32	30	39	36	31	30	30	10
11	67	57 T	64	56	46	80	49	62	33	34	34	30	42	37	32	30	30	11
12	70	62 T	67	58	47	84	51	65	34	35	35	30	44	38	33	30	30	12
13	73	66 T	70	60	48	88	54	68	36	37	37	30	46	40	34	30	30	13
14	77	71 T	73	62	50	92	56	71	37	39	39	32	49	41	35	31	30	14
15	80	76 T	75	64	51		59	74	39	40	41	35	51	42	36	33	30	15
16	83	81 T	78	66	52		61	77	40	42	42	38	53	44	37	35	30	16
17	87	85 T	81	69	54		63	80	42	44	44	40	56	45	38	37	31	17
18	90	90 T	84	71	55		66	83	43	45	46	43	58	46	39	39	32	18
19	93	95 T	87	73	57		68	86	45	47	48	46	61	48	40	41	34	19
20	97	100 T	90	75	58		71	89	46	49	49	48	63	49	41	44	36	20
21	100	104 T	92	77	59		73	92	48	50	51	51	65	50	42	46	37	21
22	104	109 T	95	79	61		76	95	49	52	53	54	68	52	43	48	39	22
23	107	114 T	98	81	62		78	98	51	54	55	57	70	53	44	50	41	23
24	110	119 T	101	83	63		80	101	53	55	56	59	72	54	45	52	42	24
25	114		104	86	65		83	104	54	57	58	62	75	56	46	54	44	25

26	46	56	47	57	77	65	60	59	56	107	85	66	88	106	117	26
27	47	59	48	58	80	68	62	60	57	110	88	67	90	109	120	27
28	49	61	49	60	82	70	63	62	59	114	90	69	92	112	120	28
29	50	63	50	61	84	73	65	64	60	117	93	70	94	115	120	29
30	52	65	51	62	87	76	67	65	62	120	95	71	96	118	120	30
31	54	67	52	64	89	78	69	67	63	120		73	98	120	120	31
32	55	69	53	65	91	81	70	69	65	120		74	100	120	120	32
33	57	71	55	66	94	84	72	70	66			76	103	120	120	33
34	59	74	56	68	96	87	74	72	68			77			120	34
35	60	76	57	69	99	89	76	74	69			78			120	35
36	62	78	58	70	101	92	77	75	71			80			120	36
37	64	80	59	72	103	95	79	77	73			81			120	37
38	65	82	60	73	106	97	81	78	74			82			120	38
39	67	84	61	74	108	100	83	80	76			84			120	39
40	69	86	62	76	110	103	84	82	77			85			120	40
41	70	89	63	77		106	86	83	79			86			120	41
42	72	91	64	78		108	88	85	80			88			120	42
43	74	93	65	79		111	90	87	82			89			120	43
44	75	95	66	81		114	91	88	83			91			120	44
45	77	97	67	82			93	90	85			92			120	45
46	79	99	68	83			95	92	86			93			120	46
47	80		69	85			97	93	88			95			120	47
48	82		70	86			98	95	89			96			120	48
49	84		71				100	97	91			97			120	49
50	85		72					98	93			99				50
51	87		73					100	94			100				51
52	89		74					102	96			101				52
53	90		75					103	97			103				53
54	92		76					105	99			104				54
55	93		77					107	100			106				55

(Continued)

TABLE C-1 (Continued)

Raw Score	VRIN	TRIN	F_1	F_2	F	L	K	Hs	D	Hy	Pd	Mf	Pa	Pt	Sc	Ma	Si	Raw Score
56					107				102	108					78		95	56
57					108				103	110					79		97	57
58					110					112					80		98	58
59					111					113					81		100	59
60					112					115					82		102	60
61					114										83		103	61
62					115										84		105	62
63					116										85			63
64					118										86			64
65					119										87			65
66					120										88			66
67															89			67
68															90			68
69															91			69
70															93			70
71															94			71
72															95			72
(M)	6.09	9.58	5.95	8.27	14.22	3.62	11.51	7.04	22.35	20.80	20.37	20.57	14.53	20.70	28.60	23.01	28.70	(M)
(SD)	2.97	2.10	3.55	4.71	7.34	2.47	4.10	3.30	6.50	6.04	5.71	3.67	4.21	7.56	9.74	4.67	6.05	(SD)

Linear T-score conversions for MMPI-A Validity and Clinical Scales for 13-year-old Females (N = 144)

Raw Score	VRIN	TRIN	F_1	F_2	F	L	K	Hs	D	Hy	Pd	Mf	Pa	Pt	Sc	Ma	Si	Raw Score
0	33	92 F	36	36	34	35	30	30	30	30	30	120	30	30	30	30	30	0
1	36	88 F	40	38	36	40	30	33	30	30	30	120	30	30	30	30	30	1
2	39	83 F	43	40	37	45	30	36	30	30	30	120	30	30	30	30	30	2
3	43	79 F	46	42	39	50	30	39	30	30	30	118	30	30	30	30	30	3
4	46	74 F	49	44	40	54	33	41	30	30	30	115	30	30	30	30	30	4
5	49	70 F	52	46	41	59	35	44	30	30	30	112	31	30	30	30	30	5
6	52	65 F	56	48	43	64	38	47	30	30	30	109	33	30	30	30	30	6
7	56	61 F	59	50	44	69	40	50	30	30	30	106	36	31	31	30	30	7
8	59	56 F	62	52	46	74	43	53	30	30	30	103	38	31	32	30	30	8
9	62	52 F	65	54	47	79	46	56	31	30	30	100	40	32	33	30	30	9
10	65	53 T	68	56	48	83	48	58	32	30	31	97	43	34	34	30	30	10
11	69	57 T	72	59	50	88	51	61	33	32	33	94	45	35	35	30	30	11
12	72	62 T	75	61	51	93	53	64	35	34	35	91	48	36	36	30	30	12
13	75	66 T	78	63	53	98	56	67	36	35	37	88	50	38	37	30	30	13
14	78	70 T	81	65	54	103	58	70	38	37	39	85	52	39	38	30	30	14
15	82	75 T	85	67	55		61	73	39	39	41	82	55	40	39	33	30	15
16	85	79 T	88	69	57		63	75	40	41	42	80	57	42	40	35	30	16
17	88	84 T	91	71	58		66	78	42	43	44	77	60	43	41	38	30	17
18	91	88 T	94	73	60		68	81	43	44	46	74	62	45	42	40	32	18
19	95	93 T	97	75	61		71	84	45	46	48	71	64	46	43	42	33	19
20	98	97 T	101	77	62		74	87	46	48	50	68	67	47	44	45	35	20
21	101	102 T	104	79	64		76	90	47	50	52	65	69	49	45	47	36	21
22	104	106 T	107	81	65		79	92	49	51	54	62	72	50	46	49	38	22
23	108	111 T	110	83	66		81	95	50	53	56	59	74	51	47	52	40	23
24	111	115 T	113	86	68		84	98	52	55	57	56	76	53	48	54	41	24

(Continued)

TABLE C-1 *(Continued)*

Raw Score	VRIN	TRIN	F_1	F_2	F	L	K	Hs	D	Hy	Pd	Mf	Pa	Pt	Sc	Ma	Si	Raw Score
25	114	120 T	117	88	69		86	101	53	57	59	53	79	54	49	57	43	25
26	117	120 T	120	90	71		89	104	54	58	61	50	81	56	50	59	44	26
27	120	120 T	120	92	72		91	107	56	60	63	47	84	57	51	61	46	27
28	120	120 T	120	94	73		94	109	57	62	65	44	86	58	52	64	47	28
29	120	120 T	120	96	75		96	112	59	64	67	41	88	60	53	66	49	29
30	120	120 T	120	98	76		99	115	60	65	69	38	91	61	54	68	50	30
31	120	120 T	120	100	78			118	62	67	70	35	93	63	55	71	52	31
32	120	120 T	120	102	79			120	63	69	72	32	96	64	56	73	53	32
33	120	120 T	120	104	80				64	71	74	30	98	65	57	76	55	33
34	120				82				66	73	76	30	100	67	57	78	57	34
35	120				83				67	74	78	30	103	68	58	80	58	35
36	120				85				69	76	80	30	105	69	59	83	60	36
37	120				86				70	78	82	30	108	71	60	85	61	37
38	120				87				71	80	84	30	110	73	61	87	63	38
39	120				89				73	81	85	30	112	74	62	90	64	39
40	120				90				74	83	87	30	115	75	63	92	66	40
41	120				92				76	85	89	30		76	64	94	67	41
42	120				93				77	87	91	30		78	65	97	69	42
43	120				94				78	88	93	30		79	66	99	70	43
44	120				96				80	90	95	30		80	67	102	72	44
45	120				97				81	92	97			82	68	104	74	45
46	120				99				83	94	99			83	69	106	75	46
47	120				100				84	96	100			85	70		77	47
48	120				101				85	97	102			86	71		78	48
49	120				103				87	99	104				72		80	49
50	120				104				88	101					73		81	50
51	120				105				90	103					74		83	51

Raw Score	VRIN	TRIN	F_1	F_2	F	L	K	Hs	D	Hy	Pd	Mf	Pa	Pt	Sc	Ma	Si	Raw Score
52					107				91	104					75		84	52
53					108				93	106					76		86	53
54					110				94	108					77		87	54
55					111				95	110					78		89	55
56					112				97	111					79		91	56
57					114				98	113					80		92	57
58					115					115					81		94	58
59					117					117					82		95	59
60					118					118					83		97	60
61					119										84		98	61
62					120										85		100	62
63					120										86			63
64					120										87			64
65					120										88			65
66					120										89			66
67															90			67
68															91			68
69															92			69
70															93			70
71															94			71
72															95			72
(M)	5.27	9.43	4.26	6.9	11.16	3.08	10.74	7.02	22.81	21.23	20.06	26.03	13.00	21.93	26.44	22.23	29.74	(M)
(SD)	3.08	2.23	3.11	4.81	7.18	2.07	3.93	3.53	7.10	5.66	5.34	3.40	4.17	7.25	10.09	4.22	6.47	(SD)

TABLE C-2 (Content Scales)

Linear T-score conversions for MMPI-A Content Scales for 13-year-old Males

Raw Score	A-anx	A-obs	A-dep	A-hea	A-aln	A-biz	A-ang	A-cyn	A-con	A-lse	A-las	A-sod	A-fam	A-sch	A-trt	Raw Score
0	30	30	30	30	30	30	30	30	30	37	30	30	30	30	30	0
1	30	30	33	31	31	33	30	30	30	39	33	30	30	30	30	1
2	30	32	35	33	34	36	30	30	30	41	36	30	30	32	30	2
3	33	35	37	34	38	40	32	30	30	43	39	31	30	35	32	3
4	36	38	39	36	41	43	35	30	33	45	42	34	30	39	34	4
5	38	41	41	38	44	47	38	30	36	48	45	36	32	42	36	5
6	41	44	43	40	47	50	42	31	38	50	48	39	34	45	39	6
7	44	48	46	42	50	54	45	33	41	52	51	42	36	49	41	7
8	47	51	48	44	53	57	48	36	43	54	54	45	38	52	43	8
9	49	54	50	46	56	61	52	38	46	56	57	48	40	55	45	9
10	52	57	52	48	59	64	55	41	49	59	60	51	43	59	47	10
11	55	60	54	50	62	68	58	44	51	61	63	54	45	62	50	11
12	58	63	57	52	65	71	62	46	54	63	66	57	47	65	52	12
13	60	66	59	54	68	75	65	49	57	65	69	60	49	69	54	13
14	63	69	61	56	71	78	68	51	59	67	72	63	51	72	56	14
15	66	72	63	58	74	82	72	54	62	70	75	66	53	75	58	15
16	69		65	59	77	85	75	56	64	72	78	69	55	79	61	16
17	71		67	61	80	89	79	59	67	74		72	58	82	63	17
18	74		70	63	83	92		61	70	76		74	60	86	65	18
19	77		72	65	86	96		64	72			77	62	89	67	19
20	80		74	67	89			67	75			80	64	92	69	20
21	82		76	69				69	78			83	66		71	21

	22	23	24	25	26	27	28	29	30	31	32	33	34	35	36	37
22			78	71								86	68		74	
23			80	73								89	70		76	
24			83	75								92	73		78	
25			85	77									75		80	
26			87	79									77		82	
27				81									79			
28				83				72					81			
29				85									83			
30				86					80				86			
31				88					83				88			
32				90									90			
33				92									92			
34				94									94			
35				96									96			
36				98												
37				100												
(M)	9.26	7.78	9.00	11.08	7.09	5.89	8.49	13.54	10.52	6.06	6.70	9.64	13.48	7.41	11.22	
(SD)	3.63	3.22	4.60	5.19	3.28	2.85	2.98	3.91	3.81	4.55	3.28	3.42	4.65	2.98	4.55	

(Continued)

TABLE C-2 *(Continued)*
Linear T-score conversions for MMPI-A Content Scales for 13-year-old Females

Raw Score	A-anx	A-obs	A-dep	A-hea	A-aln	A-biz	A-ang	A-cyn	A-con	A-lse	A-las	A-sod	A-fam	A-sch	A-trt	Raw Score
0	30	30	30	30	30	33	30	30	30	30	30	30	30	30	30	0
1	30	30	32	31	32	36	30	30	30	32	30	30	30	32	32	1
2	30	30	34	33	35	39	30	30	32	35	33	30	30	35	35	2
3	32	31	36	35	38	42	30	30	35	39	37	33	30	38	38	3
4	35	34	39	37	41	46	30	30	38	42	41	36	31	41	41	4
5	38	38	41	39	45	49	34	30	40	46	45	39	33	45	45	5
6	41	42	44	41	48	52	38	30	43	49	49	41	35	48	48	6
7	44	45	46	43	51	55	42	30	46	53	53	44	37	51	51	7
8	47	49	48	44	54	59	46	33	48	56	57	47	39	54	54	8
9	50	52	51	46	58	62	49	35	51	60	61	50	41	57	30	9
10	53	56	53	48	61	65	53	38	54	63	65	53	43	60	48	10
11	56	59	55	50	64	68	57	41	56	66	69	55	45	63	50	11
12	59	63	58	52	67	71	61	44	59	70	73	58	47	66	53	12
13	62	66	60	54	70	75	65	46	62	73	77	61	49	70	56	13
14	65	70	63	56	73	78	68	49	64	77	81	64	51	73	58	14
15	68	73	65	58	76	81	72	52	67	80	85	67	53	76	61	15
16	71		67	60	80	84	76	54	70	84	89	69	55	79	64	16
17	74		70	61	83	88	80	57	72	87		72	57	82	67	17
18	77		72	63	86	91		60	75	91		75	59	85	69	18
19	80		74	65	89	94		62	77			78	61	88	72	19
20	83		77	67	92			65	80			81	63	91	75	20
21			79	69				68	83			84	65		77	21

	(1)	(2)	(3)	(4)	(5)	(6)	(7)	(8)	(9)	(10)	(11)	(12)	(13)	(14)	(15)
22				71								86	67		80
23				73								89	69		83
24				75								92	71		85
25				76									73		88
26				78				70					75		91
27				80					85				76		
28		82		82					88				78		
29		84		84									80		
30		86		86									82		
31		89		88									84		
32		91		90									86		
33				91									88		
34				93									90		
35				95									92		
36				97											
37				99											
(M)	9.03	8.41	8.73	10.94	6.49	5.36	9.18	14.41	8.64	6.25	6.25	9.04	13.48	6.73	10.87
(SD)	3.34	2.84	4.20	5.32	3.22	3.10	2.63	3.73	3.77	2.88	2.50	3.57	5.11	3.20	3.70

TABLE C-3 (Supplementary Scales)

Linear T-score conversions for MMPI-A Supplementary Scales for 13 year-old Males and Females

Raw Score	Males						Raw Score	Females						Raw Score
	MAC-R	ACK	PRO	IMM	A	R		MAC-R	ACK	PRO	IMM	A	R	
0	30	31	30	30	30	30	0	30	32	30	30	30	30	0
1	30	35	30	30	30	30	1	30	36	30	30	30	30	1
2	30	40	30	30	30	30	2	30	41	30	30	30	30	2
3	30	44	30	30	30	30	3	30	45	30	30	30	30	3
4	30	49	30	30	31	30	4	30	49	30	30	30	30	4
5	30	54	30	30	32	30	5	30	53	30	31	32	30	5
6	30	58	30	31	34	30	6	30	58	30	33	34	30	6
7	30	63	30	32	35	30	7	30	62	30	35	35	31	7
8	30	67	32	34	37	33	8	30	66	30	37	37	34	8
9	30	72	34	36	38	35	9	30	71	33	38	39	36	9
10	30	77	36	37	40	38	10	30	75	35	40	39	39	10
11	30	81	38	39	41	41	11	30	79	37	42	40	41	11
12	26	86	40	41	43	44	12	30	83	40	44	42	44	12
13	28	90	42	43	44	46	13	30	88	42	45	44	46	13
14	31		44	44	46	49	14	33		45	47	45	48	14
15	33		46	46	47	52	15	35		47	49	47	51	15
16	36		48	48	49	54	16	38		49	50	48	53	16
17	38		51	49	50	57	17	40		52	52	50	56	17
18	41		53	51	52	60	18	43		54	54	52	58	18
19	43		55	53	53	62	19	46		57	56	53	61	19
20	46		57	54	55	65	20	48		59	57	55	63	20
21	48		59	56	56	68	21	51		61	59	57	66	21
22	51		61	58	58	70	22	53		64	61	58	68	22
23	53		63	59	59	73	23	56		66	63	60	71	23
24	56		65	61	60	76	24	58		68	64	62	73	24
25	58		67	63	62	78	25	61		71	66	63	76	25
26	61		69	64	63	81	26	63		73	68	65	78	26
27	63		71	66	65	84	27	66		76	70	67	81	27

Table 1

Score	(M) 14.63 (SD) 4.05	(M) 6.97 (SD) 6.08	(M) 15.72 (SD) 5.76	(M) 16.26 (SD) 4.20	(M) 4.20 (SD) 2.34	(M) 20.76 (SD) 3.93
28						
29						
30						
31						
32	83	68	71	78		
33	85	70	73	80		
34	88	72	75	83		
35	90	73	77	85		
36	93	75	78	87		68
37	95	76	80	90		71
38		78	82	92		73
39		80	83	95		76
40			85	97		79
41			87			81
42			89			84
43			90			86
44			92			89
45			94			91
46			96			94
47			97			96
48						99
49						101
50						104
51						106
52						109
53						112
54						114
55						117
56						119
57						120

Table 2

Score	(M) 14.42 (SD) 3.37	(M) 16.93 (SD) 6.76	(M) 17.46 (SD) 5.95	(M) 16.74 (SD) 4.82	(M) 4.22 (SD) 2.17	(M) 21.68 (SD) 3.99
28						
29						
30						
31						
32	86	66	68	73		
33	89	68	69	75		
34	92	69	71	78		
35	94	71	73	80		
36	97	72	74	82		66
37	100	74	76	84		68
38		75	78	86		71
39		77	79	88		73
40			81	90		76
41			83			78
42			85			81
43			86			83
44			88			86
45			90			88
46			91			91
47			93			93
48						96
49						98
50						101
51						103
52						106
53						108
54						111
55						113
56						116
57						118

T-SCORE CONVERSIONS FOR MMPI-A BASIC VALIDITY AND CLINICAL SCALES, CONTENT AND SUPPLEMENTARY SCALES, AND THE HARRIS-LINGOES AND *Si* SUBSCALES

Note. Reprinted from Butcher, James N., Williams, Carolyn L., Graham, John R., Archer, Robert P., Tellegen, Auke, Ben-Porath, Yossef S., and Kaemmer, Beverly. *MMPI-A (Minnesota Multiphasic Inventory—Adolescent): Manual for Administration, Scoring, and Interpretation.* Copyright © 1992 by the Regents of the University of Minnesota.

TABLE D-1
Uniform and Linear T-score Conversions for Validity and Clinical Scales (Boys)

Basic Profile Scales

Raw	VRIN	TRIN	F_1	F_2	F	L	K	Hs	D	Hy	Pd	Mf	Pa	Pt	Sc	Ma	Si	Raw
0	36	101F	40	40	39	37	30	31	30	30	30	30	30	30	30	30	30	0
1	39	96F	42	42	40	42	30	35	30	30	30	30	30	30	30	30	30	1
2	42	90F	45	44	42	46	30	38	30	30	30	30	30	30	30	30	30	2
3	45	85F	47	46	43	50	30	41	30	30	30	30	30	32	31	30	30	3
4	48	79F	50	48	44	55	32	43	30	30	30	30	30	33	33	30	30	4
5	51	73F	52	50	45	59	34	45	30	30	30	30	32	35	34	30	30	5
6	54	68F	55	52	46	63	36	47	30	30	30	30	35	36	35	30	30	6
7	57	62F	57	54	47	67	38	49	30	30	30	30	38	37	36	30	30	7
8	60	57F	60	56	49	72	40	50	30	31	30	30	40	38	38	30	30	8
9	63	51F	63	58	50	76	42	52	32	32	31	30	42	39	39	30	30	9
10	66	54T	65	60	51	80	44	54	34	32	33	30	44	41	40	32	30	10
11	69	60T	68	62	52	84	46	55	36	34	35	30	46	42	41	34	31	11
12	72	66T	70	64	53	89	49	58	38	35	37	30	48	43	41	35	32	12
13	75	71T	73	66	55	93	51	60	40	36	39	32	50	44	42	37	33	13
14	78	77T	75	68	56	97	53	63	41	38	41	34	52	45	43	38	35	14
15	81	82T	78	70	57		55	65	43	39	42	37	54	46	44	39	36	15
16	83	88T	80	72	58		57	68	45	41	44	39	57	47	45	41	37	16
17	86	93T	83	74	59		59	71	46	43	45	42	60	48	45	42	38	17
18	89	99T	85	76	60		61	74	48	45	47	44	63	49	46	43	40	18
19	92	105T	88	78	62		63	76	50	46	48	47	66	50	47	45	41	19
20	95	110T	90	80	63		65	79	51	48	50	49	69	51	47	46	42	20
21	98	116T	93	82	64		68	82	53	50	51	52	73	53	48	48	44	21
22	101	120T	95	84	65		70	84	55	52	53	54	76	54	49	50	45	22
23	104	120T	98	86	66		72	87	56	54	55	57	79	55	50	52	46	23
24	107	120T	101	88	68		74	90	58	56	57	59	82	57	50	54	47	24
25	110		103	90	69		76	92	60	58	58		85	58	51	56	49	25

n																n
26	50	59	52	60	88	62	62	59	62	95	78	70	92	106	113	26
27	51	62	53	62	92	64	65	61	65	98	80	71	94	108	116	27
28	53	65	54	64	95	67	67	63	67	100	82	72	96	111	119	28
29	54	68	55	65	98	69	70	64	69	103	84	74	98	113	120	29
30	55	72	56	67	101	72	72	66	71	106	87	75	100	116	120	30
31	56	75	57	69	104	74	75	68	73	108		76	102	118	120	31
32	58	78	59	71	107	77	78	69	75	111		77	104	120	120	32
33	59	81	60	72	111	79	80	71	77			78	106	120	120	33
34	60	84	61	74	114	82	83	72	79			79			120	34
35	62	87	63	76	117	84	85	74	81			81			120	35
36	63	90	64	78	120	87	88	76	83			82			120	36
37	64	93	66	79	120	89	90	77	85			83			120	37
38	65	96	67	81	120	92	93	79	88			84			120	38
39	67	100	68	83	120	95	95	81	90			85			120	39
40	68	103	70	85		97	98	82	92			87			120	40
41	69	106	71	86		100	101	84	94			88			120	41
42	70	109	73	88		102	103	86	96			89			120	42
43	72	112	74	90		105	106	87	98			90			120	43
44	73	115	75	92		107	108	89	100			91			120	44
45	74	118	77	94			111	90	102			92			120	45
46	76	120	78	95			113	92	104			94			120	46
47	77		80	97			116	94	106			95			120	47
48	78		81	99			118	95	108			96			120	48
49	79		82				120	97	111			97			120	49
50	81		84					99	113			98			120	50
51	82		85					100	115			100			120	51
52	83		87					102	117			101			120	52
53	85		88					104	119			102			120	53
54	86		89					105	120			103			120	54
55	87		91					107	120			104			120	55

(Continued)

TABLE D-1 *(Continued)*

Basic Profile Scales

Raw	VRIN	TRIN	F_1	F_2	F	L	K	Hs	D	Hy	Pd	Mf	Pa	Pt	Sc	Ma	Si	Raw
56					106				120	108					92		88	56
57					107				120	110					94		90	57
58					108					112					95		91	58
59					109					113					97		92	59
60					110					115					98		94	60
61					111										99		95	61
62					113										101		96	62
63					114										102			63
64					115										104			64
65					116										105			65
66					117										106			66
67															108			67
68															109			68
69															111			69
70															112			70
71															113			71
72															115			72
73															116			73
74															118			74
75															119			75
76															120			76
77															120			77

Uniform and Linear T-score Conversions for Validity and Clinical Scales (Girls)

Basic Profile Scales

Raw	VRIN	TRIN	F_1	F_2	F	L	K	Hs	D	Hy	Pd	Mf	Pa	Pt	Sc	Ma	Si	Raw
0	36	110F	40	40	39	38	30	30	30	30	30	120	30	30	30	30	30	0
1	40	104F	43	42	41	43	30	32	30	30	30	120	30	30	30	30	30	1
2	43	97F	46	44	42	49	30	35	30	30	30	120	30	30	30	30	30	2
3	47	91F	50	47	43	54	31	38	30	30	30	118	30	30	30	30	30	3
4	50	85F	53	49	45	59	33	40	30	30	30	115	30	31	32	30	30	4
5	54	78F	56	51	46	64	35	42	30	30	30	112	32	33	33	30	30	5
6	58	72F	59	53	48	70	37	44	30	30	30	110	34	34	35	30	30	6
7	61	65F	63	55	49	75	40	46	30	30	30	107	37	35	36	30	30	7
8	65	59F	66	57	50	80	42	48	30	30	30	104	39	36	37	30	30	8
9	68	53F	69	60	52	85	44	49	30	30	30	102	41	37	38	31	30	9
10	72	54T	72	62	53	90	46	51	31	30	32	99	43	38	39	33	30	10
11	75	60T	76	64	55	96	49	53	33	30	34	96	45	39	40	34	30	11
12	79	67T	79	66	56	101	51	54	34	32	36	94	47	40	41	36	31	12
13	82	73T	82	68	57	106	53	56	36	33	38	91	49	41	42	36	33	13
14	86	79T	85	70	59	111	56	58	38	35	40	88	52	42	43	37	34	14
15	89	86T	89	73	60		58	61	40	36	41	86	54	43	43	38	35	15
16	93	92T	92	75	61		60	63	41	38	43	83	56	44	44	39	36	16
17	96	99T	95	77	63		62	65	43	39	44	80	59	45	45	41	38	17
18	100	105T	98	79	64		65	68	45	41	46	77	62	46	45	42	39	18
19	103	111T	102	81	66		67	70	46	42	47	75	65	47	46	43	40	19
20	107	118T	105	83	67		69	72	48	44	48	72	68	48	47	45	41	20
21	110	120T	108	86	68		72	75	50	46	50	69	71	49	47	46	43	21
22	114	120T	112	88	70		74	77	52	48	51	67	73	50	48	48	44	22
23	117	120T	115	90	71		76	79	53	49	53	64	76	51	48	50	45	23
24	120	120T	118	92	73		78	82	55	51	55	61	79	52	49	52	46	24

(Continued)

TABLE D-1 (Continued)

Basic Profile Scales

Raw	VRIN	TRIN	F_1	F_2	F	L	K	Hs	D	Hy	Pd	Mf	Pa	Pt	Sc	Ma	Si	Raw
25	120		120	94	74		81	84	57	53	57	59	82	53	50	55	48	25
26	120		120	96	75		83	86	59	55	59	56	85	55	51	58	49	26
27	120		120	99	77		85	89	61	58	62	53	88	56	51	61	50	27
28	120		120	101	78		88	91	63	60	64	51	91	58	52	64	51	28
29	120		120	103	79		90	93	65	62	67	48	93	59	53	68	53	29
30	120		120	105	81		92	96	67	65	69	45	96	61	54	71	54	30
31	120		120	107	82			98	69	67	72	43	99	63	55	75	55	31
32	120		120	109	84			101	71	70	74	40	102	65	56	78	56	32
33	120		120	112	85				73	72	77	37	105	67	58	82	58	33
34	120				86				75	74	79	35	108	68	59	85	59	34
35	120				88				77	77	82	32	111	70	60	89	60	35
36	120				89				79	79	84	30	113	72	62	92	61	36
37	120				91				81	82	86	30	116	74	63	96	63	37
38	120				92				83	84	89	30	119	76	65	99	64	38
39	120				93				85	86	91	30	120	78	66	103	65	39
40	120				95				87	89	94	30	120	79	68	106	66	40
41	120				96				89	91	96	30		81	69	109	68	41
42	120				97				91	94	99	30		83	71	113	69	42
43	120				99				93	96	101	30		85	72	116	70	43
44	120				100				95	98	104			87	74	120	71	44
45	120				102				97	101	106			88	75	120	73	45
46	120				103				99	103	109			90	77	120	74	46
47	120				104				101	106	111			92	78		75	47
48	120				106				103	108	114			94	80		76	48
49	120				107				105	111	116				81		78	49
50	120				109				107	113					83		79	50

51	80	84		110		51
52	81	86	109	111		52
53	82	87	111	113	115	53
54	84	89	113	114	118	54
55	85	90	115	115	120	55
56	86	92	117	117	120	56
57	87	93	119	118	120	57
58	89	95	120	120	120	58
59	90	96		120	120	59
60	91	98		120	120	60
61	92	99		120		61
62	94	101		120		62
63		102		120		63
64		104		120		64
65		105		120		65
66		107		120		66
67		108				67
68		110				68
69		111				69
70		113				70
71		114				71
72		116				72
73		117				73
74		119				74
75		120				75
76		120				76
77		120				77

TABLE D-2
Uniform T-score Conversions for Content Scales (Boys)

Content Scales

Raw	A-anx	A-obs	A-dep	A-hea	A-aln	A-biz	A-ang	A-cyn	A-con	A-lse	A-las	A-sod	A-fam	A-sch	A-trt	Raw
0	32	32	32	31	33	36	30	30	30	34	30	32	30	31	30	0
1	35	35	35	35	36	41	32	30	31	39	34	35	32	36	32	1
2	37	38	38	39	40	45	35	33	34	42	38	37	35	39	35	2
3	39	40	41	42	42	48	38	35	36	45	41	39	37	42	38	3
4	41	42	43	44	45	50	40	36	38	47	43	41	39	44	40	4
5	43	44	45	46	47	53	42	38	40	49	46	43	40	46	42	5
6	45	46	47	48	49	55	44	39	42	52	49	45	42	48	43	6
7	47	48	49	49	52	58	46	40	43	54	52	47	43	50	45	7
8	49	51	51	50	54	62	48	41	45	58	56	49	44	53	46	8
9	52	54	52	52	58	66	51	42	47	62	62	51	46	56	48	9
10	54	58	54	53	62	70	54	43	49	66	69	53	47	60	50	10
11	57	63	57	54	66	74	58	45	52	71	75	55	48	65	52	11
12	59	67	59	55	70	77	64	46	54	75	81	58	50	69	55	12
13	63	72	61	57	74	81	69	48	57	79	88	60	51	74	58	13
14	66	77	64	59	78	85	74	50	61	84	94	63	53	78	61	14
15	69	82	66	62	82	89	79	53	64	88	100	66	54	82	65	15
16	72		69	64	87	93	85	57	68	92	106	69	57	87	69	16
17	75		71	67	91	97	90	60	72	97		72	59	91	73	17
18	79		74	69	95	101		65	75	101		75	62	96	77	18
19	82		77	72	99	105		69	79			78	64	100	81	19
20	85		79	74	103			74	83			81	67	105	85	20
21	88		82	77				78	86			83	70		88	21

22	92	86		90	82	80	84
23	96	89		94		82	87
24	100	92	72			85	89
25	104		75			87	92
26	108		78			90	94
27			81			92	
28			83			95	
29			86			97	
30			89			100	
31			91			102	
32			94			105	
33			97			108	
34			100			110	
35			102			113	
36			105			115	
37			108			118	

TABLE D-2
Uniform T-score Conversions for Content Scales (Girls)

Content Scales

Raw	A-anx	A-obs	A-dep	A-hea	A-aln	A-biz	A-ang	A-cyn	A-con	A-lse	A-las	A-sod	A-fam	A-sch	A-trt	Raw
0	30	30	31	30	33	36	30	30	30	33	31	32	30	31	30	0
1	33	33	34	34	37	41	30	31	32	37	35	36	30	35	33	1
2	36	36	36	37	41	45	33	33	35	40	38	39	33	39	36	2
3	39	38	39	39	43	48	36	35	38	43	40	41	35	42	38	3
4	41	40	41	42	46	50	38	37	40	45	43	43	37	45	40	4
5	43	42	43	44	48	53	40	38	43	47	45	45	39	47	42	5
6	44	43	44	45	50	55	42	40	45	50	48	47	40	50	43	6
7	45	45	46	47	53	58	44	41	47	52	52	49	42	53	45	7
8	47	48	48	49	55	62	46	42	49	55	56	51	43	56	46	8
9	48	51	49	50	59	65	49	43	51	58	61	53	44	59	48	9
10	50	54	51	52	62	69	52	44	53	62	66	55	45	63	50	10
11	52	59	52	53	66	73	57	45	56	65	72	58	46	67	52	11
12	54	64	54	55	69	76	62	46	59	69	77	60	48	71	54	12
13	57	70	56	56	73	80	67	48	63	73	82	63	49	75	57	13
14	61	75	58	58	77	84	72	50	66	77	87	66	50	79	60	14
15	65	81	61	60	80	87	77	53	70	81	93	69	52	83	64	15
16	69		63	62	84	91	83	56	74	84	98	72	54	87	67	16
17	73		66	64	87	95	88	60	77	88		75	56	90	71	17
18	77		68	66	91	98		64	81	92		78	58	94	75	18
19	81		71	68	94	102		68	85			81	61	98	78	19
20	85		73	70	98			72	88			84	64	102	82	20
21	89		76	72				77	92			86	67		85	21

22	78	74	81	96	89	70	89	22
23	81	76		99	92	73	93	23
24	83	78			95	75	96	24
25	86	80				78	100	25
26	88	82				81	104	26
27		84				84		27
28		86				87		28
29		88				90		29
30		90				92		30
31		92				95		31
32		95				98		32
33		97				101		33
34		99				104		34
35		101				107		35
36		103						36
37		105						37

TABLE D-3
Linear T-score Conversions for Supplementary Scales (Boys and Girls)

Supplementary Scales

Raw	Boys MAC-R	ACK	PRO	IMM	A	R	Raw	Girls MAC-R	ACK	PRO	IMM	A	R	Raw
0	30	34	30	30	30	30	0	30	35	30	31	30	30	0
1	30	38	30	30	31	30	1	30	39	30	33	30	30	1
2	30	42	30	32	32	30	2	30	43	30	35	31	30	2
3	30	46	30	33	34	30	3	30	47	30	36	32	30	3
4	30	50	30	35	35	30	4	30	51	30	38	33	30	4
5	30	54	30	37	37	31	5	30	56	30	39	34	30	5
6	30	59	30	38	38	33	6	30	60	30	41	36	30	6
7	30	63	30	40	39	35	7	30	64	30	42	37	32	7
8	30	67	31	41	41	38	8	30	68	30	44	38	35	8
9	30	71	33	43	42	40	9	30	72	31	46	40	38	9
10	30	75	35	44	44	42	10	30	77	34	47	41	40	10
11	30	79	37	46	45	44	11	30	81	36	49	42	43	11
12	30	83	40	48	46	47	12	31	85	39	50	44	46	12
13	32	87	42	49	48	49	13	34	89	41	52	45	49	13
14	34		44	51	49	51	14	36		43	54	46	52	14
15	36		46	52	51	54	15	39		46	55	48	55	15
16	39		49	54	52	56	16	41		48	57	49	58	16
17	41		51	56	53	58	17	43		51	58	50	60	17
18	43		53	57	55	60	18	46		53	60	51	63	18
19	45		56	59	56	63	19	48		55	61	53	66	19
20	48		58	60	58	65	20	51		58	63	54	69	20
21	50		60	62	59	67	21	53		60	65	55	72	21
22	52		62	64	60	70	22	55		63	66	57	75	22
23	54		65	65	62	72	23	58		65	68	58	78	23
24	57		67	67	63	74	24	60		67	69	59	80	24

n					
25	83	61	71	70	63
26	86	62	73	72	65
27	89	63	74	75	68
28	92	64	76	77	70
29	95	66	77	79	72
30	98	67	79	82	75
31	100	68	81	84	77
32	103	70	82	87	80
33	106	71	84	89	82
34		72	85	91	84
35		74	87	94	87
36			88	96	89
37			90		92
38			92		94
39			93		97
40			95		99
41			96		101
42			98		104
43			100		106
44					109
45					111
46					113
47					116
48					118
49					120

n					
25	76	65	68	69	59
26	79	66	70	71	61
27	81	67	72	74	63
28	83	69	73	76	66
29	86	70	75	78	68
30	88	71	76	80	70
31	90	73	78	83	72
32	92	74	79	85	75
33	95	76	81	87	77
34		77	83	89	79
35		78	84	92	81
36			86	94	84
37			87		86
38			89		88
39			91		90
40			92		93
41			94		95
42			95		97
43			97		99
44					102
45					104
46					106
47					108
48					111
49					113

TABLE D-4
Linear T-score Conversions for Harris-Lingoes and Si Subscales (Boys)

Raw	D_1	D_2	D_3	D_4	D_5	Hy_1	Hy_2	Hy_3	Hy_4	Hy_5	Pd_1	Pd_2	Pd_3	Pd_4	Pd_5	Raw
								Subscales (D, Hy, & Pd)								
0	30	30	30	35	36	32	30	34	36	30	32	30	30	30	32	0
1	32	31	35	39	41	38	33	38	39	36	37	35	35	32	36	1
2	35	36	42	43	46	44	37	42	43	44	42	41	42	37	41	2
3	37	41	48	47	51	49	41	46	46	51	48	48	48	42	45	3
4	39	46	55	52	56	55	46	50	50	59	53	54	54	46	49	4
5	42	51	62	56	61	61	50	54	53	66	59	60	61	51	53	5
6	44	56	68	60	66	66	54	58	57	74	64	67	67	55	57	6
7	46	61	75	64	71		58	62	60	81	69	73		60	61	7
8	49	66	82	68	76		63	66	64		75	79		65	65	8
9	51	71	89	72	81		67	70	67		80			69	69	9
10	53	76	95	76	85		71	74	71					74	73	10
11	56	81	102	80			76	77	74					78	78	11
12	58	86		84			80	81	78					83	82	12
13	60	91		88				85	82							13
14	63	96		92				89	85							14
15	65			96				93	89							15
16	67								92							16
17	70								96							17
18	72															18
19	75															19
20	77															20
21	79															21
22	82															22
23	84															23
24	86															24
25	89															25
26	91															26
27	93															27
28	96															28
29	98															29

Subscales (Pa, Sc, Ma, & Si)

Raw	Pa_1	Pa_2	Pa_3	Sc_1	Sc_2	Sc_3	Sc_4	Sc_5	Sc_6	Ma_1	Ma_2	Ma_3	Ma_4	Si_1	Si_2	Si_3	Raw
0	35	30	30	31	37	37	34	33	35	31	30	30	30	30	38	30	0
1	39	36	34	34	43	41	38	38	38	38	30	36	31	33	43	31	1
2	42	42	40	37	48	46	42	43	41	45	30	43	37	36	47	34	2
3	46	49	45	40	54	50	46	48	44	52	33	49	42	40	52	37	3
4	50	55	50	43	59	55	50	53	47	59	38	55	48	43	57	40	4
5	53	61	56	46	65	59	53	57	50	66	43	62	53	46	62	42	5
6	57	67	61	49	71	64	57	62	53	73	48	68	58	49	67	45	6
7	60	73	66	53	76	68	61	67	56		52	74	64	53	72	48	7
8	64	79	72	56	82	73	65	72	59		57	81	69	56	77	51	8
9	68	85	77	59	87	77	69	77	62		62		75	59		54	9
10	71			62	93	82	73	82	65		66			62		57	10
11	75			65	98		77	86	68		71			65		60	11
12	78			68			81		71					69		63	12
13	82			71			85		74					72		66	13
14	86			74			88		77					75		69	14
15	89			77					80							72	15
16	93			80					83							75	16
17	96			83					86							77	17
18				86					89								18
19				89					92								19
20				92					95								20
21				95													21

TABLE D-4
Linear T-score Conversions for Harris-Lingoes and Si Subscales (Girls)

Subscales (D, Hy, & Pd)

Raw	D_1	D_2	D_3	D_4	D_5	Hy_1	Hy_2	Hy_3	Hy_4	Hy_5	Pd_1	Pd_2	Pd_3	Pd_4	Pd_5	Raw
0	30	30	30	35	33	31	30	33	34	30	30	31	30	30	31	0
1	31	30	33	39	37	37	34	37	37	35	35	38	36	31	35	1
2	33	35	39	43	42	43	38	40	40	43	40	45	43	35	39	2
3	35	40	46	47	46	48	42	44	44	51	45	52	49	39	43	3
4	37	46	52	50	51	54	46	47	47	58	51	59	55	44	47	4
5	40	51	58	54	56	60	50	51	50	66	56	65	61	48	51	5
6	42	57	64	58	60	65	55	55	53	74	61	72	67	53	55	6
7	44	62	71	62	65		59	58	57	81	66	79		57	59	7
8	46	67	77	66	70		63	62	60		71	86		62	63	8
9	48	73	83	70	74		67	65	63		77			66	67	9
10	50	78	89	73	79		71	69	66					71	71	10
11	52	84	96	77			75	72	70					75	75	11
12	55	89		81			80	76	73					80	79	12
13	57	95		85				80	76							13
14	59	100		89				83	79							14
15	61			92				87	83							15
16	63								86							16
17	65								89							17
18	68															18
19	70															19
20	72															20
21	74															21
22	76															22
23	78															23
24	80															24
25	83															25
26	85															26
27	87															27
28	89															28
29	91															29

Subscales (Pa, Sc, Ma, & Si)

Raw	Pa_1	Pa_2	Pa_3	Sc_1	Sc_2	Sc_3	Sc_4	Sc_5	Sc_6	Ma_1	Ma_2	Ma_3	Ma_4	Si_1	Si_2	Si_3	Raw
0	35	30	31	30	37	36	34	31	34	32	30	31	30	31	40	30	0
1	39	36	36	33	43	41	38	35	37	39	30	37	30	34	45	30	1
2	42	41	41	36	48	45	41	40	40	47	30	44	35	37	51	33	2
3	46	46	46	39	54	50	45	44	43	55	30	50	41	40	56	36	3
4	50	51	51	42	59	54	49	49	46	63	34	57	47	43	61	39	4
5	53	57	56	46	65	58	52	54	49	70	39	64	52	46	67	41	5
6	57	62	61	49	70	63	56	58	52	78	44	70	58	49	72	44	6
7	61	67	66	52	76	67	60	63	54		49	77	64	52	78	47	7
8	64	73	72	55	81	71	63	68	57		54	83	70	55	83	49	8
9	68	78	77	58	87	76	67	72	60		59		75	58		52	9
10	72			61	93	80	71	77	63		65			62		55	10
11	76			64	98		75	82	66		70			65		58	11
12	79			67			78		69					68		60	12
13	83			70			82		72					71		63	13
14	87			73			86		75					74		66	14
15	90			76					78							68	15
16	94			79					81							71	16
17	98			83					83							74	17
18				86					86								18
19				89					89								19
20				92					92								20
21				95													21

T-SCORE CONVERSIONS FOR BASIC MMPI-A SCALES PERMITTING ESTIMATES OF THE MARKS AND BRIGGS ADOLESCENT T-SCORE VALUES PROVIDED IN DAHLSTROM, WELSH, AND DAHLSTROM (1972)

Note. Adapted from Butcher, James N., Williams, Carolyn L., Graham, John R., Archer, Robert P., Tellegen, Auke, Ben-Porath, Yossef S., and Kaemmer, Beverly. *MMPI-A (Minnesota Multiphasic Personality Inventory—Adolescent): Manual for Administration, Scoring, and Interpretation*. Copyright © 1992 by the Regents of the University of Minnesota.

TABLE E-1

T-score Values for MMPI-A Basic Scales for Adolescent Males Ages 14 and Below Based on Marks and Briggs Norms (Dahlstrom, Welsh, and Dahlstrom, 1972)

Raw	L	F	K	Hs	D	Hy	Pd	Mf	Pa	Pt	Sc	Ma	Si	Raw
0	32	42	30	34	30	30	30	30	30	30	32	30	30	0
1	39	44	30	37	30	30	30	30	30	32	33	30	30	1
2	46	46	30	40	30	30	30	30	30	33	35	30	30	2
3	51	47	30	43	30	30	30	30	30	34	36	30	30	3
4	56	48	31	46	30	30	30	30	33	36	37	30	30	4
5	61	50	33	49	30	30	30	30	35	37	38	30	30	5
6	66	52	35	52	30	30	30	30	38	38	39	30	30	6
7	71	53	37	55	30	30	30	30	41	40	40	30	30	7
8	76	54	39	58	32	31	30	30	44	41	41	31	30	8
9	80	56	41	61	35	33	32	30	46	43	42	33	30	9
10	85	58	43	64	37	36	35	30	49	44	43	35	30	10
11	90	59	45	67	39	38	37	31	52	45	44	37	30	11
12	95	60	48	70	41	40	39	35	55	47	45	39	31	12
13	100	62	50	73	43	42	42	38	57	48	46	41	33	13
14	105	64	52	76	46	44	44	41	60	49	47	43	34	14
15		65	54	79	48	47	46	43	63	51	48	45	35	15
16		66	56	82	50	49	49	47	65	52	50	47	37	16
17		68	58	84	54	51	51	50	68	54	51	49	38	17
18		69	60	87	57	53	53	53	71	55	52	50	40	18
19		70	62	90	59	56	56	55	74	56	53	52	41	19
20		71	64	95	61	58	58	59	76	58	54	54	42	20
21		73	66	99	63	60	60	62	79	59	55	56	44	21
22		75	68	102	66	62	62	65	82	60	56	58	46	22
23		77	70	105	68	64	65	67	84	62	57	60	47	23
24		78	72	108	70	67	67	71	87	63	58	62	49	24
25		79	74	111				74	90	65	59	64	50	25

26	51	66	60	66	93	76	69	69	72	114	76	81
27	53	68	61	67	95	79	72	71	75	117	79	83
28	54	70	62	69	98	83	74	73	77	120	81	84
29	56	72	63	70	101	86	76	75	79		83	85
30	57	74	65	71	104	88	79	78	81		85	87
31	58	76	66	73	106	91	81	80	83			89
32	60	78	67	74	109	95	83	82	86			90
33	61	80	68	75	112	98	86	84	88			91
34	62	82	69	77	114	100	88	87	90			93
35	64	84	70	78	117	102	90	89	92			95
36	65	86	71	80	120	106	93	91	95			96
37	66	88	72	81	120	109	95	93	97			97
38	68	90	73	82	120	112	97	95	99			99
39	69	92	74	84	120	114	100	98	101			101
40	70	94	75	85		117	102	100	103			102
41	72	96	76	86		120	104	102	106			103
42	73	98	77	88		120	106	104	108			105
43	75	100	78	89		120	109	107	110			107
44	76	101	80	91		120	111	109	112			108
45	77	103	81	92			113	111	115			109
46	79	105	82	93			116	113	117			111
47	80		83	95			118	115	119			113
48	81		84	96			120	118	120			114
49	83		85					120	120			115
50	84		86					120	120			117
51	85		87					120	120			119
52	87		88					120	120			120
53	89		89					120	120			120
54	91		90					120	120			120
55	92		91					120	120			120

(Continued)

TABLE E-1 (Continued)

Raw	L	F	K	Hs	D	Hy	Pd	Mf	Pa	Pt	Sc	Ma	Si	Raw
56		120			120	120					92		93	56
57		120			120	120					93		95	57
58		120				120					95		96	58
59		120				120					96		98	59
60		120				120					97		99	60
61		120									98		100	61
62		120									99		102	62
63		120									100			63
64		120									101			64
65		120									102			65
66		120									103			66
67											104			67
68											105			68
69											106			69
70											107			70
71											108			71
72											110			72
73											111			73
74											112			74
75											113			75
76											114			76
77											115			77

T-score Values for MMPI-A Basic Scales for Adolescent Females Ages 14 and Below Based on Marks and Briggs Norms (Dahlstrom, Welsh, and Dahlstrom, 1972)

Raw	L	F	K	Hs	D	Hy	Pd	Mf	Pa	Pt	Sc	Ma	Si	Raw
0	31	44	30	36	30	30	30	120	30	30	32	30	30	0
1	39	46	30	39	30	30	30	120	30	30	34	30	30	1
2	46	47	30	41	30	30	30	120	32	32	35	30	30	2
3	50	49	30	44	30	30	30	118	34	33	36	30	30	3
4	55	51	30	46	30	30	30	115	36	34	37	30	30	4
5	59	54	31	49	30	30	30	112	38	36	38	30	30	5
6	64	56	33	51	30	30	30	109	40	37	40	30	30	6
7	69	57	35	54	30	30	31	107	43	39	41	30	30	7
8	73	59	38	56	30	30	34	104	45	40	42	32	30	8
9	78	61	40	59	32	30	36	101	47	42	43	35	30	9
10	83	64	42	61	34	30	38	99	49	43	45	37	30	10
11	87	65	44	64	36	31	40	97	51	44	46	39	30	11
12	92	66	47	66	38	33	42	95	54	46	47	41	32	12
13	97	69	49	69	41	35	44	91	56	47	48	43	33	13
14	101	71	51	71	43	38	46	88	58	49	49	45	34	14
15		72	53	74	45	40	49	86	60	50	51	47	35	15
16		74	56	76	47	42	51	84	62	52	52	49	37	16
17		76	58	79	49	44	53	80	65	53	53	51	39	17
18		79	60	81	52	46	55	77	67	54	54	54	40	18
19		81	62	84	55	49	57	75	69	56	56	56	42	19
20		82	65	86	57	51	59	73	71	57	57	58	43	20
21		84	67	89	59	53	61	69	73	59	58	60	44	21
22		86	69	91	62	55	64	66	75	60	59	62	45	22
23		89	71	94	64	58	66	64	78	62	60	64	47	23
24		90	73	96	66	60	68	62	80	63	62	66	48	24
25		91	76	99	68	62	68	58	82	64	63	68	49	25

(Continued)

TABLE E-1 (Continued)

Raw	L	F	K	Hs	D	Hy	Pd	Mf	Pa	Pt	Sc	Ma	Si	Raw
26		94	78	101	70	64	70	55	84	66	64	70	51	26
27		96	80	104	72	66	72	53	86	67	65	72	52	27
28		99	82	106	74	69	74	51	89	69	67	75	53	28
29		100	85	109	76	71	76	47	91	70	68	77	54	29
30		101	87	111	78	73	79	44	93	72	69	79	56	30
31		104		113	80	75	81	42	95	73	70	81	57	31
32		106		116	83	78	83	40	97	74	71	83	58	32
33		107			85	80	85	36	99	76	73	85	59	33
34		109			87	82	87	33	102	77	74	87	61	34
35		111			89	84	89	31	104	79	75	89	62	35
36		114			91	86	92	30	106	80	76	91	63	36
37		116			93	89	94	30	108	82	77	94	65	37
38		117			95	91	96	30	110	83	79	96	67	38
39		119			97	93	98	30	113	84	80	98	68	39
40		120			99	95	100	30	115	86	81	100	69	40
41		120			102	98	102	30		87	82	102	71	41
42		120			104	100	104			89	84	104	72	42
43		120			106	102	107			90	85	106	73	43
44		120			108	104	109			92	86	108	75	44
45		120			110	106	111			93	87	110	76	45
46		120			112	109	113			94	88	113	77	46
47		120			114	111	115			96	90		78	47
48		120			116	113	117			97	91		80	48
49		120			118	115	119				92		81	49
50		120			120	118					93		82	50

51	52	53	54	55	56	57	58	59	60	61	62	63	64	65	66	67	68	69	70	71	72	73	74	75	76	77
83	85	86	87	88	90	92	94	95	96	97	99															
95	96	97	98	99	101	102	103	104	106	108	109	110	112	113	114	115	117	118	119	120	120	120	120	120	120	120
							120	120	120	120	120	120	120	120	120	120										
120	120	120	120	120	120	120																				
120	120	120	120	120	120	120	120	120	120	120	120	120	120	120	120											
51	52	53	54	55	56	57	58	59	60	61	62	63	64	65	66	67	68	69	70	71	72	73	74	75	76	77

TABLE E-2

T-score Values for MMPI-A Basic Scales for Adolescent Males Age 15 Based on Marks and Briggs Norms (Dahlstrom, Welsh, and Dahlstrom, 1972)

Raw	L	F	K	Hs	D	Hy	Pd	Mf	Pa	Pt	Sc	Ma	Si	Raw
0	32	41	30	36	30	30	30	30	30	30	33	30	30	0
1	39	43	30	39	30	30	30	30	30	31	34	30	30	1
2	46	44	30	41	30	30	30	30	31	32	35	30	30	2
3	50	45	30	44	30	30	30	30	33	34	36	30	30	3
4	55	46	30	46	30	30	30	30	35	35	37	30	30	4
5	59	48	32	48	30	30	30	30	37	37	38	30	30	5
6	63	50	34	51	30	30	30	30	40	38	39	30	30	6
7	67	51	37	53	30	30	30	30	42	39	40	30	30	7
8	72	52	39	55	30	32	30	30	44	41	41	30	30	8
9	76	53	41	58	30	34	30	30	46	42	42	32	30	9
10	80	55	43	60	31	36	32	31	48	44	43	34	30	10
11	85	56	45	62	33	38	34	33	50	45	44	36	30	11
12	89	57	47	65	36	40	37	36	52	46	45	38	31	12
13	93	58	49	67	38	42	39	39	54	48	46	40	32	13
14	98	60	51	69	40	44	41	41	56	49	47	42	34	14
15		61	53	72	43	46	43	43	58	51	48	43	35	15
16		62	55	74	45	48	45	46	60	52	49	45	36	16
17		63	58	76	47	50	47	49	63	54	50	47	38	17
18		65	60	79	49	52	49	51	65	55	51	49	39	18
19		66	62	81	53	54	52	53	67	56	52	51	40	19
20		67	64	85	56	57	54	57	69	58	53	53	42	20
21		68	66	88	58	59	56	60	71	59	54	55	44	21
22		70	68	91	61	61	58	62	73	61	55	57	46	22
23		71	70	93	63	63	60	64	75	62	56	59	47	23
24		72	72	95	65	65	62	67	77	64	57	61	48	24
25		73	74	98	67	67	64	70	79	65	58	63	50	25

26	51	65	59	66	81	72	66	67	70	100	76	75
27	52	66	60	68	83	74	69	69	72	102	78	76
28	54	68	61	69	86	78	71	71	74	105	81	77
29	55	70	62	71	88	81	73	73	77	107	83	78
30	56	72	63	72	90	83	75	75	79	109	85	80
31	58	74	64	73	92	85	77	77	81	112		81
32	59	76	65	75	94	88	79	79	83	114		82
33	60	78	66	76	96	91	81	81	86			83
34	62	80	67	78	98	93	84	83	88			85
35	63	82	68	79	100	95	86	85	90			86
36	64	84	69	81	102	98	88	87	92			87
37	66	86	70	82	104	101	90	89	95			88
38	67	87	71	83	106	104	92	91	97			90
39	69	89	72	85	109	106	94	94	99			91
40	70	91	73	86	111	109	96	96	101			92
41	71	93	74	88		112	99	98	104			93
42	73	95	75	89		114	101	100	106			95
43	74	97	76	90		116	103	102	108			96
44	75	99	77	92		119	105	104	111			97
45	77	101	78	93			107	106	113			98
46	78	103	79	95			109	108	115			100
47	79		80	96			111	110	117			101
48	81		81	98			114	112	120			102
49	82		82				116	114	120			103
50	83		83					116	120			105
51	85		84					118	120			106
52	87		85					120	120			107
53	89		86					120	120			108
54	90		87					120	120			110
55	91		88					120	120			112

(Continued)

TABLE E-2 (Continued)

Raw	L	F	K	Hs	D	Hy	Pd	Mf	Pa	Pt	Sc	Ma	Si	Raw
56		113			120	120					89		93	56
57		114			120	120					90		94	57
58		115				120					91		95	58
59		117				120					92		97	59
60		118				120					93		98	60
61		119									94		99	61
62		120									95		101	62
63		120									96			63
64		120									97			64
65		120									98			65
66		120									99			66
67											100			67
68											101			68
69											102			69
70											103			70
71											104			71
72											105			72
73											106			73
74											107			74
75											108			75
76											109			76
77											110			77

T-score Values for MMPI-A Basic Scales for Adolescent Females Age 15 Based on Marks and Briggs Norms (Dahlstrom, Welsh, and Dahlstrom, 1972)

Raw	L	F	K	Hs	D	Hy	Pd	Mf	Pa	Pt	Sc	Ma	Si	Raw
0	31	43	30	37	30	30	30	120	30	30	32	30	30	0
1	38	45	30	39	30	30	30	116	30	31	34	30	30	1
2	45	46	30	41	30	30	30	113	31	32	35	30	30	2
3	49	47	30	43	30	30	30	111	33	33	36	30	30	3
4	53	50	30	46	30	30	30	109	36	35	37	30	30	4
5	58	52	32	48	30	30	30	106	38	36	39	30	30	5
6	62	54	34	50	30	30	30	103	40	37	40	31	30	6
7	66	55	36	52	30	30	30	101	42	39	41	33	30	7
8	70	57	38	55	30	30	30	100	44	40	42	35	30	8
9	75	59	40	57	30	30	32	97	47	41	43	37	30	9
10	79	61	42	59	32	30	34	94	49	43	44	39	30	10
11	83	62	45	61	34	31	36	92	51	44	45	41	31	11
12	88	63	47	64	37	33	38	90	53	45	46	42	32	12
13	92	66	49	66	39	35	40	87	55	47	47	44	33	13
14	96	68	51	68	41	37	42	84	58	48	48	46	35	14
15		69	53	70	43	39	44	82	60	49	49	48	36	15
16		70	56	72	45	42	46	79	62	51	50	50	38	16
17		73	58	75	47	44	48	76	64	52	51	52	40	17
18		75	60	77	52	46	51	73	66	53	53	54	41	18
19		77	62	79	54	48	53	71	68	55	54	56	42	19
20		78	64	81	56	50	55	69	71	56	55	57	44	20
21		79	67	84	58	52	57	66	73	58	56	59	45	21
22		82	69	86	60	54	59	63	75	59	57	59	45	22
23		84	71	88	62	56	61	61	77	60	58	61	46	23
24		85	73	90	65	58	63	59	79	62	59	63	48	24

(Continued)

TABLE E-2 (Continued)

Raw	L	F	K	Hs	D	Hy	Pd	Mf	Pa	Pt	Sc	Ma	Si	Raw
25		86	75	93	67	60	65	56	82	63	60	65	49	25
26		89	77	95	69	62	67	53	84	64	61	67	50	26
27		91	80	97	71	64	69	51	86	66	62	69	52	27
28		93	82	99	73	66	71	49	88	67	63	70	53	28
29		94	84	102	75	68	74	45	90	68	64	72	54	29
30		95	86	104	78	70	76	42	93	70	65	74	55	30
31		98		106	80	72	78	40	95	71	66	76	57	31
32		100		109	82	74	80	38	97	72	68	78	58	32
33		101			84	76	82	35	99	74	69	80	59	33
34		102			86	79	84	32	101	75	70	82	61	34
35		104			88	81	86	30	103	76	71	83	62	35
36		107			90	83	88	30	106	78	72	85	64	36
37		109			93	85	90	30	108	79	73	87	66	37
38		110			95	87	92	30	110	80	74	89	67	38
39		111			97	89	95	30	112	82	75	91	68	39
40		114			99	91	97	30	114	83	76	93	70	40
41		116			101	93	99	30		85	77	95	71	41
42		117			103	95	101	30		86	78	96	72	42
43		118			106	97	103	30		87	79	98	73	43
44		120			108	99	105			89	80	100	75	44
45		120			110	101	107			90	82	102	76	45
46		120			112	103	109			91	83	104	77	46
47		120			114	105	111			93	84		79	47
48		120			116	107	113			94	85		80	48
49		120			119	109	116				86		81	49
50		120			120	111					87		82	50

51					120		120
52					120		120
53					120		120
54					120		120
55					120		120
56					120		120
57					120		120
58	84	88			120	113	120
59	85	89			120	115	120
60	86	90			120	118	
61	88	91			120	120	
62	89	92			120	120	
63	91	93			120	120	
64	93	94			120	120	
65	94	95			120	120	
66	95	97				120	
67	97	98					
68	98	100					
69	99	101					
70		102					
71		103					
72		104					
73		105					
74		106					
75		107					
76		108					
77		109					
		110					
		112					
		113					
		114					
		115					
		116					
		117					

TABLE E-3

T-score Values for MMPI-A Basic Scales for Adolescent Males Age 16 Based on Marks and Briggs Norms
(Dahlstrom, Welsh, and Dahlstrom, 1972)

Raw	L	F	K	Hs	D	Hy	Pd	Mf	Pa	Pt	Sc	Ma	Si	Raw
0	31	40	30	33	30	30	30	30	34	30	30	30	30	0
1	38	42	30	36	30	30	30	30	35	30	32	30	30	1
2	44	44	30	39	30	30	30	30	36	31	33	30	30	2
3	49	45	30	42	30	30	30	30	37	33	35	30	30	3
4	53	46	30	45	30	30	30	30	39	34	36	30	30	4
5	58	47	31	47	30	30	30	30	40	36	37	30	30	5
6	62	49	33	50	30	30	30	30	42	37	38	30	30	6
7	67	50	36	53	30	30	30	30	43	39	39	30	30	7
8	71	51	38	56	30	30	30	30	45	40	40	30	30	8
9	76	53	40	59	31	30	30	30	46	42	41	30	30	9
10	80	54	42	62	33	32	32	30	48	43	42	32	30	10
11	85	55	45	64	36	34	34	31	49	45	43	34	30	11
12	89	56	47	67	38	37	36	35	51	46	44	36	30	12
13	94	58	49	70	40	39	38	39	52	48	45	38	31	13
14	99	59	51	73	42	41	41	41	54	49	46	40	32	14
15		60	54	76	45	43	43	43	55	51	48	43	34	15
16		61	56	78	47	45	45	47	57	52	49	45	35	16
17		63	58	81	49	47	47	50	58	54	50	47	37	17
18		64	60	84	53	50	49	53	60	55	51	49	38	18
19		65	63	87	56	52	51	55	61	56	52	51	39	19
20		66	65	91	58	54	53	59	63	58	53	53	41	20
21		68	67	95	60	56	56	62	64	59	54	55	43	21
22		70	70	98	63	58	58	65	66	61	55	58	45	22
23		71	72	101	65	61	60	67	67	62	56	60	46	23
24		72	74	104	67	63	62	71	68	64	57	62	48	24
25		73	76	107	69	65	64	74	70	65	58	64	49	25

26	51	66	59	67	71	76	66	67	71	109	79	75
27	52	68	61	68	73	79	69	69	74	112	81	77
28	54	70	62	70	74	83	71	71	76	115	83	78
29	55	73	63	71	76	86	73	73	78	118	85	79
30	56	75	64	73	77	88	75	76	80	120	88	80
31	58	77	65	74	79	91	77	78	83	120		82
32	59	79	66	76	80	95	79	80	85	120		83
33	61	81	67	77	82	98	82	82	87			84
34	62	83	68	79	83	100	84	85	89			86
35	63	85	69	80	85	103	86	87	92			87
36	65	88	70	82	86	107	88	89	94			88
37	66	90	71	83	88	110	90	91	96			89
38	68	92	72	85	89	112	92	93	98			91
39	69	94	74	86	91	114	95	96	101			92
40	71	96	75	87	92	117	97	98	103			93
41	72	98	76	89		120	99	100	105			94
42	73	100	77	90		120	101	102	107			96
43	75	103	78	92		120	103	104	110			97
44	76	105	79	93		120	105	106	112			98
45	78	107	80	95			107	109	114			99
46	79	109	81	96			110	111	116			101
47	81		82	98			112	113	119			103
48	82		83	99			114	115	120			104
49	83		84				116	117	120			105
50	85		85					120	120			106
51	86		86					120	120			108
52	88		88					120	120			109
53	90		89					120	120			110
54	92		90					120	120			112
55	93		91					120	120			113

(Continued)

TABLE E-3 (Continued)

Raw	L	F	K	Hs	D	Hy	Pd	Mf	Pa	Pt	Sc	Ma	Si	Raw
56		114			120	120					92		95	56
57		115			120	120					93		96	57
58		117				120					94		98	58
59		118				120					95		99	59
60		119				120					96		100	60
61		120									97		102	61
62		120									98		103	62
63		120									99			63
64		120									101			64
65		120									102			65
66		120									103			66
67											104			67
68											105			68
69											106			69
70											107			70
71											108			71
72											109			72
73											110			73
74											111			74
75											112			75
76											114			76
77											115			77

T-score Values for MMPI-A Basic Scales for Adolescent Females Age 16 Based on Marks and Briggs Norms (Dahlstrom, Welsh, and Dahlstrom, 1972)

Raw	L	F	K	Hs	D	Hy	Pd	Mf	Pa	Pt	Sc	Ma	Si	Raw
0	30	41	30	35	30	30	30	120	30	30	32	30	30	0
1	36	43	30	37	30	30	30	120	30	30	33	30	30	1
2	42	44	30	40	30	30	30	120	30	30	34	30	30	2
3	47	46	30	42	30	30	30	118	30	32	35	30	30	3
4	51	48	30	44	30	30	30	116	32	33	36	30	30	4
5	56	50	33	47	30	30	30	112	35	34	38	30	30	5
6	60	52	35	49	30	30	30	109	37	36	39	30	30	6
7	64	53	37	51	30	30	30	106	40	37	40	30	30	7
8	69	55	39	54	30	30	30	104	42	38	41	30	30	8
9	73	57	41	56	30	30	31	101	45	40	42	32	30	9
10	78	59	44	58	30	30	33	98	48	41	43	35	30	10
11	82	60	46	61	30	32	36	96	50	42	44	37	30	11
12	86	62	48	63	32	34	38	94	53	44	45	39	30	12
13	91	64	50	65	34	36	40	90	55	45	46	41	30	13
14	95	66	52	67	36	38	42	87	58	46	47	44	31	14
15		67	55	70	38	40	44	84	61	48	48	46	32	15
16		68	57	72	40	42	47	82	63	49	49	48	33	16
17		71	59	74	43	44	49	78	66	50	50	50	35	17
18		73	61	77	45	46	51	75	68	52	51	53	37	18
19		75	63	79	48	48	53	73	71	53	52	55	38	19
20		76	66	81	51	50	55	70	74	54	53	57	39	20
21		77	68	84	53	52	57	67	76	56	54	59	41	21
22		80	70	86	55	54	60	64	79	57	55	62	42	22
23		82	72	88	57	56	62	61	81	58	56	64	43	23
24		83	74	91	59	57	64	59	84	60	58	66	44	24
25		84	77	93	61	59	66	55	87	61	59	68	46	25

(Continued)

TABLE E-3 *(Continued)*

Raw	L	F	K	Hs	D	Hy	Pd	Mf	Pa	Pt	Sc	Ma	Si	Raw
26		86	79	95	63	61	68	52	89	62	60	71	47	26
27		89	81	98	65	63	71	50	92	64	61	73	48	27
28		91	83	100	67	65	73	47	94	65	62	75	49	28
29		92	85	102	69	67	75	43	97	66	63	77	51	29
30		93	88	105	71	69	77	40	99	67	64	80	52	30
31		95		107	73	71	79	38	102	69	65	82	53	31
32		97		109	75	73	82	36	105	70	66	84	54	32
33		98			77	75	84	32	107	71	67	86	55	33
34		100			79	77	86	30	110	73	68	89	57	34
35		102			81	79	88	30	112	74	69	91	58	35
36		104			83	81	90	30	115	75	70	93	60	36
37		106			85	83	92	30	118	77	71	95	62	37
38		107			87	85	95	30	120	78	72	98	63	38
39		109			89	87	97	30	120	79	73	100	64	39
40		111			92	89	99	30	120	81	74	102	65	40
41		113			94	91	101	30		82	75	104	67	41
42		114			96	93	103	30		83	77	106	68	42
43		116			98	95	106	30		85	78	109	69	43
44		118			100	97	108			86	79	111	70	44
45		120			102	99	110			87	80	113	72	45
46		120			104	101	112			89	81	115	73	46
47		120			106	103	114			90	82		74	47
48		120			108	105	116			91	83		75	48
49		120			110	107	119				84		77	49
50		120			112	109					85		78	50
51		120			114	111					86		79	51
52		120			116	113					87		80	52
53		120			118	115					88		82	53

54					54
55					55
56					56
57					57
58					58
59					59
60					60
61					61
62					62
63					63
64					64
65					65
66					66
67					67
68					68
69					69
70					70
71					71
72					72
73					73
74					74
75					75
76					76
77					77

83 84 86 88 89 90 91 93 94

89 90 91 92 93 94 95 97 99 100 101 102 103 104 105 106 107 108 109 110 111 112 113 114

117 119 120 120 120 120 120

120 120 120 120

120 120 120 120 120 120 120 120 120 120 120 120 120

TABLE E-4

T-score Values for MMPI-A Basic Scales for Adolescent Males Age 17 Based on Marks and Briggs Norms (Dahlstrom, Welsh, and Dahlstrom, 1972)

Raw	L	F	K	Hs	D	Hy	Pd	Mf	Pa	Pt	Sc	Ma	Si	Raw
0	30	39	30	35	30	30	30	30	30	30	31	30	30	0
1	37	41	30	38	30	30	30	30	30	30	32	30	30	1
2	43	43	30	40	30	30	30	30	30	30	33	30	30	2
3	47	44	30	43	30	30	30	30	30	32	34	30	30	3
4	51	45	30	45	30	30	30	30	31	33	35	30	30	4
5	55	47	31	48	30	30	30	30	34	35	36	30	30	5
6	59	49	34	50	30	30	30	30	37	36	37	30	30	6
7	63	50	36	53	30	30	30	30	40	38	38	30	30	7
8	68	52	38	55	32	30	30	30	43	39	39	30	30	8
9	72	54	40	58	34	30	30	30	46	41	40	31	30	9
10	76	56	42	60	35	32	30	31	49	42	41	33	30	10
11	80	57	45	63	37	34	32	33	52	44	43	35	30	11
12	81	58	47	65	39	36	34	37	55	45	44	37	30	12
13	84	60	49	68	41	38	36	40	58	47	45	39	30	13
14	93	62	51	70	43	40	39	42	61	48	46	41	32	14
15		63	53	73	44	42	41	44	64	50	47	43	33	15
16		65	56	75	46	44	43	47	67	52	48	45	35	16
17		67	58	78	48	46	46	50	70	53	49	48	36	17
18		68	60	80	51	48	48	53	72	55	50	50	38	18
19		69	62	83	54	49	50	55	75	56	51	52	39	19
20		71	64	87	55	51	52	58	78	58	52	54	41	20
21		73	67	90	57	53	55	61	81	59	53	56	43	21
22		76	69	93	59	55	57	63	84	61	55	58	45	22
23		78	71	95	61	57	59	66	87	62	56	60	47	23
24		79	73	98	63	59	62	69	90	64	57	62	49	24
25		80	75	100	64	61	64	72	93	65	58	65	50	25

26	52	67	59	67	96	74	66	63	66	103	78	82	26
27	53	69	60	69	99	77	69	65	68	105	80	84	27
28	55	71	61	70	102	80	71	67	70	108	82	85	28
29	56	73	62	72	105	83	73	68	72	110	84	87	29
30	58	75	63	73	108	85	75	70	73	113	86	89	30
31	59	77	64	75	111	87	78	72	75	115		91	31
32	61	79	66	76	114	91	80	74	77	118		92	32
33	62	82	67	78	117	94	82	76	79			93	33
34	64	84	68	79	120	96	85	78	81			95	34
35	65	86	69	81	120	98	87	80	83			97	35
36	67	88	70	82	120	102	89	82	84			98	36
37	68	90	71	84	120	105	91	84	86			100	37
38	70	92	72	86	120	107	94	86	88			102	38
39	71	94	73	87	120	109	96	87	90			104	39
40	73	96	74	89		113	98	89	92			105	40
41	74	99	75	90		116	101	91	93			106	41
42	76	101	77	92		118	103	93	95			108	42
43	77	103	78	93		120	105	95	97			110	43
44	79	105	79	95		120	108	97	99			111	44
45	80	107	80	96			110	99	101			113	45
46	82	109	81	98			112	101	102			115	46
47	83		82	99			114	103	104			117	47
48	85		83	101			117	105	106			118	48
49	86		84				119	107	108			119	49
50	88		85				120	108	110			120	50
51	89		86				120	110	112			120	51
52	91		88				120	112	113			120	52
53	93		89				120	114	115			120	53
54	95		90				120	116	117			120	54
55	97		91				120	118	118			120	55

(Continued)

TABLE E-4 (Continued)

Raw	L	F	K	Hs	D	Hy	Pd	Mf	Pa	Pt	Sc	Ma	Si	Raw
56		120			120	120	120				92		98	56
57		120			120		120				93		100	57
58		120					120				94		101	58
59		120					120				95		103	59
60		120					120				96		104	60
61		120									97		106	61
62		120									99		107	62
63		120									100			63
64		120									101			64
65		120									102			65
66		120									103			66
67											104			67
68											105			68
69											106			69
70											107			70
71											108			71
72											109			72
73											111			73
74											112			74
75											113			75
76											114			76
77											115			77

T-score Values for MMPI-A Basic Scales for Adolescent Females Age 17 Based on Marks and Briggs Norms (Dahlstrom, Welsh, and Dahlstrom, 1972)

Raw	L	F	K	Hs	D	Hy	Pd	Mf	Pa	Pt	Sc	Ma	Si	Raw
0	30	40	30	31	30	30	30	120	30	30	30	30	30	0
1	35	42	30	34	30	30	30	120	30	30	31	30	30	1
2	41	43	30	36	30	30	30	117	30	30	32	30	30	2
3	45	45	30	38	30	30	30	115	30	30	33	30	30	3
4	49	47	30	41	30	30	30	113	33	31	35	30	30	4
5	54	49	31	43	30	30	30	109	35	33	36	30	30	5
6	58	51	33	45	30	30	30	106	38	34	37	30	30	6
7	62	52	36	48	30	30	30	104	41	36	38	30	30	7
8	66	54	38	50	30	30	30	102	44	37	39	32	30	8
9	70	57	41	52	30	30	30	99	47	39	40	34	30	9
10	74	59	44	55	30	30	31	96	50	40	41	37	30	10
11	79	60	46	57	30	30	33	94	53	42	43	39	30	11
12	83	62	49	59	32	31	35	92	56	43	44	41	30	12
13	87	64	51	61	35	33	37	88	59	44	45	43	30	13
14	91	66	54	64	37	35	40	85	61	46	46	45	30	14
15		67	56	66	39	37	42	83	64	47	47	47	30	15
16		69	59	68	41	39	44	80	67	49	48	50	31	16
17		72	61	71	43	41	47	77	70	50	49	52	33	17
18		74	64	73	47	43	49	74	73	52	50	54	35	18
19		76	66	75	50	45	51	71	76	53	52	56	37	19
20		77	69	77	52	47	54	69	79	55	53	58	38	20
21		79	71	80	54	49	56	65	82	56	54	60	39	21
22		81	74	82	56	51	58	62	84	58	55	63	41	22
23		83	76	84	58	53	61	60	87	59	56	65	42	23
24		84	79	87	60	55	63	58	90	60	57	67	43	24
25		86	81	89	62	57	65	54	93	62	58	69	45	25

(Continued)

TABLE E-4 (Continued)

Raw	L	F	K	Hs	D	Hy	Pd	Mf	Pa	Pt	Sc	Ma	Si	Raw
26		89	84	91	65	59	67	51	96	63	60	71	46	26
27		91	86	93	67	61	70	49	99	65	61	73	47	27
28		93	89	96	69	63	72	47	102	66	62	76	49	28
29		94	91	98	71	65	74	43	105	68	63	78	50	29
30		96	94	100	73	67	77	40	108	69	64	80	51	30
31		99		103	75	69	79	38	110	71	65	82	53	31
32		101		105	78	71	81	36	113	72	66	84	54	32
33		102			80	73	84	32	116	74	68	86	55	33
34		104			82	75	86	30	119	75	69	89	57	34
35		106			84	77	88	30	120	77	70	91	58	35
36		109			86	79	91	30	120	78	71	93	60	36
37		111			88	81	93	30	120	79	72	95	62	37
38		112			90	83	95	30	120	81	73	97	63	38
39		113			93	85	98	30	120	82	74	99	65	39
40		116			95	87	100	30	30	84	76	101	66	40
41		118			97	89	102	30		85	77	104	67	41
42		119			99	91	104	30		87	78	106	69	42
43		120			101	93	107	30		88	79	108	70	43
44		120			103	95	109			90	80	110	71	44
45		120			105	97	111			91	81	112	73	45
46		120			108	99	114			93	82	114	74	46
47		120			110	101	116			94	84		75	47
48		120			112	103	118			95	85		77	48
49		120			114	105					86		78	49
50		120			116	107					87		79	50
51		120			118	109					88		81	51
52		120			120	111					89		82	52
53		120			120	113					90		83	53

Raw						Raw
54	120	120	115	92	85	54
55	120	120	117	93	86	55
56	120	120	119	94	88	56
57	120	120	120	95	90	57
58	120		120	96	91	58
59	120		120	97	93	59
60	120		120	98	94	60
61	120			101	95	61
62	120			102	97	62
63	120			103		63
64	120			104		64
65	120			105		65
66				106		66
67				108		67
68				109		68
69				110		69
70				111		70
71				112		71
72				113		72
73				114		73
74				116		74
75				117		75
76				118		76
77				119		77

LACHAR-WROBEL CRITICAL ITEMS

Lachar-Wrobel Critical Items

MMPI-A Item No.	MMPI Item No.	Direction Scored	MMPI-A Content
			Psychological Discomfort
Anxiety and Tension			
14	13	T	I work under a great deal of tension.
16	16	T	I am sure I get a raw deal from life.
165	186	T	I frequently notice my hand shakes when I try to do something.
205	238	T	I have periods of such great restlessness that I cannot sit long in a chair.
209	242	F	I believe I am no more nervous than most others.
244	287	F	I have very few fears compared to my friends.
279	335	T	I cannot keep my mind on one thing.
281	337	T	I feel anxiety about something or someone almost all the time.
300	352	T	I have been afraid of things or people that I knew could not hurt me.
375	407	F	I am usually calm and not easily upset.
402	543	T	Several times a week I feel as if something dreadful is about to happen.
Depression and Worry			
2	2	F	I have a good appetite.
3	3	F	I wake up fresh and rested most mornings.
10	9	F	I am about as able to work as I ever was.
62	76	T	Most of the time I feel blue.
70	86	T	I am certainly lacking in self-confidence.
71	88	F	I usually feel that life is worthwhile.*
124	142	T	I certainly feel useless at times.
158	178	F	My memory seems to be all right.
173	168	T	There is something wrong with my mind.
255	301	T	Life is a strain for me much of the time.
283	339	T	Most of the time I wish I were dead.
318	397	T	I have sometimes felt that difficulties were piling up so high that I could not overcome them.
379	418	T	At times I think I am no good at all.
383	431	T	I worry quite a bit over possible misfortunes.
399	526	T	The future seems hopeless to me.
Deleted	139	T	(Sometimes I feel as if I must injure either myself or someone else.)

(Continued)

Lachar-Wrobel Critical Items *(Continued)*

MMPI-A Item No.	MMPI Item No.	Direction Scored	MMPI-A Content
Sleep Disturbance			
5	5	T	I am easily awakened by noise.
36	43	T	My sleep is fitful and disturbed.
134	152	F	Most nights I go to sleep without thoughts or ideas bothering me.
308	359	T	Sometimes some unimportant thought will run through my mind and bother me for days.
353	31	T	I have nightmares every few nights.
Deleted	559	T	(I have often been frightened in the middle of the night.)

Reality Distortion

MMPI-A Item No.	MMPI Item No.	Direction Scored	MMPI-A Content
Deviant Beliefs			
39	35/331	T	If people had not had it in for me, I would be much more successful.*
95	110	T	Someone has it in for me.
102	119	F	My speech is the same as always (not faster or slower, no slurring or hoarseness).*
132	121	T	I believe I am being plotted against.
136	123	T	I believe I am being followed.
155	151	T	Someone has been trying to poison me.
286	284	T	I am sure I am being talked about.
294	347	F	I have no enemies who really wish to harm me.
314	364	T	People say insulting and vulgar things about me.
315	275	T	Someone has control over my mind.
332	291	T	At one or more times in my life I felt that someone was making me do things by hypnotizing me.
337	293	T	Someone has been trying to influence my mind.
428	200	T	There are persons who are trying to steal my thoughts and ideas.
Deleted	197	T	(Someone has been trying to rob me.)
Deleted	551	T	(Sometimes I am sure that other people can tell what I am thinking.)
Deviant Thinking and Experience			
29	33	T	I have had very peculiar and strange experiences.

(Continued)

Lachar-Wrobel Critical Items *(Continued)*

MMPI-A Item No.	MMPI Item No.	Direction Scored	MMPI-A Content
92	66	T	I see things or animals or people around me that others do not see.
116	134	T	At times my thoughts have raced ahead faster than I could speak them.
278	334	T	Peculiar odors come to me at times.
287	341	T	At times I hear so well it bothers me.
296	349	T	I have strange and peculiar thoughts.
299	350	T	I hear strange things when I am alone.
387	464	F	I have never seen a vision.
433	48	T	When I am with people, I am bothered by hearing very strange things.*
439	184	T	I often hear voices without knowing where they come from.*
Deleted	420	T	(I have had some very unusual religious experiences.)

Characterological Adjustment

Substance Abuse

MMPI-A Item No.	MMPI Item No.	Direction Scored	MMPI-A Content
161	156	T	I have had periods in which I carried on activities without knowing later what I had been doing.
247	215	T	I have used alcohol excessively.
Deleted	460	F	(I have used alcohol moderately (or not at all).)
Deleted	466	F	(Except by a doctor's orders I never take drugs or sleeping powders.)

Antisocial Attitude

MMPI-A Item No.	MMPI Item No.	Direction Scored	MMPI-A Content
24	28	T	When people do me a wrong, I feel I should pay them back if I can, just for the principle of the thing.*
32	38	T	I have sometimes stolen things.*
80	56	T	I have been suspended from school one or more times for bad behavior.*
101	118	T	In school I have sometimes been sent to the principal for bad behavior.*
213	250	T	I don't blame people for trying to grab everything they can get in this world.*
224	205	T	At times it has been impossible for me to keep from stealing or shoplifting something.
238	280	T	Most people make friends because friends are likely to be useful to them.
249	294	F	I have never been in trouble with the law.
354	269	T	I can easily make other people afraid of me, and sometimes do it for the fun of it.

(Continued)

Lachar-Wrobel Critical Items *(Continued)*

MMPI-A Item No.	MMPI Item No.	Direction Scored	MMPI-A Content
Family Conflict			
19	21	T	At times I have very much wanted to leave home.
79	96	F	I have very few quarrels with members of my family.
119	137	F	I believe that my home life is as pleasant as that of most people I know.
269	245	T	My parents and family find more fault with me than they should.
Problematic Anger			
81	97	T	At times I have a strong urge to do something harmful or shocking.
128	145	T	At times I feel like picking a fistfight with someone.
201	234	T	I get mad easily and then get over it soon.
367	381	T	I am often said to be hotheaded.

Other Categories

Sexual Concern and Deviation			
31	37	F	I have never been in trouble because of my sex behavior.
59	74	T/F[a]	I have often wished I were a girl. (Or if you are a girl) I have never been sorry that I am a girl.
159	179	T	I am worried about sex.*
251	297	T	I wish I were not bothered by thoughts about sex.
Deleted	20	F	(My sex life is satisfactory.)
Deleted	69	T	(I am very strongly attracted by members of my own sex.)
Deleted	133	F	(I have never indulged in any unusual sex practices.)
Deleted	519	T	(There is something wrong with my sex organs.)
Somatic Symptoms			
4	36	F	I seldom worry about my health.
17	23	T	I am troubled by attacks of nausea and vomiting.
25	29	T	I am bothered by an upset stomach several times a week.*
37	44	T	Much of the time my head seems to hurt all over.
41	47	T	Once a week or oftener I suddenly feel hot all over, for no real reason.*

(Continued)

Lachar-Wrobel Critical Items *(Continued)*

MMPI-A Item No.	MMPI Item No.	Direction Scored	MMPI-A Content
44	55	F	I am almost never bothered by pains over my heart or in my chest.*
50	62	T	Parts of my body often feel like they are burning, tingling, or "going to sleep."*
54	68	F	I hardly ever feel pain in the back of my neck.*
56	72	T	I am troubled by discomfort in the pit of my stomach every few days or oftener.
97	114	T	Often I feel as if there is a tight band around my head.*
106	125	T	I have a great deal of stomach trouble.
138	154	F	I have never had a fit or convulsion.
152	174	F	I have never had a fainting spell.
157	175	F	I seldom or never have dizzy spells.
167	189	T	I feel weak all over much of the time.
168	190	F	I have very few headaches.
175	194	T	I have had attacks in which I could not control my movements or speech but in which I knew what was going on around me.
210	243	F	I have few or no pains.
214	251	T	I have had blank spells in which my activities were interrupted and I did not know what was going on around me.
231	273	T	I have numbness in one or more places on my skin.*
239	281	F	I do not often notice my ears ringing or buzzing.
275	330	F	I have never been paralyzed or had any unusual weakness of any of my muscles.
Deleted	544	T	(I feel tired a good deal of the time.)

Note. A total of 12 Lachar-Wrobel critical items were deleted in the development of the MMPI-A.

( ) Indicates original MMPI item content.

*Item reworded on MMPI-A.

[a]Critical direction for this item is T for males and F for females.

WIGGINS CONTENT SCALE ITEMS RETAINED IN THE MMPI-A

Note. MMPI-A items reproduced by permission. Copyright © 1992 by the Regents of the University of Minnesota.

Wiggins Content Scale Items Retained in the MMPI-A

MMPI Item No.	MMPI-A Item No.	Direction Scored	MMPI-A Content
SOC: Social Maladjustment (27/22)[a]			
52	43	True	I prefer to pass by people I know but have not seen for a long time, unless they speak to me first.*
57	46	False	I am a very sociable person.*
91	75	False	I do not mind being made fun of.
99	82	False	I like to go to parties and other affairs where there is lots of loud fun.
171	151	True	It makes me uncomfortable to put on a stunt at a party even when others are doing the same sort of things.
172	154	True	I frequently have to fight against showing that I am bashful.
180	160	True	I find it hard to make talk when I meet new people.
201	178	True	I wish I were not so shy.
267	227	True	When in a group of people I have trouble thinking of the right things to talk about.
292	248	True	I am likely not to speak to people until they speak to me.
304	257	True	In school I find it very hard to talk in front of the class.*
309	262	False	I seem to make friends about as quickly as others do.
377	316	True	At parties I am more likely to sit by myself or with just one other person than to join in with the crowd.
384	369	True	I feel unable to tell anyone all about myself.
391	319	False	I love to go to dances.
449	331	False	I enjoy social gatherings just to be with people.
450	335	False	I enjoy the excitement of a crowd.
479	336	False	I do not mind meeting strangers.
482	312	False	While in trains, busses, etc., I often talk to strangers.
502	341	False	I like to let people know where I stand on things.
521	245	False	In a group of people I would not be embarrassed to be called upon to start a discussion or give an opinion about something I know well.
547	292	False	I like parties and socials.

Items deleted by MMPI No. = 371, 453, 455, 509, and 520.

(Continued)

Wiggins Content Scale Items Retained in the MMPI-A *(Continued)*

MMPI Item No.	MMPI-A Item No.	Direction Scored	MMPI-A Content
DEP: Depression (33/31)[a]			
8	9	False	My daily life is full of things that keep me interested.
41	35	True	I have had periods of days, weeks, or months when I couldn't take care of things because I couldn't "get going."
61	49	True	I have not lived the right kind of life.
67	53	True	I wish I could be as happy as others seem to be.
76	62	True	Most of the time I feel blue.
79	60	False	My feelings are not easily hurt.
88	71	False	I usually feel that life is worthwhile.*
94	78	True	I do many things which I regret afterwards (I regret things more or more often than others seem to).
104	88	True	I don't seem to care what happens to me.
106	90	True	Much of the time I feel as if I have done something wrong or evil.
158	139	True	I cry easily.
202	219	True	I believe I am a condemned person.
207	179	False	I enjoy many different kinds of play and recreation.
209	230	True	I believe my sins are unpardonable.
210	236	True	Everything tastes the same.
217	185	True	I frequently find myself worrying about something.
259	218	True	I have difficulty in starting to do things.
305	259	True	Even when I am with people I feel lonely much of the time.
337	281	True	I feel anxiety about something or someone almost all the time.
338	285	True	I have certainly had more than my share of things to worry about.
339	283	True	Most of the time I wish I were dead.
374	320	True	At periods my mind seems to work more slowly than usual.
379	360	False	I very seldom have spells of the blues.
396	372	True	Often, even though everything is going fine for me, I feel that I don't care about anything.
407	375	False	I am usually calm and not easily upset.
413	392	True	I deserve severe punishment for my sins.
414	377	True	I am apt to take disappointments so keenly that I can't put them out of my mind.

(Continued)

Wiggins Content Scale Items Retained in the MMPI-A *(Continued)*

MMPI Item No.	MMPI-A Item No.	Direction Scored	MMPI-A Content
487	340	True	I feel like giving up quickly when things go wrong.
517	415	True	I cannot do anything well.
526	399	True	The future seems hopeless to me.
543	402	True	Several times a week I feel as if something dreadful is about to happen.

Items deleted by MMPI No. = 390, and 518

FEM: Feminine Interests (30/16)[a]

1	1	False	I like mechanics magazines.
74	59	True	I have often wished I were a girl. (Or if you are a girl) I have never been sorry that I am a girl.
77	61	True	I enjoy reading love stories.
78	64	True	I like poetry.
81	66	False	I think I would like the kind of work a forest ranger does.
92	76	True	I would like to be a nurse.
132	114	True	I like collecting flowers or growing house plants.
140	122	True	I like to cook.
149	131	True	I keep a diary.*
219	186	False	I think I would like the work of a building contractor.
221	188	False	I like science.
223	190	False	I very much like hunting.
283	241	False	If I were a reporter I would very much like to report sporting news.
300	254	False	There never was a time in my life when I liked to play with dolls.
552	403	False	I like to read about science.
562	407	True	The person to whom I have been most attached and whom I have most admired is a woman (mother, sister, aunt, or other woman).*

Items deleted by MMPI No. = 70, 87, 126, 203, 261, 295, 423, 434, 463, 537, 538, 554, 557, and 563.

MOR: Poor Morale (23/20)[a]

84	68	True	These days I find it hard not to give up hope of amounting to something.
86	70	True	I am certainly lacking in self-confidence.

(Continued)

Wiggins Content Scale Items Retained in the MMPI-A *(Continued)*

MMPI Item No.	MMPI-A Item No.	Direction Scored	MMPI-A Content
122	105	False	I seem to be about as capable and smart as most others around me.
138	121	True	Criticism or scolding hurts me terribly.
142	124	True	I certainly feel useless at times.
244	211	True	My way of doing things is apt to be mis-understood by others.
264	223	False	I am entirely self-confident.
321	270	True	I am easily embarrassed.
357	306	True	I have several times given up doing a thing because I thought too little of my ability.
361	311	True	I am inclined to take things hard.
382	368	True	I wish I could get over worrying about things I have said that may have injured other people's feelings.
389	370	True	My plans have frequently seemed so full of difficulties that I have had to give them up.
395	371	True	The future is too uncertain for a person to make serious plans.
397	318	True	I have sometimes felt that difficulties were piling up so high that I could not over-come them.
398	327	True	I often think, "I wish I were a child again."
411	326	True	It makes me feel like a failure when I hear of the success of someone I know well.
418	379	True	At times I think I am no good at all.
431	383	True	I worry quite a bit over possible misfor-tunes.
531	400	True	People can pretty easily change my mind even when I have made a decision about something.*
555	404	True	I sometimes feel that I am about to go to pieces.

Items deleted by MMPI No. = 375, 416, and 549.

REL: Religious Fundamentalism (12/1)[a]

| 115 | 126 | True | I believe in a life hereafter. |

Items deleted by MMPI No. = 58, 95, 98, 206, 249, 258, 373, 483, 488, 490, and 491.

(Continued)

Wiggins Content Scale Items Retained in the MMPI-A *(Continued)*

MMPI Item No.	MMPI-A Item No.	Direction Scored	MMPI-A Content
AUT: Authority Conflict (20/20)[a]			
59	47	True	I have often had to take orders from someone who did not know as much as I did.
71	55	True	I think a great many people exaggerate their misfortunes in order to gain the sympathy and help of others.
93	77	True	I think most people would lie to get ahead.
116	99	True	I enjoy a race or game more when I bet on it.*
117	100	True	Most people are honest chiefly because they are afraid of being caught.*
118	101	True	In school I have sometimes been sent to the principal for bad behavior.*
124	107	True	Most people will use somewhat unfair means to get what they want.*
250	213	True	I don't blame people for trying to grab everything they can get in this world.*
265	225	True	It is safer to trust nobody.
277	234	True	At times I have been so entertained by the cleverness of some criminals that I have hoped they would get away with it.*
280	238	True	Most people make friends because friends are likely to be useful to them.
294	249	False	I have never been in trouble with the law.
298	252	True	If several people find themselves in trouble, the best thing for them to do is to agree upon a story and stick to it.
313	263	True	A person who leaves valuable property unprotected is about as much to blame when it is stolen as the one who steals it.*
316	265	True	I think nearly anyone would tell a lie to keep out of trouble.
319	267	True	Most people inwardly dislike putting themselves out to help other people.
406	325	True	I have often met people who were supposed to be experts who were no better than I.
436	330	True	People generally demand more respect for their own rights than they are willing to allow for others.

(Continued)

Wiggins Content Scale Items Retained in the MMPI-A *(Continued)*

MMPI Item No.	MMPI-A Item No.	Direction Scored	MMPI-A Content
437	361	True	It is all right to get around the law if you don't actually break it.
446	323	True	I enjoy gambling for small stakes.

Items deleted = none.

PSY:Psychoticism (48/40)[a]

16	16	True	I am sure I get a raw deal from life.
22	21	True	At times I have fits of laughing and crying that I cannot control.
24	20	True	No one seems to understand me.
27	22	True	Evil spirits possess me at times.
33	29	True	I have had very peculiar and strange experiences.
35	39	True	If people had not had it in for me, I would be much more successful.*
40	45	True	Most anytime I wold rather sit and daydream than do anything else.*
48	433	True	When I am with people, I am bothered by hearing very strange things.*
50	250	True	My soul sometimes leaves my body.
66	92	True	I see things or animals or people around me that others do not see.
73	58	True	I am an important person.
110	95	True	Someone has it in for me.
121	132	True	I believe I am being plotted against.
123	136	True	I believe I am being followed.
127	109	True	I know who is responsible for most of my troubles.
136	118	True	I often wonder what hidden reason another person may have for doing something nice for me.*
151	155	True	Someone has been trying to poison me.
168	173	True	There is something wrong with my mind.
184	439	True	I often hear voices without knowing where they come from.*
194	175	True	I have had attacks in which I could not control my movements or speech but in which I knew what was going on around me.
200	428	True	There are persons who are trying to steal my thoughts and ideas.
232	199	True	I have been inspired to a program of life based on duty which I have since carefully followed.

(Continued)

Wiggins Content Scale Items Retained in the MMPI-A *(Continued)*

MMPI Item No.	MMPI-A Item No.	Direction Scored	MMPI-A Content
275	315	True	Someone has control over my mind.
278	235	True	I have often felt that strangers were looking at me critically.
284	286	True	I am sure I am being talked about.
291	332	True	At one or more times in my life I felt that someone was making me do things by hypnotizing me.
293	337	True	Someone has been trying to influence my mind.
299	253	True	I think that I feel more intensely than most people do.
312	264	True	I dislike having people around me.*
317	266	True	I am more sensitive than most other people.
334	278	True	Peculiar odors come to me at times.
341	287	True	At times I hear so well it bothers me.
345	291	True	I often feel as if things are not real.*
347	294	False	I have no enemies who really wish to harm me.
348	295	True	I tend to be on my guard with people who are somewhat more friendly than I had expected.
349	296	True	I have strange and peculiar thoughts.
350	299	True	I hear strange things when I am alone.
364	314	True	People say insulting and vulgar things about me.
400	324	True	If given the chance I could do some things that would be of great benefit to the world.
464	387	False	I have never seen a vision.

Items deleted by MMPI No. = 197, 198, 420, 433, 448, 476, 511, and 551.

ORG: Organic Symptoms (36/31)[a]

23	17	True	I am troubled by attacks of nausea and vomiting.
44	37	True	Much of the time my head seems to hurt all over.
46	40	False	My judgment is better than it ever was.
68	54	False	I hardly ever feel pain in the back of my neck.*
103	87	False	I have little or no trouble with my muscles twitching or jumping.
108	93	True	There seems to be a fullness in my head or nose most of the time.

Wiggins Content Scale Items Retained in the MMPI-A *(Continued)*

MMPI Item No.	MMPI-A Item No.	Direction Scored	MMPI-A Content
114	97	True	Often I feel as if there is a tight band around my head.*
119	102	False	My speech is the same as always (not faster or slower, no slurring or hoarseness).*
154	138	False	I have never had a fit or convulsion.
156	161	True	I have had periods in which I carried on activities without knowing later what I had been doing.
159	141	True	I cannot understand what I read as well as I used to.
161	143	True	The top of my head sometimes feels tender.
174	152	False	I have never had a fainting spell.
175	157	False	I seldom or never have dizzy spells.
178	158	False	My memory seems to be all right.
185	193	False	My hearing is apparently as good as that of most people.
186	165	True	I frequently notice my hand shakes when I try to do something.
187	169	False	My hands have not become clumsy or awkward.
188	166	False	I can read a long while without tiring my eyes.
189	167	True	I feel weak all over much of the time.
190	168	False	I have very few headaches.
192	172	False	I have had no difficulty in keeping my balance in walking.
243	210	False	I have few or no pains.
251	214	True	I have had blank spells in which my activities were interrupted and I did not know what was going on around me.
273	231	True	I have numbness in one or more places on my skin.*
274	233	False	My eyesight is as good as it has been for years.
281	239	False	I do not often notice my ears ringing or buzzing.
330	275	False	I have never been paralyzed or had any unusual weakness of any of my muscles.
332	276	True	Sometimes my voice leaves me or changes even though I have no cold.
335	279	True	I cannot keep my mind on one thing.

(Continued)

Wiggins Content Scale Items Retained in the MMPI-A *(Continued)*

MMPI Item No.	MMPI-A Item No.	Direction Scored	MMPI-A Content
405	374	False	I have no trouble swallowing.

Items deleted by MMPI No. = 496, 508, 540, 541, and 560.

FAM: Family Problems (16/16)[a]

21	19	True	At times I have very much wanted to leave home.
65	86	False	I love my father, or (if your father is dead) I loved my father.*
96	79	False	I have very few quarrels with members of my family.
137	119	False	I believe that my home life is as pleasant as that of most people I know.
212	181	True	My family treats me like a child.*
216	184	True	There is very little love and companionship in my family as compared to other homes.
220	258	False	I love my mother, or (if your mother is dead) I loved my mother.*
224	191	True	My parents often object to the kind of people I go around with.*
226	194	True	Some of my family have habits that bother and annoy me very much.
239	206	True	I have been disappointed in love.
245	269	True	My parents and family find more fault with me than they should.
325	302	True	The things that some of my family have done have frightened me.
327	277	True	My mother or father often make me obey even when I think it is unreasonable.*
421	381	True	One or more members of my family are very nervous.*
516	396	True	Some of my family have quick tempers.
527	398	False	The members of my family and my close relatives get along quite well.

Items deleted = none.

HOS: Manifest Hostility (27/18)[a]

28	24	True	When people do me a wrong, I feel I should pay them back if I can, just for the principle of the thing.*
39	34	True	At times I feel like smashing things.
80	65	True	I sometimes tease animals.

(Continued)

Wiggins Content Scale Items Retained in the MMPI-A *(Continued)*

MMPI Item No.	MMPI-A Item No.	Direction Scored	MMPI-A Content
89	72	True	It takes a lot of argument to convince most people of the truth.
109	94	True	Some people are so bossy that I feel like doing the opposite of what they request, even though I know they are right.
129	111	True	Often I can't understand why I have been so irritable and grouchy.*
145	128	True	At times I feel like picking a fist fight with someone.
162	145	True	I resent having anyone trick me so cleverly that I have to admit I was fooled.*
269	354	True	I can easily make other people afraid of me, and sometimes do for the fun of it.
282	240	True	Once in a while I feel hate toward members of my family whom I usually love.
336	282	True	I easily become impatient with people.
355	303	True	Sometimes I enjoy hurting persons I love.
363	321	True	At times I have enjoyed being hurt by someone I loved.
417	378	True	I am often so annoyed when someone tries to get ahead of me in a line of people that I speak to that person about it.*
426	382	True	I have at times had to be rough with people who were rude or annoying.
468	388	True	I am often sorry because I am so irritable and grouchy.*
469	334	True	I have often found people jealous of my good ideas, just because they had not thought of them first.
536	401	True	It makes me angry to have people hurry me.

Items deleted by MMPI No. = 139, 218, 368, 393, 410, 438, 447, 452, and 495.

PHO: Phobias (27/15)[a]

128	110	False	The sight of blood doesn't frighten me or make me sick.*
131	112	False	I do not worry about catching diseases.
166	148	True	I am afraid when I look down from a high place.
176	156	False	I do not have a great fear of snakes.
182	163	True	I am afraid of losing my mind.
287	244	False	I have very few fears compared to my friends.

(Continued)

Wiggins Content Scale Items Retained in the MMPI-A *(Continued)*

MMPI Item No.	MMPI-A Item No.	Direction Scored	MMPI-A Content
351	297	True	I get anxious and upset when I have to make a short trip away from home.
352	300	True	I have been afraid of things or people that I knew could not hurt me.
353	301	False	I have no dread of going into a room by myself where other people have already gathered and are talking.
360	309	True	Almost everyday something happens to frighten me.
365	350	True	I feel uneasy indoors.
401	346	False	I have no fear of water.
473	304	True	Whenever possible I avoid being in a crowd.
499	394	True	I must admit that I have at times been overly worried about something that really didn't matter.*
553	349	True	I am afraid of being alone in a wide-open place.

Items deleted by MMPI No. = 169, 367, 385, 388, 392, 412, 480, 492, 494, 522, 525, and 539.

HYP: Hypomania (25/18)[a]

13	14	True	I work under a great deal of tension.
134	116	True	At times my thoughts have raced ahead faster than I could speak them.
181	162	True	When I get bored I like to stir up some excitement.
196	198	True	I like to visit places where I have never been before.
228	195	True	At times I feel that I can make up my mind with unusually great ease.
234	201	True	I get mad easily and then get over it soon.
238	205	True	I have periods of such great restlessness that I cannot sit long in a chair.
248	212	True	Sometimes without any reason or even when things are going wrong I feel excitedly happy, "on top of the world."
266	226	True	Once a week or oftener I become very excited.
268	228	True	Something exciting will almost always pull me out of it when I am feeling low.

(Continued)

Wiggins Content Scale Items Retained in the MMPI-A *(Continued)*

MMPI Item No.	MMPI-A Item No.	Direction Scored	MMPI-A Content
272	289	True	At times I am all full of energy.
296	298	True	I have periods in which I feel unusually cheerful without any special reason.
340	284	True	Sometimes I become so excited that I find it hard to get to sleep.
342	288	True	I forget right away what people say to me.
381	367	True	I am often said to be hotheaded.
445	386	True	I like excitement.*
500	393	True	I readily become one hundred percent sold on a good idea.
505	343	True	I have had periods when I felt so full of pep that sleep did not seem necessary for days at a time.

Items deleted by MMPI No. = 146, 372, 386, 409, 439, 465, and 506.

HEA: Poor Health (28/17)[a]

2	2	False	I have a good appetite.
10	11	True	There seems to be a lump in my throat much of the time.
18	18	False	I am very seldom troubled by constipation.
29	25	True	I am bothered by an upset stomach several times a week.*
34	470	True	I have a cough most of the time.
36	4	False	I seldom worry about my health.
51	42	False	I am in just as good physical health as most of my friends.
55	44	False	I am almost never bothered by pains over my heart or in my chest.*
72	56	True	I am troubled by discomfort in the pit of my stomach every few days or oftener.
125	106	True	I have a great deal of stomach trouble.
130	113	False	I have never vomited blood or coughed up blood.
153	135	False	During the past few years I have been well most of the time.
155	140	False	I am neither gaining nor losing weight.
163	146	False	I do not tire quickly.
193	174	False	I do not have spells of hay fever or asthma.

(Continued)

Wiggins Content Scale Items Retained in the MMPI-A *(Continued)*

MMPI Item No.	MMPI-A Item No.	Direction Scored	MMPI-A Content
230	196	False	I hardly ever notice my heart pounding and I am seldom short of breath.
279	237	True	I drink an unusually large amount of water every day.

Items deleted by MMPI No. = 14, 63, 214, 424, 462, 474, 486, 519, 533, 542, and 544.

Note. ª = Numbers in parentheses following scale names indicate the number of items in the original scale and the number of items retained in the MMPI-A, respectively.

* = MMPI-A item modified from appearance in the original MMPI.

AUTHOR INDEX

443

SUBJECT INDEX